2000

Marc Chagall
and the Jewish Theater

Marc Chagall
and the Jewish Theater

GUGGENHEIM MUSEUM

Reproductions of cat. nos. 1–7
© State Tret'iakov Gallery, Moscow

ISBN: 0–89207–099–4

Published by the Guggenheim Museum
1071 Fifth Avenue
New York, New York 10128

Printed in the United States by Thorner Press

Front cover:
Marc Chagall, *Music,* 1920
Tempera and gouache on canvas
212.4 x 103.5 cm (83 ⁵/₈ x 40 ³/₄ inches)
State Tret'iakov Gallery, Moscow

Back cover:
Marc Chagall, *Love on the Stage,* 1920
Tempera and gouache on canvas
284.2 x 249.6 cm (111 ⁷/₈ x 98 ¹/₄ inches)
State Tret'iakov Gallery, Moscow

Frontispiece:
Emblem of the Jewish Chamber Theater, taken from
a 1919 poster printed in Petrograd.

Color photography:
Cat. nos. 1–7, from State Tret'iakov Gallery, Moscow;
nos. 1, 2 photo H. Preisig; no. 3 courtesy Fondation
Pierre Gianadda; nos. 4–7 photographed by Lee
Ewing. Cat. nos. 8, 9, 11, 14, from Musée national d'art
moderne, Centre Georges Pompidou, Paris; photo
Philippe Migeat, © Centre G. Pompidou. Cat. nos. 10,
12, 13, 15–20, from the collection of Ida Chagall, Paris.
Cat. nos. 21–32, from Solomon R. Guggenheim
Museum; no. 24 photographed by Myles Aronowitz;
no. 29 by Lee Ewing; nos. 21, 31, 32 by Carmelo
Guadagno; nos. 21–23, 25–28, 30 by David Heald.

Marc Chagall and the Jewish Theater

Solomon R. Guggenheim Museum
September 23, 1992–January 17, 1993

The Art Institute of Chicago
January 30–May 7, 1993

This exhibition has been sponsored, in part, by
Lufthansa German Airlines.

 **Lufthansa**

Additional support has been provided by
The Helena Rubinstein Foundation.

Contents

Preface
Thomas Krens
viii

Foreword
Iurii K. Korolev
x

Sponsor's Statement
Jürgen Weber
xi

Introduction
Jennifer Blessing
xii

**Chagall's Auditorium:
"An Identity Crisis of Tragic Dimensions"**
Susan Compton
1

**Chagall: Postmodernism and
Fictional Worlds in Painting**
Benjamin Harshav
15

Catalogue to the Exhibition
65

Texts and Documents
Edited by Benjamin Harshav
Translated by Benjamin and Barbara Harshav
133

Bibliography
Benjamin Harshav
200

Afterword
Gregory Veitsman
205

Marc Chagall and the Jewish Theater appears at the Guggenheim Museum SoHo while *The Great Utopia: The Russian and Soviet Avant-Garde, 1915–1932*, the comprehensive exhibition of one of the principal Modernist movements of the twentieth century, is on display at the Solomon R. Guggenheim Museum. *The Great Utopia* presents the fruits of the avant-garde's attempt to restructure an entire society — economically, socially, and culturally — in the face of a tremendous political upheaval, the Russian Revolution. Artists became integral participants in the formation of the Soviet government. They also strove to create new forms for art and utilitarian objects that would function purposefully to bring about and encourage change. Stranded in Russia during a visit with his fiancée before World War I, Marc Chagall participated in revolutionary debates about art and politics. He was appointed the Commissar of Art for the region of Vitebsk and founded an art academy and museum in his official capacity. At the academy, Chagall's teachings were challenged by Kazimir Malevich, who succeeded in convincing the school's students of the primacy of his Suprematism. *The Great Utopia* serves as an excellent background for *Marc Chagall and the Jewish Theater* by providing the context within which Chagall, in 1920, undertook his commission for the State Jewish Chamber Theater. *Marc Chagall and the Jewish Theater*, in turn, can be viewed as a counterpoint to *The Great Utopia* in that it presents the work of an artist whose methods of representation, enigmatic symbolism, and abstract individualist ideology left him at odds with many of his fellow artists and hastened his departure from Russia.

These exhibitions have been both blessed and plagued by the myriad changes in the former Soviet Union. The opening of previously restricted archives and the willingness to cooperate with Western scholars and institutions have led to a wealth of new studies on the pre- and postrevolutionary periods and to exhibitions of works that may not have been removed from storage in the Soviet Union, much less been lent to museums in other countries. An exhibition of Chagall's murals for the Jewish Theater was unthinkable a few short years ago. The rapidity of change in the Russian political situation in recent years created unique logistical and technical difficulties that had to be overcome. Without the dedicated commitment of our Russian partners, as well as of many individuals and institutions in Europe and the United States, this show would not be possible.

We are most indebted to Iurii Korolev, Director of the State Tret'iakov Gallery, Moscow, and his staff. Among them, Lidiia Romashkova, Chief Registrar and Deputy Director, played a key role. The Tret'iakov Gallery has cared for Chagall's seven murals for the Jewish Theater since 1950, when they were admitted to the museum. These paintings would not be on display today without the meticulous restoration work led by Aleksei Kovalev, Director of the Restoration Department, and his team, including Leonid Astaf'ev and Galina Iushkevich.

The participation of Evgenii Sidorov, the Minister of Culture of the Russian Federation, was vital to the success of the project.

A number of collectors and institutions were extremely generous in agreeing to lend us important works with the short notice that resulted from our scheduling requirements. Madame Ida Chagall, daughter of the artist, selflessly lent nine sketches from her collection. Our exhibition would be incomplete without these essential works related to the commission for the Jewish Theater. We must also thank Meret Meyer, Ida Chagall's daughter, for facilitating the transmission of photographs. The contribution of Franz Meyer, the author of the artist's first catalogue raisonné, was indispensable to the exhibition.

The Musée national d'art moderne, Centre Georges Pompidou, Paris lent additional theater drawings, including the preparatory sketch for the Guggenheim's *Green Violinist*. We offer our special thanks to Dominique Bozo, President of the Centre Georges Pompidou, and Germain Viatte, the Musée national d'art moderne's Director. Additional assistance was offered by Curator Didier Schulmann, who is compiling the Chagall catalogue raisonné for the museum, and Collection Registrar Viviane Faret, who helped us navigate the loan procedures for the popular works.

The State Bakhrushin Museum, Moscow, under the direction of Valerii Gubin, lent four sketches by Chagall's contemporaries who designed productions for the Jewish Theater. We have been the beneficiaries of this museum's profound contribution to the preservation and restoration of theatrical objects from the early Soviet period, including an extensive archive of documentary material. The Central State Archive for Literature and Art, Moscow, directed by Natal'ia Volkova, generously lent rare 1920s posters for the theater, among them an important broadsheet believed to be the first poster mentioning Chagall.

In 1991, the murals were exhibited en suite for the first time in the West, at the Fondation Pierre Gianadda in Martigny, Switzerland, which sponsored their restoration. We must thank the foundation's President Leonard Gianadda as well as Christoph Vitali, Director of the Schirn Kunsthalle Frankfurt. Their institutions' exhibitions and catalogues provided both inspiration and substantial new material on Chagall's murals. Mr. Vitali lent the Guggenheim numerous historical photographs and provided important technical advice.

Marc Chagall and the Jewish Theater might never have been realized without the assistance of Lufthansa German Airlines and its Chairman, Jürgen Weber. Nicolas V. Iljine, Manager of Public Affairs, arranged and coordinated extensive transportation services, and his enthusiastic interest throughout the show's development was a continuously important source of encouragement. Through his capable offices we were able to obtain much of the documentary material that is the basis of the informational component of the exhibition. Additional support was provided by the Helena Rubinstein Foundation, for which we are grateful.

Preface and Acknowledgments

Valentin Rivkind, Deputy Director of the Vuchetich All-Union Artistic Production Association (VUART), Moscow, was instrumental in securing all loans of art from Russia, a very complicated task due to the volatile political and economic situation. The assistance and enthusiasm of Zel'fira Tregulova, art expert and Deputy Chief of the exhibition department at VUART, was fundamental to the realization of this project. She was a model of efficiency and grace under pressure.

Marc Chagall and the Jewish Theater has profited from the initiatives taken by Russian scholars. Aleksandra Shatskikh's extensive research into the life and work of Chagall is amply demonstrated by her contributions to the Schirn Kunsthalle Frankfurt's catalogue. Our knowledge of the commission for the Jewish Theater has been greatly enriched by her work. We are also grateful to Zara Abdulaeva for her research on the Jewish Theater, which we relied upon for the production history presented in the exhibition.

Christiane Bauermeister of Ost-West-Kultur facilitated communication between various parties in Russia and New York. In Moscow, we benefited from the participation of Rada Abdulaeva, Liubov' Chistiakova, Irina Duksina, Matvei Geizer, Natal'ia Iakimova, Boris Karad'ev, Tat'iana Klim, Elena Korenevskaia, Alla Lukanova, Rada Mamedova, Vjatscheslaw Nechaev, Anait Oganessian, Igor Pal'min, Il'ia Plotkin, Ekaterina Seleznova, Mikhail Shvydkoi, and Boris Zingerman. We also received help from Aleksei Bessobrasov, St. Petersburg; Natan Fedorowskii, Berlin; David Hasan, Helsinki; Sam Norich, New York; and Elena Rakitin, Frankfurt.

The dedication of and sheer hard work by Guggenheim staff members made this exhibition possible. In spring 1992, a team was created to bring the exhibition to fruition, which included Michael Govan, Deputy Director, and Maryann Jordan, Director of External Affairs, who quickly began to mobilize the museum's resources.

Jennifer Blessing, Assistant Curator for Research, spearheaded the curatorial organization of the exhibition. She was ably assisted by Emily Locker, Project Research Assistant, whose Russian-language skills and meticulous attention to detail were a tremendous asset. At crucial moments, Carmen Giménez, Curator of Twentieth-Century Art, participated in loan negotiations; and Jane Sharp, Project Associate Curator for *The Great Utopia*, lent her expertise to the Chagall show when needed. Sharon Corwin, Curatorial Intern, solved numerous problems of logistics during her short summer tenure.

The Technical Services staff, headed by Pamela Myers, Administrator for Exhibitions and Programming, took on the task of designing, planning, and mounting this exhibition in six short months. Peter Costa, Senior Museum Technician, was key to its installation. Andrew Law Simons, associate designer, designed the didactic component of the exhibition; he also designed the the catalogue based on a format by Massimo Vignelli. The commitment of the Publications Department, led by Anthony Calnek, Managing Editor, was no less essential to the success of this project. Despite numerous other obligations, Mr. Calnek, Laura Morris, Assistant Editor, and Jennifer Knox, Editorial Assistant, responded to their labors with fortitude and good spirits.

Paul Schwartzbaum, Assistant Director for Technical Services and Chief Conservator, was involved in the exhibition from its inception. His expertise in overseeing the care of the murals and in negotiating technical issues has been indispensable. Jan Adlmann, Director of Special Programs, organized the symposium Two Lectures/New Insights: Marc Chagall's Jewish Theater Project in conjunction with the 92nd Street Y. Among the many other staff members who made contributions were Lynne Addison, Associate Registrar, who handily took over the responsibilities of the exhibition midstream after joining the museum, and Heidi Rosenau, the Public Affairs Coordinator responsible for the Chagall exhibition, who discharged her duties with intelligence and grace.

Finally, we owe our thanks to this catalogue's contributors, who committed themselves to the project despite our short deadlines. Dr. Susan Compton, the eminent Chagall specialist, and Dr. Benjamin Harshav, J. and H. Blaustein Professor of Hebrew and Comparative Literature at Yale University, have made immeasurable contributions to Chagall scholarship. Barbara Harshav translated, with Dr. Harshav, the extensive selection of primary texts included herein. Gregory Veitsman, former Assistant Director for Technical Services at the State Tret'iakov Gallery, shares his recollections of Chagall in the afterword.

—Thomas Krens
Director, The Solomon R. Guggenheim Foundation

Foreword

The monumental murals Marc Chagall created in 1920 for the State Jewish Chamber Theater in Moscow (GOSEKT) were the last works the master made in his native land. His artistic achievement was immediately recognized by critics and art scholars. Therefore, after the theater was closed in 1949, it was no accident that the State Tret'iakov Gallery, the country's leading museum, acquired the panels for their permanent collection. There, cared for by restorers and curators, the murals were kept on drums because of their large size. They were unrolled to check for damage on a regular but infrequent basis because of the fragility of their backing and paint layers. When the artist visited the Tret'iakov Gallery in 1973, he was delighted by the careful treatment the murals had received, and he signed and dated them at that time. Until perhaps the late 1960s, he had not even known that the works had survived.

During the many years the murals were in storage our experts could only undertake measures to protect the panels. There was no possibility of restoration, and there was nowhere large enough to display them in the museum's old exhibition galleries. When the museum underwent major reconstruction and plans were made to expand exhibition space, the question of displaying kinds of paintings never shown before arose. We wrestled with the difficulties of restoring and exhibiting such works as Chagall's theater panels and Vrubel's panel *Princess Greza*. The singular history of Chagall's murals — including their creation in the extreme conditions of postrevolutionary Russia, the nature of their materials (tempera and gouache on thin linen), their subsequent fate determined by dramatic twists and turns such as the theater's move from Bol'shoi Chernyshevskii Lane to Malaia Bronnaia Street, and the far-from-ideal storage conditions from 1938 through the war — was reflected in their appearance. The restorers had to deal with wrinkling of the backing, weak threads holding the damaged parts of the linen together, scratches, and large areas where the paint was missing or flaking. They also had to reinforce Chagall's canvas. This extremely complicated work was carried out by the Tret'iakov Gallery's restorers, Aleksei Kovalev (the director of the department, who developed a unique method for treating the murals), Leonid Astaf'ev, and Galina Iushkevich.

The obstacle of the cost of such a complicated restoration project was overcome by means of international collaboration. It was decided that the murals would be exhibited in various countries throughout the world until the reconstruction of the museum was complete. The high quality of the restoration, which won a prize in Ferrara in 1991, enabled an extensive exhibition tour. The paintings were first shown in Switzerland, at the Fondation Pierre Gianadda, Martigny, which financed the restoration. The exhibition then traveled to the Schirn Kunsthalle Frankfurt, the State Tret'iakov Gallery, Moscow, and the State Russian Museum in St. Petersburg. In all of these exhibitions, which proved to be very successful, the murals were shown in the context of Chagall's Russian period. Now the murals have reached North America and New York, the

most distant place on the tour.

I wish to express my profound thanks to my colleague Thomas Krens, the Director of the Solomon R. Guggenheim Foundation, and Deputy Director Michael Govan for bringing the exhibition *Marc Chagall and the Jewish Theater* to the United States.

I would especially like to thank Nicolas V. Iljine, Manager of Public Affairs of Lufthansa German Airlines, for his enormous interest in the exhibition and the energy he devoted toward it. I hope all visitors to the exhibition will enjoy their encounter with Chagall's legendary panels, the only great works of a monumental scale the artist created in Russia, which, the critics of the 1920s agreed, were his best works.

—Iurii K. Korolev
General Director
State Tret'iakov Gallery, Moscow

Sponsor's Statement

The legendary, monumental murals Chagall created in 1920 for the auditorium of Moscow's State Jewish Chamber Theater are, as the artist himself described them, his most important works of art. They express many of the major influences that formed the artist's life and work, fusing into perfect harmony his Jewish and Russian background and traditions with European Modern art trends.

Like no other artist of his time, Chagall was able to combine traditional themes with Modern painting in a very special and symbolic form of expression. He thus created an ensemble that contains its own message for and language of the different cultures. The masterpieces were exhibited in 1991 in Frankfurt's Schirn Kunsthalle. We are now especially proud to enable their first showing in America.

For Lufthansa, our traditional commitment to cultural understanding and artistic expression is evidenced in our support of this extraordinary exhibition. Our association with great art and great artists provides better communication across different cultures, frontiers, and geographic boundaries. It is, after all, what Lufthansa is all about — linking people with people throughout the world.

This exhibition in particular honors an artist who coined what is perhaps the most beautiful phrase ever written about art: "Paint is the lifeblood of the artist."

—Jürgen Weber
Chairman of the Executive Board
Lufthansa German Airlines

In November 1920, the State Jewish Chamber Theater moved into a residence in Moscow provided by the Soviet government. Adjoining rooms on the second floor of the house, which had belonged to a wealthy merchant, L. I. Gurevich, before apparently being confiscated during the Revolution, were converted into a small auditorium capable of seating 90 people on benches.[1] Marc Chagall, who was by then known internationally, was hired to design the sets and costumes for the troupe's inaugural production of three one-act plays by Sholem Aleichem, which opened on January 1, 1921. In the last few weeks of 1920, in the midst of civil war and famine, the artist produced an ensemble of paintings for the theater's three walls, the stage curtain, and the ceiling, creating an environment for the production that extended beyond the stage. The small hall became known as Chagall's Box.[2] Its surviving seven paintings (the curtain and ceiling canvases were lost) form the core of the Guggenheim's exhibition.

Marc Chagall and the Jewish Theater is designed to present these murals within a framework that illuminates the circumstances of their creation, from Chagall's artistic process and aesthetic decisions to the conditions under which he worked. To that end, the exhibition is divided into two components; the first, its nucleus, consists of the murals and related art works by Chagall. Included are studies for the paintings, which demonstrate the artist's working methods and techniques, as well as his set and costume sketches for the *Sholem Aleichem Evening*. Also on display are works by the artist in the Guggenheim's collection, ranging from the early *Portrait of the Artist's Sister Aniuta* (1910, cat. no. 21), painted before Chagall made his pivotal trip to Paris; to masterpieces of his first Parisian period, such as *Paris Through the Window* (1913, cat. no. 23); to important reprises of earlier canvases, including *Green Violinist* (1923–24, cat. no. 30). Chagall created the latter painting, a virtual replica of the Jewish Theater's *Music* (1920, cat. no. 4), in Paris from a sketch he had brought with him from Moscow, probably the drawing in the exhibition on loan from the Musée national d'art moderne, Centre Georges Pompidou, Paris (*The Green Violinist* [study for *Music*], 1920, cat. no. 11).[3] Chagall frequently re-created images that he had painted years before, as if to have souvenirs of works that were lost to him. This exhibition unites the various versions of the fiddler for the first time.[4]

The second component of the exhibition is a presentation of documentary material concerning the Jewish Theater and the Chagall commission. Historical photographs, sketches, and posters — some unpublished and previously unknown in the West — and explanatory text panels indicate the period and atmosphere in which the murals were created. One section is devoted to the history of the Jewish Theater from its founding in 1918 through 1928. Other segments provide background information on Chagall's activities during his second and final Russian period, from 1914 to 1922, on the original installation of the murals, and on the history of the paintings after their creation.

By his own account, Chagall was determined to create a visual manifesto for the Jewish Theater in this commission.[5] Foiled in earlier attempts to design theatrical productions, he saw this as an opportunity to assert his beliefs about a new direction for the theater (and perhaps also for art and revolution). At the Jewish Theater, Chagall found himself among a group of young people who were trying to define the nature of their company. The events of 1917 had provided a tabula rasa for the Jewish Theater, upon which Chagall could inscribe his own codes. That Chagall perceived himself as a kind of Moses giving the law to the Israelites is clear in his grand statement, the nearly twenty-six-foot-long mural *Introduction to the Jewish Theater* (1920, cat. no. 1), in which he painted himself being carried by Abram Efros, the theater critic who suggested him for the commission, to Aleksei Granovskii, the theater's director. The two tablets of the Ten Commandments appear behind the artist's head.

Through a natural outgrowth of his painterly vocabulary, Chagall presented a kaleidoscopic panoply of ecstatic figures in this work, which suggested an anti-rational model of carnivalesque abandon for the theater. This conceptualization of theater was not entirely new; Russian directors such as Vsevolod Meierkhol'd and Aleksandr Tairov were exploring the legacy of commedia dell'arte and other popular theatrical spectacles before Chagall began work on the murals.[6] Granovskii was already disposed to that kind of dramatic treatment through his studies under Max Reinhardt, the progressive Austrian director. Yet Chagall presented a unique, and uniquely Jewish, approach. Through specifically Jewish visual puns, Yiddish inscriptions, and references to the festivities of Jewish weddings and Purim — a Jewish analogue to carnival in its emphasis on ludicrous masquerades and outrageous intoxication — he posited a distinctive model for the Jewish Theater.[7]

This model was not without political implications. In a 1940 paper, Mikhail Bakhtin (1895–1975), a Russian literary scholar who was Chagall's contemporary, described carnival as a populist, utopian conception of the world.[8] He found a critique of established power in its flouting of conventional behavior and established norms and in its inversion of standard hierarchies. Although Bakhtin studied the Renaissance world of Rabelais, many of his observations about the dialectical representation of human form — the "classical" versus the "grotesque" body — can be applied to Chagall's work in general, and his murals in particular. The classical body is the idealized, regularly proportioned, and decorously realistic figure, while the grotesque body, the body of carnival, is a lewdly comic explosion of ill-proportioned parts. Grotesque realism, in its emphasis on the debased aspects of the human figure, challenges the authority of the normative, or bourgeois standard. Carnival, along with its elements of feasting, dancing, parody, and raucous laughter, embraces the grotesque, and as such resists the principles of the dominant culture.

Carnivalesque merrymaking and grotesquerie are

predominant in *Introduction to the Jewish Theater*. Non-naturalistic figures abound: men with rubbery legs twisted like pretzels, violinists with heads hovering over their bodies, and acrobats walking on their hands. Quizzical, off-color vignettes, such as a man pissing on a pig, a boy's circumcision, and a man with a boot in his mouth, appear amidst the festive revelers. The other paintings in the theater ensemble sustain the jocular tone. Four paintings representing the Arts of Music, Dance, Drama, and Literature were hung on the wall opposite *Introduction*. Above them was a frieze, *The Wedding Table* (1920, cat. no. 3), depicting a whimsical feast. All of these works have been connected to the festivities of Jewish weddings, and all teem with colorful, humorous details.[9]

The murals take on added significance when viewed within the context of the Russian Revolution and its immediate aftermath. Chagall's riotous tumult of figures and hues, a Jewish harlequinade, is more than a playful fantasy; it asserts the priority of a specific ethnic culture against the hegemony of Russian society, from which the artist had been institutionally excluded since youth. Chagall often portrayed the people of the shtetl with sympathy, among them badchanim, fiddlers, and hasidim derived from the environment in which he was raised. Yet in the murals the unconventional behavior of these personages suggests a new world order. Chagall's inclusion of *Purimspieler*[10] increases the revolutionary signification of the paintings because the festival of Purim commemorates the victory of Persian Jews over Haman, a repressive foe. To Russian Jews, who had been the victims of suppression and persecution for centuries, Christian tsars and their governments were but latter-day Hamans.

While celebrating the new theater, Chagall may have used his Purim-carnival to rejoice at the troupe's victory over their Haman, that is at the fall of the tsar, who had suppressed Yiddish theater. In *Introduction to the Jewish Theater*, the vignette of a Jew urinating on a pig, which Chagall placed in the lower-right corner, the area of the painting where signatures are traditionally placed, may be interpreted as a sign of his subversive intent because the act can be viewed as a profanation of Christianity.[11] Chagall, as always, couched the reference in the deceptively naïve abandon of an upside-down world.[12]

Chagall's paintings for the Jewish Theater are probably his strongest political statement on canvas, yet they fit wholly within the world view expressed in his earlier work, an oeuvre marked by a poetic symbolism rooted in his personal cultural life. Within the ensemble, the canvas that most clearly presents Chagall's individualist utopian vision is *Love on the Stage*, which hung on the entrance wall of the theater and would be the image the audience saw while leaving the theater. The ethereal white-on-white painting of dancers in a pas de deux presents the theme of two lovers floating in the air, which Chagall returned to repeatedly throughout his life. With this symbolism he seemed to suggest that love, ultimately, was the most important subject and, perhaps, inspiration for the new Jewish theater.

If these lovers are a bride and groom, they are linked to the wedding performers depicted in the theater paintings of the Arts and to *The Wedding Table*.[13] The wedding, ubiquitous in Yiddish drama, is a festive celebration of a new beginning, and as such bears potential political implications akin to those of the Purim-carnival. Solomon (Shloyme) Mikhoels, the Jewish Theater's star and Chagall's dear friend, indicated the significance of the wedding in his remarks about a production he directed in 1945:

Our task is to show that you cannot destroy a people. No matter how we may bleed, we will go on as a people, and we will continue to celebrate weddings and give birth to children. . . . A wedding is the bond of life and bearing children, the beginning of a new life.[14]

Four years after he made this statement, Mikhoels was murdered by order of Joseph Stalin, escalating the repression of the Jewish Theater that had begun in the late 1920s, when all avant-garde theater was scrutinized by the Soviet state. The dream of a new world imagined by Russian artists, designers, and architects was ultimately quashed when the government rethought its support of avant-garde culture as a pedagogic means. The Jewish Theater, accused of undermining the goals of the Revolution, received the same criticism that was meted out to many cultural organizations and individuals. This repression may be a measure of the power, whether paranoically conceived or real, that the theater was believed to possess. Perhaps for the sake of self-preservation, the Jewish Theater censored itself, becoming progressively more conservative in the 1930s.

The fate of Chagall's murals was inextricably tied to that of the theater for which they were painted. During the purges of 1937, the paintings were rolled up and stored beneath the theater's stage for protection. In 1950, when the theater was closed by order of the state, the State Tret'iakov Gallery obtained the murals.

After four years in Paris, the capital of the European avant-garde, Chagall returned to his country in 1914 on the brink of international recognition. Swept up in the chaos and euphoria of the Revolution, he obtained positions and commissions with regularity, yet his plans were rejected with equal frequency. His designs for various experimental theatrical productions were sought after, then misunderstood or disliked; he organized an art academy and museum as the Commissar of Art for his native region, only to be rejected by his students, who had absorbed the Suprematism of Malevich. He was asked to design the inaugural production for the Jewish Theater in Moscow, yet he had a falling-out with the management of the theater and was never paid. The artist left Russia in 1922 disillusioned and disappointed by the vicissitudes of his vocation in his homeland.

Chagall's paradoxical reception in the Soviet Union continued for decades. As an émigré and a Jew, Marc Chagall was officially persona non grata, yet he was the country's most famous visual artist of the twentieth century. When he visited the Soviet Union in 1973, apparently as part of a political maneuver related to the dawn of détente, he was given a hero's welcome, despite a virtual press blackout.[15] The fate of the murals, which had lain in storage for years, was unknown to him for decades. During his visit, they were unrolled for him to sign, but this event did not lead to their restoration and exhibition. It was not until the mid-1980s that it became possible for the masterpieces of his second Russian period to go on display. In 1991, Chagall's extant paintings for the theater were exhibited together for the first time in fifty-four years; their exhibition at the Guggenheim Museum SoHo is their first appearance in the United States.[16] This catalogue marks the occasion.

Chagall's playful, fantastic scenes and seemingly childish handling of paint have frequently caused viewers to presume that an exotic, naïf artist created them. In fact, the opposite is true. Chagall was, in many ways, an extremely arcane painter, loading his canvases with texts and subtexts directed at particular audiences, ranging from the francophile avant-garde to his loved ones in the shtetl. A single painting may contain buried references to a French poem and a Yiddish proverb, Suprematist and Orphist formal means, and subject matter that includes the Eiffel Tower and a Hasidic couple. The authors of this exhibition catalogue make Chagall's multiple cultural affiliations abundantly clear while exemplifying two different approaches to the artist's work. Dr. Susan Compton, an expert on Chagall, has written an essay illuminating Chagall's art-historical context. Her thorough knowledge of both the French and Russian avant-gardes has enabled her to describe the myriad sources for the Jewish Theater murals.

Dr. Benjamin Harshav, J. and H. Blaustein Professor of Hebrew and Comparative Literature at Yale University, discusses the socio-historical and cultural legacy of Russian Jews from the Pale of Settlement, helping the reader to understand both the environment in which Chagall was raised and the references to it in his work. One of the world's foremost scholars of Yiddish, Dr. Harshav describes the role of this language in Chagall's oeuvre, while clarifying specific textual references in the paintings. Dr. Harshav and Barbara Harshav have translated and edited an extensive collection of primary documents by and about Chagall and relating to the Jewish Theater, many never before available in English.

Chagall's murals for the Jewish Theater are of tremendous historical and aesthetic value. They indicate the artist's achievement at a pivotal time in his career, summarizing his stylistic development on a monumental scale and foreshadowing the concerns of his future work. For contemporary viewers, they may also be compelling because they suggest a position vis-à-vis the role of politics in an artist's oeuvre, an issue contentiously debated today. Chagall was a painter who insisted on emphasizing his identity while remaining technically sophisticated. For him 1920 was a time

of intense political awareness; yet ultimately his ideology remained personal, destined, he believed, to communicate with all humanity.

—Jennifer Blessing
Assistant Curator for Research
Guggenheim Museum

Notes

1. Alexandra Shatskich [Aleksandra Shatskikh], "Marc Chagall and the Theatre," in *Marc Chagall: The Russian Years 1906–1922*, exh. cat. (Frankfurt: Schirn Kunsthalle, 1991), p. 77. Isaac Kloomok in "The State Jewish Theater of Moscow," in *Marc Chagall: His Life and Work*, exh. cat. (New York: Philosophical Library, 1951), p. 55, claims that the house was confiscated.

2. James Johnson Sweeney, *Marc Chagall*, exh. cat. (New York: The Museum of Modern Art, 1946), p. 44.

3. Angelica Zander Rudenstine, *The Guggenheim Museum Collection: Paintings 1880–1945*, vol. 1 (New York: Solomon R. Guggenheim Museum, 1976), pp. 76–77, fig. c.

4. Chagall's painting *Music* or the Guggenheim's *Green Violinist* inspired the 1964 production of *Fiddler on the Roof*, which was designed by Boris Aronson, author of an early monograph on the artist. (Joseph P. Swain in *The Broadway Musical: A Critical and Musical Survey* [New York and Oxford: Oxford University Press, 1990], p. 260, notes the influence of the Guggenheim canvas on *Fiddler on the Roof*.)

5. In his autobiography, *My Life*, which he began in 1921, he described his inspiration: "Ah, I thought, here is an opportunity to do away with the old Jewish theatre, its psychological naturalism, its false beards. There on these walls I shall at least be able to do as I please and be free to show everything I consider indispensable to the rebirth of the national theater." (Marc Chagall, *My Life*, Elisabeth Abbott, trans. [New York: The Orion Press, 1960], p. 162.)

6. See Avram Kampf, "Art and Stage Design: The Jewish Theatres of Moscow in The Early Twenties," in *Tradition and Revolution*, Ruth Apter-Gabriel, ed., exh. cat. (Jerusalem: The Israel Museum, 1988), pp. 125–42; and Konstantin Rudnitsky, *Russian and Soviet Theater 1905–1932*, Dr. Lesley Milne, ed., Roxane Permar, trans. (New York: Harry N. Abrams, 1988).

7. For detailed descriptions of the murals see Matthew Frost, "Marc Chagall and the Jewish State Chamber Theatre," in *Russian History*, vol. 8, parts 1–2 (1981), pp. 90–107; Ziva Amishai-Maisels, "Chagall and the Jewish Revival: Center or Periphery," and Avram Kampf, "Art and Stage Design" in Apter-Gabriel, *Tradition and Revolution*, pp. 71–100; Kampf, "The Quest for a Jewish Style," in *Chagall to Kitaj: Jewish Experience in Twentieth Century Art*, exh. cat. (London: Lund Humphries in association with Barbican Art Gallery, 1990), pp. 14–43; and Amishai-Maisels, "Chagall's Murals for the State Jewish Chamber Theatre," in Vitali, *Marc Chagall: The Russian Years 1906–1922*, pp. 107–27.

8. Mikhail Bakhtin, *Rabelais and His World*, Hélène Iswolsky, trans. (Bloomington: Indiana University Press, 1984, submitted as a dissertation in 1940; first published in Moscow, 1965; first published in English by MIT Press in 1968); for a discussion of Bakhtin's works see also Peter Stallybrass and Allon White, *The Politics and Poetics of Transgression* (Ithaca: Cornell University Press, 1986).

9. As characterized by Bakhtin, grotesque bodies are oversized and protuberant and engage in activities considered impolite. In the vertical paintings, Chagall's figures are chunky and ponderous or lanky and angular. An examination of the tiny vignettes reveals more grotesqueries, for example, the small figure beside the house in the upper left section of the painting *Music*. In a 1974 interview with Margit Rowell, the artist described this figure as a man "qui fait caca."

10. *Purimspieler* are itinerant players who perform at Purim. Kampf describes the Purim atmosphere of the paintings in "Art and Stage Design," p. 129; and "The Quest for a Jewish Style," p. 33. Amishai-Maisels in "Chagall's Murals for the State Jewish Chamber Theatre," p. 116, connects one of the acrobats in Chagall's *Introduction to the Jewish Theater* to the festival of Purim.

11. Amishai-Maisels, "Chagall's Murals for the State Jewish Chamber Theatre," p. 118.

12. Chagall's use of the world of the carnival and circus became more pronounced, and perhaps secular, in his later work. In 1974, he stated, "Le cirque pour moi c'est une énorme réalité. Nous somme tous des personnages des cirque.'" (Quoted in Rudenstine, *The Guggenheim Museum Collection: Paintings 1880–1945*, p. 78.)

13. Amishai-Maisels in "Chagall's Murals for the State Jewish Chamber Theatre," p. 121, identifies the wedding canopy in *Love on the Stage*.

14. Quoted by Nahma Sandrow, "The Soviet Yiddish State Theaters: GOSET," in *Vagabond Stars: A World History of Yiddish Theater* (New York: Harper and Row, 1977), p. 248.

15. This information was relayed to me by Gregory Veitsman, former Assistant Director for Technical Services at the State Tret'iakov Gallery, who is working on a book about that museum. See his Afterword in this book, pp. 205–07.

16. Restoration of the three largest paintings, sponsored by the Fondation Pierre Gianadda, Martigny, Switzerland, began in late 1989. The ensemble of paintings was exhibited at the Fondation Pierre Gianadda, March 1–June 9, 1991; Schirn Kunsthalle Frankfurt, June 15–August 25, 1991; State Tret'iakov Gallery, Moscow, fall 1991–winter 1992; and State Russian Museum, St. Petersburg, spring 1992. The single paintings *Dance* and *Music* were exhibited in 1987 at the State Tret'iakov Gallery, Moscow; and in 1989–90 at the Bunkamura Museum of Art, Tokyo; Kasama Nichido Museum, Ibaraki; and the Nagoya City Art Museum.

Chagall's Auditorium: "An Identity Crisis of Tragic Dimensions"

Susan Compton

There cannot be many instances of an artist being invited to design the sets for a play and so exceeding his commission that he made the whole auditorium into an extension of the stage. Yet this is what Marc Chagall did in November–December 1920, when he transformed an unpromising room in an ordinary Moscow house into a spectacular setting for the State Jewish Chamber Theater.[1] The company had been set up in 1919 to perform plays in Yiddish, the traditional language spoken by Jews in Eastern Europe. When the group failed to find suitable premises in Petrograd, they were offered two floors of a building on Bol'shoi Chernyshevskii Lane in Moscow, which had become the home of another Jewish theater company in April 1920; they accepted, moving to Moscow in November 1920, and the two groups merged. The company immediately began rehearsing their first production scheduled for the new space, an evening of three one-act plays by Sholem Aleichem, for which Chagall had been commissioned to design the sets and costumes. From opening night on New Year's Day 1921, the audience found so much to look at in the theater that Abram Efros, the artistic director, spent as much time explaining the pictures on the walls as the plays on the stage. Efros, co-author of a recently published monograph, *The Art of Marc Chagall*, was well equipped to provide answers to his questioners.[2] But because he did not leave any record of his explanations, most of what we know about Chagall's role in the State Jewish Chamber Theater has come from the artist's own memoirs, *My Life*.[3] In those pages, Chagall wrote a vivid account of the conditions in which he worked, describing how he painted the canvases on the floor while workmen built a stage at one end, and how he continued to paint while the actors rehearsed on it.[4] When he was done, his paintings — in tempera and gouache on canvas — decorated all the walls and even the ceiling of the theater: four vertical panels between the windows on one side, on the themes of Music, Dance, Drama, and Literature (cat. nos. 4–7), and a narrow frieze depicting a wedding feast (cat. no. 3) above them; one long composition, *Introduction to the Jewish Theater* (cat. no. 1), on the windowless wall opposite; a single panel, *Love on the Stage* (cat. no. 2), between the two entrance doors at the back of the theater; the stage curtain; and the ceiling painting, which depicted flying lovers and was described by James Johnson Sweeney in 1946 as "conceived as a sort of mirror in an interwoven pattern of grays, blacks and whites, suggesting a reflection of the colors and forms on all sides and beneath it."[5] In 1924, the canvases were taken from their original setting to the new home of the Jewish Chamber Theater, a former concert hall in Malaia Bronnaia Street, to which the company moved when their success required seating for more than the eighty accommodated by their old theater.[6] Because Chagall's large works were painted like theater sets on canvas, rather than directly on the wall, they were easily rehung in the foyer of the new building.

During Chagall's lifetime these theater decorations were little known in the West — where they remained unseen except in photographs — and so the scale of the original undertaking went unrecognized. His friends in Paris saw something of his vision when the company toured Western Europe in the late 1920s, and they no doubt recognized that the style of acting in the *Sholem Aleichem Evening* was inspired by his sets, which were still in use. But the murals remained in obscurity in the theater on Malaia Bronnaia Street for the next twenty years.

A tangible reminder in New York of the project was *Green Violinist*, a second version of one of the murals, *Music*; Chagall made *Green Violinist* in Paris in 1923–24, and it is now in the Guggenheim Museum's collection (cat. no. 30). In 1946, this painting (then still in the artist's possession) was exhibited in

fig. 1
Chagall painting a study for Introduction to the Jewish Theater *(cat. no. 8), 1920.*

New York at Chagall's retrospective at the Museum of Modern Art and fully discussed in the context of the State Jewish Chamber Theater in the catalogue.[7] The watercolor study for *Introduction to the Jewish Theater* (cat. no. 8) was also shown at the same exhibition, along with some of the costume and set designs. Soon afterward, the company was disbanded and its Moscow theater expropriated when Stalin carried out a persecution of the Jews. Apparently through the initiative of artist Aleksandr Tyshler, Chagall's canvases were taken to the State Tret'iakov Gallery for safekeeping.[8] Chagall did not see the works again until 1973, when he was invited to sign them at the Tret'iakov on his visit to Moscow. All the canvases had survived except the ceiling painting. Unfortunately, Chagall did not live to see the conservation work that has enabled the surviving murals to be exhibited again; they had deteriorated while being kept rolled up for more than forty years.[9]

The present exhibition thus provides one of the first opportunities to consider Chagall's theater murals in the context of his own art and of that of his friends and acquaintances in the worlds of theater and art. Ideas underlying the scheme for the series of paintings can be shown to hark back to the beginning of Chagall's life as an artist, and to reflect his upbringing in Vitebsk. This essay is devoted to exploring certain aspects of his work in relation to Russian and French writing and art. (His background in a Yiddish-speaking community and its effect on his art are discussed elsewhere in this book.) Previously, many writers have relied too heavily on Chagall's memoirs, accepting them as though they were an objective account of his life. Chagall's *My Life* should rather be seen as a response to the 1918 publication in Russian of Vasilii Kandinskii's *Reminiscences*, that artist's carefully self-selected artistic autobiography, originally published in German in 1913.[10]

It is true that the themes in Chagall's art are very often autobiographical; and *My Life* and the memoirs of his wife, Bella,[11] give fascinating insights into his childhood background. However, once he began to study art, Chagall was not as cut off from the Russian and French avant-garde as he later claimed. He liked to perpetuate the notion (put forward by his first biographers) that he was "an original primitive," but despite the apparent naïveté of his imagery, he was actually quite sophisticated and knowledgeable in matters of art.[12]

Chagall's sophistication is apparent in his creation of a fully integrated decorative scheme for the auditorium of the State Jewish Chamber Theater as well as his handling of pictorial space in the individual parts, and the complete work may be compared with decorative schemes by Russian artists known to him. Among the most prominent were those made in Berlin shortly afterward by Kandinskii and by two of Chagall's former colleagues at the Art School in Vitebsk, Ivan Puni (Jean Pougny) and El Lissitzky (which were reconstructed for the Venice Biennale in 1976 as examples of environmental art in the twentieth century[13]). Puni's was the earliest, made at the gallery Der Sturm in Berlin in 1921; it was less ambitious than the other two, because Puni covered only one of the gallery walls with his numbers, letters, and a tumbling acrobat, cut from colored paper. In contrast, Lissitzky's *Proun Room*, first shown at the Grosser Berliner Kunstausstellung in 1923, was a complete interior, for which he made designs on the floor and the ceiling, painted the walls, and constructed three-dimensional, painted reliefs for the corners, using combinations of squares and rectangles in black, gray, and white.[14] Kandinskii planned his *Musical Environment* for an unjuried exhibition in Berlin, also in 1923 — a group of huge murals, with abstract elements typical of his contemporary paintings, on a black background in an octagonal room.[15]

Only now can the differences between these Berlin schemes and Chagall's in Moscow be fully appreciated. Chagall's "box" — as the Moscow theater he had decorated was soon nicknamed — may have inspired these other Russian artists to produce their schemes in Berlin, but, unlike his own and, to a lesser extent, Puni's, the creations by Lissitzky and Kandinskii were art taken to the limits of abstraction. Although Chagall used abstract elements freely throughout the murals, he never confined himself to what he regarded as the narrow path of abstraction. "Although I love all painting, provided that its elements are pure," he told an interviewer in 1949, ". . . abstract art is so intolerant. Everything has to give way, the romantic, the figurative. . . . Even Cubists never went as far as to say: *Seulement nous* [ourselves alone]." [16] However, the greatest difference between Chagall's design and his compatriots' slightly later ones is that his decorations were not made solely for an exhibition. His scheme was intimately connected with the action on the stage and, when the curtain was raised, the "fourth wall" opened onto an imaginary world, made real by the actors. Chagall's plan took this into account: he prepared the audience for the stage performance by his *Introduction to the Jewish Theater*, which filled the long wall of the auditorium and led the eye toward the stage curtain; between the windows of the wall opposite this lively mural, and on the frieze above, the spectators could see his interpretations of characters and props probably inspired by An-ski's play *The Dybbuk*.[17] Once the performance ended and they turned to leave the theater, they faced another scene, *Love on the Stage*, on the exit wall. Chagall's theater was therefore closer in feeling, though not in style, to the nightclubs or cabarets decorated by avant-garde artists that were such a feature of artistic life in Petrograd and Moscow. Chagall frequented the Stray Dog and the Comedian's Halt in the capital when he lived there from 1915 to 1917; he must have also known the Café Pittoresque and the Poets' Café, which opened in Moscow shortly before he began work on the murals. The Comedian's Halt provided the closest prototype: its walls were covered with large figure paintings by Boris Grigorev.[18] Chagall knew the place well, as he had painted the backdrop for one of the theatrical productions that was staged at the club in 1916, a musical sketch called *To Die Happy*.[19]

The director who gave Chagall this first opportunity to work in the theater was Nikolai Evreinov, recently described by the author of an essay on Chagall as "a friend of Meyerhold." [20] Perhaps the author's reason for linking Evreinov and Vsevolod Meierkhol'd in this way was to connect Chagall's earlier work for Evreinov at the Comedian's Halt with the designs for plays by Nikolai Gogol' that Chagall made for Meierkhol'd's Hermitage Studio Theater in 1919.[21] It also serves to place Chagall firmly in the theatrical camp opposed to Konstantin Stanislavskii, the director of the Moscow Art Theater, whose realistic style Chagall criticized in *My Life*.[22] But Evreinov was a director with his own ideas and had been responsible for the seasons of Old Time Theater staged in St. Petersburg while Chagall was a student there from 1907 to 1910.[23] In those years, there were frequent debates on the nature of Russian theater and its future, mainly between factions supporting realism and symbolism. Chagall must have been fully aware of the arguments, because both of his teachers at the Zvantseva School were working for the stage at the time. Lev Bakst, who taught him painting, was then designing sets and costumes for Sergei Diaghilev's ballets, which were rehearsed in St. Petersburg before being taken to Paris. Mstislav Dobuzhinskii, who taught Chagall drawing, designed stylized sets and costumes for the two medieval mystery plays that Evreinov put on in his first season in 1907–08, and naturalistic ones for Stanislavskii's production of *A Month in the Country* in 1909.[24]

Chagall understated his early interest in the theater. He entirely omitted Dobuzhinskii's name from his memoirs, even though he began writing them not long after Dobuzhinskii had designed one of the early productions of the State Jewish Chamber Theater and had taught with him for some months at the Art School in Vitebsk.[25] In *My Life* he did write about Bakst, conveying something of the dandyism of this "actor in life." He also remembered asking his permission to try to paint a backdrop for the ballet *Narcisse*; the production stayed in his memory, for the dancer in Chagall's mural *Dance* is closer to Bakst's costume designs for the Bacchantes in *Narcisse* than to any of his own earlier work.[26]

Despite Chagall's failure to mention Evreinov in *My Life*, the director's ideas made a lasting impression on him at the beginning of his career, and Chagall's approach to painting remained close to Evreinov's ideas on theater.[27] In an article in 1908, Evreinov had set out his theatrical principles, which seem to have been a factor in Chagall's frequent choice of dramatic moments of everyday life as subject matter for his paintings. Evreinov claimed that theater is basic to man and that historically it developed before art of any other kind, even antedating religion and aesthetics. He argued that primitive man guards against monotony in his everyday life by using such events as marriage or death as opportunities to organize spectacles; and that from these, there is only a small psychological step to theater. Dismissing naturalism, he said that theatrical illusion depends on showing an *image* of the subject rather than the actual subject, on developing a *representation* of action, not simply action itself. Theater should create its own spiritual values and not serve some external idea or morality. Pure realism and pure symbolism were for him irreconcilable with true theater — the first because it unnecessarily duplicates life; the second because it interferes with the direct enjoyment of what we see.[28] From 1908 on, Chagall chose to depict the rites of life: birth, marriage, and death in different non-naturalistic styles. Even before he left the Zvantseva School for Paris, he had exhibited his *Dead Man* (1908) at the school's exhibition at the offices of the journal *Apollon*; he had also painted a remarkable *Birth* (1910), as well as a *Russian Wedding* (1909),[29] in which the characters that he would later paint in the State Jewish Chamber Theater murals make their first appearance, though in a style that shows his admiration of the work of Paul Gauguin at that time.

There are other reasons for Chagall's attraction to such subjects, particularly the theory of "real symbols" put forward by the poet Viacheslav Ivanov, who lived in his "Tower" on the top floor of the building that housed the Zvantseva School. Ivanov believed that artists should make use of everyday things to "enable us to become aware of the interrelationship and meaning of what exists not only in the sphere of earthly, empirical consciousness, but in other spheres too." Moreover, Ivanov wrote, "as a midwife eases the process of birth, so should [the artist] help things to reveal their beauty,"[30] an idea that almost crudely underlies Chagall's first painting of birth, which is dominated by the central figure of a midwife holding up the newborn child.[31] Yet, over the following years Chagall's approach remained close enough to Evreinov's ideas for the director to be content to allow him to use a version of an existing composition, *The Drunkard*,[32] as the backdrop at the Comedian's Halt. It created the right ambience because, although fantastic, it was neither too realistic nor too symbolic. In the field of Russian theater design, where artists generally took great care to relate their work precisely to the play, this was a rare case of an artist simply adapting one of his paintings for a stage set. But Chagall's backdrop, his coloring the hands and faces of the actors for the production, and even his murals for the State Jewish Chamber Theater would not have taken

the form they did without the stimulus of living in Paris, where he had painted *The Drunkard*. In that city he was even more closely in contact with new ideas generated by painters and poets than he had been in St. Petersburg.

Although he spent barely four years in Paris — from 1910 to 1914 — during that time the young Russian developed from a student of promise into an artist of international stature. In 1911, he painted a larger, revised version of *Russian Wedding*, called simply *Wedding*, giving it a friezelike composition in which a procession takes place on a stagelike space, with similar figures but complicated by colored, abstract shapes in the brilliant hues that he began using soon after he arrived in Paris.[33] By the end of 1911, he had painted a new version of *Birth*, dividing the canvas into several scenes, each containing its own episode, which he sent back to Russia for inclusion in a Mir Iskusstva (World of Art) exhibition.[34] By the time he returned to Vitebsk at the end of June 1914, Chagall's most recently exhibited paintings rivaled in scale and complexity those of more experienced French artists such as Henri Le Fauconnier, Albert Gleizes, and Jean Metzinger. All three taught at the Académie de la Palette (attended by Chagall) and produced large canvases for exhibition at the Salon des Indépendants.

Chagall's paintings on view at the Salon in spring 1914 included *The Fiddler* (fig. 2),[35] a particularly significant work because it is the precursor of the mural *Music*, the only one in the series with a direct antecedent. Although a violinist had led the procession in *Russian Wedding*, and the instrument was dear to Chagall because he had learned it as a boy, *The Fiddler* may also contain a historical reference. The Estonian violinist Edward Sormus was performing in 1912 at fund-raising events in Paris when Anatolii Lunacharskii reported in the Russian-language Parisian newspaper how Sormus, at the time of the abortive Revolution of 1905, had led demonstrations through the streets of St. Petersburg, playing his violin.[36] Some of the elements in the background of *The Fiddler* — such as the footprints in the snow (one red as though bloodstained) and heads piled one above the other (suggesting a crowd) — indicate that Chagall may have been inspired by the story. When he based *Music* on the same composition, after the successful Revolution of 1917, he altered the details but kept the same device of using a variety of elements behind a central figure. In both *The Fiddler* and *Music*, these interpolated background elements are much smaller than the dominant figure in the foreground. The association of fragments of events and places separated in time and space, which he had invented for *The Fiddler*, became the most notable characteristic of the entire theater-murals project.

This device (which he later termed "psychic construction") is intimately bound up with the poetry of the artist's Parisian friends. He mentioned several writers in *My Life* — André Salmon, Max Jacob, Blaise Cendrars, and Guillaume Apollinaire — but Cendrars and Apollinaire contributed the most to his art. Apollinaire's interest in Chagall was greatest at the very end of the painter's stay in Paris. He provided a poem as the introduction to Chagall's exhibition at the gallery Der Sturm in Berlin in 1914,[37] and also wrote a review of the show (which was published in Paris soon after Chagall returned to Vitebsk). In the review, Apollinaire described him as "an extremely varied artist, capable of painting monumental pictures, and he is not inhibited by any system."[38] As the champion of modern art, whose articles in avant-garde journals defined emerging art movements, he thus placed Chagall outside the Parisian mainstream; and he confessed to preferring Chagall's more recent work, giving *Paris Through the Window* (now in the Guggenheim Museum's collection; cat. no. 23) as an example. His choice is not surprising, for the Janus-headed

figure in the foreground has been identified as representing the poet himself, and the human-faced cat on the windowsill has been seen as a reference to a line from one of his own poems: "Your father was a sphinx and your mother the night."[39] This connection between Apollinaire's poetry and Chagall's painting is reinforced by the small yellow heart painted on the Janus-headed figure's outstretched hand, corresponding to the black heart around which Chagall had written his dedication to Apollinaire in his painting *Homage to Apollinaire*.[40]

Chagall saw more of Cendrars than of Apollinaire in Paris, and it was Cendrars who provided titles for many of Chagall's pictures, including *Paris Through the Window*.[41] The various snippets of experience from which Chagall composed this window-painting reflect the dislocated imagery of Cendrars's poetry. Note, for instance, some lines that Cendrars wrote in 1913:

It's raining electric light bulbs
Montrouge Gare de l'Est subway North-South
*   river boats world*
Everything is halo
Profundity
In the Rue de Buci they're hawking l'Intransigeant
*   and* Paris-Sports
The airdrome of the sky is on fire, a painting
*   by Cimabue.*[42]

Cendrars piles one idea upon another intuitively without any apparent logical connection, as in the accidental juxtaposition of advertising posters on walls or fragments of overheard conversation, in order to reflect modern life and its multiple means of communication.

Apollinaire used similar sources and juxtaposed his images in this seemingly random fashion in the poems he named *Calligrammes*, where the printed words not only carry their expected meanings but are clustered together on the page in novel arrangements to form literal pictures. He defended them from the charge that they were incomprehensible as written language by saying that the fragments of language were now tied together by an ideographic, instead of a grammatical, logic. He felt that this made no psychological difference to the poem, even though the intuitive spatial arrangement was quite the opposite of reasoned order. Apollinaire's poems and this explanation were printed in *Les Soirées de Paris* after Chagall had left for the opening of his 1914 exhibition in Berlin.[43]

Chagall's quotation of disconnected visual elements in his recently completed *Fiddler* parallels Apollinaire's use of verbal ones. Indeed, Apollinaire's defense could be adapted to read as a defense of works such as *The Fiddler*, where the normal relation of parts to the whole is absent, conventions of scale are ignored, and spatial logic is replaced by unaccountable jumps from one part of the picture to another. Viewers who had barely accustomed themselves to "reading" Cubist space — with its quotations from "real life" in the form of snippets of words — must have been confused by the absence of anything like the geometric framework that served to relate one element with another in a Cubist painting. Instead, their eyes must have moved restlessly from the little blue tree on the right, with its population of songbirds, to the composite figure on the left, with the three heads imposed on a single body. They must have found quite incomprehensible the juxtapositions of a house with a foot, a leg with a stool, and a stool with a

---

fig. 2
The Fiddler, 1912–13.
Oil on canvas, 188 x 156 cm (74 x 61 3/8 inches).
Stedelijk Museum, Amsterdam.

church tower; only in the upper part of the picture — where a row of houses preserved its congruent proportions — could they find a reliable type of order. Yet, a particular aspect of Cubism described by Albert Gleizes and Jean Metzinger in their treatise on Cubism, published in 1912, applies to *The Fiddler*: "The painter has the power of rendering as enormous things that we regard as infinitesimal, and as infinitesimal things that we know to be considerable: he changes quantity into quality."[44] In addition, viewers of *The Fiddler* might be reminded of Cimabue or other primitive Italian masters. In the review mentioned above, Apollinaire suggested yet another link, describing Chagall as "a colorist imbued with an imagination that occasionally finds its source in the fantasies of Slavic folk illustration but always goes beyond them."[45] Russian woodblock prints, so popular with avant-garde artists in Russia at the time, often show figures enlarged according to their importance in the story. As is invariably the case in Chagall's paintings at all stages in his career, a multiplicity of ideas underlay his inventions.

It may seem strange that Chagall's *Fiddler*, conceived in Paris, is so much further from Cubism than *Music* and its later counterpart, *Green Violinist*. In Paris in 1913, however, Chagall rejected rigorous Cubism after showing a large picture at the Salon des Indépendants in spring 1913 under the title *Couple sous l'arbre (Couple Under a Tree)* — obviously Adam and Eve.[46] The entwined figures of Adam and Eve are close in style to Russian Cubo-Futurist paintings such as those that Liubov' Popova painted in 1914–16 on her return to her homeland from Paris (where she had studied in the same Académie de la Palette as Chagall).[47] Chagall, however, found that style too cerebral and he became interested in an offshoot of Cubism, Orphism. This was a movement named and promoted by Apollinaire, who summarized the first exhibition of Orphist paintings in March 1913: "[Orphism] unites painters of quite different characters all of whom have, by their researches, arrived at a more subjective, more popular, more poetic vision of the universe and of life."[48] He admired the work of its chief exponent and theorist, Robert Delaunay, whose work has often been compared to Chagall's.[49] Chagall became friends with Delaunay and his Russian wife, Sonia, and in 1913 attended a dance hall, the Bal Bullier, with them and a group of their friends every Thursday. During that year Sonia Delaunay painted evocations of the lights and the movement of the colorful dancers in what she named her "simultaneous" paintings. Some of her canvases were very large (though not as large as Chagall's *Introduction to the Jewish Theater*) and her interlocking circles, with traces of dancing figures entirely painted in bright colors, produce a luminous effect. The memory of her work may have contributed to Chagall's decision to break up his flat background with segments of circles when he came to paint the theater murals.

This connection may seem rather remote, especially as Chagall was not interested in Orphism taken to the extremes of pure abstraction, in which the subject matter was progressively reduced until only color and form remained. Yet, in 1913–14, he painted a figure of *Orpheus* (whose name had inspired the art movement) reclining on a colored hillock.[50] Chagall emphasized the hero's lyre in this painting, which suggests that he was fully aware of the symbolic aspect of Orpheus as the "ideal embodiment of the poet whose song had the power of illumination . . . giving meaning to the mystery of life."[51] Such a view stems from nineteenth-century French poetry and was the basis of Apollinaire's use of the Orphic theme in his own. In *Le Bestiaire*, Apollinaire had interspersed his poems about animals with poems about Orpheus, and one of the woodcuts that Raoul Dufy made for this book is dominated by an enlarged figure of the mythical hero surrounded by abstract space, in which a tiny Eiffel Tower as well as an equally small Egyptian pyramid emerge from a multitude of lines.[52] Dufy's illustration may even have provided a further prototype for Chagall's *Fiddler* composition. Yet another instance of the connections between Apollinaire's poetry and Chagall's work is found in some almost untranslatable lines from *Cortège d'Orphée*, which may have inspired the image of *The Drunkard*: "he saw his cut-off head is the sun / and the moon his sliced neck."[53]

After Chagall returned to Russia, during the six years before he painted his murals, he chose themes that were less easily connected with contemporary poetry. He relinquished birth and death, although love dominated his pictures after his marriage to Bella in 1915. Among other subjects, he painted a different type of wedding scene in a completely different style from the ones he had done before. This black, white, and gray drawing on paper, entitled *Jewish Marriage* (fig. 3), shows a non-naturalistic but dramatic indoor scene: in a stagelike space, a bride and groom sit at the head of a table with caricatured guests in front of a "backdrop" view of the local town through a curtain-framed window. From the "wings," a figure anticipating the one in the mural *Drama* floats in, bearing wine for the feast; "downstage," a woman enlivens the proceedings by dancing with a male reveler, admittedly in a more earthbound way than her later counterpart in the mural *Dance*. The watercolor is reminiscent of studies that Chagall made at the beginning of 1917, when he was commissioned to provide wall-paintings for the school attached to the chief synagogue in Petrograd. The project was never realized, but some of Chagall's preparatory works for it have survived, including a watercolor of a secular scene, *Visit to the Grandparents*, and scenes of two religious festivals, *Feast of the Tabernacles* (in gouache) and *Purim* (in oil),[54] as well as two final sketches, *Purim* and *The Baby Carriage*,[55] both greatly simplified in comparison with the *Purim* oil and *Visit to the Grandparents*. Many of the details in these final sketches are similar to those for the theater murals — indeed, at the top of the *Introduction to the Jewish Theater* there is a drawing of the façade of the St. Petersburg building in which they were to have been housed.[56] But, although activity is suggested in both designs — a striding figure and a seller of sweets in one; a woman knitting, another woman painting, and figures apparently pushing the pram in the other — there is none of the sweeping sensation of movement expressed by the figures in the later murals. *Purim* features a large figure in the foreground and smaller ones in the background, as in *The Fiddler*, but here they are silhouetted against a plain white background, with no anticipation of the Cubist touches that were to dominate *Music*.

Chagall explored a great many ways of composing pictures after his return to Russia. He drew portraits and even townscapes "from life" and usually added his own quirky details; he transformed interior views by choosing unusual viewpoints; he invented a bird's-eye view combining a recognizable town with stylized figures floating in the sky. He was well aware of the inventions of other Russian avant-garde artists because he took part in exhibitions that included a wide range of contemporary artists.[57] Sometimes he found inspiration in unexpected sources, such as Aristarkh Lentulov's *Ornéisme*.[58] However, whereas Lentulov often used real lace and tassels, gluing them to his canvases, Chagall soaked lacy cloth in paint and used it to transfer patterns to canvas or paper — a device that he employed extensively in the theater murals. The technique can be studied in close-up in a work on paper from 1920 known as *The Dream* (and belonging to the Guggenheim Museum; cat. no. 27).

In Russia in 1917, general interest in Cubism — and more specifically, Pablo Picasso's use of unusual textures — was stimulated by a study of the artist by poet and critic Ivan Aksenov.[59] This Russian monograph (the first on Picasso in any language) provoked considerable response among artists. Chagall himself investigated the formal possibilities of Cubism again, particularly in two rather different paintings, *The Apparition*,[60] and *Anywhere Out of This World* (its title borrowed from a prose-poem by Charles Baudelaire).[61] Chagall's close-up figures in blue and white, hovering in the dreamlike space of his Cubistic *Apparition*, may be compared with Natan Al'tman's earlier *Portrait of Anna Akhmatova*,[62] which has a similar, Cubistic background. *Anywhere Out of This World*, with its simple coloring and emphasis on texture, has some formal resemblance to David Shterenberg's *Table with a Roll* of 1919.[63] The connection between the last two and conventional Cubism may seem remote, as Shterenberg's composition of a tabletop with a dish and a bread roll is nearly abstract, but the principal feature of both works is an area of thick white paint worked in places with a house-painter's graining comb. (This refers to the "Polemical Supplement" that Aksenov had added to his account of Picasso's art in which he discussed the artist's use of texture, mentioning the use of such a comb.[64]) These three Russian artists had all lived in Paris for several years before 1914, but it was not easy to see Picasso's work, except in his studio or his dealer's gallery, as he did not submit work to exhibitions there. Furthermore, Shterenberg (considerably older than the other two) had studied at the Ecole des Beaux-Arts, and Al'tman (the youngest) had attended Marie Vasil'ev's Russian Academy in Paris, so Chagall was the only one with a Cubist-oriented background. However, in Moscow, artists were able to study Picasso at first hand because the city already boasted the largest number of his paintings outside Paris. The best collection of Picasso's work in Russia belonged to Sergei Shchukin, who had bought many of Picasso's Cubist paintings from 1909 onward and regularly opened his Moscow house to artists. However, it is not certain that the Jewish artists had the opportunity to see the collection until they gained citizenship after the February Revolution in 1917; this allowed all Jews to travel without a permit for the first time and gave artists an opportunity to visit this remarkable collection and see works by Gauguin and Henri Matisse as well as Picasso. A renewed concern with French art was an important corrective to what might have become a provincial attitude, especially for Shterenberg, Chagall, and Al'tman, who in 1919 founded the Moscow branch of the League of Culture, an organization dedicated to the promotion of Jewish art.[65] They did not believe that art, in order to be Jewish, should be stylistically restricted, and each developed an international approach, remaining close enough in their aims to share an exhibition in spring 1922, which featured the second public display of Chagall's murals.[66]

When Chagall began designing the theater murals, his decision to allot a complete wall to a single subject meant that he had to invent a far more complex composition than he had proposed for the Petrograd synagogue-school murals. The disproportion of length to height suggested a friezelike, compartmentalized composition, which he could have based on his 1911 pictures of *Birth* and *Wedding*. Alternatively, he could have followed the example of Sonia Delaunay in her Orphist rendering of the Bal Bullier. He seems, however, to have found help in Gleizes's and Metzinger's book on Cubism, where the following passage reads like a recipe for the way he composed his *Introduction to the Jewish Theater*:

We must also contrive to cut up by large restful surfaces all regions in which activity is exaggerated by excessive contiguity. In short, the science of design consists in instituting relations between straight lines and curves. A picture which contained only straight lines or curves would not express life. It would be the same with a picture in which

fig. 3
Jewish Marriage, *1910s.*
Gouache, india ink, pen, and brush on paper,
mounted on cardboard, 20.5 x 30 cm (8 x 11 3/4 inches).
Collection of Zinaida Gordaeva, St. Petersburg.

curves and straight lines exactly compensate one another, for exact equivalence is equal to zero. . . . What the curve is to the straight line, the cold tone is to the warm tone in the domain of color.[67]

Chagall indeed "cut up" the extensive surface of his twenty-six-foot-long canvas by using straight lines and curves. But instead of the fragmented arrangement of thin verticals, horizontals, and adjoining curves so characteristic of Picasso's Cubist work — and of Gleizes's and Metzinger's — Chagall joined his lines with bands of color so that they sweep across the canvas in great diagonals and become parts of large triangles. His curves form segments of circles, so large that they form interlocking worlds within the composition. In addition, although his curves and straight lines never "compensate one another," nor, "in the domain of color," do his cold tones evenly balance the warm, he imparts a sensation of movement — alien to Cubism, though not to Orphism — to this mural, and to the entire scheme.

It would be foolish to suggest that Chagall simply read or re-read Gleizes's and Metzinger's *Cubism*[68] in 1920 because he was faced with a compositional problem. A more likely reason was the publication at the Art School in Vitebsk of a fellow-teacher's book on the development of twentieth-century art, Kazimir Malevich's *On New Systems in Art*, which was published in December 1919 in an edition handmade by the school's graphic workshop.[69] Chagall referred to it as "our edition" in a note on a letter that he wrote in April 1920, when he was evidently still on reasonable terms with Malevich.[70] Nonetheless, Chagall's firsthand experience of the full range of Modernist art in Western Europe must have raised doubts in his own mind about his colleague's analysis of Cubism. Furthermore, although Malevich showed an extraordinary grasp of the principles of Cubism in his earlier paintings (especially considering that he had then traveled no further from Moscow than Petrograd), he had used the style as his stepping-stone to non-objective Suprematism, which he still espoused in 1919–20. The emblem of Suprematism was his 1915 *Black Square*, which he saw as a breakthrough in the history of art. He explained that Suprematism was the beginning of a new culture: "The square is not a subconscious form. It is the creation of intuitive reason. The face of the new art"; with his painting of a black square on a white ground he had reduced painting to "zero," building on Gleizes's and Metzinger's phrase "exact equivalence is equal to zero."[71]

Chagall quoted Malevich's "zero-form" in the mural *Music*, where a small black square hovers over one of the houses in the background, near the right-hand edge. He balanced this on the left side, not by a complete black circle, typical of Suprematism, but by a black wedgelike segment more typical of recent black paintings by Aleksandr Rodchenko, a younger artist who had opposed his *Black on Black* paintings to Malevich's latest *White on White* at the Tenth State Exhibition in 1919.[72] Those attuned to the subtleties of non-objective art may have recognized Chagall's comment on this recent battle of white and black in his mural *Love on the Stage*, in which the outlines of the transparent figures of two ballet dancers embracing emerge from an interplay of geometric forms executed in gradations of grays. But unlike Malevich, who had eliminated all but squares, polygons, and curved abstract forms from his white paintings in this show, or Rodchenko, who had based some of his apparently abstract black forms on recent astronomical events,[73] Chagall retained references to the world as we know it in his riposte. He indicated the floorboards of a steeply raked stage by means of parallel lines; he placed a screen behind and to the left of the dancers — not unlike the one he used as scenery for *It's a Lie*, on e of the plays in the *Sholem Aleichem Evening* — and topped it with a shaded

fig. 4
Collage, *1921.*
Pencil, pen, ink, and collaged elements (including a fragment of the invitation to the exhibition of Chagall's Jewish Theater murals) on paper, 34.2 x 27.9 cm (15 ³/₈ x 11 inches).
Musée national d'art moderne, Centre Georges Pompidou, Paris.

rectangle whose scalloped edge hints at the traditional canopy present at all Jewish weddings. Furthermore, he did not reduce his colors simply to shades of white and black but connected the tableau with the frieze above the windows, *The Wedding Table*, by adding a few arcs and lines of similar color. He even used touches of color in the ballerina's legs and in one of the two tiny figures in the foreground.

The different ways that Chagall painted dancers in his theater murals — the barely outlined figures of *Love on the Stage*, the rounded forms of the Hasidic dancers of his *Introduction* with their delicately painted costumes, and the baroque figure in *Dance* herself, with her heavily modeled face — show his continuing fascination with a variety of styles. Shortly before beginning work on the murals he had studied paintings of dancers by Rodchenko and Varvara Stepanova at the Nineteenth State Exhibition (1920). Brief entries in Stepanova's diary for November 1920 record several visits by Chagall to the show and his interest in their work, to the extent of his asking to visit their studio.[74] Her diary also gives her own verdict on her dancers — that they represented an impasse in her work — and Chagall must have hoped that his own stylistic inventions would serve as a model for the future of art. With the benefit of hindsight, it is clear that his murals had little chance of success with these artists, who, by the time he was able to exhibit them, were moving so decisively toward Constructivism.[75] Nevertheless, Chagall explored a style closer to theirs when he made an abstract *Collage* (fig. 4)[76] — not in 1920, as he later signed it, but in 1921, when the exhibition of his theater murals took place (part of the invitation for that Twenty-Third State Exhibition of June 1921 is pasted on as one of the collage elements). The only Russian collages that resemble it in any way are by Rodchenko and Stepanova, dated 1918 and 1919.[77] Such flirtation with near abstraction is untypical of Chagall, but it shows how he remained open to different ways of creating art after he had finished work on the murals.

He was anxious for general recognition for the murals, and the June 1921 exhibition was held as a result of his own initiative. He wrote to the theater management shortly after he had finished the murals, assuring them that he had proved his love for Jews but that he equally loved Russians and other nationalities.[78] Expediently, he said that he wanted "the masses" to see the paintings; but he must have been anxious that artists should discuss them, as well as that his work should have official, as well as ethnic, approval. His *Introduction to the Jewish Theater* served a dual purpose, as a manifesto for his art and also for the new theater itself. Because the murals were not made for exhibition per se — in contrast to the installations by Puni, Lissitzky, and Kandinskii discussed earlier — Chagall was so anxious that they should be considered as works of art that he made sure that they were shown to the general public as soon as possible.

Chagall's theater murals, though on the whole not very abstract, are not very realistic, as might be expected in view of his early closeness to Evreinov. In the mural *Introduction*, the abstract geometric elements that form the background double as screens, partially eclipsing some figures, musical instruments, and even an angel trumpeter — a somewhat "realistic" effect that is counterbalanced by the deliberate incompleteness of the main figures, which are missing heads or legs, arms or hands. It is as though, like the elements of his *Collage*, they were simply components in the artist's repertoire. Paradoxically, however, these imperfect figures create an illusion of a reality that is more convincing to a viewer from the modern world than any of the socialist pageantry that was to become the norm in Soviet Russia within a decade, and the murals survived in place until 1937, longer than the so-called

Formalist art of Malevich, Rodchenko, Lissitzky, or Kandinskii. What saved Chagall, perhaps, is that almost everything that is represented in the murals is sufficiently lifelike for viewers to recognize them: the three principal figures (Efros presenting Chagall to Granovskii, the director of the theater); the details of their everyday world, such as the somewhat Cubist glass of milk being served by the caretaker (who is described in *My Life*[79]); the musicians throughout the mural, modeled on the real musicians in the theater; and the actors portrayed in Chagall's rainbow-colored fantasy in the right-hand section of the mural. Here — literally at a higher level — Shakespeare's Hamlet (for such is the figure behind the cow[80]) points back to the dancers at a Hasidic wedding (which Chagall also describes in *My Life*[81]). In the foreground the artist's wife, Bella (herself an aspiring actress) and their little daughter, Ida, applaud this new world that extends to the very edge of the mural. In the bottom-right corner it ends in a witty image of a Jewish villager (the artist himself?) urinating on an unclean pig — a separate, rectangular picture that Chagall repeated on a small scale in black and white while he was living in Berlin.[82]

Chagall must have been delighted to learn that the canvases finally found their permanent home in the State Tret'iakov Gallery, where they can be considered as statements not simply of his birthright but of his achievement as an artist. This is particularly significant because Chagall resisted attempts to allow himself to be classed as an exclusively Jewish painter. His friend the Hebrew poet Hayim Nakhman Bialik sought his advice when a new art museum for Tel Aviv was being planned in 1931, and Chagall fought for an international collection rather than a museum limited to art by Jewish artists who had settled in Palestine.[83] And when he founded his own Museum of the Biblical Message in 1973 in Nice, near his adopted home in the South of France, he expressed the wish that religious art by painters and sculptors of all nationalities should be shown in exhibitions there.[84] In 1921, a review of the exhibition of the murals claimed that Chagall's *Introduction to the Jewish Theater* represented an "identity crisis of tragic dimensions, a point at which any word and any talk whatsoever would be as out-of-place as at somebody's deathbed." To the reviewer, the tragedy was that the artist lacked the means "to reproduce the unending complexity of each single atom of our world, on which the eyes of our contemporaries are fixed."[85] But Chagall had already found that pertinent references to the real world can make art more powerful — and certainly more accessible — than pure abstraction or strict naturalistic representation. As he demonstrated throughout his career, the world of art reflects a world of another dimension that cannot be revealed through geometry but is embodied in love. His position was surprisingly similar to the conclusion reached by Gleizes and Metzinger: "Henceforth by the study of all the manifestations of physical and mental life, the painter will learn to apply them. But if he ventures into metaphysics, cosmogony, or mathematics, let him content himself with obtaining their savour, and abstain from demanding of them certitudes which they do not possess. At the back of them he finds nothing but love and desire."[86]

Notes

1. See Alexandra Shatskich [Aleksandra Shatskikh], "Marc Chagall and the Theater," in Christoph Vitali, ed., *Marc Chagall: The Russian Years 1906–1922*, exh. cat. (Frankfurt: Schirn Kunsthalle, 1991), p. 80. This is the source that I have used throughout for facts on the theater. The company is often referred to in the literature as the State Jewish Kamerny Theater; *kamerny* is Russian for "chamber."

2. For Efros's account of Chagall's murals and the production, see his essay, "The Artists of the Granovsky Theater," from *Iskusstvo*, vol. 4, nos. 1–2 (1928), pp. 62–64, trans. in Vitali, *Marc Chagall: The Russian Years 1906–1922*, p. 91. The monograph that Efros had co-authored was A. Efros and Ia. Tugendkhol'd, *Iskusstvo Marka Shagala* (Moscow: Helikon, 1918). A new translation appears in this book on pages 134–43.

3. Marc Chagall, *Ma Vie*, preface by André Salmon, trans. from the Russian to French by Bella Chagall (Paris: G. Charensol, 1931); reissued in 1957, and trans. from the French to English by Dorothy Williams as *My Life* (New York: Oxford University Press, 1989). For the earlier history of this text, see Susan Compton, *Marc Chagall, My Life — My Dream: Berlin and Paris 1922–1940* (Munich: Prestel / New York: Te Neues Publishing Company, 1990), p. 196.

4. Chagall, *My Life*, p. 160. There are subtle differences between this text and Chagall's lesser-known version, published in English translation from the Yiddish original (in *The Jewish World*, vol. 2 [1928]), as "My Work in the Jewish Kamerny Theatre," in Aleksandr Kamensky, *Chagall: The Russian Years 1907–1922*, trans. from the French by Catherine Phillips (London: Thames and Hudson, 1989), pp. 359–60.

5. James Johnson Sweeney describes the ceiling in his *Marc Chagall*, exh. cat. (New York: The Museum of Modern Art, 1946), p. 46; and Shatskich, citing the unpublished memoirs of A. V. Asarkh-Granovskaia, identifies the subject as "Flying Lovers" in her essay in Vitali, *Marc Chagall: The Russian Years 1906–1922*, p. 88 (note 6). This interpretation strengthens Ziva Amishai-Maisels's identification of the theme of some of the murals as being inspired by the play *The Dybbuk* (see note 17 below).

6. The company had moved at the end of 1921 to Malaia Bronnaia Street, but still used the theater at Bol'shoi Chernychevskii Lane for studio productions until 1924. See Shatskich's essay in Vitali, *Marc Chagall: The Russian Years 1906–1922*, pp. 80–81.

7. The project is discussed and illustrated in Sweeney, *Marc Chagall*, pp. 44–48.

8. Tyshler's part in saving the murals was recalled by Granovskii's widow, A. V. Asarkh-Granovskaia, in conversation with Alexandra Shatskich in 1975; see Shatskich's essay in Vitali, *Marc Chagall: The Russian Years 1906–1922*, p. 81.

9. The canvases, which were no doubt regarded unfavorably at that time as "Formalist," were rolled up and stored under the stage in the summer of 1937 and, from 1950, were left rolled up in the State Tret'iakov Gallery storeroom. See Shatskich's essay in Vitali, *Marc Chagall: The Russian Years 1906–1922*, p. 81.

10. V. V. Kandinskii, *Tekst khudozhnika (Stupeni): 25 reproduktsii s kartin 1902–1917 gg. 4 vin'etki* (Moscow: Izdanie Otdela Izobrazitel'nykh Iskusstv Narodnogo Komissariata po Prosveshcheniiu, 1918), a Russian translation of Kandinskii's *Rückblicke, 1901–1913* (Berlin: Der Sturm [1913]).

11. Bella Chagall's memoirs were first published as *Brenendicke Licht* (New York: Book League of the Jewish Peoples Fraternal Order, 1945) — trans. into English by Norbert Guterman as *Burning Lights* (New York: Schocken Books, 1946) — and *Di Ershte bagegenish* (New York: 1947); the text was trans. into French by Ida Chagall as *Lumières allumées* (Paris: Gallimard, 1973), then trans. from the French into English by Barbara Bray as *First Encounter* (New York: Schocken Books, 1983).

12. Tugendkhol'd described Chagall's art as like that of a child in the monograph that he co-authored with Efros (see note 2 above). See also J. P. Hodin's 1949 interview, "Marc Chagall: In Search of the Primary Sources of Inspiration," in *The Dilemma of Being Modern: Essays on Art and Literature* (London: Routledge and Kegan Paul, 1956), p. 43.

13. Photographs of the interiors by Puni and Kandinskii are reproduced in *Thirty-Seventh Biennale di Venezia: Environment. Participation. Cultural Structures*, exh. cat., vol. 1 (Milan: Alfieri, 1976), p. 189.

14. Lissitzky's diagram of his "Proun Room" at the exhibition hall of the Lehrter Bahnhof is reproduced in Sophie Lissitzky-Küppers, *El Lissitzky: Life, Letters, Texts*, Helene Adwinckle and Mary Whittal, trans. (London: Thames and Hudson, 1968), fig. 189; a translation of his account of the room from the periodical *G* (July 1923) is given there on p. 365.

15. For Kandinskii's room, see Clark V. Poling, "Kandinsky at the Bauhaus in Weimar, 1922–1925," in *Kandinsky: Russian and Bauhaus Years 1915–1933*, exh. cat. (New York: Solomon R. Guggenheim Museum, 1983), pp. 40–41.

16. Chagall, in Hodin interview (see note 12 above), p. 44.

17. For this interpretation, see Ziva Amishai-Maisels, "Chagall's Murals for the State Jewish Chamber Theater," in Vitali, *Marc Chagall: The Russian Years 1906–1922*, pp. 122–25. She connects the scheme with An-ski's *The Dybbuk*, which the author apparently gave Chagall to read, wanting him to design sets and costumes for it.

18. See John E. Bowlt, *The Silver Age: Russian Art of the Early Twentieth Century and the "World of Art" Group* (Newtonville, Mass.: Oriental Research Partners, 1979), opposite p. 125, for a photograph of the interior of the Comedian's Halt. Franz Meyer gives the name as Prival Komediante Theater in his *Marc Chagall: Life and Work* (New York: Abrams, n.d.), p. 289; this is corrected to Comedian's Halt in Matthew Frost, "Marc Chagall and the Jewish State Chamber Theater," in *Russian History*, vol. 8, p. 92.

19. See Frost, ibid., p. 92, note 10, where he cites a letter from Mme A. A. Evreinova to John E. Bowlt, April 14, 1980, stating that *To Die Happy* was written by Sasha Chernyi and set to music by Nikolai Evreinov.

20. Nikolai Nikolaevich Evreinov, 1879–1953; the essay is by Alexandra Shatskich in Vitali, *Marc Chagall: The Russian Years 1906–1922*, pp. 76–88.

21. Matthew Frost states that Chagall's designs for Gogol''s *Marriage* and *The Gambler* of 1919 were also requested by Evreinov (see Matthew Frost, "Marc Chagall and the Jewish State Chamber Theater," in *Russian History*, vol. 8, p. 92); the plays were to be staged at the Hermitage Studio Theater in St. Petersburg, which was founded on the initiative of Meierkhol'd. See Susan Compton, *Chagall*, catalogue for 1985 exhibition at the Philadelphia Museum of Art and the Royal Academy of Arts, London (New York: Abrams, 1985), cat. no. 61 and fig. 40, pp. 198–99.

22. Chagall, *My Life*, pp. 160–61.

23. For an account of the Old Time (or Antique) Theater, see Bowlt, *The Silver Age*, pp. 116–17.

24. Color reproductions of Dobuzhinskii's work are included in Alla Gusarova, *Mstislav Dobuzhinskii: Zhivopis': Graphika. Teatr* (Painting. Graphic Art. Stage Design) (Moscow: Izobrazitel'noe Iskusstvo, 1982). For his influence on Chagall, see "The Russian Background" in Compton, *Chagall*, p. 32.

25. Dobuzhinskii is identified as the director of the State School of Art when it opened at 10 Voskresenksaia Street, Vitebsk, on January 30, 1919, in Kamensky, *Chagall: The Russian Years 1907–1922*, p. 275.

26. Bakst is described as an "actor in life" in Bowlt, *The Silver Age*, p. 225. Chagall's account of Bakst (in *My Life*, pp. 89–93) hints at the "double standard" of his teacher, who changed his name from Rozenberg to Bakst and then his religion, converting to Lutheranism to marry in 1903. Bakst's reversion to Judaism after his divorce in 1910 may account for Chagall's enigmatic paintings *Circumcision* and *The Holy Family*, reproduced in Kamensky, *Chagall: The Russian Years 1907–1922*, pp. 35 and 43. Bakst's set for *Narcisse* is reproduced in color in *The Decorative Art of Léon Bakst* (London: The Fine Art Society, 1913; reprinted, New York: Dover Paperback, 1972), plate 34; costumes for the Bacchantes from *Narcisse*, plates 31 and 54.

27. Evreinov's most radical theatrical invention was his monodrama (a play with a single character — the writer himself), which was published in Nikolai Kul'bin, ed., *Studiia impressionistov*, (St. Petersburg: N. I. Butkovskoi, 1910). It is discussed in Susan Compton, *The World Backwards: Russian Futurist Books 1912–17* (London: The British Library, 1978), pp. 46–49. The title of Chagall's mural *Love on the Stage* resembles the title of Evreinov's monodrama *The Representation of Love*.

28. Evreinov summarized the article in his French text, referring to it as "Apologie de la théâtralité," and citing its publication in 1908 in a newpaper that he calls *Le Matin* (he gives no further details, but presumably he means the Russian newspaper *Utro Rossii*); see Nicolas Evreinoff [sic], *Histoire du Théâtre russe* (Paris: Editions du Chêne, 1947), pp. 375–77.

29. In Compton, *Chagall*, these paintings are reproduced and discussed in detail: *The Dead Man*, 1908, cat. no. 3, pp. 155–56; *Russian Wedding*, 1909, cat. no. 9, p. 160; *Birth*, 1910, cat. no. 10, pp. 160–61. *The Dead Man* is now in the collection of the Musée national d'art moderne, Centre Georges Pompidou, Paris. The exhibition of works by pupils at the Zvantseva School took place in the offices of *Apollon*, April 20–May 9, 1910.

30. V. Ivanov, "Dve stikhii v sovremennom simvolizme (Two Elements of Contemporary Symbolism)," in *Zolotoe runo*, April/May 1908.

31. *Birth* (Kunsthaus, Zurich) is discussed further in Compton, *Chagall*, p. 34, cat. no. 10, p. 161.

32. *The Drunkard* (collection of Hans Neumann, Caracas) is reproduced in color in Kamensky, *Chagall: The Russian Years 1907–1922*, p. 321, with the date given as 1921; Meyer, following the inscription on the canvas, dates the painting 1911–12. Chagall repeated the composition in a gouache, painted around 1923, reproduced in color in *The First Russian Show: A Commemoration of the Van Diemen Exhibition Berlin 1922*, exh. cat. (London: Annely Juda Fine Art, 1983), p. 90.

33. *The Wedding* (Musée national d'art moderne, Centre Georges Pompidou, Paris), is reproduced in color and dated 1910 in Meyer, *Chagall*, p. 113.

34. *Birth* (The Art Institute of Chicago) is reproduced and discussed in Compton, *Chagall*, cat. no. 18, pp. 166–67. That entry was written before the publication of the letter and sketch of the composition sent by the artist to the secretary of the World of Art exhibiting society, which indicates that he had sent the canvas to Moscow; see M. Chagall, "Letter to K. V. Kandaurov of November 14, 1911," in Vitali, *Marc Chagall: The Russian Years 1906–1922*, pp. 144–45. The same picture seems to have been shown at the Salon des Indépendants in 1913.

35. *The Fiddler* (Stedelijk Museum, Amsterdam, on loan from the P. A. Regnault collection, Netherlands State Collection) is reproduced in color in Compton, *Chagall*, p. 75.

36. A. V. Lunacharskii, in *Parizhskii vestnik*, no. 47, November 23, 1912. The story of Edward Sormus is mentioned in R. C. Williams, *Artists in Revolution* (London: Scolar, 1977), pp. 53 and 210 (note 50), but the name is transliterated there as Eduard Syrmus. For the connection between this painting and Dobuzhinskii's post-1905 revolutionary art, see Compton, *Chagall*, p. 33. Note also that after the October Revolution in 1917, Lunacharskii was the commisar who authorized Chagall's official appointment.

37. G. Apollinaire, "Rotsoge; au peintre Chagall," exh. cat. in *Der Sturm*, Berlin, vol. 5 (May 1914), p. 19; English trans. in Sweeney, *Chagall*, p. 102. Chagall's work was exhibited at the gallery Der Sturm in a two-person show with Alfred Kubin in May 1914; his solo exhibition was in June.

38. Guillaume Apollinaire, *Apollinaire on Art: Essays and Reviews 1902–1918*, LeRoy C. Breunig, ed., Susan Suleiman, trans. (New York: Viking Press, 1972), p. 400.

39. George T. Noszlopy identifies the head as modeled on "Apollinaire's famous 'Roman profile' . . . while it follows the iconography of the *Beardless Janus*, a Roman coin in the Bibliothèque nationale, Paris." The line that he refers to (the original French is "Ton père fut un sphinx et ta mère une nuit") is from "Le Larron" (The thief), in *Alcools*. See Noszlopy, "Apollinaire, Allegorical Imagery and the Visual Arts," *Forum for Modern Language Studies*, vol. 9, no. 1 (January 1973), pp. 72–73, note 91.

40. *Homage to Apollinaire*, 1911–12 (Stedelijk Van Abbemuseum, Eindhoven), reproduced and discussed in Compton, *Chagall*, cat. no. 22, p. 170.

41. See Angelica Zander Rudenstine, *The Guggenheim Museum Collection: Paintings 1880–1945* (New York: Solomon R. Guggenheim Museum, 1976), p. 64.

42. Blaise Cendrars, "Contrastes" (October 1913), *Du monde entier au coeur du monde* (Paris: Denoël, 1947), pp. 56–57; English trans. in Roger Shattuck, *The Banquet Years: The Origins of the Avant-Garde in France, 1885 to World War I*, rev. ed. (London: Jonathan Cape, 1969), p. 337.

43. Gabriel Arbouin [pseudonym for Guillaume Apollinaire], "Devant l'idéogramme d'Apollinaire," *Les Soirées de Paris*, no. 26/27 (July–August 1914), p. 383.

44. Albert Gleizes and Jean Metzinger, *Du Cubisme* (Paris: Eugène Figuière, 1912), here quoted in English from Albert Gleizes and Jean Metzinger, *Cubism* (London/Leipzig: T. Fisher Unwin, 1913), p. 26.

45. See note 38 above.

46. *Adam and Eve*, 1912 (St. Louis Art Museum), reproduced and discussed in Compton, *Chagall*, cat. no. 26, pp. 173–74.

47. Examples of these paintings by Popova are reproduced in Angelica Zander Rudenstine, ed., *The George Costakis Collection: Russian Avant-Garde Art* (New York and London: Thames and Hudson, 1981).

48. G. Apollinaire, review of the Salon des Indépendants, March 25, 1913, quoted in English translation in Virginia Spate, *Orphism: The Evolution of Non-Figurative Painting in Paris 1910–1914* (Oxford: Clarendon Press, 1979), p. 73.

49. See, for example, Sherry A. Buckberrough, *Robert Delaunay: The Discovery of Simultaneity*, Studies in the Fine Arts: The Avant-Garde, no. 21 (Ann Arbor: UMI Research Press, 1982), pp. 149–50.

50. *Orpheus* (private collection) is reproduced in Meyer, *Chagall*, p. 212.

51. Spate, *Orphism*, p. 61.

52. See *Apollinaire: Selected Poems*, trans. and with intro. by Oliver Bernard (Baltimore, Maryland: Penguin Books, 1965); Dufy's *Orpheus* is reproduced on p. 19.

53. G. Apollinaire, *Le Bestiaire, ou Cortège d'Orphée* (Paris: Deplanche, 1911).

54. In Compton, *Chagall*, see: *Visit to the Grandparents* (private collection), cat. no. 50, p. 192; *The Feast of the Tabernacles* (private collection), cat. no. 51, pp. 192–93; *Purim* (Philadelphia Museum of Art, Louis E. Stern Collection), cat. no. 52, p. 193.

55. These two sketches are reproduced in color in Kamensky, *Chagall: The Russian Years 1907–1922*, p. 259.

56. Ziva Amishai-Maisels, "Chagall and the Jewish Revival: Center or Periphery?" in Ruth Apter-Gabriel, ed., *Tradition and Revolution: The Jewish Renaissance in Russian Avant-Garde Art 1912–1928*, exh. cat. (Jerusalem: Israel Museum, 1987), p. 89.

57. Chagall had exhibited in group exhibitions including *The Year 1915*, Moscow, May 1915; *Contemporary Russian Painting*, St. Petersburg, 1916; *Jack of Diamonds*, Moscow, November 1916; and *Contemporary Russian Painting*, St. Petersburg, November 1916–January 1917. See listings in Donald Gordon, *Modern Art Exhibitions, 1900–1916* (Munich: Prestel, 1974). Chagall's *Over the Town* (State Tret'iakov Gallery) was first shown at the last of these exhibitions, according to V. P. Lapshin, *Khudozhestvennaia zhizn' Moskvy i Petrograda v 1917 godu* (Artistic life of Moscow and Petrograd in the year 1917) (Moscow: Sovetskii khudozhnik, 1983), pp. 27 and 305.

58. Like Chagall and Popova, Lentulov had studied in Paris at the Académie de la Palette in 1911. For reproductions of Lentulov's paintings, see E. B. Murina and S. G. Dzhafarov, *Aristarkh Lentulov* (Moscow: Sovetskii khudozhnik, 1990).

59. I. A. Aksenov, *Pikasso i okrestnosti* (Picasso and environs) (Moscow: Tsentrifuga, 1917).

60. *The Apparition* (collection of A. K. Gordeeva, St. Petersburg) is reproduced in color in Kamensky, *Chagall: The Russian Years 1907–1922*, p. 287.

61. *Anywhere Out of This World* (private collection) is reproduced in color in Kamensky, *Chagall: The Russian Years 1907–1922*, p. 249. The date 1915 and Western signature were added later by Chagall; Meyer dates the painting 1917–18 in his *Chagall*, p. 264. Baudelaire gave the title of his prose-poem in English because the phrase was taken from Thomas Hood, "The Bridge of Sighs," as quoted in Edgar Allen Poe's *Poetic Principle*; see Charles Baudelaire, *Flowers of Evil and Other Works (Les Fleurs du Mal et Oeuvres choisies)*, Wallace Fowlie, ed. (New York: Bantam Books, 1964), pp. 150–53.

62. Al'tman's *Anna Akhmatova*, 1914 (State Russian Museum, St. Petersburg) is reproduced in color in *Natan Al'tman, 1889–1970* (Moscow: Sovetskii khudozhnik, 1978), unpaginated catalogue of an exhibition held at the State Bakhrushin Museum, Moscow, 1978.

63. Shterenberg's *Table with a Roll*, 1919 (State Russian Museum, St. Petersburg) is reproduced in color in Phyllis Freeman, ed., Sharon McKee, trans., *Soviet Art, 1920s and 1930s: Russian Museum, Leningrad* (New York: Harry N. Abrams, 1988), fig. 157, p. 151.

64. Part of Aksenov's "Polemical Supplement" is trans. by Christine Thomas in *A Picasso Anthology: Documents, Criticism, Reminiscences*, Marilyn McCully, ed. (London: Arts Council of Great Britain/Thames and Hudson, 1981), pp. 113–18.

65. See Grigori Kasovsky, "Chagall and the Jewish Art Programme," in Vitali, *Marc Chagall: The Russian Years 1906–1922*, p. 57.

66. In March 1922, the Moscow League of Culture held an exhibition at the theater on Bol'shoi Chernychevskii Lane that included work by Al'tman and Shterenberg as well as Chagall's murals and costume and set designs. See Shatskich in Vitali, *Marc Chagall: The Russian Years 1906–1922*, p. 88. An earlier exhibition of the murals with Chagall's set and costume designs had taken place at the theater in June 1921.

67. Gleizes and Metzinger, *Cubism* (1913 edition), pp. 32–33 (see note 44).

68. Gleizes and Metzinger, *Du Cubisme*, trans. into Russian by E. Nizen (St. Petersburg, 1913).

69. K. S. Malevich, *O novykh sistemakh v iskusstve* (On new systems in art) (Vitebsk, 1919). A shortened version was issued in 1920, as *Ot Sezanna do suprematizma. Kriticheskii ocherk.* (From Cézanne to Suprematism) ([Moscow]: Izdanie otdela Izobrazitel'nykh Iskusstv Narkomprosa [1920]).

70. M. Chagall, "Letter to Pavel Davidovitch Ettinger 1920," in Vitali, *Marc Chagall: The Russian Years 1906–1922*, pp. 73–75.

71. Malevich unveiled his *Black Square* at the *0.10* exhibition held in St. Petersburg in December 1915 at N. E. Dobychina's gallery; Chagall may have seen it, as he was working in the capital then. Malevich's display was dominated by *Black Square*, which he positioned high across a corner (not flat against a wall). The quotation is from Malevich, *Ot kubizma i futurizma k suprematizmu. Novyi zhivopisnyi realizm* (From Cubism and Futurism to Suprematism. The new painterly realism) (Moscow, 1916), the third edition of the artist's statement that Malevich issued for *0.10*, as trans. in John E. Bowlt, ed. and trans., *Russian Art of the Avant-Garde: Theory and Criticism 1902–1934*, rev. ed. (London: Thames and Hudson, 1988), p. 133.

72. The *Tenth State Exhibition: Nonobjective Creation and Suprematism* was held in April 1919 in Moscow.

73. See Susan Compton, "Kazimir Malevich: A Study of the Paintings, 1910–1935" (Ph.D. diss., University of London, Courtauld Institute of Art, 1982), pp. 217–18.

74. See V. Stepanova, "Diary entries on the XIXth State Exhibition," *Sieben Moskauer Kunstler/Seven Moscow Artists 1910–1930*, exh. cat. (Cologne: Galerie Gmurzynska, 1984), pp. 257 and 260. There is an installation photograph of this exhibition on p. 253; Stepanova's *Dancers and Figures*, shown at the exhibition, are reproduced in color on pp. 275, 281, 288, and 289.

75. The debates on composition versus construction held in early spring 1921 in Moscow at the Institute of Artistic Culture (Inkhuk) are chronicled in Christina Lodder, *Russian Constructivism* (New Haven and London: Yale University Press, 1983), pp. 83–94.

76. Chagall's *Collage* (Musée national d'art moderne, Centre Georges Pompidou, Paris) is reproduced in color in Kamensky, *Chagall: The Russian Years 1907–1922*, p. 313.

77. Two collages by Rodchenko are reproduced in A. N. Lavrent'ev, *A. M. Rodchenko/V. F. Stepanova* (Mastera sovetskogo knizhnogo iskusstva [About soviet book art]) (Moscow: Kniga, 1989): *Burevestnik*, 1919, fig. 51; and *Bilet No. 1*, 1919, fig. 63. Several collages by Stepanova (intended for the book *Gly-Gly* by A. Kruchenykh) are reproduced in *Alexander Rodtschenko und Warwara Stepanowa*, the catalogue for an exhibition at the Wilhelm-Lehmbruck-Museum, Duisburg, and Staatliche Kunsthalle, Baden-Baden, 1983, pp. 213–15; those on pp. 213 and 214 are closest to Chagall's.

78. M. Chagall, "Letter to the Management of the State Jewish Kamerny Theater," in Vitali, *Marc Chagall: The Russian Years 1906–1922*, p. 89; the letter is dated 12/II.21 (February 12, 1921). A new translation appears in this book on page 173.

79. Chagall, *My Life*, p. 158.

80. See the caption to the detail of the figure behind the cow's head at the far right of the mural, reproduced in Sweeney, *Chagall*, p. 45. The identification must have come from Mikhoels, the company's principal actor, who spent the year 1942 in New York as a Soviet cultural emissary, or from Chagall, who lived in New York from 1941 to 1948.

81. Chagall, *My Life*, p. 36.

82. *Man with Pig*, 1922–23, lithograph, edition of 35 copies, published by Paul Cassirer, Berlin; reproduced in Compton, *Chagall*, p. 258.

83. For an account of Chagall's involvement with the project for an art museum at Tel Aviv, see Tami Katz-Frieman, "Founding the Tel Aviv Museum 1930–36," *The Tel Aviv Museum Annual Review*, vol. 1 (1982). A summary is given in the Chronology in Compton, *Chagall*, pp. 264–65.

84. The Musée national message biblique Marc Chagall opened in Nice in 1973 to house a permanent collection of Chagall's biblical paintings; it also includes a space for temporary exhibitions and a concert/lecture hall.

85. Alexander Vetrov, "On Chagall," from *Ekran* (November 1921), Jerry Payne, trans., in Vitali, *Marc Chagall: The Russian Years 1906–1922*, p. 93. The article is a review of the exhibition held earlier in the year.

86. Gleizes and Metzinger, *Cubism* (1913), p. 64 (see note 44).

Chagall: Postmodernism and Fictional Worlds in Painting

Benjamin Harshav

Introduction

In November–December 1920, Marc Chagall designed the first production and painted murals for the new State Yiddish Chamber Theater in Moscow. The murals challenged the boundaries between stage and audience, the artist and the object of his painting, realism and abstraction, the religious past and secular present. They embodied the intersection of a quadruple revolution: revolution in the theater, revolution in painting, social and political revolution in Russia, and the Modern Jewish Revolution, which brought Jews into the center of European culture.

It was a time of upheaval. The old culture in Russia was swept away — many members of the intelligentsia had left or were terrorized — and these multiple revolutions were carried out by imaginative, ideological, and daring young people who believed in the reappraisal of all values and in the need for a new language of art. Their context was the intellectual and artistic fermentation at the beginning of the twentieth century, which, encouraged by the new political and social order, moved from small avant-garde circles on the periphery of national cultures to their very center.

By 1908, Cubism was established in Paris; in February 1909, Filippo Tommaso Marinetti launched Italian Futurism, which was soon disseminated throughout Europe; in 1912, Expressionism had crystallized in Germany and Imagism emerged in English poetry. In Russia, avant-garde creativity engulfed all the arts; the first manifesto of the Russian Cubo-Futurists appeared in 1912, a succession of radical trends revolutionized painting, and a wave of experiments transformed the Russian theater. To many artists, the political revolutions of 1917 seemed allied to the creation of an entirely new civilization; they also led to government support for innovation in all the arts.

At the same time, the traditional Jewish world in Russia was uprooted. In August 1914, World War I broke out. By order of the Russian army, a million and a half Jews were expelled from their homes in the border areas, often with only twenty-four-hours' notice. Russia was losing the war on its front and the German army occupied large areas of Russian territory. In February 1917, a democratic revolution in Petrograd deposed the tsar. Over five million Russian Jews, confined for a hundred and fifty years to a large geographical ghetto, the Pale of Settlement, were suddenly granted equal rights. In October 1917, the Bolsheviks took power. The liberation of the Jews — the last oppressed social "class" in Russia — was one of the exciting events in Revolutionary Russia and served as an exemplary case in the eyes of enlightened world opinion. Peace with the Germans was concluded; but Civil War broke out and raged for three years. For the first time in modern history, large-scale massacres of Jews erupted in the Ukraine, leaving about a hundred thousand dead and several hundred thousand homeless.

Parallel to the advent of Modernism, a cultural renaissance swept through Jewish communities in Russia and elsewhere from the end of the nineteenth century. A powerful secular Jewish literature in both Yiddish and Hebrew, and Jewish political and cultural movements revitalized Jewish society, and were followed by the revival of folklore, music, painting, and theater. Painting in the European sense was forbidden in the Jewish tradition, but a new breed of secular Jewish painters entered the general European art scene; Chagall was the best known of them. Born in Russia in 1887, he studied art in St. Petersburg and spent the years between 1910 and 1914 in Paris. After a famous exhibition in Berlin, he returned to Russia, where he remained until 1922. Following the Bolshevik Revolution, he was appointed Commissar of Art in Vitebsk, where he established a People's Art School and invited some of

fig. 5
Detail of Introduction to the Yiddish Theater *(cat. no. 1).*

the best Russian artists as teachers; but the school was overwhelmed by the radical avant-garde (led by Kazimir Malevich and El Lissitzky) and Chagall moved to Moscow, where he accepted an invitation to design the sets for the first production of the new Yiddish Theater: three one-act plays by Sholem Aleichem. In a creative fury, he also painted murals for the walls, enclosing the whole theater in one Chagallian environment.

The State Yiddish Chamber Theater opened in Moscow on January 1, 1921. Within a few years, it became one of the most esteemed theaters in Russia and in Europe. The English critic Huntley Carter called the theater "unequalled in Europe." Similar views were expressed when it toured Germany and Western Europe in 1928.

The strength of the State Yiddish Chamber Theater lay in a combination of avant-garde art, a multimedia perception of the totality of a theater experience, and the evocation of a grotesque and emotive fictional world based on the exotic and vibrant Jewish past. As in Chagall's paintings, this fictional world added a mythological dimension to the mere formal innovations of the new, leftist theater. No doubt it was Chagall's vision that gave the theater this new direction and its inherent strength. The interaction of four creative minds — Chagall, Sholem Aleichem, the Yiddish Theater's director Aleksei Granovskii, and the lead actor Mikhoels — in the context of the quadruple revolution resulted in a watershed event in painting and in theater.

The Yiddish Theater was not intended to be a part of Jewish parochial culture. As Granovskii wrote in a programmatic brochure of 1919, "Yiddish theater is first of all a theater in general, a temple of shining art and joyous creation — a temple where the prayer is chanted in the Yiddish language."[1] Chagall, in his *Leaves from My Notebook*,[2] published in Moscow in 1922, boasted that the Jews, who had produced Christianity and Marxism for the world, would produce art for it as well; he took pride in the Modern Jewish Revolution, yet he did not have exclusively "Jewish" art in mind. Both Chagall and the theater he influenced understood that art needs not only form and ideology but a specific fictional world; for them, Jewish thematics were part of the authentic, concrete material that constitutes art — *universal* art.

This study is presented in two complementary parts: 1) An essay in four chapters, which intends, first of all, to elucidate Chagall's murals and give the reader a sense of the character and history of the Yiddish Theater. Beyond that, however, this essay encompasses the nature and poetics of Chagall's art in the age of Modernism, and Chagall's relation to Jewish culture, especially to Yiddish language, which he spoke and in which he wrote poetry and essays; and 2) A selection of texts and documents, which includes two early books on Chagall and on the Yiddish Theater, memoirs, reviews, and discussions of the Yiddish Theater in time of Revolution. Most of these texts, written in several languages, are here translated for the first time into English. This section also includes the first translation into English of Chagall's own writings in Yiddish: his memoirs, poems, essays, and selected letters, all of which reveal a little-known side of his personality.

A note to the reader
In Yiddish, the word *Yiddish* means both "Yiddish" and "Jewish," the language and the nation (the same is true of the Russian word *evreiskii*). Therefore, in English "Yiddish" culture denotes "Jewish" culture as well (and vice versa), and the reader must keep both connotations in mind. The original Russian name for the theater was Gosudarstvenni Evreiskii Kamernyi Teatr (GOSEKT). Scholars, in translating the name into English, have used both State Jewish Chamber Theater and State Yiddish Chamber Theater to refer to the institution. I have chosen the latter translation here, because the defining trait of the theater was based on language rather than any national content. (Furthermore, another Jewish theater, HaBima, also emerged in Moscow at the time, but performed plays in Hebrew.) After 1924, the word "chamber" was dropped from GOSEKT's name. From then on, it was known simply as the State Yiddish Theater (GOSET). For simplicity's sake, in this essay the term Yiddish Theater is used for the institution throughout its lifespan.

All quotations from other languages, except where noted, are translated from their original language by the author.

Acknowledgments
This essay was written in a very short time, which included a trip to Moscow with my collaborator Barbara Harshav to study little-known archival sources. I would like to thank the staffs of the Russian archives where many extant documents of the Yiddish Theater (liquidated by Stalin in 1949) are kept in meticulous order: CGALI (Central State Archive for Literature and Art), its Director Natal'ia Borisovna Volkova, and the head of the reading room Elena Ermilovna Gafner; and the State Bakhrushin Museum, its Deputy Director Tat'iana Borisovna Klim, archivist of the Decoration Division Irina Naumovna Duksina, and the specialists at the Manuscript Division; as well as many friends in Moscow who helped with information and discussions, including Svetlana Dzhafarova, Assar Eppel, Aleksandr Kantsedikas, Grigorii Kazovskii, Boris Messerer, Aleksandra Shatskikh, and Sergei Tartakovskii. I also wish to thank the YIVO in New York, in particular Marek Webb, Dina Abramovitch, Eleonor Mlotek, and Zachary Becker; as well as Yosl Birshteyn in Jerusalem, Nava Schreiber in New York, and especially Rachael Wilson at Yale. All of them were kind, knowledgeable, and helpful. Barbara Harshav, as always, improved the shape of my writing. Anthony Calnek was an understanding and demanding editor who pulled my scholarly text in reader-friendly directions.

A postmodernist in the age of Modernism

Marc Chagall was the first conscious, even deliberate postmodernist. His meteoric rise and later devaluation, his strengths and his weaknesses are inherent in that principle of his art. Like a whirlwind he moved from one trend of the avant-garde to another, from one national context to another, absorbing some techniques and tendencies, then retreating into his own world.

In his paintings we can find quasi-geometric articulations of forms derived from Analytic Cubism; Orphism's predilection for circles in space; a Fauve-inspired exuberance for colors that overflow the boundaries of objects; the precise chromatic shapes of Suprematism; the dynamic movement and strong diagonal gestures of Futurism; pre-Expressionist deformations of human faces and figures; a dreamlike arrangement of objects in represented space, anticipating Surrealism; and even minute and multiple decorative ornaments (ornament was anathema to the avant-garde) typical of the Russian Mir Iskusstva (World of Art) movement in the beginning of the century. In Chagall's work, the seemingly disparate components fuse into one functional unity in each painting, often in an asymmetrical, uneasy, but ultimately justified balance.

Chagall's paintings have, perhaps unfairly, been judged from a perspective of purism — the ascetic use of a well-delimited discourse of art. Thus, they have been termed "eclectic." Today, in an age of postmodernism, we can surely question the validity of a "pure" language as the highest value in art or poetry. French Symbolism and its Anglo-American offshoots promoted the principle of "pure poetry," a suggestive, musical, even "magical" art, that focused on the "language" of poetry at the expense of anything that other kinds of discourse, such as prose, ideology, or philosophy, can do. The trends of art and literature that revolted against Symbolism in various European countries, beginning with the Italian Futurists, also promoted a pure language of art, no matter how "impure" the materials they used may have been. Yet, simultaneously, the purity of genres and artistic media was overruled, their boundaries deliberately broken: poetry became prosaic and dramatic, prose became lyrical, painting used words, and words themselves were used to create graphic images. Moreover, representatives of pure styles, such as Pablo Picasso or Malevich, were eclectic in diachrony: they changed their style every so often, while Chagall did not.

The terms "Modernism" and "postmodernism" do not denote any single idea, essence, monolithic style, or defined zeitgeist permeating all artists, all works, and all aspects of art in a given period. This is not the place for a careful analysis of the nature of such trends. Suffice it to say that Modernism experimented with all possibilities of the language of art; it produced a galaxy of trends, often in direct opposition to one another — some with particular labels (Futurism, Expressionism, Suprematism, Constructivism), some embodied in the work of unaffiliated artists (Paul Klee, Bertolt Brecht, Chagall).

At a certain point, the internal succession of Modernist trends tired of its own evolution, and the term "postmodernism" emerged in the 1970s.[3] But, since "Modernism" was not one essence, "postmodernism" could not be a unified phenomenon either. In architecture, for example, the Modernism of the Bauhaus and the International Style implied streamlined simplicity, functionality, cultural neutrality, and impersonality; hence the postmodernist interest in ornament, quotations from earlier styles, "impure" language, and the personal imprimatur of the architect. In literature, on the contrary, high Modernism meant elitist, difficult, metaphorical, and allusive poetry and fiction, while the reaction brought relaxation, more direct language, social engagement, and eclecticism.

We may describe postmodernism as an attitude critical of, but also acutely aware of, the achievements of many Modernist trends, styles, and breakthroughs. Postmodernism, by its very name, implies the use of possibilities opened by Modernism — and closed as well, for if innovation is the overriding principle of art, then those explored possibilities were exhausted at the moment of their discovery. It also implies the relativization of all Modernist theories and styles, the evocation of earlier styles and masters,[4] and the poetic license of eclecticism. Above all, it implies a personal voice dominating the functional integration of art. The importance of form is not ignored but, rather than being an impersonal style good for all themes and places, it is made specifically functional within each individual work of art and its context, culturally dependent, and subsumed under the unity and continuity of the artist's personal style and world. In these respects, Chagall was a postmodernist even as Modernism was unfolding.

Of course, Chagall was a major figure in the age of Modernism. He shared some basic assumptions with most Modernist trends: an opposition to mimesis in the sense of directly depicting a scene in time and space; an opposition to "realism"; the deformation of represented figures and objects; the granting of autonomy to and foregrounding of all aspects of the language of art, such as spatial forms, geometric figures, or color. Without the successive Modernist trends, there would have been no Chagall. Yet, without Chagall in the general landscape, the Modernist age would be lacking something. As one critic put it, "We think of Marc Chagall as the painter-poet of the twentieth century. He shares this distinction only with Paul Klee."[5] Chagall was not considered an innovator of any theoretically defined language of art — for his deformations of human figures, subversions of the laws and continuities of observed reality, dreamlike compositions, and *portmanteau figures* were all innovations not in language but in the fictional world presented in art — yet this in itself was a new language. And at least for this reason he was a much more important and universal artist than recent attitudes have tended to allow.

Chagall was never a group player, neither in an art group nor in any "Jewish" coterie; he was never perceived as a Cubist or Surrealist, or anything else, but only as "Chagall" — his personality defined the unity of his art. He came close to several of the new waves somewhat late, absorbed some lessons, and consumed anything that suited him into an all-encompassing fictional world, appropriated by Chagall under the construct of his own biography.

The stations of Chagall's development as an artist

Chagall was born in 1887 in a Yiddish-speaking suburb of Vitebsk, the capital of a Russian province in the Pale of Settlement (today, Belarus). He learned the fancy word *khudozhnik* (artist) from a boy in his Russian high school, then went to study with a local artist, Yehuda (Iurii) Pen. Pen was representative of the late-nineteenth-century Russian school of *Peredvizhniki* (Wanderers), who moved academic painting from Neoclassicism to a descriptive realism and populism. Furthermore, in his paintings he stressed Jewish topics and symbols and the so-called "genre of the trivial," drawn from the mores of Jewish daily life.[6] Pen was aware of the renaissance in Jewish cultural ideology, subscribed to Martin Buber's Berlin journal *Ost und West*, and trained several Jewish artists, including El Lissitzky, who came from the neighboring Smolensk Province, and Osip Zadkin. From Pen, Chagall learned the basics of drawing and portrait painting, and adopted an interest in Jewish themes. In 1921, Chagall wrote to Pen, "You raised a great generation of Jewish artists."[7]

Ambitious and resourceful, Chagall left Pen, probably in 1907, and went to St. Petersburg, where Russian art was a generation ahead. As a Jew, he could not live there legally,[8] but he managed somehow, and was supported by several Jewish patrons, notably the influential lawyer Maxim Vinaver,[9] one of the first Jewish members of the Russian Duma (parliament), who bought some of Chagall's paintings. In St. Petersburg, Chagall studied with Lev Bakst, a major figure of the aestheticist World of Art movement. Chagall was somewhat late (the journal *World of Art* had ceased publishing in 1906), but he absorbed the general post-Fauve mood nonetheless.

The prevalent intellectual movement in Russia at the beginning of the century was Symbolism, which was, in general terms, a movement of art for art's sake. At its center was Symbolist poetry, which combined emphases on poetic form and on the transcendental. By the time Chagall moved to St. Petersburg, Symbolist and aestheticist trends had spilled over into other arts. From the ivory tower of the poets, Symbolism had moved to such applied arts as theater sets and costumes; Sergei Dhiagilev's Ballet Russe showcased Bakst's stage designs and costumes, which eventually made a strong impact in Paris.

From Bakst, Chagall learned the autonomous value of rich colors, minute and precise ornaments (which the influential art critic Iakov Tugendkhol'd ascribed to a Jewish national ethos[10]), and the desire to create decorations for the theater. In St. Petersburg, he was also impressed by the tendencies of Symbolism in painting, the value of folk art, and the penchant for oriental, mystical, and legendary scenes. He even wrote Russian Symbolist poems himself. In this world of assimilated Jews merging with the Russian aristocratic intellectual scene, Chagall learned to fuse influences from Christian art with his Jewish motifs: elements of Christian iconography, Russian icons, and the *lubok* (a colorful Russian folk print with a narrative theme) meld in his work with images of the Jewish tradition. There were no contradictions inherent in these intersecting influences, for they all inhabited one consciousness. Indeed, that duality was at the foundation of modern Jewish culture in general.

Chagall soon felt that both Pen and Bakst were old-fashioned — Chagall's Neoprimitivist[11] and absurd distortions of reality were beyond his teacher's understanding — and, sponsored by Vinaver, he set out for Paris, the art capital of the world. A radical, avant-garde revolution in poetry, painting, and graphics was already brewing in Russia in 1910, when Chagall departed. In his absence, several of his paintings were exhibited with the avant-garde, but he was far away and did not participate in the cathartic experience of the Russian Cubo-Futurists, Rayonists, and similar groups.

In Paris, again somewhat late, Chagall deepened his links to Fauvism and discovered that Cubism was already an accepted norm. He adapted principles from those art movements to his own work, yet his poetic deformations and re-creation of the world of his past also anticipated Surrealism and Expressionism; they struck Guillaume Apollinaire as *sur-naturel*. Chagall lived mostly among foreign artists, including quite a few Jews eager to embrace the latest discoveries in painting and arguing about the problematics of a new Jewish art. He soon came in contact with several young French poets and painters who were influential in the debates of the avant-garde: Blaise Cendrars, Apollinaire, André Salmon, Robert and Sonia Delaunay, and others. Analytic Cubism had already been absorbed and artists were taking it in different directions. In response to the Delaunays' Orphism, Chagall too foregrounded the interplay of vivid colors and adopted the emblem of the

Eiffel Tower and the circle motif. In 1914, through Apollinaire's mediation, he was discovered by Herwardt Walden, editor of the influential German avant-garde journal *Der Sturm*, who organized an exhibition in Berlin for Chagall, thus building him up as an important figure in the emergence of Expressionist painting.

In 1914, Chagall traveled to Russia, married Bella Rosenfeld, and, because of the war, remained there. He returned to Vitebsk and refreshed his memory of his mythological city and his family's hometown of Lyozno, painting ostensibly realistic, detailed pictures of people, houses, cemeteries, and churches. In Petrograd (as St. Petersburg was called between 1914 and 1924), he was received as a Russian painter famous in Paris and Berlin. In 1918, the first book about him appeared (it was published in Berlin in a German translation in 1921); written by Abram Efros and Tugendkhol'd, it set the terms of Chagall criticism.[12]

After the Revolution, Chagall was appointed Commissar of Art in Vitebsk; for a while he was swept up by the winds of Revolution and mobilized his art in its cause, preparing propagandistic posters to be displayed around the city. He also established the People's Art School in Vitebsk, inviting some of the best painters of the day, including Lissitzky and Malevich, to teach in that provincial town. Those two were leaders of the radical and purist avant-garde and effectively pushed Chagall out of the school.[13] Aside from the incompatibility of personal ambitions, Chagall was too eclectic and thematic (or "objective," to use Malevich's negative term) for their taste. Thus he came to Moscow and accepted the commission for the new State Yiddish Chamber Theater.

Fictional world as a language of art

Like the ideal of "pure poetry," pure art to the avant-garde meant the acceptance of one language that dominated each work. In their period of Analytic Cubism, for example, Picasso and Braque made each painting according to the Cubist views of perception and text formation; each painting was a new variant, a new exploration of possibilities within this framework. Similarly, Lissitzky was a master of stylized Jewish themes (influenced by Chagall) when illustrating Yiddish books, and rendered them in a stylistically pure way; but when he discovered Suprematism and went on to create his Constructivist *Prouns,* his paintings changed entirely, becoming pure executions of that Constructivist language. The same may be said of Jean Arp, Vasilii Kandinskii, Malevich, Vladimir Tatlin, and many others who developed the various contradictory styles of the avant-garde. For them, at any given moment, the poetics of their art was like a spoken language: one speaks either French or English or Russian, but not all in the same sentence. In Yiddish, however, one *can* speak several languages in the same sentence. Chagall appropriated the languages of art and placed them side by side in the same painting. He used various elements of Modernist discourse as strains of texture formation integrated in a complex, kaleidoscopic, and contrapuntal whole. We may call this attitude *demonstrative eclecticism.*

In Chagall's work, all the strains of Modernist discourse that he learned in Vitebsk, St. Petersburg, and Paris are intertwined with another discourse: the evocation of what in literary theory is called a *fictional world.*[14] His fictional world is based on selections of representative items from several historical and personal domains, refracted through the prism of a self-constructed, simplified, and mythologized biography. Chagall's adoption of a fictional world differs from its use in literature in one key sense: an author creates a separate fictional world, with its own characters and situations, for each novel, whereas in Chagall's oeuvre, all paintings refer to one total fictional universe, a construct outside of the paintings, but to which *all* those paintings refer. This fictional world was removed from and strange to the eyes of his audiences in St. Petersburg or Paris, which were attracted to its exoticism. Chagall's achievement — using a strange fictional world as a language — was understood by his friend Cendrars, who wrote of the artist:

Suddenly he paints
He takes a church and paints with a church
He takes a cow and paints with a cow
With a sardine
With heads, hands, knives
He paints with a bull's pizzle
He paints with all the foul passions of a little Jewish city
With all the heightened sexuality of provincial Russia [15]

Chagall himself expressed this idea on several occasions:

Before the war of 1914, I was accused of falling into "literature." Today people call me a painter of fairy tales and fantasies. Actually, my first aim is to construct my paintings architecturally — exactly as the Impressionists and Cubists have done in their own fashion and by using the same formal means. The Impressionists filled their canvases with patches of light and shadow; the Cubists filled them with cubes, triangles, and cones. I try to fill my canvases in some way with objects and figures treated as forms . . . sonorous forms like sounds . . . passionate forms designed to add a new dimension which neither the geometry of the Cubists nor the patches of the Impressionists can achieve. [16]

In this statement, he defines his goals not in terms of ideology, autobiography, or national nostalgia but of composition: "to fill my canvases." The "objects and figures" of his fictional world are seen as "forms" that fulfill the same function as Impressionist light and shadow or Cubist cubes and cones.

Critics are often amazed at the wealth of topics, figures, and objects presented in Chagall's paintings. As Norbert Lynton wrote:

His subjects outreach any listing: birth, death, hardship, contentment, domesticity, isolation, social events, the longings and the delights of love, rabbis and poets, family, Bella, their daughter Ida, Vava, himself in many guises, crucifixions of Christ and others, the Russian Revolution, the Old Testament, angels, The Magic Flute, Orpheus, *Daphnis and Chloë, the circus, acrobats, cows, cocks, donkeys, fish, clocks, most of these with and without violins, flowers, Vitebsk, Paris, the Eiffel Tower. It is best not even to start imagining the other possible lists, of the materials he worked in, the many functions his art serves, the art and artists that he has allied himself to from early ikons to Modernists via shop-signs and ancient symbols, lest our heads spin off our shoulders in precisely the way he describes.* [17]

Yet for the most part those various items are not depictions of individual objects in the world but represent several recognizable domains throughout Chagall's art: old Jews of the recent religious past, as seen from the distance of a secular generation; Christian officials and peasants of the village; his own, invented "Vitebsk" as the symbolic small town of a distant Jewish world; another version of "Vitebsk," with its churches symbolizing provincial Russia; animals in that world, often humanized; his child-bride Bella and loving couples; Jesus Christ as the suffering Jew; Paris with the emblematic Eiffel Tower and the window of his studio; and, later in his career, anonymous Jewish masses, crossing the Red Sea or facing the Holocaust; and the world of the Bible. All those domains were internalized as the fictional universe of one

individual, carried around the globe in the artist's memory and consciousness.

Chagall's contemporary Yisoskhor Rybak painted Cubist synagogues of different towns; Chagall placed all objects and persons in his imaginary Vitebsk, making them elements of the painter-poet's memory and imagination. Only a few paintings (especially in certain periods of his work) were made as direct depictions of objects in nature. Rather, nature was reduced to a few individuals, such as his flower bouquets, a river representing time, and the colorful sky. His repeated personal world consisted of Bella and an occasional image of his parents; he painted his brother and sisters only once or twice (he did not use them as part of his *language*). After Bella's death, she continued to appear as the image of love. So did his common-law wife Virginia Haggard and their son David, in a Christian emblem of mother and son.

In Chagall's paintings, individuals of these fictional domains appear as modular units in a large mosaic. Their boundaries often melt and several adjacent individuals overlap and interact in what we may call *portmanteau figures*: man and animal; Christ and a praying Jew and Chagall himself; geometric forms, patches of color, and the human body; the Eiffel Tower with human legs. The repetitive use of such individuals, their appearance as emblematic representatives of specific fictional domains, and the general paucity of new items turned them into a recognizable Chagallian vocabulary. In Paris during the teens this fictional world as a language of art attracted great attention. Art, to some, seemed to have been reduced to innovations in form, two-dimensional space, color, and composition. But in Chagall's paintings an authentic, persistent world, so exotic, whimsical, and different from our own, appeared. This successful reception was repeated in Berlin in 1914, in Russia during World War I and the Revolutionary period, and in France after Chagall's return in 1923.

Attention to this world was reinforced by the painter's ambivalent perception of it. His images ranged from the grotesque to the sentimental, transformed through a series of drastic, antirealistic devices. Spectators and critics were tempted to construct "explanations" or conjectures — often as shaky as the figures themselves — and shift from direct sensuous painterly values to the domain of meaning and ideology. His work was often perceived as a forerunner of Surrealism, which shifted the focus of painting from the medium to the subconscious world of the painter and the presentation of unrealistic, fantastic spaces. Chagall, the re-creator of a lost world, became the "poetic" painter, the painter of a social or personal dreamworld, the surrealist, the visionary, the mystic, the master of a chaotic subconscious, or the naïve narrator of a strange biography, for which he sometimes supplied stories. For example, in *My Life*, written in 1923, Chagall related a visit to Lyozno in which he found his grandfather sitting on the roof, the source for the image in the 1908 painting *The Dead Man*. Whether the story is apocryphal is immaterial; the salient point is Chagall's attempt to domesticate the unrealistic events of his painting in "facts" or psychological attitudes, as did many of his critics. Ironically, if successful, this would explain away the very effect on which the painting depends; it would turn his art into realistic depiction.

Many Modernist trends promoted the impersonal in art and poetry, suppressing the private emotions and biography of the individual artist in favor of the creation of independent aesthetic objects and innovation in the language of art: at one time, Russian Futurists did not sign their texts; Cubists emphasized the impersonal style of art; T. S. Eliot wrote of the "expression of *significant* emotion, emotion which has its life in the poem and not in the history of the poet. The emotion of art is impersonal"[18]; later in the century, Structuralists and Deconstructionists excluded the author from the understanding of his or her own text.

Chagall promulgated an opposite view. In his art, personal biography is dominant and the depicted world is determined subjectively. Chagall thematized his biography in his art and writings and made it the arbiter of his authentic style. The justification for combining heterogeneous elements of style and reality was provided by the accidental, biographical unity of the artist's consciousness. To be sure, this individual experience contained public, basic stereotypes about the domains he evoked: the mystery of mundane life; the transformation of the Jews; the sad decline and mental strength of old, religious Jewry; the image of the provincial Russian town; and the depth, irrationality, and mysterious warmth of folkways and conventions. But Chagall sought to convince us that those were parts of his own, personal biography, and his self-conscious naïveté justified the unsophisticated perceptions of that world.

Since the language of Chagall's art is based on his life and fictional world, treatment of those rather than geometric forms became the focus of critical attention; thus, deformations of figures are discussed not for their own sake (as forms in space), and color is discussed not for its autonomous expressive values, but for what they do to the fictional world. A scholar of Chagall's art is compelled to study his biography and cultural context as primary sources of his language, iconography, and meaning. Jewish elements too are part of the language with which he forms a painting and expresses his emotions on love or the mysteries of life. This does not make him an exclusively "Jewish" artist any more than William Faulkner is an exclusively "Southern" writer; in both, the local specificity is the way they see the world — it becomes the "language" of their universally valid art.

Introspectivism

The theory of simultaneity in art and the interpenetration of planes was promoted, somewhat crudely, in Italian Futurism. In a manifesto for a 1912 exhibition in Paris, *The Exhibitors to the Public*, the Futurists stated:

In painting a person on a balcony, seen from inside the room, we do not limit the scene to what the square frame of the window renders visible; but we try to render the sum total of visual sensations which the person on the balcony has experienced; the sun-bathed throng in the street, the double row of houses which stretch to right and left, the beflowered balconies, etc. This implies the simultaneousness of the ambient, and, therefore, the dislocation and dismemberment of objects, the scattering and fusion of details, freed from accepted logic, and independent from one another.[19]

The last sentence applies to Chagall's art as well. In his work, however, it is not the consciousness of a depicted figure but of the artist himself that motivates such a "dismemberment of objects." Furthermore, a painting by Chagall does not represent one momentary experience, but involves different modules from several times and places, stored in the fictional repertoire inhabiting his mind.

Chagall's perception finds an affinity in theories of the Yiddish Introspectivist poets, who wrote their manifesto in New York in 1919. They determined that all topics and domains of modern life and culture were legitimate subjects for poetry, provided they were presented "in an introspective and fully individual manner":

For us, everything is "personal." Wars and revolutions, Jewish pogroms and the workers' movement, Protestantism and Buddha, the Yiddish school and the Cross, the mayoral elections and a ban on our

language — all these may concern us or not, just as a blond woman and our own unrest may or may not concern us. If it does concern us, we write poetry; if it does not, we keep quiet. In either case we write about ourselves because all these exist only insofar as they are in us, insofar as they are perceived introspectively.[20]

Thus, the social and political world are part of the artist's internalized panorama. Experience cannot be isolated or limited to the here and now of an externally observed scene:

When the poet, or any person, looks at a sunset, he may see the strangest things which, ostensibly, have perhaps no relation to the sunset. This, the series of associations and the chain of suggestions, constitutes truth, is life, much as an illusion is often more real than the cluster of external appearances we call life. . . . We insist that the poet should give us the authentic image that he sees in himself and give it in such a form as only he and no one else can see it.[21]

The Introspectivists wrote that "the poet must really listen to his inner voice, observe his internal panorama — kaleidoscopic, contradictory, unclear or confused as it may be."[22] Although Chagall was not connected to the Introspectivists, his cultural background and perceptions were similar to theirs. This may have something to do with the Yiddish language, which was their common native tongue. Yiddish, as has been well argued by ideological Yiddishist linguists, especially Max Weinreich, is considered a language of fusion, combining such disparate components as parts of German, Slavic, the Holy Tongue (Hebrew and Aramaic), and an international vocabulary. We must stress, however, that the various components of Yiddish, though ostensibly fused into one language, retain evidence of their origin, and may be played with, interchanged, and juxtaposed in a stylistic or pluricultural game. Yiddish provides a multilingual perspective in its very existence.

English, a language of fusion too, seems to its users as one language. Yiddish speakers, however, were always conscious of its component languages. Almost by definition, Yiddish speakers were, to differing extents, simultaneously speakers and readers of several other languages and were well aware of the multireligious and multicultural perspectives in which they existed. As I have argued elsewhere, Yiddish is also an amazingly *open* language: speakers could enlarge the Hebrew part — beyond what is ostensibly "merged" in Yiddish — and they could indulge in learned discourse; or enlarge the German vocabulary and shift the phonetics in order to speak and read German; or they could expand the Slavic elements and shift to Russian.[23]

Chagall's mind moved in the same direction. His fusion of heterogeneous components in one painting mirrors the world of Yiddish, especially of those Yiddish speakers who rapidly assimilated into general culture. He could not learn painting without learning the Christian tradition in it, and he merged that knowledge with the Jewish knowledge of his childhood.

Indeed, Chagall's move from a provincial, ignorant Yiddish milieu to the centers of Russian and French Modernist art was part of the Modern Jewish Revolution, the total secularization of masses of Jews and their entrance into general European culture.[24] He and his contemporaries entered the history of European culture from the outside, just as a radical upheaval was transforming that very history. For the curious and eager newcomers, history appeared as a synchronic "imaginary museum" (to use André Malraux's term). Like Chagall in the Louvre, one could run from one room to another and choose items regardless of their historical context. Chagall's generation began with Modernism, then recapitulated some of the very European past that had been subverted by Modernism! In a speech delivered in Yiddish in New York, Chagall himself observed:

I love "contrasts" in which the harmonious truth is hidden. I think about one of many examples, in which various poles of art meet somewhere. Here is the classical Realist Pushkin with his profoundly chiseled meter and the ardent Romantic Baudelaire — veiled in dreams of enchanted, poisonous flowers — nevertheless they meet somewhere in their ultimate authenticity. I recall the last art experiments in Paris where, next to a painting by an old medieval primitive such as Giotto, a Picasso may hang, and next to him, the pre-Renaissance artist Mantegna; and next to our {i.e. Jewish} Modigliani a Byzantine icon can hang; — and several paintings by the Naturalist artist and Revolutionary Gustav Courbet, who, during the Paris Commune, toppled the Vendome Column to the ground, can hang along with the magic Renaissance artist Giorgione, and so on . . . And this is not "eclecticism" — on the contrary.[25]

Like Introspectivist Yiddish poetry, Chagall's art was *kaleidoscopic* (the Introspectivists' key term). In his paintings, he presented a precarious but colorful balance of variegated splinters of a chaotic world. To justify the unity of a painting, its subject had to be introspective too, that is, the disjointed and heterogeneous elements had to cohabit one personal, internalized world, conditioned by the accidents of the artist's biography and the flights of his imagination. Furthermore, in Chagall's best paintings, there is an internal equilibrium, a *balancing of heterogeneous centers of gravity* between various strata and parts of the painting. His compositions are not determined solely by spatial forms, color, nor the fictional world in itself, but by an ambivalent, shifting emphasis from one stratum to another. These two principles — introspectivism and the balancing of heterogeneous elements in each painting — are among the defining traits of Chagall's art.

Chagall and the semiotics of Jewish discourse

In addition to the multilingual, multicultural perspective inherent in the culture of Yiddish and in the existential situation of that generation, Chagall exhibits other basic features of what might be called the "semiotics of Jewish discourse." It would take us too far afield to explain this notion in detail, but we may mention a few conspicuous aspects.

The founding book of Jewish consciousness is the Bible. The Bible is an "encyclopedic" book (as Northrop Fry wrote), encompassing all available genres: poetry, stories, prophecy, wisdom, law, and historiography. Those genres are embedded in a narrative, stretching, in the Jewish Bible, from the creation of the world to the list of generations in *Chronicles*. After the Biblical narrative ends, history is finished. The Biblical text has been reinterpreted into a panhistoric and pangeographic system of rules and beliefs. A major precept of interpretation has been, "There is no 'earlier' and no 'later' in the Bible" — any quote may be used for any purpose at hand. While Christians have interpreted Biblical events as prefigurations of the life of Jesus, Jewish learning uses Biblical texts as an inexhaustible source of law and language.

Accordingly, typical Jewish texts (in the Talmudic tradition as well as in popular writings and sermons) do not have one unfolding logical structure or one, directionally continuous narrative. Directionality, which gives a certain logical or narrative discipline to the unfolding of a text in the Western tradition, subordinates each detail or event to the continuous chain, making it functional either for the plot or for the argument. In Jewish Diaspora texts, however, directionality is set aside and each detailed observation is treated as an autonomous value. Every detail is taken out of its narrative chain and observed close up; it does not lose the reader's

interest, for it belongs to one total universe, which endows each detail with rich meaning and depth. Hence, any detail could be parallel to anything else, any textual reference could evoke any other text in the library, supporting it or serving as an opposite. To be sure, there are Jewish folklore stories, but popular narrative texts tend to be short, moralistic, or anecdotal. Especially associative were the structures of the oral performances by rabbis and popular preachers (such as the Magid of Slutsk in Chagall's *Green Jew* {1914}), for they had to depart from the given, fixed weekly portion of the Bible to whatever topics of the day or of morality interested them.

In the traditional Jewish milieu, talk and argument were important and privileged, for it was not enough just to know the law, one had to explain it, using all arguments on each side of every issue and disproving the "wrong" ones. This mode of religious and educational discourse, studied and practiced by every male in the family, permeated social communication and family life. A cluster of attitudes, developed in the universe of religious texts and the methods of teaching, was folklorized, and became second nature to typical Jewish verbal behavior, especially in Eastern Europe, where there was a dense educational network and a codified linguistic tool — Yiddish — to absorb it all and give it the sanction of privileged communicative behavior. Various aspects of it were then transferred to other languages by such assimilated Jews as Franz Kafka, Sigmund Freud, Saul Bellow, or Chagall. This semiotics of Jewish discourse can be described as a cluster of tendencies, common — though neither obligatory nor exclusive — to Jewish verbal behavior in that period.

Such "Jewish discourse" is talkative, argumentative, contrary, associative. Its typical traits include answering with examples, anecdotes, parables, or questions, rather than with direct, logical replies; seeing the smallest detail as symbolic for universal issues; delving into the meanings, connotations, and associations of a single word; and leaping from a word or concrete item to abstract generalizations and theories. In general, it was not the logical continuity of the text but the coherence of the represented universe that guided the discourse. It all made sense when it was subordinated to one total, religious universe; when that universe was no longer based on the religious system, substitute totalities were sought. In Freud's and Chagall's perception, that totality was one person's consciousness. Thus, in Freud, every word or detail or connotation could be symbolic for the whole personality, and could evoke any other detail in the individual's universe of discourse; as Peter Gay put it, Freud's goal was "to draw the map of human experience as crisscrossed by the roads of analogy."[26]

Specific characteristics of that Jewish discourse were influenced by an intersection of communicational habits from both the learned tradition and the existential situation of the Jews. For example, the inferiority-superiority complex of Kafka's protagonists, and of Chagall's self-understanding, came from the religious notion that the Jews are the "chosen people" on the one hand, combined with their actual existential condition (of a "fallen aristocracy of the mind," chosen for suffering as well) on the other. The penchant for abstraction and generalization, in which a detail is unimportant in itself unless it can be seen as representing the "rules of the game," has been derived from both the learned tradition and from the lack of contact with nature. Even when such individuals joined European cultures, they embraced first the abstract, learned language of literature and philosophy, rather than the specific, dialectal language of real people.

Chagall's work embodies many features of this typical cluster of Jewish discourse. His paintings are filled with many colorful, concrete details, animals, or flowers, but those are mostly abstractions, taken out of their realistic context; they are selected, emblematic representatives of his fictional domains, and, beyond them, of a global perception of "nature," "love," or "light." No continuity of space, time, and causality is required. His compositions and remembered asides are guided by private associations. Yet the details themselves are given intensive attention, as endowed with symbolic value; indeed, they are perceived as belonging to one total universe — which is now, however, a fictional and personal one (as in Freud's patients). His paintings are talkative — they have a lot to say and try to say it all. There is no better example for Chagall's folksy use of "Jewish discourse" than his associative, metaphorical, whimsical autobiography — and the tour de force of this style, the *Introduction to the Yiddish Theater* (cat. no. 1).

Chagall directly evoked several social and cultural domains of interest to his contemporaries. But he did it by creating a personalized fictional world, recollected through introspection. Indeed — paradoxical as it may seem — individualism was a prominent feature of Jewish behavior. In spite of the stringent religious rules and conventions imposed on daily behavior in the small town, and the strong, folklorized stereotypes of an ahistorical and collective world-view of the community, personal effort was the mainspring of Jewish life. The two most prestigious activities in Jewish society were learning and trade; a Yiddish proverb conjoins them in a rhyme, *tóyre iz di beste skhóyre* (learning is the best merchandise). For success in either of them, individual effort is required. Indeed, Jews did not work in factories or fields, and even Jewish tailors, shoemakers, peddlers, and other artisans (a third of the Jewish population in Vitebsk at Chagall's time) had very few helpers. With the Modern Jewish Revolution, this prevalent tendency toward individualism was enhanced even further as each person broke the strong chains of a conventional and religious community: hence the high value assigned in this period to autobiography and to poetry, genres focusing on individual consciousness. Introspection gave the individual the truth of his internal world and internal strength. A Jewish-German writer argued that every poet is a Jew, whether he was born one or not, because Jews are the ultimate individualists in the atomistic big city.[27]

Chagall's capricious and willful compositions and behavior were part of that individualism. He threw a temper tantrum when the Yiddish Theater's director Aleksei Granovskii put a real towel on his painted stage, and he broke the chairs in the Hadassah synagogue in Jerusalem when he discovered that his magnificent Biblical windows were buried in a tiny edifice. Nevertheless, his fame and general reception were due in part to his appeal to the most common stereotypes of Jewish and non-Jewish life.

Thinking About Picasso

Before moving on to Chagall's murals, let us discuss some basic principles of his art as they apply to two examples. Chagall was quick to learn the languages of Modernist art, and agile in distancing himself from them. This gesture of independence is common in Chagall's typical style, which I call *demonstrative eclecticism*. This demonstrative eclecticism can be seen in a black-ink drawing of 1914, probably made upon Chagall's return to Russia, which is known by the misleading title *Thinking About Picasso* (fig. 6). In it, a house is drawn with simple geometric shapes, resulting in a two-dimensional, flat presentation; its schematic doors and windows look like letters of some elementary language. Traversing its roof are two stripes with simplified shaded and white areas; one stripe bleeds from the triangle roof to the square house — a gesture indicating the autonomy of spatial forms. In the upper-left

corner of the drawing is an inverted four-square structure echoing the house's geometry — perhaps it is an abstraction of the house, or of a folded paper representing a house, or a hieroglyph of a home with triple "roofs" pointing downward and to the sides, uncertain of the direction of gravity.

The central house itself floats diagonally; divorced from any street or ground (though embellished with a decorative brick-like foundation) it seems to defy gravity. Placed as it is in the center of the drawing, the house forms a diamond, capriciously challenging the rectangular paper on which it is drawn. In Chagall's abbreviated alphabet, the house signals his own provincial home, or his return to it in an unreal world and with a topsy-turvy echo above it. Both the house and its abstraction have spiral-like doodles, perhaps indicating smoke, music, or even a snail's enclosure in his own world. A lavish tail and snout are attached to the house, transforming it into the metaphor of a fox. (Chagall seems to say that, returning to his own home base, however unreally floating in the air, he "outfoxed" Picasso.)

Text, written in a childish hand and in schematized, simplified letters, floats like smoke above the roof. The letters (which are printed, as in a caption) declare in Russian, *Shagal nadoel mne dumaia {o} pikaso* (I am sick of Chagall thinking [about] Picasso.) The "about" ("o" in Russian) is missing, unless we find it in the spiral protruding from the chimney; thus the text could also read, "thinking Picasso." The "o," however, *does* appear in the shortened version of the text below. Here it reads, *Dumaia o Pik* (Thinking about Pic); in a Picasso-like pun, Chagall uses the first syllable of that artist's name, "pik," which in Russian means "peak," in this case the summit of art. The placement of this inscription, however, suggests as a subtext a popular though vulgar Yiddish idiom, *ikh hob im in tokhes* (I have him in my ass, i.e., I don't give a damn about him).

In the upper-right corner is a cloud, derived from Symbolist painting, from which a long arm stretches down (an allusion to Michelangelo?) to touch (with the famous tip of a finger) the inverted foot of the topsy-turvy Chagall. The soft, rounded Symbolist area in the upper right is set in opposition to the Cubist forms in the center. The representation of Chagall utilizes a third stylistic language and is clearly a gesture against Cubism. Essentially, it is a simplified drawing of a human figure with a recognizable face; rudimentary shading indicates a three-dimensional body with rounded limbs. It is not broken down into shards of semigeometric areas, as in an Analytic Cubist portrait. It seems to represent the young Chagall (twenty-seven years old at the time), lying leisurely in the grass, and suddenly waking up with a start to think how not to think about Picasso. But, at the same time, it exhibits a drastic antirealistic gesture — the naturalistic human figure is bent ninety degrees in an entirely unnatural way. It could be read, "I don't give a damn about reality if I have to fill out a corner of my drawing."[28] The clownishly inverted left foot and the free-floating house placed in his inverted lap indicate the willful arrangement of a fictional world and invite the spectator to interpret it and provide a context and a narrative. If Picasso's paintings send us to rethink art, Chagall's send us to rethink reality and, simultaneously, to read the prototypical biography of the painter, especially here, where he is both the maker of the drawing and its protagonist, the focus of its internal point of view, which organizes the drawing while looking away from it.

This drastic break in the naturalistic depiction of a human figure (it cannot be predicted when moving along the "normal" body) can be described by the metaphor of the "catastrophe theory."[29] It is cognate to Kafka's drastic breaks of realistic credibility in the midst of an otherwise pedantic, realistic

fig. 6
Thinking About Picasso, *1914.*
Black ink on paper, 19.1 x 21.6 cm (7 ¹/₂ x 8 ⁵/₈ inches).
Musée national d'art moderne, Centre Georges Pompidou, Paris.

description. In "Blumfield, an Elderly Bachelor," for example, two little balls pop up suddenly in a bachelor's apartment and keep bouncing up and down. In "The Judgment," Georg Bendemann commits suicide for no reason that is detectable in what preceded it. And the first chapter of *The Trial* opens with the strange, implausible event of K.'s non-arrest arrest; then, taking that catastrophe for granted, there is a step-by-step description in almost tedious detail of an arrest (that may be a "mistake" or a "joke") until, suddenly, K. says, "This is not capital punishment yet" — and a whole new dimension of reality is introduced. Such sudden "catastrophes" — and their smaller forerunners, strange (in Kafka) or teasing (in Chagall) — stir us to question the realism of the work of art as a whole, or the different order of meaning we are invited to give the text.

One difference between fiction and painting, however, is that fiction is linear — we get to the catastrophe only when we get to it (for that reason, Kafka often announces the basic catastrophe in the first sentence), while in painting the catastrophe may appear in the midst of a figure, though our eye finds it immediately, even before we figure out the naturalistic parts of the figure. It is a perfect example of the central literary device that the Russian Formalists called *ostrannenie* (making strange), which calls the reader's attention to the text as an artificial object made by its author rather than an illusion of a "world." (Brecht borrowed the concept for his key term *verfremdung* [alienation], denoting the breaking down of the realistic illusion in theater.) Sometimes, Chagall did not need much — one major "catastrophe" — to call our attention to the strangeness of the painting, as in the reverse bending of the body here.

In the case of *Thinking About Picasso*, the basic catastrophe — the defiance of normal human anatomy — is joined by secondary catastrophes and willful deformations such as the house that defies gravity and runs off as a fox, and the topsy-turvy abstraction of the house in the upper-left corner, looking down on it all in an inverted perspective. Such willful catastrophes, drastic breaks in a normal, realistic flow, appear in many forms and were Chagall's trademark from the beginning. Indeed, Chagall was a lyrical joker, an optimist of an absurdist world perception, a comedian Kafka. Their affinity is especially obvious in the "realization of metaphors" — a technique that is not metaphoric at all, but, on the contrary, takes every metaphor literally and depicts it as a fact in the fictional world, making that world itself absurd. Such is the huge insect that Gregor Samsa actually turns into in Kafka's "Metamorphosis"; or, in *Over Vitebsk* (1915–20), Chagall's depiction of a Jew with a sack who actually "goes over the houses" (a Yiddish idiom meaning "is a beggar").

The basic units of this drawing are modules selected from Chagall's fictionalized world, arranged to fill, in asymmetrical balance, the entire sheet of paper. No continuity or direction of time, space, and causality are given a chance here. The composition places a three-dimensional figure (the person) along with a two-dimensional object (the image of the house) in a demonstratively two-dimensional space. No single principle is responsible for the overall order of the painting; a focus of attention at one end is not echoed but compensated for by a different focus of attention on the other end. This new kind of composition, of *asymmetrical balancing of opposite centers of gravity*, is a concomitant of the heterogeneity of styles and fictional domains in Chagall's painting; in the same painting, no continuity is either necessary in his represented world or in his style, for where one fails, the other takes over. Thus, Chagall foregoes both the options of an "inherent" organization of the represented world and of Cubist, Renaissance, or any other formal symmetries; instead he juggles elements of both

to fill his pictorial space.

The modular elements assembled in *Thinking About Picasso* and in more complex paintings enter various negotiations of metaphoricity, analogy, inclusion, counterpoint, and composition. We can explain how they operate together in one object of art. But why the specific selection of those modules rather than others? This question can be answered only in a Yiddish manner, with the question, "Why not?" Or, better, with a Yiddish riddle: "What is green, hangs on the wall, and whistles? — A herring. Why hangs on the wall? — I hung it there. Why green? — It's my herring, I can paint it as I want. And why whistle? — So you have something to ask." Chagall knew a lot about herrings (his father carried barrels of them every day), and he painted them as he felt (especially green). In some sense, this colloquial anecdote describes the composition of a Chagall painting, even the murals for the Yiddish Theater. But in a deeper sense, the justification of this hodgepodge assembly derives from the fact that all accidental and discontinuous individuals cohabiting one canvas are linked to a unified Chagallian universe, permeating his whole oeuvre, in which each of them makes sense.

Color and spatial form

Color complicates the issue immensely — and Chagall placed a great emphasis on it. As many critics have pointed out, the liberation of color from the boundaries of depicted objects is a basic trait of Modernist painting. Artists as diverse as Vincent van Gogh, Henri Matisse, and Kandinskii recognized color as an independent expressive force, having spiritual or musical qualities that affect the viewer in an unmediated way. Kandinskii wrote in Munich in 1912, "Generally speaking, color directly influences the soul. Color is the key-board, the eyes are the hammers, the soul is the piano with many strings. The artist is the hand that plays, touching one key or another purposively, to cause vibrations in the soul."[30]

Kandinskii was influenced by Wilhelm Worringer, a professor of aesthetics in Munich who, in his book *Abstraktion und Einfühlung* (*Abstraction and Empathy*, 1908) promoted the theory that abstract art is one of the two alternating options in art history: abstraction, which generates unlimited geometric patterns, and empathy, which results in closed paintings depicting transient human and natural figures. Chagall was not necessarily familiar with Worringer's writings, but his theories were present in the intellectual and artistic air of the period. In his paintings, Chagall combined both poles — abstraction *and* empathy — and this attitude also influenced his treatment of color. For Chagall, color had both an abstract function, influencing the spectator directly, and an expressive function, interacting with the presented world. Indeed, he often emphasized both aspects in the same painting, with some color areas subordinated to the outlines of figures and spatial forms, and others independent and dominant in parts of the painting. This is a juggling act in which each painting exhibits an asymmetrical equilibrium of painterly and representational forces. He treated all other strata that operate in his works in a similarly dual manner.

Generally speaking, we may distinguish five major strata that interact in most paintings: individuals (human and animal figures and objects); social functionality of the individuals; continuity of a presented world; spatial form; and color. The first three are aspects of the presented world, while the last two

fig. 7
I and the Village, *1911.*
Oil on canvas, 192.1 x 151.4 cm (75 ⁵/₈ x 59 ⁵/₈ inches).
Collection, The Museum of Modern Art, New York.
Mrs. Simon Guggenheim Fund.

are aspects of the organized canvas. In different periods of his life, Chagall autonomized and deformed one or several of these strata, while simultaneously evoking their presence. Thus, perspective was suggested and then subverted; human figures were deformed, yet offered to our attention; the continuities of a presented world were disrupted, yet indicated, emphasizing the disruption.

In traditional, realistic painting (admittedly, a generalization lumping together a great variety of things) all five strata basically overlap (or make believe they do). Even so, both spatial form and color may create autonomous patterns, such as symmetry or perspective in a Renaissance painting, or patterns of a color dispersed in various parts of the canvas, or quasi-abstract shaping of colors on a drapery. And yet, the appearance and boundaries of each color and spatial pattern are, on the whole, "motivated" (to use a Russian Formalist term) realistically; they are justified by the nature of the depicted objects. This coordination between strata became shaky in the age of Modernism. In various trends of Modernism, one stratum or another was subverted; for example, Marcel Duchamp's objets trouvés defy the social functionality of real (nonart) objects. In abstract painting, there may be no presented individuals at all, and the first three strata are absent.

Paul Cézanne promoted semigeometric forms in space; their very principle seems to be in opposition to the flowing, curvilinear forms of living nature. But nonetheless he motivated those semigeometric bodies by objects found in his depicted nature (e.g., buildings among trees) as well as — and here is a leap — by the nature of his metalanguage, the brush strokes executed on a canvas. The next generation did not worry about natural motivation, but broke up a tree or a face into separate color areas, or (in Cubism) broke up the human figure into semigeometric independent units, with their autonomous shadings of lighter and darker hues. Chagall did both: he played between realism and nonrealism in all five strata, and shifted his emphasis mid-painting from one stratum to the other. Let us look at an example.

I and the Village

The famous painting *I and the Village*, in the collection of the Museum of Modern Art, New York (fig. 7), was produced in Paris in 1911–12 from a distance of memory. (A later, gouache and watercolor version is in the collection of the Guggenheim Museum; cat. no. 31.) That distance is underscored by the unrealistic, impossible proportions and continuities between the modules of presented "reality"; if it had been intended as a depiction of reality, it would be either absurd or incompetent or both. Only the simultaneous existence of the figures and scenes in memory can justify such disproportions and incongruous continuities. It is as if the artist were saying, "Those are the things I remember simultaneously, and I shall put them wherever I find space on the canvas."

Most of the canvas is occupied by the heads of a young man and of an animal (presumably a calf), looking into each other's eyes, as is underscored didactically by the thin line linking them. From the title *I and the Village* (given by Cendrars), the viewer may assume that the green head is Chagall's and the village is represented through its livestock. (In Yiddish folk semantics, "village" indicated the world of the "goyim," the Christian peasants; see Chapter 4, "Chagall's Cultural Context.") The green man, however, wears a cross — which may be explained in this interpretation as Chagall trying to identify himself with the Christian village. Partial overlapping of two individuals or two opposing categories is frequent in Chagall's work; parallel to the portmanteau words of Modernist literature, they may be called *portmanteau figures*. In his paintings, we often encounter portmanteau figures in combinations such as human/animal, man/woman, child/old person, animate/inanimate, and, as here, Jew/Christian.

If, however, one assumes that the green man is not Chagall, but the representation of an authentic man of the village, Chagall may still be discovered peeping out of the black, gaping space of the Church and observing it all. (Adherents of the former interpretation have suggested that the small figure is a priest, but his face could easily be Chagall's.) Of course, in Chagall's world they may both represent Chagall. In any case, two internal, "naïve" points of view are established, through which the other parts of the village world are perceived: the point of view of the green man in the foreground, his gaze fixed on the animal head with the rest of the scene perhaps in the back of his mind; and the point of view of the smaller man looking out of the village church onto the free scene of emotions. Simultaneously, however, an external point of view is present, that of the painter-poet, who does not hide behind his work of art but manipulates the strata of the painting at will, for any spectator to see.

Though the painting emphasizes a "world," there are several conspicuous geometric forms independent of the figures of that world, claiming for themselves a competing, quasi-geometric principle of organization. Most conspicuous is the imprecise circle in the center, which cuts through and unifies the man and the animal. This circle is echoed by a smaller circle with inverted red and white colors, intersecting the major one, but not related to any presented figures. Furthermore, the geometric principle is repeated in several semicircular lines, drawn in a nonconcentric manner. That includes two intersecting ovoids through the calf's head, as well as several continuations of one oval in almost-straight lines. Some of the outlines of the objects and figures are also involved in the geometric network; like verbal ambiguities in poetry, they participate in both systems. Crisscrossing diagonal lines divide the great circle like spokes of a wheel, touch the outlines of the two faces, and create five sections with different functions in the fictional world of the picture. The upper wedge forgoes geometry to create a horizon, or the upper limits of a globe, where the peasant pair and the village houses are placed (almost realistically — but for the woman and two houses standing on their heads).

Thus, spatial figures may act as independent geometric bodies or they may be motivated by realistic objects and dependent on their shape. Competition exists between the two principles of composition as does mutual reinforcement. The overall semigeometric organization of space compensates for any discontinuity in the fictional space of the presented village; where one fails, the other takes over. As is often the case in his work, Chagall doesn't know what to do with distance in a depicted landscape: he paints a rising, almost vertical ground, feels uncomfortable with its awkward perspective, and fills it in with figures, whether contiguous with the surrounding reality or not.

The same holds for color. Colors, many and bright, are delineated with clear-cut boundaries, but within each division they are alive, constantly shifting, interacting. Color deviates from the natural function of an object's surface in two major ways: an "unnatural," unexpected color covers the surface of an individual; or colors create spatial areas in their own right, as a different kind of reality, shifting the emphasis from the presented world to the surface of the painting itself. An example of the former in *I and the Village* is the green face; the color is precisely delineated by the form of the face (though the boundaries of the face itself are guided in part by the spatial forms), but its incongruity makes a statement so strong we don't feel that most of the head is cut out of the picture.

Indeed, it is the relation between the human head and the animal head that counts here, rather than the presentation of a whole human or animal figure. The same green reappears as an independent agent throughout the painting, one of several unifying motifs. The peasant houses are also painted in strong, jolly colors — in a country where buildings and garb are usually gray, and where Maiakovskii caused a scandal of sorts by wearing a yellow sweater in the capital! The white in the upper slice would, in another painting, suggest snow, but the man with the scythe and the bouquet below suggest harvest time, and thus turn the white into an unnatural color as well, indicating vacuous space rather than physical ground.

The same double-directed relationship we observe between geometric forms and the fictional world holds true of the relationship between color and spatial forms: in part, colors are confined within the limits of the semigeometric figures, and, in part, they glide outside the spatial form. Red, subordinated to the geometric form in the circles, spills over their boundaries and becomes a dominant, sweeping space of its own on the lower left, which is echoed throughout the picture. The strong confrontation of the two opposing colors, green and red, creates the central organizing power in the color composition of the painting, tied together by the circular form. It is this alliance that foregrounds the blue and the black of the sky in the background. But the colors, too, do not organize the space as a whole and retreat in the upper part, giving way to the dominance of the fictional world: the peasant pair and the line (rather than street) of houses strung in a row. Thus three competing principles of composition, based on three strata — presented world, spatial form, and color — intersect, reinforcing and complementing one another.

The disproportion in the sizes of the objects is not entirely antiperspectival. The two friends in love, young man and animal, are shown close up and large, while the smaller village is indicated in the background. But there is no transition in represented space between them (in the form of streets, roads, or fields) — just a rising white, globelike surface. A possibility of perspective is suggested and then defied and discontinued. The same is true for the head, disproportionately occupying the bulk of the church. The contours of the two frontal figures and some of the houses look almost like flat paper cutouts (though there is some roundness in the middle of the bodies). On the other hand, the peasants, the milking scene, the fingers, and the fruit are three-dimensional. What we have is not an overall perspective but multiple planes placed one behind the other. Yet the order of the planes is sometimes confused. Thus, the visor of the young man's hat is both part of the front plane and a foundation of the house in the distance. And the small milking scene is placed in the large animal head, reversing perspective and forcing a nonrealistic reading.

The shifting dominance of the major strata — color, geometric form, and human and social space — is echoed in the shifting functions at work in the picture. The animal head seems to be a calf (with a cow indicated in its head); functionally, in this painting, the calf is a beloved to whom the young man stretches a bunch of grapes or a bouquet of flowers; and the man himself wears the hat of a school uniform and a cross, identifying himself (if he is Chagall) with the "goyish" village and its love of animals. Even human love, indicated in the inverted man-woman pair, is the simple, healthy love of a working peasant and a sensuous village woman, who invites him home with a generous gesture of her hands. We can say, with Roman Jakobson, that here "every metonymy is a metaphor," every two items placed side by side may evoke a metaphoric construct by the reader. Thus, the boy's loving look and offer of a bouquet to the calf transforms the animal into a metaphor of his beloved. This is underscored by several additional metonymies: the parallelism between this couple and the peasant couple in the background; the motherly function of the cow in the embedded milking scene; the strings of beads on the necks of the boy and the calf; the similarity of the milking woman to the woman in the peasant couple; and the line (conspicuous when the picture is inverted, as Chagall did when he painted it) that leads from the scythe, through the woman's gesture, to the young man's eye.

The principles described above are, of course, not ubiquitous in all of Chagall's work. Rather, I have sought to describe a set of basic options that grew, developed, and changed with time, and from which Chagall selected various aspects and possibilities in the course of his life. A full account of Chagall's art would need a careful historical description.

Chapter 2: Chagall's Murals

A total painting environment

The murals Chagall made for the State Yiddish Chamber Theater in Moscow were a landmark for both the painter and the theater. The theater was transformed from a small actors' studio producing traditional plays in a generally Stanislavskiian manner to one embracing Chagall's avant-garde conception of Modern art, combined with his vision of Sholem Aleichem and the totality and vitality of topsy-turvy Jewish existence. In a few years it became one of the most celebrated theaters in Europe. Chagall himself did not recover from the exhilarating experience of having created a huge object of public art — he kept repeating, "Give me a wall!" — until he made his great stained-glass windows, tapestries, and ceilings in churches, synagogues, and opera houses after World War II.

Founded in 1919 in Petrograd, the Yiddish Chamber Theater moved to Moscow in the end of 1920, where its second birth occurred. Abram Efros, the art critic who co-authored the first book about Chagall,[31] was appointed artistic director of the theater; he persuaded the director, Aleksei Granovskii, to commission Chagall to design the stage sets for the first production in Moscow. Chagall had just been defeated by the radical abstractionists Malevich and Lissitzky in his own People's Art School in Vitebsk, and a commission from Moscow was welcome, even though it was for a separate Jewish (rather than general) institution. The opening production was to be the *Sholem Aleichem Evening*, with two one-act plays by that Yiddish writer — *Agents: A Joke in One Act* and *Mazel Tov: A Comedy in One Act* — as well as his *It's a Lie*, a prose dialogue. Because these were light pieces — almost caricatures — Granovskii could fill in the texts with a theatrical conception of the *gesamtkunstwerk* he had brought from Germany and perfected into a meticulously choreographed multimedia event. Simultaneously, Chagall used the opportunity to impose on the theater his vision of a grotesque, tragicomic Jewish world, disappearing yet brimming with vitality.

In the cold winter of 1920, as civil war raged in the Soviet Union and as the center of power moved from Petrograd to Moscow, rehearsals went on and Chagall painted in a fury. The Yiddish Theater was located on Bol'shoi Chernyshevskii Lane in central Moscow, in the nationalized house of a Jewish businessman, L. I. Gurevich. Gurevich, who apparently fled after the Revolution, had built the three-story mansion in 1902 and lived with his family on the second floor. (Stars of David still embellished the tiles of the corridors when the troupe moved in; fig. 17.) The second floor, including the large reception room and some adjacent spaces, was turned into a theater that held ninety seats. The actors were given living quarters in the same building.

Aleksandr Tairov, the director of the Russian Chamber Theater, had promoted a new perception of the artist's function: rather than painting the backdrop decoration alone, the artist constructed the whole, three-dimensional stage. But Chagall went beyond even this radical notion, embracing the entire auditorium in a Chagallian painting ensemble. Within forty days,[32] working singlehandedly, he painted a twenty-six-foot-long canvas, *Introduction to the Yiddish Theater* (cat. no. 1); four tall images of the Arts (which contributed to the new theater according to Granovskii's conception): *Music, Dance, Drama,* and *Literature* (cat. nos. 4–7); a long frieze, *The Wedding Table* (cat. no. 3); and an almost translucent square image, *Love on the Stage* (cat. no. 2). In sum, the murals covered all the walls, and, according to some sources, the ceiling was painted as well. Thus, instead of seeing a painting in a theater, the audience experienced a performance within a Chagallian four-wall space. It was soon nicknamed "Chagall's box." A critic described the impression:

The task that confronted the artist — to paint the auditorium of the theater — challenged him to a dialogue between the auditorium and the stage. The auditorium, presumably embodying life itself, life standing against the stage, speaks in Chagall's Introduction to the Yiddish Theater *about the ever-theatrical nature of mundane life itself, about life itself being drunk on the elixir of theatricality, about Chagall's paintings connecting the ties between the Harlequinade of the stage and the Harlequinade of mundane life.*[33]

Chagall hated any naturalistic disturbance and pitched a temper tantrum when Granovskii, in the Stanislavskiian tradition, hung a *real* towel on the stage. Chagall even painted the rags that were bought to make costumes, and covered the actors' bodies and faces with colorful dots. As Efros tells it:

He obviously considered the spectator a fly, which would soar out of its chair, sit on Mikhoels's hat and observe with the thousand tiny crystals of its fly's eye what he, Chagall, had conjured up there. . . . On the day of the premiere, just before Mikhoels's entrance on the stage, he clutched the actor's shoulder and frenziedly thrust his brush at him as at a mannequin, daubing dots on his costume and painting tiny birds and pigs no opera glass could observe on his visored cap, despite repeated, anxious summonses to the stage.[34]

The actors were thus perceived as moving Chagallian figures. This coincided with Granovskii's theory that, since the normal human state is silence, actors should pop up out of silence and go back to it. Efros wrote of the production, "The best places were those in which Granovskii executed his system of 'dots' and the actors froze in mid-movement and gesture, from one moment to the next. The narrative line was turned into an assembly of dots."[35] But this was contrary to the usual conception of theater as a three-dimensional, dynamic art. Efros shrewdly understood the problem:

The wholeness of the spectator's impression was complete. When the curtain rose, Chagall's wall panels and the decorations with the actors on the stage simply mirrored each other. But the nature of this ensemble was so untheatrical that one might have asked, why turn off the light in the auditorium, and why do these Chagallian beings move and speak on the stage rather than stand unmoving and silent as on his canvases.[36]

The stage and the walls mirrored each other because Chagall used images of the actors for his painted carnival. Chagall wouldn't abide by the traditional three-dimensionality of the theater any more than he would limit himself to two dimensions in painting: within a demonstratively two-dimensional surface he rendered figures as *both* two- and three-dimensional. And, as we see in his murals, two-dimensionality itself is often presented in a multiplanar perspective. If some figures seem to move in and out of his painted world, it is a fulfillment of his larger conception: his own wife and child peep out from between two flat color stripes in the *Introduction,* and the major figures of the painted theater leap above geometric space altogether. The actors, to Chagall, merely provided another degree of animation in a two-and-a-half-dimensional space. Nevertheless, Efros concluded, "[Chagall] never understood that he was the clear and undisputable victor, and that, in the end, the young Yiddish theater had struggled because of this victory."[37]

fig. 8
Detail of Introduction to the Yiddish Theater *(cat. no. 1).*

fig. 9
Detail of Introduction to the Yiddish Theater *(cat. no. 1).*

Introduction to the Yiddish Theater:
The multiplanar canvas:

Let us first walk into the auditorium as it was and then return to the history and nature of that tragic Yiddish Theater.

As we enter the theater and look at the huge mural to our left, *Introduction to the Yiddish Theater*, a powerful, sweeping movement carries us forward; yet the movement is constantly impeded by groups of figures, bizarre activities, and ever-changing painterly events, making it a long journey indeed. In most of his paintings, Chagall's figures hover over the depicted scenery, but here there is no such setting at all, no houses, streets, town, or stage. The authority of space is transferred from the fictional world to another stratum, the geometric areas formed by Suprematist-like stripes and Orphic-like circles. Colorful figures float on this spaceless canvas, brought together in three functional groups: the management of the theater, the musicians, and the comedians. The painting is framed on each side by a cow and a human figure in a red shirt, and many smaller groups, individuals, and vignettes appear throughout the painting. Within each human grouping, there is no realistic space but rather a conceptual conjunction that unites them. We cannot imagine, for example, an *actual* scene in which Chagall, touching Granovskii with his palette, is carried in Efros's arms while a midget serves tea to the trio. It is rather a realization of the dead metaphor, "Efros brought Chagall to Granovskii."

Basically, the composition is organized in three circles with margins on either end. The circles increase in diameter from left to right, and their upper arcs rise from a distance of about one quarter below the top of the canvas to the very top. In addition to the circles, there are conspicuous stripes and triangles, with well-defined boundaries, as well as lines, segments, and radii, all of which overlap the circles. From the Suprematists, Chagall learned the value of abstract geometric figures, defined in sharp outlines as if made by a ruler, and usually monochromatic. The geometric forms he used in the *Introduction* enabled him to hold such a long work of art together. For years afterward, he was proud and jealous of this achievement. He attempted another massive composition in the long "political" quasi-mural *The Revolution* (1937); yet he had to cut it into several parts, for he could not handle the unity of a painting larger than the length of his arms — until the grills of his stained-glass windows, which he designed later in life, resolved the problem.

The use of Suprematist elements in the midst of this lively work is, of course, a profanation. Malevich sought to achieve "a 'desert' in which nothing could be perceived but feeling," the rediscovery of pure art not "obscured by the accumulation of 'things.'"[38] And along comes Chagall, using a complex structure of geometric figures as a *ground* for his human figures to walk on!

One of the first things that strikes us is the strong black diagonal stripe at the center of the canvas. We recognize this gesture in other post-Revolutionary paintings by Chagall as the realization of his name in Russian, which means "he strode." (Maiakovskii came up with a rhyme: *Shagal / Shagal*, "He strode / Chagall.") To the left of this black diagonal, and parallel to it, is Efros's footless black leg. In the right half of the painting we have a parallel move: the faint, pastel stripes, although oriented downward, are stacked so that as a band of colors they also move upward in the same diagonal. Indeed, if we look at all the precisely organized diagonal stripes and lines, we see that a huge flattened "W" underlies the composition, uniting the canvas — circles, people, and all. The movement upward and forward is further reinforced by the band of human figures that occupies precisely half of the height of the mural and moves slowly from its lower to its upper half. This colorful band represents the theater, whereas the paler images and vignettes all around it represent Chagall's fictional and personal world.

A Yiddish inscription is written on top of the first circle with "square" Hebrew letters. It is conspicuously placed above the red arc that brings together the three dominant figures of the theater: artistic director Efros, painter Chagall, and director Granovskii. To understand it, we must turn first to a study for the *Introduction* (cat. no. 8). On it, these words read: **EFROS IKSVONARG LAGASh**. (Inscriptions on the murals are rendered here in bold type; when the inscription is in inverted Yiddish, it is rendered in bold italic type.) The first surprise is Efros's name, which, in Hebrew, is usually spelled (consonants only) APRT; but here we have the new Soviet Yiddish spelling, with all its vowels, **EFROS**. His name and revolutionary stride underline the message: Energy! Revolution! (In the state? In the theater? In painting?) The other two words look like total gibberish, a collection of Yiddish letters; only if we read the text letter by letter, in the opposite direction (as if it were Russian), can we decipher the names ShAGAL GRANOVSKI.

On the final canvas, however, the names are distorted further than on the study. Of **LAGASh**, all that remains is **. . . AG . . . Sh**, with vestiges of something in between; and even **EFROS** has only **EF . . . S**, with paler outlines of the rest. Inside the words, however, in place of missing letters, there are tiny drawings, of Chagall painting at his easel and of the professorial Efros reading a book. Thus, Chagall combined two systems, letters and ideograms, to represent people. The strangest distortion is of Granovskii's name: instead of the inverted **IKSVONARG**, as it appears on the study, we read **IKTIKTUNARG** on the mural. Chagall often erased parts of a written message (as he deleted parts of a human body), but rarely (if at all) did he add to a written word. Perhaps because he was fed up with the theater director, Chagall began distorting his name from the Yiddish side. In Yiddish, "S" is close to "T" and easily changed; **IKT** could indicate the initials of Idish Kamer Teatr[39] and is repeated twice. To squeeze the longer text into the allotted space, the beginning of the word on the Yiddish side was given in much smaller letters (the study has them all of the same size). When writing from both directions, the beginning of **GRAN{ovski}** meets the double **IKT**, leaving a small space. Hypothetically, the thin letter "U" was the only one that would fit into the space; this may be yet another game of Chagallian deformations.

Inversions and mirror-images of words were in fashion; indeed, the Russian Futurists boasted of having invented *perevertni* (inverted rhymes). Yet Chagall's unusual spelling, with most letters arranged from left to right, indicates the direction of the reader's walk along the canvas toward the stage. It may also indicate the new, European direction Yiddish culture was taking.[40] Chagall, himself a Jewish intellectual moving into general culture, sometimes signed his name in two directions simultaneously: MARC *LAGASh* — first name in French letters, last name in inverted Yiddish — or even M*RAC*, with the "M" and the "C" in Latin letters and the "AR" in inverted Yiddish. The names on the mural thus signal the viewer's eyes to move in the direction of the stage and in the direction of Russian culture.[41]

The circus of intersecting circles, stripes, sections, and triangles acts as the ground under the figures. It also usurps the role of perspective. Chagall painted little figures that emerge from between the planes, thus creating depth between them. As a result, the flat surfaces, used in Modernist art to emphasize the two-dimensionality of the canvas, here create a multiplanar perspective.

Some parts of the individual figures look like paper cutouts

(for example, Mikhoels's blue shirt in the center of the mural; fig. 9), but most figures have three-dimensional characteristics, either through their rounded bodies or through cubistic formations of body and clothing (for example, Chagall's yellow suit). From group to group, perspectives are often inverted — for example, some miniature figures (implying that we are seeing them at a distance) appear not *beyond* but *before* the larger figures. The same ambiguity permeates Chagall's treatment of time. Preparations for the theater, performances themselves, as well as reminders from the Jewish religious and folkloristic past are all presented simultaneously. In a typical postmodernist gesture, Chagall thus blurs the boundary between object-language (describing the presented objects) and metalanguage (describing the painter's language and himself).

In sum, space, time, and perspective are all evoked in the painting and are presented in discontinuous, disrupted bursts. The spectator's position is not taken for granted either. Chagall was furious that chairs were placed in the auditorium, thus fixing the place of the spectators. Apparently, he wanted them to go back and forth from mural to mural. The spectator's distance needs to be variable: to grasp the whole, one must stand at a distance; to understand the activities of the social groups, one needs a middling view, far enough to absorb one third of the canvas but close enough to recognize the figures; and to read the minute inscriptions and embroideries, one must press one's nose up to the canvas.[42]

The *Introduction* is characterized by a gay celebration of colors; some are bold and saturated (in the left half of the painting), some are pale and ornamented (mostly toward the right), some are subtle. Color, though almost entirely subordinated to the boundaries of the figures and geometric bodies, occasionally revolts against the domination of spatial form: the yellow on the margins of the middle circle flows over the geometric boundary into the space above, where it becomes a background for the little sketched figures; similarly, in the lower-right triangle the diffuse orange, though contained in geometric boundaries, permeates the fiddler, bird, and synagogue in the background, as if merging all the disproportionate objects in one level of color and depth; and in the lower-right corner, several colored stripes cover the indecent scene of a boy urinating on a pig.

Thus, each major stratum of the painting is subordinated to other strata in parts of the canvas and asserts its independence in others. Where one stratum is interrupted, another takes over. The general principles of Chagall's art apply to the murals: several stylistic strains may interact in one figure or texture; several figures may overlap partially; deformation or distortion may act on any established figure or artistic stratum; disproportion of the sizes of figures is universally accepted; and any surface of one thing may become the background of another.

The paucity of means available to Chagall in the winter of 1920 is obvious, but he used anything he could lay his hands on. The mural was painted on thin Dutch bedsheets sewn together, with a poorer lining behind it. He used gouaches as well as kaolin with paint and water[43] (in several cases, he left the dripping or mopped-up paint stains as part of the texture), sawdust, and pencil; he dipped lace in paint, pressed it to the canvas, and then removed it, leaving its impression in some areas of the canvas (for example, on the dress of the female dancer), and drew similar tiny patterns with a brush.

The art of comedy

Chagall's surrealist perception of both art and life, his turning away from the realism and psychologism that still reigned in the Russian theater, his unsentimental emphasis on the vitality of traditional Jewish folk culture — these traits infected the

fig. 10
Detail of Introduction to the Yiddish Theater *(cat. no. 1).*

spirit of the theater and influenced its later achievements.

The Yiddish writer Dovid Bergelson wrote that he welcomed the Russian Revolution but did not know how to write "proletarian" fiction — although he knew exactly how the Jewish bourgeois puts his slippers under his bed, he had no idea what the proletarian would do (indeed, there were no Jewish proletarians yet, and they had no slippers). This was a general problem of the new Soviet Russian theater and of literature as well; plays that promoted the new society were sloganeering and vacuous, for they did not embody any real society, any specific, concrete world. The importance of Chagall's role in the theater lay in his embracing the genre of the carnivalesque (as later formulated by the Russian cultural critic Mikhail Bakhtin), the topsy-turvy world that had reigned in medieval fairs. It was precisely through the carnival that Chagall was able to introduce the old, subverted world as a real, tangible substance of a work of art. This enabled the theater to fill its productions with a fictional world populated by rich archetypes, flesh-and-blood popular characters, widely shared jokes, and an inimitable and endearing language. And although these characters were grotesque and out of touch with reality, they also were inspired by flights of fantasy and poetry, and by an ahistorical sense of an absurd and comic human dignity.

By turning that fictional world upside down, Chagall saved it. Later, the Yiddish Theater could be either sentimental or politically obnoxious and rudely critical, even anti-Semitic (showing the "Yid" in full bloom, as Efros described it [44]); yet the tangible existence and vitality of the lost Jewish world was preserved, and resounded in the minds of the viewers, even gentiles or assimilated Jews in Russia and in Western Europe. There was no narrative, only a "world" — and it could be reproduced with plotless plays, characters with no psychology or grounding in reality, and dialogue with no subtlety. The leap that Jewish literature, art, and theater made from a medieval carnivalesque or comedic art to the age of Revolution — leapfrogging realism and psychology — made it seem fresh and Modernist. In this sense Chagall learned a great lesson from his new understanding of the master. Chagall wrote, "I was angry at the small town guys who read Sholem Aleichem and laughed all the time just for the sake of laughing. I, on the contrary, didn't laugh so much and thought that Sholem Aleichem was a 'Modernist' in art." [45] Chagall may have been influenced by his first accepted theater work in the Petrograd cabaret Comedians' Resting Place, but Sholem Aleichem's influence is unmistakable.

Chagall promoted awareness of the Jewish folk tradition, which has no language of tragedy. Entertainment and folk literature are fragmentary, anecdotal, joking, melodramatic, with no narrative or continuous structures; this is the mode of comedy. The traditional Jewish world, fictionalized in Yiddish literature, could be resurrected on the Soviet stage as an entertainment only in the genre of comedy.

Chagall's perception prevailed. In 1919–20, the Yiddish players still called themselves "actors" and attempted serious drama; after Chagall and Sholem Aleichem, they called themselves "comedians." For fifteen years they did not approach serious tragedy. Mikhoels's stunning success as King Lear in 1935 was the victory of a comedian turned tragic actor.

Unlike graven images, theater is not forbidden in the Bible. Rather, the prohibition against it in Jewish tradition stems from a ban against the Hellenistic entertainment enjoyed in Palestine in the early centuries of the common era. But comedians and clowns were not considered part of theater. Indeed, the European Renaissance concept of "comedians" enjoyed a long tradition. In Yiddish, they were called *Purim-shpiler, komediantn,* also derogatorily *Komedyanshtshikes.* A later version of the *Sholem Aleichem Evening* was titled *A Spectacle of Comedians*. Chagall's *Introduction* is a manifesto for that antirealistic, antitragic art.

The *Introduction* is, in general, a celebration of Jewish culture and a vindication of Jewish dignity. As Chagall proudly wrote in his *Leaves from My Notebook*, "I am too shy to say what this little nation can show," implying primarily that it could produce great, universal Art (through Chagall himself), as earlier it had produced Christianity and Marxism. Radical Jewish vignettes appear on the right margins of the work. In the upper-right corner, an adult is being "Jewified" — we can clearly see the circumcision tool. In the lower-right corner a circumcised (and therefore Jewish) boy urinates on a pig — a gesture of defiance against the Christian world (fig. 10). It is as though Chagall were saying, "We will produce art in spite of all our enemies" (in Yiddish, a triumphant stance, meaning "we shall overcome," has this formulaic addition, *oyf tselokhes ale sonim*).[46] Having painted this scene of defilement, he covered it over with three bars. Chagall was extremely ambivalent about the Jewishness of his art, and actually caused a small scandal when the management of the theater refused to open the auditorium as an exhibition to the general public; he argued that his art was being seen only by the hundred Jews who came to the theater, while he wanted a wider audience composed of many nationalities.[47]

Interpreting the large mural

The literary-minded viewer would attempt to "explain" each detail in the mural and the intentions and messages Chagall inscribed in them. But if we succeed in doing so, why do we need a painting at all? The observation of the fine Russian scholar Boris Zingerman is closer to the truth:

In many paintings, he naively and insistently demonstrates his encyclopedia, "the world of Chagall": the sight of his native Vitebsk, next to it the sight of Paris, a wooden grandfather clock, a fish, a sled, lovers, a fiddle, patriarchal relatives, domestic animals, candleholders and acrobats. . . . In vain are the attempts to provide a univalent, rational or symbolic interpretation of Chagall's recurrent poetic images, reading them as a combination of signs, a rebus one can decipher. . . . Chagall's paintings are dominated by the magic of atmosphere, the mystery of a subtext you can never transform into a text.[48]

And yet, a few specific observations are necessary in order to gain access into this Chagallian world.

In the first group of figures on the left, the artistic director Abram Efros brings Chagall to the theater, and Chagall offers his palette to the director Granovskii (fig. 11). The German-educated, serious Granovskii wears a formal tie and jacket, but his legs perform a quadrille, a gesture indicating that he accepts the notion of merriment. The midget serving tea fits Chagall's description of the janitor Ephraim, who served Chagall milk mixed with water.[49] Behind Chagall is a red background, covered with thin outlines of synagogue art, including the stone tablets (only four of the Ten Commandments are indicated here — by their first or last words: no, no, no, no!), a lion and other ornaments, and a *bimah* (synagogue platform) drawn as if it were a Constructivist stage.

Four figures in the center enact the only traditional Jewish art: music. Indeed, the group is a *kapelye* of *klezmers* (a band of musicians), directed by the cymbalist, who resembles the theater's first composer, Lev Pulver. The musicians are actors. This is a realization of a metaphor: in Yiddish, *zey shpiln* means both "they play music" as well as "they perform in a play." A goat, Chagall's representative (it was also painted on the curtains), opens the performance. The bodies of the actors are deformed in a Chagallian manner, limbs scattered in space.

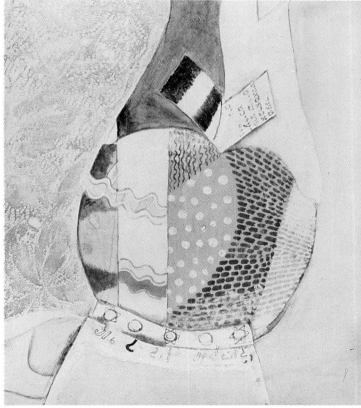

figs. 11–12
Details of Introduction to the Yiddish Theater *(cat. no. 1).*

One can recognize specific actors of the Moscow theater. Ironically, they all wear hats, to indicate that they *act* as a traditional Jewish group (the secular actors of the Yiddish Soviet theater certainly didn't cover their heads indoors). While the theater managers are bare-headed, the hats worn by the figures in the second and third groupings indicate the enactment by a secular culture of its religious past.

A basic problem existed for modern Jewish artists: how should secular Jews, who look like everybody else, be represented? In Jewish literature, the problem was solved by locating every story in the shtetl, though the writer and his readers no longer lived there. The shtetl was the prototypical locus of Jewish iconography, with its distinctive and separate garb, milieu, and discourse. The painter, too, had to mark his secular Jews with emblems of the religious world. Thus, the revolutionary actors wear hats, and the cymbalist wears a Jewish *kapote* (long coat), though it is light blue rather than the traditional black.

With the same logic, in the next major grouping on the right, a Jew is depicted with philacteries on one arm and on his forehead, indicating that he is in the most solemn moment, in mid-prayer (fig. 5). But he stands on his hands, head down, like an acrobat! On his belt is an inscription in childish, longhand Yiddish letters: *ikh balavezekh ikh* (I play pranks, frolic, am naughty, mischievous, have fun.)[50] His neighbor, wearing a skullcap, has written on his belt, in the same childish longhand letters: *ikh bin akrob{at}* (I am an acrobat). There were no acrobats in the Yiddish Theater; Chagall inserted them as his way of indicating the upheaval of the old Jewish world and the entertainment achieved in the meantime.

In the same grouping, an actor in a different kind of play points his gun, in a theatrical gesture, through the twisted legs of the praying acrobat. This may well be Uriel Acosta, the hero of the German playwright Karl Gutzkow's drama by that name, which was one of the first plays performed by Granovskii's theater in Petrograd and revived in Moscow shortly after the *Sholem Aleichem Evening*. Uriel Acosta (1585–1640) was a converso born in Portugal who moved to Amsterdam, where he underwent circumcision and returned to Judaism. He wrote an antireligious book, was excommunicated by the rabbis, recanted, and eventually committed suicide with a pistol. The figure (depicted with different attributes on his left and right sides), the pistol, and the circumcision scene to his right support this conjecture. Uriel Acosta was seen as a hero by secular Jews who wanted to be cosmopolitan, both Jewish and antireligious at the same time.

Several more actors crowd behind the acrobats (the woman has been identified as the actress Sara Rotbaum, the man with jacket and tie as Benyomin Zuskin). Behind Rotbaum, we see a newspaper clipping with printed headline letters, **YIDISHE K**[amer], and, perpendicular to it, [tea]**TR**,[51] superimposed on an old newspaper with the word **BAVEGUNG** (movement, usually used for a political or cultural trend).

The middle acrobat has a list of great Yiddish writers stuck between his legs (fig. 12): **Mend[ele-]Abramovitz Peretz Sholem Aleichem Bil** [Bal-Makhshoves?] [Der] **Nis**[ter]. The first three — Mendele Abramovitz, Y. L. Peretz, and Sholem Aleichem — are the "classic" trio of modern Yiddish literature, all of whom died during World War I. The last two, hesitantly indicated, are Yiddish writers of Chagall's generation: Der Nister, who wrote a children's book that Chagall illustrated, and his friend the Yiddish literary critic Bal-Makhshoves (Dr. Elyashev). Dr. Elyashev also appears near the bottom of the canvas, directly below the gun-holding actor. Together with Bella Chagall and daughter Ida, he greets Marc, who comes down to them under an umbrella (perhaps it is the ubiquitous umbrella carried by the Sholem Aleichem character

Menakhem-Mendel). To the right, Chagall, in a hat and sitting on top of a thin branch, welcomes his parents. The building in the orange triangle resembles a traditional grave; the Yiddish inscription **P N**, which stands for *po nikbar* (here lies) is accompanied by the letters *T A* (for Yiddish Theater, in reverse, Russian order). To the left, someone is being kicked in his mouth and silenced (bringing to mind the Yiddish expression *farshtop im dos moil*, stop his mouth, i.e. shut him up) — could it be Malevich?

This edifice is echoed at the top center by the silhouette of a temple (it also bears the stone tablets), perhaps alluding to Granovskii's conception of the Yiddish theater as "a temple of shining art and joyous creation — a temple where the prayer is chanted in the Yiddish language."[52] This, too, is welcomed by a happy Chagall figure, also with an umbrella.

We also notice elements of Chagall's shtetl, lovingly drawn on Mikhoels's white belt, which is decorated with a lace fringe. And the smallest treasure of all: on the flutist's only leg, above the black vertical and horizontal stripes, there are Yiddish/Hebrew inscriptions, written in childish, clear, unconnected longhand letters, listing Chagall's immediate family: **feyge ite** [mother] **yhzkl** [father, in Hebrew] / **mshe** [Marc's Hebrew name "Moyshe"] **blanh** ["Bella-Anna" — Anyuta] / **roze mariyaske** [sisters] / **dovid** [brother] **zisle** [sister Zina] **leyke mane** [the twin sisters Liza and Manya] / **berte** [his wife Bella, by her Yiddish name] **ide** [daughter Ida] / **mnahem mendl** [grandfather, spelled half in Hebrew, half in Yiddish][53] **ba** [unfinished] / **basheve** [grandmother[54]] **avrhm neyah** [uncles Abraham and Noah].[55] For the most part, these are Hebrew names, spelled in a half-Yiddishized way, as they are pronounced; some are spelled with Russified forms.

On the far left, we find several isolated vignettes within Suprematist spaces. The art historian Ziva Amishai-Maisels speculates that the upper vignette represents the isolation of the theater in its first year in Petrograd, where Granovskii "talked to the lamp" (a Yiddish idiom meaning "gets no response"), for there were no Yiddish-speaking masses in that city.[56] The image below is of a worker waiting to applaud — in Moscow, closer to the Pale, Jewish working people, NEP tradespeople, students, and government officials were then streaming into the city.

The most puzzling images are of a cow and red-shirted person on both ends of the painting. One possible interpretation is that the green cow, with its aggressive horns, represents Chagall's art, forcefully entering the situation. (In the painting *Literature* we see a similar animal, mooing "Chagall" in Yiddish.) Indeed, Chagall favored green: his face in *I and the Village* is green; so is the face of the fiddler in *Music*; in his earlier work for the Petrograd cabaret Comedians' Resting Place, Chagall painted the faces of all the actors green; he used the green cow as his emblem in revolutionary Vitebsk; and in the *Introduction*, the circle in the center, which focuses the "play" around it, is a saturated green.

Who, then, are the attending figures? The figure doing a split on the left, according to the account of Chagall's son-in-law, is Mikhoels, with the attributes of folk art and play-acting. He welcomes the menacing, powerful Chagall; this fits in with the various accounts of Mikhoels's sudden conversion to Chagall's conception and art, and his subsequent influence on the whole troupe in this direction. Below, a shofar blower emerges from a wooden synagogue ornament, heralding and welcoming the newcomer.

The red-shirted man at the far right is not necessarily the same as that on the left — their hats, noses, and chins are different. His feet are in water, a method used by rabbinical scholars to relax or to keep awake when studying late at night. With his visor hat, he may be a worker, representing the proletarian audience for which, presumably, the theater was performing. Or could the figure at the right be Granovskii, resting in satisfaction at the feet of the calmed cow? In this case, the chicken legs under the board on which Granovskii sits may indicate that his enterprise is precarious — it stands on "chicken legs," as the Yiddish idiom would have it. He seems to be satisfied with the cow that now rests, topsy-turvy like the acrobats, after having charged in and revolutionized the theater.

Chagall's *Introduction* and Picasso's *Guernica*
In many ways, *Introduction to the Yiddish Theater* plays a role in Chagall's oeuvre similar to that of *Guernica* in Picasso's. Both are murals, made by invitation of a central cultural body of their respective cultures, both of which were in "diaspora" (Picasso's was commissioned in Paris in January 1937 by the Spanish government in exile). Both were made for a public purpose, expressing a political and cultural position. Neither Chagall nor Picasso were overtly political artists, but both eagerly responded to a public invitation and mobilized their entire stock of images for the purpose, and the commission became a quintessential encyclopedia of their previous work.

For Picasso, in the midst of a period of stylistic hesitation, the commission gave new motivation to the use of his techniques. For Chagall, after a brief and stormy period of propaganda painting in Vitebsk, it also came at a crossroads.

Picasso's mural was a summation of major artistic trends, in his case Cubism, Futurism, Expressionism, Surrealism, and political art. In Chagall's mural, various contradictory trends are also brought together, but in a pluralistic balance; in Picasso's painting they are fused within each figure. Picasso's organic perception of art versus Chagall's dazzling market-fair display is manifested in their color schemes as well: Picasso's painting is almost monochromatic, while Chagall's is a celebration of many colors and hues.

Both artists use the irrational, nonverbal, and empathic power of animals: in Picasso's vision it is the Spanish bull (representing Picasso himself) and the heroic horse-cum-statue, while in Chagall's it is the green cow (also self-representative) and such shtetl animals as goats, chickens, and fish.

Both artists confronted a similar task of organizing a large, unwieldy mural. Picasso's is slightly more than twice as long as it is wide, whereas Chagall's is almost three times as long. As Rudolf Arnheim has pointed out, "Picasso prevented the composition from falling to pieces by the symmetrical correspondence of the flanks — the bull at the left, the falling woman at the right — and the roughly equilateral triangle culminating in the oil lamp.[57] Chagall's mural was longer and could not be integrated in one pyramid; hence his use of the "W" and the three semicircles as an underlying structure.

There are additional devices to unify the murals. In both, a dynamic pulls the viewer with it. As Arnheim notes, "Any compositional movement toward the left . . . runs against the tide, because for psychological reasons the observer's glance proceeds freely from left to right whereas it is impeded in the opposite direction."[58] In Picasso's mural, there is a "movement of the wave of figures . . . directed toward the bull" (on the left), counteracting the normal, rightward current. In Chagall's mural, on the contrary, the basic movement is from left to right. It is plausible, however, that Arnheim's psychological rule applies only to cultures writing from left to right; the Jewish viewer, who writes from right to left, would have felt a tension while viewing Chagall's mural. There are similar images bracketing both works: a powerful cow or bull dominates the leftmost parts of the canvases, while a person at the right summarizes the mood of each painting — a scream in Picasso's and relaxed acceptance in Chagall's.

The difference between Picasso and Chagall may be compared to the difference between tragedy and comedy. Picasso presents the Aristotelian unities of time, space, and action; Chagall displays a plurality of all three. The genre of comedy does not require one purposeful action, but rather prefers anecdotes, immediate effects following each other. It is the heroic gesture of a Spaniard and a Communist versus Jewish utopian hope and self-irony.

The different social purposes and cultural backgrounds of the two artists account for the different conception of the whole, yet in both murals we can see the stocktaking of several waves of Modernism and the political urge of the artist to go beyond the problems of art itself. Both plunged into the work with extreme intensity. There was also a practical difference: Picasso had time and could afford to make dozens of sketches and choose any materials that suited him, while Chagall had a paucity of time and materials at his disposal.

The four Jewish muses, a wedding feast, and *Love on the Stage*
The four paintings that hung to the audience's right in the auditorium represent the four "Jewish muses." The Russian invitation to the exhibition of Chagall's murals called them "Music, Dance, Drama, Literature," but Chagall, in his Yiddish memoir on his work in this theater, published in 1928,[59] called them "klezmers, a wedding jester, women dancers, a Torah scribe" — traditional Jewish professions, which may be grasped as the folk origins of the new Jewish arts.

The four traditional professions depicted here are part of Yiddish rather than Hebrew culture. Even the Hebrew Torah scribe in *Literature* is transformed into a secular figure: on his scroll he has written **amol iz {geven}** — "once upon a time," the conventional opening of a Yiddish folktale. Above the scribe, a cow moos "Chagall" (with an inverted, Russian-directed "L"), while above a small figure carries a chair inscribed **Der T**[eatr] (the theater). The *badkhan* (wedding jester) makes everybody cry or laugh with his improvised grotesque, and often bawdy, rhymes. The dancing woman, wearing a flowery peasant dress, dances to the Hebrew wedding song *kol khosn, kol kale* ("the voice of the groom, the voice of the bride"), inscribed on the hem of her dress and outside it, which is also part of a Yiddish ceremony.

Above the four Arts hung a long frieze, *The Wedding Table*. It consists of two halves painted as mirror images — though one is turned upside down. The Hebrew inscriptions on it read **kosher le-pesakh** (kosher for Passover) and **carmel** (wine from Eretz-Israel, a Zionist element naïve Chagall was unafraid to use in the Soviet Union). The food, however, is not part of a Passover meal — it has no specific Passover dishes and includes challah (a festive Jewish food, but forbidden on Passover). During Passover and the Sabbath, the richest meals in Jewish life are served, hence their symbolic value for this wedding celebration. Chagallian creations, such as a humanized fish and a gymnasium student (in uniform) are also served, along with a live chicken.

It is tempting to assume that the murals are indicative, in a very general way, of the three skits to be performed here: the four musicians are "four agents," the acrobats perform "a lie" (the actual "lie" in the dialogue is the real truth, only turned upside down), and the wedding feast represents the double wedding at the culmination of *Mazel Tov*.

Across from the stage is a painting that is atypical for Chagall, and is known by a poetic title, *Love on the Stage*. Painted in airy hues, mostly shifting between gray and silver, it is composed of geometric figures with a rounded thickness reminiscent of Fernand Léger or early Malevich. It exhibits an impressionistic mood superimposed on cubistic forms. With effort, we can discern the dancing couple at the upper right, in a very "un-Jewish" embrace, face to face and dancing a ballet movement, as hinted by the swinging blue tights on the woman's legs. This is a purely secular, lyrical image.

The socks on the man bear tiny red inscriptions in Yiddish. On the right foot we read K[amer] (Chamber) and **AIDISh** (Yiddish) *RTAET* (Theater) written in five printed letters on each side. "Yiddish" is written in one direction, "Theater" in the opposite.

On the other shoe we have a more puzzling text:

...	L						
P	Sh	M	L	Kh	A	T	
R	L	...	...	M			
...	O						

When we read the text in columns from top to bottom and from right to left (here copied in the English direction) and interpolate the missing letters, we have **Y. L. Peretz Shalom Aleichem A T** (Yiddish Theater). Some letters have faded or were obscured by Chagall.

Underlying the composition is a huge, stylized Shin (the Hebrew letter "Sh," as in *Shaday*, God's name on a mezuza, attached to every Jewish door frame), made of the rounded geometric arms and the red diagonal between them. We can also discern, on the same level, a large "G," and in the lower half of the panel, an "L." The three large cubistic letters of Chagall's name in its Hebrew spelling, ShGL, are as subtle and elusive as the figure of love itself.

One might look at the whole room, "Chagall's box," in light of Efros's understanding of Chagall and the Yiddish theater as an art sprung from nowhere, with no history or tradition, therefore an "art of three times," encompassing its own present, past, and future.[60] Indeed, the large *Introduction* is a summation of Chagall's work as a whole, but without the dark, mystical visions of his early years and without the figures of old, pious Jews. It is a celebration of Chagall's and the actor's generation as they try to enact the past, to extract its folk spirit, joy, and artistic values for the present. It is a procession onward and upward, to an unknown future, which they will reach by turning their world upside down. Yet they are not facing the future, but the audience of the festival. On the right-hand wall, the past is presented, the four towering figures, looming large above their shtetl world. And on the back wall, an image of universal Love, with no specifically Jewish attributes, evokes a translucent, veiled vision of the future.

Chagall's art, in general, developed in this direction, from a fictional world grounded in the past and reclaimed by means of deformation — to the abstract notion of human love, as diffuse as the colors of his later paintings. He came to embrace the ahistorical world of the Bible, as a humanistic vision created by the Jews that will save the world from an atomic disaster.[61]

This perception of Jewish culture entailed a foreboding of its own disaster. Aecular Jewish culture, to which Chagall, Efros, and the new Yiddish Theater contributed, was imported from general European culture. It was a utopian effort to create a culture of "three times," encompassing past and future in the present, in one great burst of art. But secular Jewish culture had no true past, so it had to borrow one from the religious tradition; and it had no future of its own, so it borrowed one from the Russian Revolution. In Russia, it was wiped out by that Revolution itself. What[remains is a heroic art that captured the moment of transformation.

Chagall's work for the stage

"Chagall's box" eclipsed his stage designs, yet they too were revolutionary. His early interest in theater decorations was inspired by Bakst, who had asked Chagall, while he was still his student, to work on the ballet *Narcisse*. When Chagall returned to Petrograd during World War I, it was the center of theater experimentation and avant-garde opposition to the finicky, decorative stage backdrops of the World of Art artists.

Innovations in Russia were spurred by a new wave of little theaters that emerged in the decade before the Revolution. As the art historian Aleksandra Shatskikh has pointed out, "in the period of 1908–1917 small theaters of a semi-club semi-studio character developed everywhere — the so-called cellars, pubs, cabarets, 'little stages.' The most famous of them were *House of Interlude, Flying Mouse, Vagabond Dog, Comedians' Resting Place*."[62] Chagall's first successful production design was for one of three miniatures, "An Absolutely Joyful Song," staged by Evreinov, which opened at the Comedians' Resting Place, a cabaret, on January 23, 1917. For the play, Chagall painted the faces of all the actors green and their hands blue. In this establishment, the stage and auditorium were fused by one "unified decoration," made by S. Iu. Sudeikin and others, which might have influenced Chagall's perception of the artist's role in the theater.

In early 1919, he was commissioned to prepare the decorations and costumes for two plays by Nikolai Gogol' for the Petrograd theater Hermitage. Gogol', with his profound and hilarious comedy of life, was a major literary influence on Chagall. The production, however, was never realized.

As Commissar of Art in Vitebsk, Chagall plunged into revolutionary cultural activity, including founding a new People's Art School and organizing mass decorations around the city for celebrations marking the anniversary of the October Revolution. Vitebsk, at the intersection of the railroads from Moscow and Petrograd, exhibited a feverish cultural activity. The Russian-speaking Jewish youth, starved for culture and finally liberated, plunged into all modes of self expression. Among the many drama circles, the most active, according to Shatskikh, was the theater studio of the Y. L. Peretz Society, named for the major Yiddish writer and ideologue of modern Yiddish secular culture. Recent scholarship has revealed that Chagall became the chief artist of a new kind of Russian theater that emerged in Vitebsk, Terevsat (an acronym for Theater of Revolutionary Satire). Vitebsk was close to the front line of the Civil War and Terevsat supplied entertainment for the army as well as the city. It combined political propaganda with satire in a review based on traditions of the Russian folk theater. The Vitebsk Terevsat became a model for similar theaters in other cities.

Terevsat opened on February 7, 1919, and Chagall was its only artist for the 1919–20 season. He designed at least ten productions,[63] including costumes, makeup, and various stage objects. In April 1920, Terevsat moved to Moscow; Chagall came a month later.[64] In June 1922, Meierkhol'd became its director, and the theater was renamed Theater of the Revolution at the Moscow Soviet. Chagall designed one more production for Terevsat, *Comrad Khlestakov*, a Revolutionary parody with allusions to Gogol'.[65]

The Yiddish Theater moved to Moscow in the fall of 1920, and in November, Chagall plunged into the immense project. His stage sets were truly minimal, for lack of means and material. In his costumes and stage designs we can see a combination of naturalistic, folkloristic, and comic perceptions of Jewish poverty, on the one hand, and strong Constructivist gestures, on the other. But unlike some of those who followed, he never gave in to pure Constructivism.

The Yiddish Theater planned to perform Sholem

Aleichem's *Agents* while still in Petrograd. (For a translation of the play, see pages 164–71.) Schil'dknecht designed a realistic background of middle-class living, rich in details and colors, in the style of the World of Art. When Chagall was assigned the production design in Moscow, the only aspect of Schil'dknecht's design he took was a compartment and a half of a railroad car standing at the center. He presented the double compartment furniture with minimalist detail and unified the scene with a sweeping asymmetrical arch, breaking the realistic illusion. On top of the arch was a tiny locomotive, and an inscription in Yiddish, "**for smok**[ers]," and, in inverted Yiddish, "**III cl**[ass]."

The minimalism and poverty of that first production of *Agents* can be seen in a list of costumes and props required for the performances:

Vovsi {Mikhoels}/ for Agents */ 1. Valise, hard.*
2. Coat. 3. Briefcase. 4. Matches. 5. Letter with envelope.
6. Paper, white pages.

Krashinski {another actor} / for Agents */*
1. Small valise. 2. Briefcase. 3. Cigarette case. 4. Cigarettes.
5. Pages of white paper.

As late as January 1, 1922, the required inventory for the stage consisted of the following:

Green curtain (left side, right side); wooden window on stand; wooden moon; wooden board with painting of locomotive smokestack, on stand; white bench (of railroad car); valise with cover for Yakenhoz, same for Lanternshooter; big doll (for Davidka); whistle (wooden instrument). [66]

For *Mazel Tov*, Chagall designed a similar rounded arch and a minimalized kitchen, his emblematic goat (turned upside down) painted on the wall, minimal furniture, and several Constructivist patterns (cat. nos. 15–16). A plate above the stove has a Yiddish inscription, disintegrating into vertical and horizontal lines. The legible beginning reads **ELEY**, which could be either the beginning of [Sholem] Aleichem or the inverted name of the cook [B]eyle.

S'A Lign (*It's a Lie*) is a dialogue that takes place on a train. An ugly story about corruption is revealed little by little, as the narrator keeps protesting "it's a lie" before uncovering another detail. Apparently Chagall's design (cat. no. 17) was so minimal and abstract that it was replaced with a set by Natan Al'tman.[67] Chagall included a home in which the roof was half removed, a boot was hanging out, and a huge pencil was leaning from the ground to the ceiling. Looming above it was a ten-story-high piece of paper and a huge pen, turned lamp, illuminating the scene. The top of the paper was imprinted with tentative headline letters *HGSh* (a distortion of *Lagash*, the inverted Chagall) and **S'ALIGN S'ALIGN** ("it's a lie," "it's a lie"). One of the costumes portrays a popular bluffer, with partially obscured Yiddish inscriptions on his pants; on them, we can read **s'align** several times, **sheker** (Hebrew for "lie"), parts of *sidur* and *talis*, and perhaps the name of the corrupt rich man in the play, **Shia** [Finkelstein]. (For examples of Chagall's costume designs for the *Sholem Aleichem Evening*, see cat. nos. 18–20.)

The fate of the murals
After one year, the theater moved to a larger home on Malaia Bronnaia Street, but the murals remained behind. After 1925, the murals were displayed in the foyer of the new auditorium. Chagall left the Soviet Union in 1922, Granovskii in 1928 — thenceforth, both were considered traitors, and after the 1930s

their names were unmentionable in their country. During the purges of the 1930s, the murals were hidden and suffered damage. Somehow they arrived at the State Tret'iakov Gallery — presumably in 1950 — but were not shown. For a time, they were hidden in a dilapidated church building that was used for storage.

Mikhoels was brutally murdered by the NKVD in 1948; the theater was closed in 1949, and most of its actors were put in concentration camps or liquidated along with Soviet Yiddish writers and all other representatives of official Soviet Yiddish culture. How did Chagall's paintings, property of the State Yiddish Theater, get to the State Tret'iakov Gallery? One version has it that the Liquidation Commission gave the murals to the Tret'iakov in 1950[68]; another version, prevalent in Moscow art circles today, is that the last artistic director of the theater, Aleksandr Tyshler, when he saw that all was lost, carried the canvases on his back to the Tret'iakov.[69] One day, I am sure, the Tret'iakov Gallery will disclose the truth.

The Tret'iakov conservators did a careful job in preparing the canvases in 1991 for "the long-distance transport firstly to Germany, and then at a later date to other countries."[70] They did not attempt to restore the original colors.

The murals now display Chagall's signatures, which he applied to them on his visit to Russia in 1973. Chagall, accustomed for so long to signing his name in French, confused the two languages: on the large *Introduction*, his signature is in printed Russian letters with the exception of the "G" from the Latin rather than Cyrillic alphabet.

The fame of the Yiddish Theater

The Yiddish Theater began as a modest actors' studio in Petrograd in 1919 and moved to Moscow in 1920. By the mid-1920s, it was one of the most exciting companies in Russia and, indeed, in Europe. On a visit to Russia, the English theater critic Huntley Carter, who wrote several books on Russian avant-garde theater, said, "The work of GOSET has no equal in Europe."[71] And the German theater critic Alfons Goldschmidt, after visiting Moscow in 1925, wrote, "The Moscow State Yiddish Theater, directed by Granovskii in ensemble with the actors, embodies at least the beginning of something entirely new, while the Western European theater, in its degeneration, looks in vain for new forms."[72]

When the Yiddish Theater came to Berlin's Theater des Westens in 1928, the awe-inspiring critic Alfred Kerr began his essay with these words:

This is great art. Great art.
External image and soul-shaking. The sound of words, the sound of blood, the sound of color, the sound of images. There are calls, voices, questions, shouts, choruses. It is enjoyment and horror . . . and in the end, human communion.
That is, of course, pantomime with movement into eternity. Something wonderful.
(Great art.) [73]

Similar superlatives were expressed both by visitors to Russia and by theater critics during the troupe's tour of Western Europe in 1928. After all the formal inventions of the first quarter of the century, the avant-garde theater had exhausted its innovations, and this new company seemed to fulfill a need at a moment of crisis. It also exemplified the new culture created in the wake of the Russian Revolution and as a result of the miraculous rebirth of the Jews.

The Yiddish Theater no longer exists and the "air" (as Granovskii would have said) of that time is very distant from our own. Contemporaries of those events speak for themselves in the Texts and Documents section in this book. Among the original translations we have provided are several sources on the emergence of this theater, its methods and significance, Chagall's role in it, early responses to and analyses of the theater, the theater's role vis-à-vis the lost Jewish past, and one of the plays performed at the *Sholem Aleichem Evening*. These documents provide a vivid image of the theater in the context of its time, and there is no need to repeat it all here. Nor can we deal here with the later history of this theater under the conditions of Soviet political pressures and terror — a worthy topic in its own right. We shall, however, recapitulate the major facts and assess the key aspects of the theater's nature, achievement, and destruction.

Yiddish culture and Yiddish theater

Toward the end of the tsarist regime in Russia, new ideas were coalescing among the new class of Jewish intellectuals concerning the organized creation and promotion of a full-fledged national culture for the more than five million Jews in Russia. After the February and October Revolutions of 1917, when Jews were granted civil rights and could move to the centers of Russia, it was only natural that they tried to implement those ideas under the new regime. Thus, in 1918, in the Ukraine's capital of Kiev, there emerged an umbrella

organization, Kultur-Lige (Culture League), devoted to Yiddish national cultural. Their program declared:

Kultur-Lige *stands on three pillars: Yiddish education for the people, Yiddish literature, and Jewish art. The goal of the* Kultur-Lige *is to make our masses intelligent and make our intelligentsia Jewish. . . .*
The goal of Kultur-Lige *is to help create a new Yiddish secular culture, in the Yiddish language, in Jewish national forms, with the vital forces of the broadest Jewish masses, in the spirit of the Jewish working masses, in harmony with their ideal of the future.*
The working field of Kultur-Lige *is the whole field of the new secular culture: the child before the school and in the school, education for the young and adult Jew, Yiddish literature, Jewish art.*[74]

The stamp of Kultur-Lige bore the inscription "Mendele, Peretz, Sholem Aleichem" — all of whom died during World War I and thus secured their status as the three "classic" writers of modern Yiddish literature. Theirs was sophisticated literature that reached the highest European standard. Deeply involved in understanding Jewish existence, their work formed a dignified foundation for a modern, secular, truly Jewish literature and culture. (Chagall was influenced by these three classic writers and included their names on the *Introduction to the Yiddish Theater*.)

Kultur-Lige emerged during the Civil War, when Kiev itself was shifting from one power to another. The war, and the exterminating pogroms of 1919 (when about a hundred thousand Jews were slaughtered and several hundred thousand were exiled from their towns), were hard on the Kiev center; but its ideas were shared by other centers in Russia and in the newly re-established Poland.

With the same spirit that led to Kultur-Lige's formation, a Jewish Theater Society was founded on November 9, 1916, in Petrograd. The Revolution disrupted all work in the capital, but its emerging cultural powers supported the rehabilitation of the Jews as part of the new Soviet policy of elevating those oppressed by the tsarist regime. On November 29, 1918, the journal *Zhizn Iskusstva* (*Life of Art*) announced the establishment of a "Yiddish workers' theater" in Petrograd, affiliated with the theater and performance department of the People's Commissariat of Education. The Jewish Theater Society implemented that decision. In February 1919, a theater studio was established and Aleksei Granovskii, who had studied in Germany and was a disciple of the famous theater director Max Reinhardt, was appointed director of the Artistic Division. After five months of intensive work, the studio became the new Yiddish Chamber Theater and began performances on July 3, 1919. But Petrograd was not the best place for Yiddish theater, and between July 7 and August 22, 1919 the company gave performances in the nearest Jewish center — Vitebsk, where Chagall was then Commissar of Art and director of the People's Art School. Chagall had no interest in this theater when it visited Vitebsk. Its designs were heavily Symbolist, and its artists impressed him as uninteresting or epigones (such as the prominent but unoriginal second-generation World of Art designer Dobuzhinskii).

During its Petrograd period, the Yiddish Chamber Theater included the works of Yiddish and non-Yiddish authors alike, producing such plays as Maurice Maeterlinck's *The Blind*, Sholem Asch's *Sin* and *Amnon and Tamar*, Gutzkow's *Uriel Acosta*, and A. Vayter's *Before Dawn*. It was an art theater that happened to perform in the Yiddish language. For lack of heat in Petrograd, the theater was closed for the 1919–20 season, yet rehearsals continued, giving Granovskii the chance to educate and form a well-trained and integrated troupe of an entirely new kind.

fig. 13
Poster from a 1924 performance, in Kiev, by the Yiddish Theater. Central State Archive for Literature and Art, Moscow.

A parallel initiative was taken in Moscow. In September 1918, the Jewish Commissariat of the Russian government founded a theater section as part of its Education Department. According to its head, B. Orshanski, the call for actors met with little response because the Jewish intelligentsia did not support the Soviet power and "sabotaged" the enterprise. For that reason they gathered some young and politically trustworthy people, with no theater experience. Thus, an independent actors' studio was founded in Moscow in 1919, which included actors of the Vitebsk Yiddish theater studio.

On April 1, 1920, the government authority chaired by Anatolii Lunacharskii transferred the Yiddish Chamber Theater from Petrograd to Moscow. When Granovskii's theater arrived in November 1920 (with only eight of the original students), it merged with the Moscow actors' studio as well as with some actors from the Vilna Troupe, a recently established Yiddish art theater.

In 1921, Granovskii's theater was renamed GOSEKT (State Yiddish Chamber Theater). Performances in Moscow began on January 1, 1921, in a hall with ninety seats and Chagall's murals. A year later, the theater moved from "Chagall's box," as it became known, to a larger auditorium, containing five hundred seats, and in 1924 it was renamed GOSET (State Yiddish Theater; for a while, it was also called the State *Academic* Yiddish Theater).

Two magical slogans guided the new Yiddish theater and gave it immense prestige: "theater as art" and "theater of the State." Finally, Jews could have an "art theater" (not unlike Stanislavskii's Moscow Art Theater) connected with the most advanced of the other arts — graphic art, literature, dance, music — and separate from the kitschy entertainment stage. And this theater was supported by the State itself — the foreign State that had been the enemy of the Jews for two thousand years — almost a Zionist vision! The Yiddish name for the theater sounded even better — Moskver Yidisher Melukhisher Teater (Moscow Yiddish *Royal* Theater). It is hard to imagine the dignity and pride its supporters felt. Their tangible hope for a new secular and elite Jewish national culture, and the revolutionary spirit that inspired this enterprise made those involved open to the trends of political revolution and the avant-garde.

In his Yiddish productions, Granovskii wanted the Jewish subject matter to represent general human values. Yet as director of the Yiddish Theater he felt a special mission, which included both raising the Jewish masses to a high cultural level and creating a national Jewish secular culture. In the archives of the theater, there is a document dating from 1920 or 1921, handwritten in Russian by Granovskii, describing the goals and organizational structure of GOSEKT. The first section reads:

General Principles

- *GOSEKT is the first and only attempt to create a permanent performing-arts theater for the Jewish nation.*

- *Because of political conditions, it was hitherto impossible to establish such a theater.*

- *Geographically, Moscow was selected, as the cultural and artistic center of the life of the whole Republic.*

- *Unlike all other nationalities inhabiting Russia, the Jews are the only ones who have no territory of their own.*

This was the succinct ideology of a political-cultural program, from which the organizational framework followed. To keep a theater of such importance alive, one needed to train personnel at all levels. As Granovskii saw it, there were to be three

separate units: a School of Stage Art, to "train the personnel of actors and directors, who are totally lacking in the Yiddish theater"; a Studio, "a laboratory to develop the forms of the Jewish theater"; and the Theater itself, "for the broad masses."

Granovskii and theater as art

Aleksei Granovskii was born Abraham Azarkh in Moscow in 1890. Moscow was out of bounds for most Jews, which means that his parents must have been well off and probably well educated and Russian speaking (it was said that he knew no Yiddish before he heard it from his actors).[75] In 1891, all of Moscow's Jews were expelled (was this the source of his nationalist feelings?). His family settled in Riga, then the third largest city of Russia. Riga has a long German tradition but had been under Russian rule for over two centuries. There, he imbibed both Russian and German language and culture, and through them, the culture of Western Europe. Riga produced such contemporary intellectuals as Sergei Eizenshtein (whose Jewish father converted to Lutheranism and became the city architect), who was two years older than Granovskii. It also produced Shloyme Mikhoels, who, like Granovskii, was born in 1890.

In 1910, Granovskii began his theater studies in St. Petersburg, and from 1911 to 1914 he studied in Germany at the Munich Theater Academy, where he worked for a season under Max Reinhardt. In 1917, he studied film directing in Sweden. Back in Petrograd in 1918, he joined the new Theater of Tragedy, which was supported by prominent intellectuals such as Maksim Gorkii and Aleksandr Blok and was devoted to promoting classical drama for the masses. There, he directed Sophocles's *Oedipus Rex* and William Shakespeare's *Macbeth* in Russian. He also directed two operas, Charles Gounod's *Faust* and Nikolai Rimskii-Korsakov's *Sadko*, and the famous German-language production of Maiakovskii's avant-garde play *Mystery Bouffe,* which was performed for the Third Congress of the Comintern. Then he strove to create a theater in Yiddish.

Granovskii and his mentors believed in the creation of Yiddish theater as *art*. The amazing Jewish cultural renaissance of the preceding fifty years had been concentrated in literature and ideology; they believed that to become a full-fledged culture, the nation needed music, plastic arts, and theater. Since theater was accepted only as an art in the most modern sense, they recognized no earlier tradition. Granovskii was to begin from absolute zero.

From the Greco-Roman period in Palestine, theater was banned in Judaism, though there were a few exceptions: Hebrew drama was written and performed in post-Renaissance Italy; Hebrew plays were written in the Haskala period, the Jewish "Enlightenment," which flowered in Berlin in the late-eighteenth century and spread to Central and Eastern Europe; and there were entertainments in Yiddish, notably the *Purim-shpil*. Nevertheless, theater in the modern, European sense was almost nonexistent in Yiddish. Avrom Goldfaden began a Yiddish theater to provide entertainment in 1876, but in 1883 the Russian government banned all theater in "jargon" (Yiddish); the ban was lifted between 1905 and 1910, then renewed until the Revolution. Yiddish popular theater, primarily low-class melodrama (such as Kafka saw and admired in Prague in 1910), blossomed in London and New York, but Granovskii, like most Yiddish highbrow writers and cultural activists, would have nothing to do with it. (New York's celebrated Second Avenue Yiddish theater was considered terrible and kitschy, degrading to Yiddish culture in America.)

During the 1905–10 period, when Yiddish theater was legal in Russia, there were important beginnings: good literary and theatrical plays were written by Peretz Hirshbeyn, Dovid

fig. 14
Aleksei Granovskii in the 1920s.

fig. 15
Chagall and Mikhoels, 1921.

figs. 16–17
Interior of the house on Bol'shoi Chernyshevskii Lane, the Yiddish Theater's first home in Moscow, as it looks today.

Pinskii, and others; excellent actors emerged, such as Ester-Rokhl Kaminski, who made a strong impact on young Mikhoels during her performances in Riga; and plays by Gorkii, Gerhard Hauptmann, Shakespeare, and Friedrich von Schiller, translated into literary Yiddish, were performed. Granovskii and his contemporaries rejected that theater too because it was individualistic, psychological, and literary. The new regime, certainly, saw those Yiddish playwrights as "bourgeois" writers, and Granovskii probably knew little about them; they were too provincial for this snobbish disciple of Reinhardt. Like Chagall, Granovskii absorbed the most recent developments in theater technique while simultaneously reaching back for its sources to the folk traditions of entertainment and *Komedyanshtshikes* that preceded the literary theater in Yiddish.

Granovskii's system

In 1918, when Granovskii undertook his mission, he announced the search for candidates to train as actors. They were required to have had no previous experience with theater, and could not be older than twenty-seven. (Granovskii himself was twenty-eight.) His selection process coincided with the political selection process in Moscow, barring anybody with "Old World" conventions or habits. Granovskii made an exception for Shloyme Vovsi, an intellectual who studied law at Petrograd University but was Granovskii's age. Vovsi had a "monkey-face" so ugly that Granovskii found him beautiful. From the beginning — and under his new stage name, Mikhoels — he was Granovskii's right-hand man and his conduit to the other actors.

In the first programmatic publication of the Yiddish Theater in Petrograd in 1919, Mikhoels described the situation:

Outside, the Revolutionary wave raged, and human eyes and too-human thoughts, scared and scattered, blinked in the chaos of destruction and becoming. . . . At a time when worlds sank, cracked and changed into new worlds, a miracle occurred, perhaps still small, but very big and meaningful for us, Jews — the Yiddish theater was born.[76]

Granovskii trained his actors ab ovo, utilizing the best resources of the avant-garde theater. They had top Russian teachers to instruct them in music, rhythm and dance, gesture, "plastic movement," and acting techniques; they also studied Yiddish literature, language, folklore, and folksongs intensively with specialists. Each actor was to be a master of all theater arts and in precise command of his body and voice. The system was similar in part to Meierkhol'd's Biomechanics; it prepared the actors to be as agile as acrobats (the circus was an inspiration for the theater, as it had been for Meierkhol'd and Eizenshtein). The stress fell on language, music, and folklore — a rich, modern Yiddish language was an avant-garde achievement in itself — as it related to the Jewish fictional world they re-enacted.

Mikhoels described the state of the students:

Two feelings struggled in our heart: the great will to create on the stage in the Jewish domain and the internal doubt in our own powers. . . . Indeed, who were we — lonely dreamers with unclear strivings; what did we bring with us — except for oppressed and bound limbs and internal tightness, complete ignorance and helplessness in stage work and stage technique — nothing. . . . Yet one thing each of us had — fiery will and readiness for sacrifice. . . . And our leader told us it was enough.[77]

For Granovskii, Man was but one of the elements of a stage production, along with the script, the music, the sets, and the lighting. But, as Mikhoels wrote, "We could only give ourselves, the Jew . . . to give the stage *Man* with a capital "M" — this became our goal." The teaching and rehearsals were conducted in Russian, yet Granovskii learned some Yiddish from the actors' speech. A typical *yekke*, assimilated to what Jews understood as high-culture German manners, Granovskii's ideal was silence — a state that was alien to the talkative Eastern European Jews who were his actors and audiences. He taught that

the word is the greatest weapon of stage creation. Its value lies not only in speech but in silence. . . . The normal state is silence. . . . The word is a whole event, a super-normal state of man. . . . The intervals of silence between utterances of phrases or words are the background from which the great, meaningful word emerges. . . .
The normal state is static. . . . The movement is an event, a super-normal state. . . . Every move must start from the static state, which is the general background from which the meaningful move emerges. . . . A movement must be logically articulated into its basic elements as a complex algebraic formula is broken down to its simple multipliers.[78]

The theater performance was a work of art, a stylized multimedia event that had nothing to do with Stanislavskii's realism. Granovskii invited the ballet master B. A. Romanov to teach his actors rhythmic movement, "plastics," and dance. When all this was drilled perfectly, rehearsals began, between 150 and 250 per production. No wonder the actors who remained admired their director; Mikhoels called him "our leader." "For us," the actor wrote, "he is the highest authority and the last word," for "only we, the students, see what is still hidden from every other eye . . . the work of self-sacrifice, the love of art and the people, the rich content, filled with ideals, which his activity breathes!"[79]

In the State Bakhrushin Museum we find Granovskii's handwritten key to the scores for actors and for the director's exposition of the play; it dates from the early twenties:

I	pause
II	long pause
I:I	long pause and change of mood
⟶	merging
word underlined	foregrounding
⌒	modulating a word
↓	end of mood
↑	beginning of mood
Mus	music
------	music continues
F. M.	end of music

Modulation of movement and voice, and shifts of mood and dynamics, gave life to the ensemble. It was between words and movement that the art of the ensemble was located. The text, like the actor, was treated as a means to the goal, and the shorter the text the better. Granovskii sought a total effect, involving every move of a multimedia polyphony, and involving every spectator in every move. Performances were so rich because they articulated every separate medium into a myriad of tiny steps, each one foregrounded and meaningful. The Yiddish Theater did not stage many productions, but almost every one was a true cultural event. Mikhoels noted his director's programmatic statement (made at the early studio stage):

fig. 18
Mikhoels as Reb Alter in Mazel Tov.

I see the ensemble performance, the stage action, as a choir action. . . . Every type, everybody's movement, everybody's acting, playing, painting, every individual action in the play is only a part of the architectonic whole. . . . Our artistic goal is the play as a whole. . . . And the value and significance of the smallest role is great in its relations to the whole dramatic construct. . . . One false performance of a word, or a move, not just of the central figure in a play but of the smallest and most overshadowed, can corrupt and cheapen the whole artistic image. [80]

This was Granovskii's theory in the first months of molding his studio. He refined this vision throughout his tenure at the Yiddish Theater. Granovskii choreographed a polyphonic and dynamic, constantly surprising stage. He was mathematically precise and pedantically meticulous about every detail.

A prominent Russian drama critic and theater professional observed:

When one sees this "Jewish acting," one cannot fail to be struck by the emotional appeal and rapidity of movement, the intensity of speech and vigor of the gestures. In its early productions, when the old repertory was being revised, poor Jews in tattered garments and comical masks of rich Jews — in frock-coats and stately, old-fashioned robes with colorful trimmings — would dart and dance about on the curious platforms and crooked staircases, in an ecstasy of delight. They were the Jews of the poorer slums. They would stand for a moment in solemn stillness, like monuments, before dashing away into the hum of the marketplace, or springing from one platform to another, or rushing down a flight of stairs and away. [81]

The importance of language was diminished in the context of the polyphonic productions. The greatest successes of the theater occurred with audiences that hardly understood Yiddish; many Russians attended its performances in Moscow, and German audiences perhaps understood only some of the words. A story about HaBima, the parallel Moscow Hebrew theater that used similar sources of Yiddish folklore, though it was still influenced by Stanislavskii's method, is telling: The actor and director Mikhail Chekhov once visited a rehearsal directed by Vakhtangov. Chekhov, who did not know Hebrew (neither, for that matter, did Vakhtangov), said to him, "I understood it all except for one scene." Vakhtangov continued to work on that scene, and on his next visit Chekhov understood it perfectly. The scene was not effective if you needed the words. The lack of a common language among the audience members encouraged Granovskii's virtuoso treatment of the nonverbal aspects of this Wagnerian *gesamtkunstwerk*.

For the same reason, ideology was unimportant as well. Like Maiakovskii and Meierkhol'd, Granovskii was willing to incorporate a socialist propaganda message in whatever play he performed — what counted to him was not the message but the effectiveness of the play's impact on the viewer. Indeed, ideology was almost an excuse for producing a play. As soon as the troupe appeared in Western Europe in 1928, Granovskii was accused by Lunacharskii of neglecting socialist ideology and the theater was summoned back to Moscow. (Granovskii, fortunately, remained in the West.)

The theater's greatness, however, did not rest solely on Granovskii's polyphonic approach, nor on his mathematically calculated scores and directing. It derived rather from the fusion of his ideas with a Jewish fictional world created by modern Yiddish literature, and elevated to art by Chagall. As in Chagall's work itself, another language was superimposed on the languages of avant-garde theater: a powerful, time-forged, fictional world, with a series of generalized but unique types.

Other Russian directors of the time merged leftist art with ideological slogans, but ideology is flimsy and transient, while

fig. 19
Chagall's set for Mazel Tov.

a fictional world with unique prototypical characters remains in the imagination of the spectator. The ideologies that were attached to GOSET's productions were easily forgotten: "They went out to curse and found themselves blessing," as one critic put it. Indeed, such estranged semi-Jews as Osip Mandelshtam and Shklovskii saw in the theater's productions the vitality (and tragic end) of the shtetl world, and paid no attention to the obvious Soviet message.[82]

This fictional world was raised to the level of a timeless myth through Granovskii's rhythm of "spots," which broke down the continuities of character and plot as if they were the subject matter of an Analytic Cubist painting. It was Chagall who taught him to depart from realism and continuity of space and time, and to embrace simultaneity of action on several levels (for which not Chagall, but his Constructivist followers, prepared multilevel stages).

The fictional world

Chagall and Granovskii were polar opposites: the former was emotional, "childish," "crazy," the very embodiment of the awakening folk type from the Jewish Pale, while the latter was rational, Europeanized, German-trained and assimilated, mostly silent, precise, and disciplined. They met at the very beginning of the Yiddish Theater in Moscow, for a production of three negligible skits, yet the collision of these two willful originals changed the course of the theater from then on.

One critic bluntly asked about Granovskii, "This alien Goy will build a Jewish theater?" The program for a Petrograd performance of his Chamber Theater carried a notice, in half-German, half-Yiddish, that typifies Granovskii's attitude: *Das publikum wert gebeten entzagen zikh fun aplodismentn um tsu behaltn di gantskeyt fun ayndruk.* (The audience is requested to refrain from applauding to preserve the wholeness of the impression.)

Granovskii's productions in Petrograd might have been perfect, but no one remembered them. It was only after Chagall's influence on the theater that its stunning effect was achieved — the *Sholem Aleichem Evening* was performed three hundred times. After Chagall's departure, Granovskii revived another good (and thematically Jewish) play, Gutzkow's *Uriel Acosta,* but it was a boring flop that endangered the very existence of the theater. Only a return to Sholem Aleichem, as seen through Chagallian eyes, put the Yiddish Theater back on center stage.

The linchpin between Granovskii and Chagall was Mikhoels. Shloyme Vovsi — Mikhoels — was born in Dvinsk, midway between Chagall's Vitebsk and Granovskii's Riga. Dvinsk, part of two different cultural worlds, shared features of both. For that reason, Mikhoels found a common language with and admiration for both Chagall and Granovskii. Mikhoels, one of eight sons of a rich merchant, received a traditional Jewish education until the age of fifteen, and was steeped in Jewish learning and folklore. Like Chagall's, his family adhered to the Byelorussian brand of Hasidism, Chabad, typified by emotionalism, warmth, and joy. Both Mikhoels and Chagall loved Jewish folk culture and knew it inside out.

However, in Western Lithuania, where Mikhoels was born, a rich man's home was influenced by the Haskala and by an admiration for Russian and German culture. When his father went bankrupt, the family moved to Riga, where Mikhoels finished a science-oriented Russian high school. He married a daughter of Yehuda-Leyb Kantor, a rabbi, doctor, *maskil* (secular, intellectual), Hebrew poet, and editor of a Russian newspaper in St. Petersburg, *Russkii Evrei* (The Russian Jew).

After being rejected by St. Petersburg University because he was a Jew, Mikhoels studied in Kiev; in 1915, however, he was admitted to the Law School of Petrograd University. But

in 1918, his attraction to acting and his commitment to Jewish culture led him to Granovskii's budding studio. As an actor, Mikhoels combined his intellectual powers, a restrained emotionalism, and the skills he had learned under Granovskii's tutelage to create one celebrated role after another. The essence of his art, however, came from Chagall: the painter was the source of the tragicomic perception of the absurdity of Jewish (and general human) existence, evoked through a demonstrative antirealism.

Almost from the beginning, the aloof Granovskii charged Mikhoels with conducting the daily work of the troupe. Mikhoels was stage director, and before each production he announced a competition for each role. Mikhoels read to them from the newly published multivolume *Jewish Encyclopedia* in Russian. Mikhoels's enthusiastic "conversion" to Chagall led to the conversion of the theater as a whole. Under Mikhoels's guidance, the actors (all of whom came from various towns in the Pale) recovered from their childhood memories the gestures, movements, intonations, and sensibilities of the Jewish shtetl world. Mikhoels and his counterpart Benyomin Zuskin (another Western Lithuanian) worked together to bring to light the subtle connotations and gestures of the disappearing Jewish world. This was knowledge that no teacher could provide; it was the source of the emotive depth that was then stylized and refined by Granovskii's system. Granovskii embraced the Jewish fictional world and integrated it into his polyphonic conception, creating theater productions that were closer to a mythological happening than to a formalist performance.

The *Sholem Aleichem Evening* was based on character types familiar from Yiddish literature and folklore. The central character of *Agents* is Menakhem-Mendel, a symbolic character based on Sholem Aleichem's book by that name, and as popular in Yiddish discourse as Hamlet is in English. Menakhem-Mendel is the prototype of a *shlemiel,* who seesaws between soaring fantasy and searing failure. A shtetl type, he attempts all Jewish *luft-parnoses* (professions in the air), such as matchmaking (*shlemiel* that he is, he brings together "a wall with a wall," a bride with a bride) and stock-market speculation (with much the same success). *Agents* provides only abbreviated glimpses of Menakhem-Mendel, but the spectators were expected to know the type. Menakhem-Mendel, acted by Mikhoels, was also the central figure of the Yiddish Theater's *200,000* (based on Sholem Aleichem's *The Great Winning Ticket*), and the later version, titled simply *Menakhem-Mendel.* In 1925, he became the hero of the film *Jewish Luck,* which boasted Granovskii as director, Lev Pulver as composer, Edward Tisse (Eizenshtein's cameraman) as cinematographer, Isaac Babel as screenwriter, Mikhoels, Zusman, and the cast of the Yiddish Theater as actors; even the train compartment used for the stage production was adapted and became the trademark of the film.

Other variants of the same fictional world were brilliantly conceived for plays based on Goldfaden's *Sorceress,* Peretz's *At Night in the Old Market Place,* and Mendele's *Travels of Benjamin the Third.* The texts were treated nonchalantly, shortened and augmented with other works by the same authors. What Granovskii kept intact were the characters and the symbolic situations.

In an interview given in Berlin in April 1928, Mikhoels formulated "the method of *scenic social analysis*":

Instead of the individual's moods, half words, half tones — explicit, burgeoning social feelings; instead of isolated heroes with private, purely subjective, limited experiences — joyful mass movements, with their noise, their dancing on the ruins of the old, their great social hopes and rational activities; instead of types — social figures that

fig. 20
At Night in the Old Market Place, *designed by Robert Fal'k.*

fig. 21
The Travels of Benjamin the Third, *designed by Robert Fal'k.*

convey the breadth of large human masses, of human collectives; instead of family conflicts, instead of "Chekhovism," instead of sadness and melancholy — large social contradictions which create the background for the whole action on the stage.[83]

No doubt, part of this language was due to the fact that Mikhoels toed the Party line; yet part of it was a true theatrical vision, which had excited European audiences. Indeed, the "crazy," unreal characters of classic Yiddish literature were social types representing a codified, stereotypical society — which is why the theater went back to the classics rather than dealing with the early twentieth-century Yiddish literature of individualism and impressionism. The ideological conflict was described by Mikhoels thus:

Looking for the means, how most sharply and conspicuously to uncover the tragic content of past Jewish life, condemned to disappear in our country, the theater showed a great diversity in evoking new stimulae in its development. To hone the characters, to perfect the stage devices, uncover new social kernels hidden in the atrocious, often-anecdotal classical figures — this was our continuing path. Isn't tragicomedy one of the phenomena typical of our contemporary epoch?[84]

This ideological conflict, combined with the artistic tensions within the polyphonic art, produced new, hybrid genres: *At Night in the Old Market Place* was dubbed "A Tragic Carnival," *The Travels of Benjamin the Third* "A Touching Epic," *200,000* "A Musical Comedy," *Trouhadec* "An Eccentric Operetta."

Granovskii did not mind being eclectic. He harnessed any and all means of the contemporary Russian and European avant-garde theater for his new concept: a surrealist perception of the fictional world of Jewish literature, refracted through the tragicomic and polyphonic, kinetic and musical, rationally calculated multimedia event. A historian of the avant-garde theater in Soviet Russia noted:

At the same time it is obvious from early accounts of their work that while they borrowed much from Meyerhold — his system of biomechanics, for instance — they had nothing in common with his intellectualization of theatrical form. They held his theories but expressed them with more drama and play of mood. Particularly is this seen in their stage settings. They believed that the decor should evolve images in the minds of the audiences — but they approached the mind through the senses. Their settings were always highly functional — look, for instance, at the settings for Goldfaden's The Witch, *three-dimensional combinations of planes, ladders and platforms arranged in a staccato picture that stabs the mind into an awareness of incoherent pain. The idea of the structure is pure Meyerhold — the carrying out of the idea has the stamp of ecstasy, mystery and unfathomable sadness. A great contribution was made by such expressionists as the artists Chagall and Rabichev, and later by Nathan Altman, Rabinovich and Falk. They lit up the stage with a series of vivid pictures, always three-dimensional and mobile, which seemed to have a life of their own, which harmonized with and enhanced the grotesquerie of the stylized movements and which underlined the inherent colour and richness in the Jewish character.*[85]

This conception could almost be a description of Chagall's art. Chagall left the Yiddish Theater after its first production, yet the artists that succeeded him were his admirers and disciples. Moreover, the conception of the theater as a whole was influenced by him, as numerous accounts claim. An unexpected witness was David Ben-Gurion, who visited Moscow in 1923.[86] Of the Yiddish Theater's production of *200,000* he noted, "They sit on roofs, ledges and stairs, don't walk but hop, don't go up but clamber, don't come down but tumble and leap — Sholem Aleichem is unrecognizable." The

set was Rabichev's, yet this is clearly the description of a Chagallian placement of characters and conception of "groundless" space. Ben-Gurion was never known for his appreciation of literature or art, but he registered what he saw. Chagall's reading of Sholem Aleichem's authentic topsy-turvy world is absolutely correct.

The German critic Max Osborn also visited Moscow in 1923, and on his return he wrote an essay on Chagall. He described *200,000* in this way:

The curtain goes up and you see a strange chaos of houses, intertwined in a Cubist manner, rising one above the other on different levels. Intersecting one another at sharp angles, they either stand below wide roofs or suddenly appear without a roof altogether, like a man taking off his hat, and display all their internal secrets. Here and there, bridges and passways are drawn; wide streets rise and fall diagonally. Meierkhol'd's Constructivist stage is embodied here in original variants. The Cubist, linear play of these forms is complemented and enriched by Cézanne colors. Your eye perceives a fantastic interpretation of a Jewish-Russian small town, presented in the narrow confines of a stage in an unusually joyful and charming formula. Before the spectator's eye, everything can happen simultaneously: the events in the tailor shop, scenes among the populace of the shtetl *who accompany the play and the experiences of the main characters as their own — a picturesque, machine-like, mimic-acrobatic choir.*

When the news arrives about the tailor's unexpected great win of a huge sum, setting the whole town into an unusual excitement, suddenly, high above the roof of one building, appears the figure of a Jew with a red beard and a green greatcoat, with a sack on his back and a staff in his hand. Instinctively I said aloud: "Chagall!" And suddenly everything became clear: this is the world of Chagall. From him, everything emerged: the young artist-decorator Rabichev's creations, Granovskii's constructions, and the accompanying music of the composer Pulver. The latter, with unusual expressiveness, embodied Oriental motifs, ancient Jewish images, and Russian songs in operatic melodies, with trumpets and kettledrums.

Later, in Mikhoels's dressing room, Osborn learned that, indeed, "Marc Chagall had played a decisive role in the development of the whole stage art of the Yiddish Chamber Theater; that, in this circle, he was considered the great originator and inspiration." He also learned that "Chagall's box" was preserved like a temple in the "House of Yiddish Theater Art" (as the former small theater was called).

It is no accident that painting exerted such an influence on the stage, no whim of a theater director attracted by the work of an artist. It was a stronger force, an inner necessity. Always, when the personality and the school of a master truly find a clear and strong expression for the cultural spirit of the time — the stage is captivated by it — and only then it is captivated. . . . Like no one else in the young Russia of our days, Chagall has the stunning power of transforming the elements of an exceedingly rich and profound artistic folk culture into colorful, dreamy visions, striking our imagination.[87]

HaBima

Monti Jakobs, the theater critic for the prestigious German newspaper *Vossische Zeitung*, began his review of the Yiddish Theater's *200,000* thus: "*HaBima*, but joyful. The same intoxication as in *HaBima*, the same *furor judaicum*, it is a play that pulls the spectator out of his seat and draws him into the strong rhythm emanating from the stage." This is not the place to discuss HaBima at length, but a few words are in order, for the two theaters are often mentioned together.

A group of young people gathered before World War I in Bialystok to create a new kind of *bima* (the Hebrew word for "stage"; *ha* is the article) in order to perform in the budding

fig. 22
Mikhoels and Chagall at their last meeting, in New York City in 1944.

spoken Hebrew language. In 1918, they arrived in Moscow and received the patronage of the great Stanislavskii, and HaBima became one of the four studios attached to his Moscow Art Theater. The young Vakhtangov, Stanislavskii's most famous disciple, became HaBima's director. In November 1918, HaBima was recognized as a Soviet State theater. With *The Eternal Jew*, *The Dybbuk,* and other plays, *HaBima* entered general theater history; its 1926 tour of Europe was a great triumph, especially in Germany, then the center of European theater.

Hebrew was the language of the holy books, but during the Modern Jewish Revolution it rapidly expanded its genres into secular literature, science, and politics. It was not easy to turn a language of religious texts into a spoken language, dealing with mundane and secular topics, yet between 1906 and 1913 the first Hebrew speakers emerged in Palestine. HaBima was an early attempt at speaking the Biblical language on stage (most of its own actors knew no Hebrew beforehand). Thus two Jewish theaters in Moscow, in two languages, emerged as Soviet State Theaters in the first years following the Revolution.

Soon the "war of the languages" was raging. Those who wanted to revive Yiddish culture in Russia saw Hebrew as a religious vestige of old times, not the language of the masses.[88] Evsektsiia (the Jewish Section of the Communist Party) battled the recognition of HaBima; its leader, Dimandshteyn, claimed that HaBima was "a whim of the Jewish bourgeoisie; the money of the Revolutionary power should not be allowed to support a theater the peasants and workers don't want." But the most illustrious Russian intellectuals of the day supported the new phenomenon in the lofty Biblical language; Gorkii and Fiodor Chaliapin wept during its performances. Leaders of the Russian intelligentsia wrote a letter to Lenin on its behalf, and the Commissar of Nationalities — Stalin himself — overruled Evsektsiia and saved HaBima.

In January 1926, the Moscow State Theater HaBima departed on its spectacular tour of Western Europe and the United States.[89] Most of the troupe did not return to Russia, and eventually re-established HaBima in Tel Aviv, where it became the Israeli National Theater.

Both HaBima and GOSET drew on the achievements of the Russian avant-garde theater, though HaBima, still in the Stanislavskii tradition, was more conservative and expressionistic. Both derived their strength from the same collective Jewish folk tradition, expressed in mass ensemble scenes and the multimedia polyphony of music, dance, sets, and stage scenes. HaBima, too, was based on the Yiddish literary tradition (Dovid Pinski's *The Eternal Jew*, An-ski's *The Dybbuk*), but translated into Hebrew. However, the solemn language of the still uncolloquial and Biblical Hebrew influenced the pathos and the elevated, heroic national style of HaBima; it did not have the humor, irony, or flexibility of moods typical of popular Yiddish. Although emanating from the same national milieu, HaBima fostered the Hebrew genre of high tragedy, oriented toward a utopian dream, while GOSET showcased the Yiddish genre of comedy, looking the tragic end of a culture straight in the eye.

Epilogue

In 1927, in recognition of their artistic contribution, Granovskii, Mikhoels, and Zuskin were awarded the title of People's Artist of the USSR. And finally, the theater was allowed to go abroad. On April 7, 1928, the Yiddish Theater performed *200,000* in Berlin, where it received more than forty reviews. Its reception surpassed anything other Russian theaters experienced, and a book was published to understand it.[90] Berlin was the center of innovative theater at the time, and

theater enjoyed the popularity of sports events in America. As many reviews indicated, "Granovskii was received in Berlin as a new theatrical messiah, a more innovative and revolutionary director than Meyerhold, Reinhardt and Piscator."[91]

GOSET traveled throughout Germany and visited Vienna and Paris, but toward the end of the year, it was forced to return to Russia. Granovskii stayed in the West; after several unsuccessful attempts, he had success with Arnold Zweig's *Sergeant Grisha,* produced in Berlin in 1930, and he also made several German films. Apparently, he fled Germany with the rise of the Nazis, and faded into oblivion. On March 11, 1937, at the age of forty-seven, one of the original theater directors of the century died in Paris. At about the same time, the great innovator Meierkhol'd, who had sold his soul to the Communists, was tortured to death in a Soviet prison.

In 1928, Mikhoels became the director of the theater. He enjoyed great fame in Russia and was accepted in Moscow's high society. He continued performing Jewish plays, insisting that this was the task of the Yiddish theater — classical and Russian plays were better performed in the Russian Chamber Theater next door. But pressures and criticism were incessant. During the purges of the thirties, Stalin's brother-in-law and right-hand man Lazar Kaganovich came to a performance. He inspired terror in the director and actors, screaming that it was a shame to show such crippled Jews, "Look at me, I am a Jew, my father was also like this: tall, broad, healthy."[92] Mikhoels immediately started rehearsing a drama, Moyshe Kulbak's *Boytre*; then Kulbak himself was arrested and liquidated and his plays were forbidden.

In 1935, Mikhoels performed one of his greatest roles — King Lear. In the early years of the theater, Mikhoels had recognized the tragic depths encompassed by comedy, and had described the theater and the contemporary human condition as "tragicomedy." Now he inverted the relationship and brought all his comic experiences to bear on this tragic role. The power and scope of the impact on the Russian theater was unforgettable.

During World War II, he became chairman of the Jewish Anti-Fascist Committee, seeking international help in the war against Hitler. In this function, he came to the United States and saw Chagall again.[93] But in 1948 he was sent to Minsk, where he was brutally murdered on Stalin's order. Most Yiddish writers, actors, and activists were arrested; some were shot, others tortured. The theater was closed, along with the Yiddish newspaper and publishing house.

Production designs from throughout the theater's brief history were placed in the State Bakhrushin Museum in Moscow. There, they were sealed in a special room along with the archives of the Russian Chamber Theater, which was also liquidated. A fire broke out at the Bakhrushin — only in this room — and the set designs were burned around the margins; the documents also suffered a layer of water damage. To this day, the causes and facts of that destruction have not been disclosed.

Other documents of the theater are kept in the excellent literary archives CGALI (Central State Archive of Literature and Art), where we were allowed access to all the papers. However, the large files of the "Liquidation Commission" of the Yiddish Theater have disappeared. For the sake of the martyrs, it would be an act of mercy to reveal exactly what happened and how.

We know very little about Chagall's early years; we don't know his mother's maiden name, for example, or when his parents died. *My Life*, his elliptical, colorful, and self-centered autobiography, is scarce on facts and notoriously unreliable.[94] Although many or most of Chagall's stories may be apocryphal, and few specific facts are known, we *can* reconstruct the cultural world in which he grew up.[95] To be sure, an artist's origins must not be confused with his art, especially when it is as complex in its cultural discourse as Chagall's. But background does provide an essential key to its understanding. Chagall worked in the modes of European painting, though his approach was strikingly different, and that difference can be explained to a large extent by the modes of Jewish discourse he brought with him. Chagall himself understood the issue when he wrote, "If I were not a Jew (with the content I put into that word) I wouldn't have been an artist, or I would be a different artist altogether."[96] We shall try to sketch here the general outlines of that context, focusing mainly on Chagall's Jewish background. The impact of Russian culture, French painting, and Modern art on his work are well known, and are not repeated here.

Empire within empire

There are many misunderstandings about the context of Chagall's childhood. This stems from a larger misunderstanding about Russian Jewry, for there is a general assumption that a Jewish religious minority existed in the midst of Russian culture, the equivalent of Jews in Germany in the 1920s or in America today. Actually, a vast Jewish "empire" had developed in Eastern Europe in the midst of a huge cultural desert.

Chagall's native city, Vitebsk, is mentioned in documents as early as the eleventh century. In the Middle Ages, the city belonged to the Grand Duchy of Lithuania, which encompassed Lithuania proper, all of what is now Belarus, parts of Latvia, some areas of Russia, and Ukraine. In the fourteenth century, Lithuania merged with Poland, which became the largest state in Europe. After the Jews were expelled from most of Western Europe, by the sixteenth century perhaps three quarters of world Jewry lived in Poland (the rest, mostly former Spanish Jews, lived in the Ottoman Empire). When Poland was devoured by its neighbors at the end of the eighteenth century, the Russian Empire took the largest chunk, including what is today central Poland, Ukraine, Belarus, Lithuania, part of Latvia, as well as Bessarabia (today's Moldavia). The Russian government did not allow Jews to live in Russia proper, and enclosed them in the occupied territories in a huge geographical ghetto called the Pale of Settlement. In time, only a few thousand Jews, the very rich and educated, were allowed to live outside the Pale, in Kiev, Moscow, St. Petersburg, or smaller cities. The Jewish masses (over five million strong) thus lived among the Empire's Western minorities, far from the centers of Russian culture and a Russian-speaking population. Thus, they preserved their own language and culture.

The demographic structure of Russian Jewry is revealing. In 1897, for example, Jews constituted only 11.8 percent of the population of Vitebsk Province, but they accounted for 66.3 percent of the population of all "small towns" in that Province, and a majority of the population of all "cities." (The distinction between "city," "town" [shtetl], and "village" was administrative and recorded in the official Russian census.) This distribution was typical for Byelorussia, and, basically, for the whole Pale.[97] The predominantly Jewish towns and cities were surrounded by a sea of "villages." Vitebsk Province included 26,590 communities, but only forty-eight of them were cities or towns with a population above 500. In the thousands of small villages, Jews constituted only 1.9 percent of the population (typically, village Jews were inn-keepers, mill owners, estate managers, and artisans, but not peasants). Until 1861, the peasants in those villages were serfs, the property of Russian or Polish landowners. Even after the serfs were granted freedom, and until the Revolution, Russia was a rigidly class-based society.

The Yiddish word *shtetl*[98] (diminutive of *shtot*, "city") in Western languages was often translated as "village" (in French, *village* from *ville*). Yet, unlike the village, the small town had no land or peasants. In Yiddish, the concept of "village" connoted something entirely different: it was a place inhabited by mostly illiterate Christian peasants, working the land with little contact to any modern technology or industry, who would come to the town market, get drunk, and exhibit their physical prowess. In Yiddish, the peasants were called *poyerim*, or the synonymous *goyim* (gentiles).

Just as the English language distinguishes between genders (for example, waiter and waitress, policeman and policewoman), so did the semiotics of that time distinguish people by their social and ethnic groups. In Russian, one could not meet just a person in the street, but a peasant or a man of the gentry, a child, an old man, a woman, a Jew, or a Jewess. In Yiddish, one met either a Jew or a goy, a bachelor or a virgin, a *sheygetz* (male gentile) or a *shikse* (female gentile). The Jewish stereotypes of the goy were mostly negative: he was dangerous, dumb (someone might have a *goyisher kop*, "the brain of a goy"), and a drunkard (a popular folksong goes: *oy, oy, shiker is a goy / shiker is er, trinken miz er / vayl er iz a goy*, "oy, oy, a drunkard is a goy / he is drunk, for he must drink / for he is a goy"). Secular Jewish culture tried to overcome that gulf, stressing the young goy's closeness to nature, his health and sexuality, and the Jewish weakness in those areas; hence Chagall's idealized goyish *Drunkard* and his idealized village in *I and the Village*. Nevertheless, the world was seen in bifurcated categories. It was not just animosity, erupting from time to time, that separated Jewish from peasant humanity, but a whole conceptual world.

The Jewish shtetl, no matter how small or unpaved, was essentially an urban location, where the people did not work the soil. Indeed, among the Jewish population of Vitebsk Province, 39 percent lived on trade and 36 percent of the breadwinners were artisans. In modern terms, the shtetl was the shopping mall of the area; it was a marketplace and a center of artisan production, where peasants came to buy and sell, and from which Jews would go to peddle their goods and skills in the surrounding villages. Rich Jews also traveled to the larger cities and other lands, aided by their common language, thus spreading a commercial network from the village to town, to Western Europe and the Russian metropolis and back.

In the cities and towns there were also churches and Russian administrative and educational institutions, and Christians comprised the ruling classes, such as the Russian administration (in which no Jews were represented), Polish and Russian landowners, Christian city householders (burghers), and even the dreaded *gorodovoy* (policemen).[99] The provincial capital was also home to semiurbanized peasants from the surrounding villages, and soldiers (mostly of peasant stock) stationed there. Whereas the peasants spoke Byelorussian (a Slavic language with hardly any literary culture before the Revolution), the language of the authorities and of the ruling culture was Russian.

Thus, the vast Jewish "empire" in Eastern Europe was based on a web of geographical centers, in which Jews regularly

constituted between half and two thirds of the population but were surrounded by masses of illiterate peasants and were dominated by a narrow layer of the ruling classes. Jews had a dense network of social and cultural institutions of their own, including an educational system, societies, synagogues and prayer houses, hospitals, cemeteries, philanthropic organizations, publishing houses, newspapers, community administrations, taxation, religious authorities, and political movements (such as Hasidim) — all under the aegis of one religious framework, officially separating the Jews from the governing Christian Orthodox Church. Contact between Jews and non-Jews was frequent, but on a very marginal range of topics having nothing to do with internal Jewish culture, learning, and consciousness. Thus, the Jews were not a minority, as they are in the West today, but a *totality* in their own culture and a *nullity* in the framework of state and territorial power.

Discourse in this autonomous world was conducted in three specifically Jewish languages: Yiddish was used for daily life, education, and letters to and from women; Hebrew was reserved for the Bible, the library of texts, written documents, and letters written between men; and Aramaic was the language of the Talmud and Rabbinic law. This extraterritorial society, defined by religion, lived in a world consolidated by the Yiddish language. In 1897, almost 98 percent of the 5.2 million Jews of the Russian Empire declared Yiddish as their language. Hebrew and Aramaic learning were embedded in Yiddish and quoted in Yiddish discourse. Yiddish contained a folklorized universe of beliefs, stories, conventions, habits of discourse, and oral and written literature. Yiddish separated the Jews from the surrounding world, but it also served as a bridge to it: Yiddish folklore absorbed many elements of European and Slavic folklore, merging it with elements of the Hebrew tradition and library. Their language contained important aspects of German, Hebrew, and Slavic. Thus, Yiddish speakers could easily glide into any of the component languages. From the end of the nineteenth century, Yiddish was the main vehicle for the Modern Jewish Revolution, manifested in the development of modern literature, ideologies, schools, and cultural institutions.

Lithuanian Jewry was characterized by an intensive and thorough approach to learning and knowledge, and it developed *yeshivas* (high-level academies). Lithuania exported rabbis, Hebrew teachers, Yiddish writers, artists, and intellectuals around the world, to Odessa, Warsaw, and St. Petersburg, to New York, New Orleans, and Paris.[100] Vilna, the Western capital of Lithuanian Jewry, was the center of the *Misnagdim* movement, which fought against irrational and ignorant Galician Hasidim. Litvaks are also said to be meticulous and naïve, even "childish."

In the eastern part of vast Jewish Lithuania, masses of simple people lived in tiny shtetls in the deep woods. In this region, where Chagall grew up, a special Hasidic movement emerged that introduced joy and optimism into the gloomy mood of orthodox Judaism; it was built on a revival of the emotional participation of simple people in religious experience. Being a Lithuanian sect, it also stressed learning and was called Chabad, a Hebrew acronym for "Wisdom, Insight, Knowledge." The founder of this movement, Shneur-Zalman of Lyady (1745–1813), was born in Lyozno, Chagall's family town. The movement is also called "Lubavitsher," for a shtetl in that area where the Shneurson dynasty resided before the Revolution. In 1909, the city of Vitebsk had two synagogues and sixty prayer houses, most of them Lubavitsher.

fig. 23
Mark, Bella, and Ida Chagall in 1917.

Chagall's cheerful disposition may have stemmed from Chabad Hasidism's cancellation of, or obliviousness to, physical existence in the name of spiritual elation. His fictional Jewish world is very different from the dour perception of the impoverished and degenerated shtetl that permeates much Jewish literature of the turn of the century.

In 1897, the city of Vitebsk had only 34,420 Jews (52.4 percent of the population), yet it became an important cultural center, producing such Jewish intellectuals as An-ski, Dr. Chaim Zhitlovsky, Yehuda Pen, and Chagall. The small population should not surprise us, for even Vilna, the "Jerusalem of Lithuania," which claimed to be the cultural center of Lithuanian religious and secular Jewry, had only 64,000 Jews at the time. The Jewish population was spread throughout Vitebsk Province, in knots of small communities, and a constant flux, cultural and economic, took place between the Provincial capital, the district towns, and the smaller shtetls. Only 20 percent of the Jews of the Province lived in Vitebsk proper, and many cultural institutions were located in smaller towns such as Lubavitsh (which numbered only 1,660 Jews), the residence of the dynastic rebbes of the Byelorussian Hasidic movement.

Chagall's ancestral home, Lyozno, located about 70 kilometers south of the city of Vitebsk, had 1,665 Jews or 67.3 percent of the population. When Chagall's family moved to Vitebsk, they lived, like many provincial newcomers, in the outskirts of the capital, and maintained contacts with the town of their origin, where part of the family still lived. But theirs was not the confined ghetto, far from any railroad and oblivious of the changes in the world, as described in Sholem Aleichem's "The Town of the Little People." The train passed through Vitebsk, bringing to it the spirits of industrialization, Russian poetry, and modern culture.

What, then, was the importance of Vitebsk? Vitebsk, the easternmost city of Poland, was taken by Russia in 1772, more than twenty years before the partitions of Poland. It was at the northeastern corner of the Pale of Settlement, relatively close to both Russian capitals. In 1897, it had a considerable Russian population (39.9 percent were Russians and Byelorussians as opposed to 52.4 percent Jews). It also was home to some Russian-speaking Jews, including those expelled from Moscow in 1891. It was an important railroad junction, where trains passed from Odessa and Kiev to St. Petersburg, and from Riga and the West to Moscow. Thus, the two capitals were easily accessible. Chagall took advantage of that proximity to escape to St. Petersburg, even though he lived there illegally; and when Granovskii's Yiddish Theater visited "the people," they went to the closest place inhabited by Jews, Vitebsk. In 1920, some of the best Russian artists joined Chagall's People's Art School in Vitebsk, where they found an eager young Jewish population awakening to modern culture and speaking Russian. And when Chagall was pushed out of that school, he had just a short ride to Moscow.

Languages
Anatolii Lunacharskii, People's Commissar of Education after the Bolshevik Revolution, appointed the painter David Shterenberg (whom he knew while in exile in Paris) as head of IZO, the division of art. As Abram Efros described him:

Shterenberg was born in Zhitomir {Ukraine}, studied in Paris, and became an artist in Moscow. He does not speak any one of the three languages, but can make himself clear in all of them. What he lacks, he substitutes with interjections and gestures. Listening to his slow speech, in which the frowning of forehead and lips, or fuzzy sounds and pauses, play the role of words and concepts — you imagine his painting as hesitant and careful. Such are the first canvases of foreigners in Paris who try to hold the brush in the French manner.[101]

Chagall was anything but hesitant, but this describes his basic situation, too; he was, like Shterenberg, a typical member of his generation and could not speak properly in any of the languages of his various cultures.

Chagall grew up in a Yiddish-speaking society, in the heartland of the Jewish masses in Russia. We know a great deal about Jewish education in that milieu and can imagine his early learning experiences. The first texts Chagall learned to read were passages from the Hebrew Bible; the oral teaching itself and all discussions were conducted in Yiddish. Normally, the Biblical text would be read accompanied by a word-for-word translation — a word in Hebrew, followed by its equivalent in Yiddish; if we were to substitute English for the Yiddish, the beginning of the Bible would be taught like this: "*bereyshis*, in the beginning, *boro*, created, *elokim*, God," etc. Chagall must have studied the Hebrew *Chumash* (Pentateuch) from the customary age of four until the age of thirteen, with at least four different teachers. Study would have been conducted every day from dawn to dusk in the teacher's *heder*, an all-male, one-class elementary school at the teacher's home; and when a child finished studying with one teacher, he would go to a higher class at the home of another teacher. The average size of a *heder* in Vitebsk Province was eight children, hence the close contact between the only *melamed* (teacher) and his pupils.

Teaching focused on reading of the holy texts, not on any oral or written expression in the language; Hebrew was not intended to be used in real-life communication. Chagall presumably advanced to study with a "Gemore-teacher." But there is no evidence of any knowledge by Chagall of Aramaic or the Talmud. Chagall was deeply impressed by the Biblical stories he heard in childhood, but throughout his life he showed little knowledge of Hebrew. In several paintings, he copied Hebrew texts from the Bible, sometimes with mistakes,[102] but never produced any sentence or even combination of two Hebrew words of his own. The spelling of the Hebrew words (which even a regular Yiddish reader should know) that appear in his numerous Yiddish texts is abysmal.

At the age of thirteen, Chagall was taken by his mother to a Russian secondary school.[103] Russian was the language of culture, and a springboard for Jews striving to accommodate the Russian power structure and to imbibe European culture; his parents, though conventionally observant, were apparently unafraid of the new secular trends. The males in Chagall's family photos wore no hats. Chagall's mother took him to Yehuda Pen's school of art, defying what was supposed to be a ban on graven images.

A fellow schoolboy and budding painter introduced Moyshe (as he was then called) to the circle that included his future wife, Bella Rosenfeld, a daughter of a prosperous merchant and Hasid. No doubt, Bella's parents spoke Yiddish at home, but the young people with whom she associated tried to speak Russian *comme il faut*, read Russian poetry, performed Russian theater, and discussed topics of Russian culture.

Bella was better educated than Chagall; she even attended Moscow University. Between them, they presumably spoke mostly Russian, especially after their daughter, Ida, was born. But Yiddish was their true language, and the Russian-educated Bella wrote her memoirs in New York in 1944 in Yiddish, explaining, "A strange thing, I wanted to write. And to write only in my stammering mother tongue which I have almost not spoken since I left my parents' home. The farther my childhood years have moved away from me, the closer they suddenly drew to me, as if they themselves were breathing into my mouth."

During their years in New York, though never politically committed, the Chagalls were in contact with leftist Yiddishist circles. It was with a leftist Yiddish publishing house, the Book League of the Jewish People's Fraternal Order, that Chagall published Bella's two autobiographical volumes after her death. In New York, even when living with his non-Jewish companion Virginia Haggard, Marc regularly read Yiddish newspapers (he did not know English) and spoke Yiddish with Max Lerner, Yosef Opatoshu, and other friends, as well as with Jews on the Lower East Side. The largest body of his extant correspondence throughout his life was with Yiddish writers, often warm, confessional, intimate, and usually both nationalistic and critical of the Jews, as many Jewish intellectuals were at the time. The numerous texts inscribed on his paintings are mostly in Yiddish or Hebrew.

No doubt, Chagall read Yiddish literature. In his younger years, Peretz, Mendele Moykher Sforim, and Sholem Aleichem made a strong impact on his world view. He carefully read all three volumes of poetry of his compatriot A. Lyesin (Walt), which he illustrated in detail (and even understood enough to doubt their "literary," i.e. modern, quality). He also read and illustrated the poetry of Dovid Hofshteyn, Abraham Sutzkever, Elkhonon Vogler, and others. And we have manuscripts of Yiddish speeches, articles, and poems in Chagall's own hand, some of which he published in the prestigious Tel Aviv–based literary quarterly *Di goldene keyt* and elsewhere.

Nevertheless, Chagall's Yiddish spelling was atrocious, and he kept apologizing for it in letters to his close friend, the Yiddish novelist Opatoshu, and to other Yiddish writers and editors. Typically, he spelled according to his own, spoken Byelorussian Yiddish dialect, confusing "S" with "Sh" and "EY" with "OY."[104] His own name, Chagall, apparently resulted from this dialect.[105]

When Chagall arrived in St. Petersburg to study art, the rich Jews who had permission to live in the capital spoke Russian. Though his teacher Lev Bakst (born in Grodno, in western Lithuania) and his first supporter, Maxim Vinaver (born in Warsaw), were Jews from the Pale, he probably talked to them in Russian. He certainly was influenced by Russian culture at the time. Nevertheless, he wrote Russian like a Babel character, employing Yiddish syntax and semantics. Still, Russian was presumably the language of his informal education and reading, and he even tried to write some poems in Russian. Late in life, his Russian was reinforced by his Russian-speaking Jewish second wife, Valentina Brodskii, who came from London to join him in France.

In France, where Marc spent most of his life and had many intellectual friends, he certainly learned to speak French. But, just as his Russian had a Yiddish subtext, so did his French have a Russian flavor. Virginia Haggard, the daughter of an English diplomat in Paris, met him in New York after he had spent many years in France. As she tells it, "We were soon conversing in French. His Russian accent was warm and colorful, and his grammatical errors made me feel less self-conscious about my own."[106] In a letter to Virginia, Chagall wrote, "I would like to write you a whole book, but I write French like a Russian pig." Chagall was always immersed in painting, not books; his language was the language of painting.

Center and periphery

Marc Chagall was born in Vitebsk on July 7, 1887 (7/7/87; he made much of his lucky number seven throughout his life).[107] The often-repeated theory, that he was actually born in the smaller town of Lyozno[108] has recently been discredited by the art historian Aleksandra Shatskikh.[109] Nevertheless, Chagall's friend, the critic Abram Efros referred to him as "the painter from Lyozno," and the Israeli President and scholar Zalman

Shazar (himself from Byelorussia) called him "our brother from Lyozno and Paris!" As young people, Chagall's parents moved from Lyozno to a house owned by his paternal grandfather in a suburb of the provincial capital Vitebsk. In the big city, they would be nicknamed "Lyezner" ("from Lyozno"); Efros recognized the impact that Lyozno images made on Chagall. When he came to Paris, Chagall could not mention such a small place as Lyozno: he was from *Vitebsk*, which he generalized as the symbol of the Pale of Settlement and provincial Russia, the source of his fictional world, and the target of his nostalgia. But in many ways he really was a provincial Lyozno boy; his early images of "Vitebsk" were closer to a suburb or a small-town scene[110] (photos of the center of Vitebsk at the time show a different city altogether), until he moved to Vitebsk proper after 1914. Yet, he liked to visit Lyozno, where the rest of the family remained, including his uncles, aunts, and remarried grandparents, and he did some semirealistic paintings there.

In a Jewish context, embracing a Lyozno ancestry was prestigious, for the founder of Chabad Hasidism was born in Lyozno. This explains the town's appeal to President Shazar, who was himself named Shneur-Zalman Rubashov, after the legendary rebbe: Chagall was a secular legend in the wake of a religious one! Like other proponents of modern Jewish culture, Chagall himself was fond of presenting a strong religious world as the roots of his secular Jewishness.

But the Chagall legend is first and foremost tied to Vitebsk, and before him the name was of little consequence. As Tugendkhol'd phrased it, the formula "Zion, Babylon, and Vilna," indicating the three symbolic centers of Jewish culture in history, became "Zion, Babylon, and Vitebsk"[111] — this is how strong his contemporaries felt about Chagall as the symbol of the renaissance of Jewish culture.

When he met his future fiancée in Vitebsk, Moyshe Shagal (or "Moshka," as his parents called him) was a poor suburban boy from the provinces. Bella's family did not quite approve of the match, aspiring painter or not. Chagall developed an ambition to get into high society, prove himself as a great artist, and win his rich and intelligent bride. Paradoxically, he succeeded by reverting in his paintings to the images of his poor, provincial past. Indeed, he strongly felt the demeaning status of his father, who declined from the level of learning set by *his* father, a Hebrew teacher, to a person steeped in drudgery and smelling of herring. It was Chagall's image of his grandfathers that inspired his paintings with awe. His father's lot reflected the impoverishment of Byelorussian Jewry, but Chagall's frustration was typical of many aspiring young Jewish intellectuals.

When Chagall came to St. Petersburg, he boldly thrust himself into the centers of Jewish high society and Russian art, simultaneously presenting the exotic images and values of what was perceived as the Jewish past, still surviving in the Pale, and of provincial Russia in general. Those images were presented from the outside, from the viewpoint of a modern, secular Jew, and of St. Petersburg's assimilated Jewish society; he depicted the past with a combination of nostalgia and admiration, and often as part of the multicultural scene of Russian provincial life. Malevich in that period depicted Russian peasants, while Chagall conjured up the small town and its deep, mysterious beliefs and customs. What he offered was not a statement but a world — which appealed to the Jews of the capital, some of whom developed a pride in their past and in the high values of popular life and folklore at the same time they were integrating into Russian Christian culture. Thus, Chagall reached people at the center by showing them the strange and vital periphery.[112]

Shortly after, ambitious Chagall moved on to the center of

fig. 24
Postcard of Vitebsk (Samkov Street).

European art. In Paris, too, he showed a fictional world to viewers preoccupied with form: an exotic world of his invented past. His Vitebsk — which came to include churches — became emblematic of Russia as well, for in France Chagall was considered a Russian painter. His paintings portrayed a different cultural world, an "other," which he made vivid to his audience at the center.

In the meantime, he also adopted emblematic images of the new domain, Paris, represented by the Eiffel Tower and the window of his studio. These emblems would now appear side by side with the Jewish and Christian images of Vitebsk. When he returned to Russia, he used images from his new past, the past of Paris. His authority in Russia was based on his fame in Paris and Berlin; the budding Yiddish Theater was proud to invite such a famous Jewish artist to design its set. Subsequently, the theater itself became famous, and Chagall drew on *its* fame. Chagall felt himself to be among the best in the art world; yet he retained the inferiority complex of a Jewish boy from the provinces. Witness how in 1952, after major solo exhibitions in New York, Paris, and London, he wrote with amazement and pride to Opatoshu that he was going to marry a woman of the rich Brodskii family from Kiev![113]

On Chagall's evolution

With time, Chagall's strength became a weakness. Through over-repetition, the images from his original fictional world, based on his retrospectively constructed childhood, lost much of their impact. The vitality of Chagall's Vitebsk derived in large part from the surreal, circuslike perspective through which he saw it. His strength as an artist came from the novelty of his fictional world and originality of his deformations, the mysterious oxymorons that permeated it, and the tensions and counterpoints between the various strata of his paintings. When the tensions were lost, the existential comedy became a sentimental decoration. With age, especially after the Holocaust, his view of the Jewish world became more sentimental, nostalgic, and stereotypical, but less deformed, imaginative, and whimsical. The physical Vitebsk was destroyed and he couldn't imagine it anymore. Similarly, after Bella's death, love too became in his paintings an abstract nostalgia.

One solution to this impasse was a shift to color, which flooded large parts of his paintings, and eventually served as the background for figures that were painted or sketched on top of it. In his classic period, deformation of color reinforced the deformation of his presented world, and vice versa. When Chagall's presented world became weakened, sentimental, and ornamental, his colors too — though beautiful in their own rich texture and light — lost the power they had aquired in their interaction and mutual reinforcement with the other strata.

Another solution was to widen the range of his media to include sculpture, porcelain, and stained-glass windows. The windows, murals, and ceilings especially had a powerful effect on large audiences — with them he repeated, to some extent, the feat of his public art in the Yiddish Theater murals. Yet most of those works were summations of his oeuvre at its current stage, translated into another medium; they were not, as the murals had been, a breakthrough in their own right.

A more substantive solution, encouraged by Ambroise Vollard, was the acquisition of new fictional domains from major works of literature — Gogol', LaFontaine, *A Thousand and One Nights* — as well as from the circus. The most important and comprehensive of those new worlds was the Bible. Like the circus, the Bible had been part of Chagall's childhood imagination. In France, Chagall incorporated the Bible into his painterly fictional world: it appeared at first in the Biblical etchings of the 1930s, still strong in Eastern European imagery, then in the colorful Biblical illustrations of the 1950s and 1960s, made in southern France and influenced by its light. Here he could combine the principle of composition by color with a public mythology.

After the Holocaust, there was a public warmth toward the all-but-annihilated world of the Jews. The Jewish world of the recent past was dead and its images exhausted, but through the Bible Chagall could again reclaim something he experienced deeply in childhood and which he could, from his peripheral perspective, offer the center. In this cynical century, his view of the Bible, embodying the highest values to humanity as a whole, may be felt as too sweet and simple a message, but if anyone could propose it, it was Chagall.

Chagall's work on the Bible in the 1930s — especially the powerful early etchings — were exclusively devoted to the first two books of the Pentateuch, which Chagall read in a new Yiddish translation.[114] These etchings focused not so much on the text itself but on basic archetypical scenes, such as "The Sacrifice of Isaac," "The Golden Calf," and "Circumcision," embellished by *Midrash* and transmitted in Jewish folklore and in stories for children. When Chagall resumed his work on the Bible in the 1950s, all twenty-four books of the Bible were available in Yehoash's Yiddish translation and he drew on all parts of the Bible[115]; he also went beyond the stock images of the Bible from his childhood, and related his works to specific textual passages.

Notes to the Introduction

1. See "Our Goals and Objectives," translated in this book, pp. 145–46.

2. Translated in this book, pp. 173–74.

Notes to Chapter 1

3. The timing of the end of Modernism has to do with the nature of the social history of ideas more than with some inherent evolution of art. It could have appeared in the "zero" stage of art, represented by Dada and Suprematism, or in the post–World War II decade.

4. As a deliberate postmodernist, Chagall often liked to emphasize pre-Modernist European painting. Although his *Homage to Apollinaire* (1911–12) was dedicated to the most avant-garde leaders of the day (Apollinaire, Canudo, Cendrars, and Walden), on the Yiddish manuscript of his autobiography written in 1925 (in the YIVO archive), he wrote an inscription in Russian — "For Rembrandt, Cézanne, my Mama, my wife" — promoting the great masters of art over the fashions of his age, and also indicating the importance of his family in the formation of his own fictional world.

5. Werner Haftmann, *Marc Chagall* (New York: Harry N. Abrams, 1973), p. 7.

6. Grigori Kasovsky, "Chagall and the Jewish Art Programme," in Christoph Vitali, ed., *Marc Chagall: The Russian Years 1906–1922*, exh. cat. (Frankfurt: Schirn Kunsthalle, 1992).

7. Chagall's letter to Pen written in Moscow on Sept. 14, 1921, was published in Alexandra Shatskich [Aleksandra Shatskikh], "Marc Chagall and Kazimir Malevich," *Shagalovskie dni v Vitebske* (special issue of *Vit'bichi*, July 3–5, 1992).

8. Around 1900, 21,000 Jews lived in St. Petersburg. They were mostly rich and influential, or professionals with university degrees.

9. Maxim Vinaver, born in Warsaw in 1862, lived in St. Petersburg and died in France in 1926. Vinaver was a founder of the Kadet (Constitutional Democratic) Party, the largest faction in the Duma in 1906, and was its vice chairman. He was active in the Society for the Promotion of Culture among Jews and headed the Historic-Ethnographic Commission, which studied the history of the Jews in Russia.

10. See his essay "The Artist Marc Chagall," translated in this book, pp. 141–43.

11. A term used to describe a trend in Russian art that spanned 1910–14 that was adopted by Chagall, Natal'ia Goncharova, Mikhail Larionov, Malevich, Vladimir Tatlin, and others. Most of the Neoprimitivists moved on to more radical, avant-garde art forms.

12. Translated in this book, pp. 134–43.

13. At least, this is how Chagall perceived the events. Aleksandra Shatskikh has argued that Chagall wanted to leave the school even before Malevich arrived, and that the students made a public appeal to keep him there. See Shatskikh, "Marc Chagall and Kazimir Malevich."

14. On the theory of fictional worlds, see Thomas G. Pavel, *Fictional Worlds* (Cambridge, Mass.: Harvard University Press, 1986). Also, see my "Fictionality and Fields of Reference: Remarks on a Theoretical Framework," *Poetics Today*, vol. 5 (1984), no. 2.

15. "Portrait," Oct. 1913, in Walter Albert, ed., *Selected Writings of Blaise Cendrars* (New York: New Directions, 1966).

16. From a speech at Mount Holyoke College, 1943, quoted in Susan Compton, *Chagall*, exh. cat. (London: Royal Academy of Arts, 1985), p. 153.

17. "Chagall 'over the Roofs of the World,'" in Compton, *Chagall*.

18. T. S. Eliot, "Tradition and the Individual Talent," in *The Sacred Wood* (London: Methuen, 1960), p. 58.

19. In Herschel B. Chipp, Peter Selz, and Joshua C. Taylor, *Theories of Modern Art: A Source Book by Artists and Critics* (Berkeley and Los Angeles: University of California Press, 1968), p. 295.

20. Translated in Benjamin and Barbara Harshav, eds. and trans., *American Yiddish Poetry: A Bilingual Anthology* (Berkeley and Los Angeles: University of California Press, 1986), p. 779.

21. Ibid., p. 776.

22. Ibid., p. 774.

23. See my book *The Meaning of Yiddish* (Berkeley and Los Angeles: University of California Press, 1990).

24. This will be discussed in my book *Language in Time of Revolution* (Berkeley and Los Angeles: University of California Press, forthcoming, 1993).

25. Speech at the Chagall-Fefer Evening, IKOR, New York, June 30, 1944; the manuscript of this speech is in the Pesakh Novick Archive, YIVO (New York).

26. Peter Gay, "Sigmund Freud: A German and his Discontents," in *Freud, Jews and Other Germans: Masters and Victims in Modernist Culture* (New York: Oxford University Press, 1978).

27. Alfred Wolfenstein, "Das neue Dichtertum der Juden," in Gustav Krojanker, ed., *Juden in der deutschen Literatur* (Berlin: Welt-Verlag, 1922).

28. James Johnson Sweeney quotes a statement by Chagall: "I fill up the empty space in my canvas as the structure of my picture requires with a body or an object according to my humor" (J. J. Sweeney, *Marc Chagall*, exh. cat. [New York: Museum of Modern Art, 1946], p. 15). We quoted above a similar and more elaborated statement from his speech at Mount Holyoke College. Of course, Chagall describes here his intuitive process of working on the canvas rather than the contents or principles of juxtaposition his critical faculty has in mind. We must also not forget that he is talking here in a period and to an audience interested in formal matters. In earlier statements he would stress his nostalgia for "Vitebsk." As we explained, both are true at the same time.

29. The French mathematician René Thom developed such a theory to be applied to economics or semiotics of language and culture. It offers a series of models representing unpredictable breaks, "catastrophes" in an otherwise regular process and graph.

30. See Chipp et. al., *Theories of Modern Art*, p. 154.

Notes to Chapter 2

31. See pp. 134–43.

32. Aleksandra Shatskikh, in Vitali, *Marc Chagall: The Russian Years 1906–1922*.

33. A. Vetrov, "On Chagall," *Ekran*, no. 7 (1921).

34. Translated in this book, pp. 153–57.

35. See p. 156.

36. See p. 156.

37. See pp. 153–57.

38. Kazimir Malevich, "The Non-Objective World," in Chipp et. al., *Theories of Modern Art*, pp. 341–42.

39. Admittedly, there is a difficulty with this explanation. At that time, Chagall's and the official Soviet spelling of the word "Yiddish" did not begin with "I" ("yud") but with "A" (the "mute aleph"): *Aidish*. Chagall used the spelling, twice, on the male dancer's shoes in *Love on the Stage*. That would imply the acronym AKT for the theater. Yet, the double repetition, the easy distortion of IKS to make IKT, and perhaps the memory of the older "Germanizing" spelling, *judish*, may explain the trick.

40. A painting by the New York Jewish artist Rafael Soyer, showing unemployed immigrants before a coffee shop with items and prices in English, is titled *Reading from Left to Right*. The alien direction of writing in the new country symbolizes the broader alienation felt by Jewish immigrants.

41. On Chagall's set design for the *Agents*, which takes place on a train car, we read in Yiddish: **FAR REIKHER**[ERS] *LK III*; the first two words mean "for smokers" (in Yiddish in the Russian train!); the last part is an inversion of the Russian label "III CL[ASS]," written in the right direction but in the wrong language.

42. Avram Kampf suggests that a "perspective of sentiment" governs the picture: "that which looms large in one's memory appears huge on the canvas" ("Chagall in the Yiddish Theater," in Vitali, *Marc Chagall: The Russian Years 1906–1922*, p. 98). Perhaps such a principle helps the writer rationalize Chagall's programmatic antirealism, but it does not really work. Can we say that any of the actors loomed larger in Chagall's memory than his own parents, wife, and child, who are quite small in the canvas? In the case of the *Introduction*, it is thematic foregrounding that governs the scale. The topic of his painting, the theater, is represented by large figures, while Chagall's own world and conceptual perspectives are inserted in the margins and interstices of space. Small size makes things no less important or less close to the artist's sentiment; on the contrary, it betrays his love for minute details and his personal world. We also see this in the small insertions of the world of his fictionalized "Vitebsk" under and on the margins of the panels representing the four Arts.

43. Conversation with Aleksei Kovalev, Director of the Restoration Department, State Tret'iakov Gallery, July 30, 1992.

44. See p. 155.

45. See p. 151. Similarly, Vladimir Maiakovskii, in his radical essay "Two Chekhovs," re-read the sentimentalized Chekhov as a great and funny master of language.

46. A practical joke performed by two boys, called "let us kill a goy," consisted of urinating together and making a cross of the two streams (symbolizing the cross on a tombstone). In the village milieu, a pig marked the most obvious difference between Jews and Gentiles.

47. See p. 173.

48. B. Zingerman, "Russia, Chagall, Mikhoels, and Others," *Teatr*, vol. 2 (1990), p. 37.

49. According to Aleksandra Shatskikh (Vitali, *Marc Chagall: The Russian Years 1906–1922*, p. 81), the figure was modeled on the actor H. S. Krashinski, but there is no proof for this.

50. The Yiddish reflexive *ikh baleve zikh* ("I entertain myself," from the Russian *balovat'sia*) is written here in one word, as in Russian, yet another example of Chagall's use of Russian spelling habits in Yiddish. The repeated *ikh* (I) at the beginning and end of the phrase is a form of folk grammar, used emphatically, as in Menakhem-Mendel's speech in *Agents*. Amishai-Maisels's translation of this expression as: "I love you" has no base in either Yiddish or Russian.

51. *Teatr* is spelled in the Russian manner, accepted by Soviet Yiddish orthography, as in the canvas *Love on the Stage*. Note also the feminine (or unfinished) form of *yidishe* rather than *yidisher*.

52. See pp. 145–46.

53. Amishai-Maisels claims that this name refers to Sholem Aleichem's hero, thus disrupting the family list and leaving the grandmother with no husband. We have no definite source for the name, but Menakhem-Mendel was common in that area, after the Hasidic rebbe "Menakhem-Mendel from Vitebsk."

54. Chagall's paternal grandmother married his maternal grandfather when their first spouses died. Those were the Lyozno grandparents he knew.

55. On the leftmost clown's green sock, the Russian inscription **P verane** is penciled in. According to Aleksei Kovalev, Director of the Restoration Department, State Tret'iakov Gallery, it signifies a green color named after the Italian painter Paolo Veronese.

56. Amishai-Maisels, in Vitali, *Marc Chagall: The Russian Years 1906–1922*, p. 112.

57. Rudolf Arnheim, *The Genesis of a Painting: Picasso's Guernica* (Berkeley and Los Angeles: University of California Press, 1962), p. 26.

58. Ibid., p. 26.

59. See p. 150.

60. See p. 148.

61. See his later speeches and essays in Yiddish, especially those translated in this book.

62. Aleksandra Shatskikh, "Marc Chagall and the Jewish Chamber Theater," unpublished manuscript.

63. For a list of productions, see A. N. Manteyfel, "The First Theater of the Revolution," *Moskva*, no. 1 (1968).

64. Shatskikh theorizes that Terevsat's move to Moscow, and not an explicit expulsion by Malevich, was the cause of Chagall's move there.

65. Chagall's involvement with revolutionary activities and his practical work for the theater before the Yiddish Theater commission were unknown until recent publications by Menteyfel and Shatskikh. Chagall's design is a rare example of his participation in propaganda art.

66. State Bakhrushin Museum, Moscow, Fond. 584, files 20, 21, 87.

67. The early announcements list Chagall as the designer of all three plays, while later ones mention Al'tman.

68. The papers of the commission were kept in CGALI (Central State Archive for Literature and Art), Moscow, Fond. 2307, Opis' 1, Unit 81: "Acts of Documentary Control of the Financial-Economic Activity of the Liquidation Commission of the Moscow State Yiddish Theater" (1950, 66 pp.); and Units 82–83: "Acts and Powers of Attorney for the Transfer and

Acceptance of Property of the Moscow State Yiddish Theater" (1950; vol. 1, 206 pp., vol. 2, 179 pp.). In 1976, however, these files were extracted from the archive and sent to *vydeleny v makulaturu* (scrap paper). Unit 3 is also missing. According to some sources, they must be preserved somewhere, perhaps by the KGB (the fate of similar files sent as "scrap paper").

69. Chaim Beyder, "Marc Chagall Returned to Russia," unpublished manuscript.

70. Alexei P. Kovaliev [Aleksei P. Kovalev], "Report on the Restoration of the Murals for the Jewish Kamerny Theatre in Moscow," in Vitali, *Marc Chagall: The Russian Years 1906–1922*, p. 134.

Notes to Chapter 3

71. *Leningradskaia krasnaia gazeta*, Aug. 30, 1926.

72. "Das jüdische Theater in Moskau," in *Das Moskauer jüdische akademische Theater* (The Moscow Yiddish Academic Theater) (Berlin: Die Schmiede, 1928), pp. 17–21.

73. In *Mit Schleuder und Harfe: Theaterkritiken aus drei Jahrzehnten* (Berlin: Hensche Iverlag, 1981).

74. *Kultur-Lige: A sakh hakl* (The Culture League: A stocktaking) (Kiev, Nov. 1919), pp. 1–3.

75. That may be an exaggeration for a Jew born in Riga; Granovskii didn't talk much anyway.

76. Mikhoels, "In our Studio," in *Dos yidishe kamer teatr* (The Yiddish Chamber Theater) (Petrograd: Jewish Theater Society, 1919), p. 22.

77. Ibid.

78. Ibid.

79. Ibid., p. 17.

80. Ibid., p. 24.

81. P. A. Markov, *The Soviet Theatre* (New York: G. P. Putnam's Sons, 1935), pp. 165–66.

82. The degree to which the Jewish tradition was merged with the so-called "internationalism" and political engagement can be seen, for example, in the program of the spectacle called "Carnival of Jewish Comedians." According to a program of May 12, 1923, it included:

Thieves' songs from Odessa and Warsaw; a Negro performance "Java Celebes"; the Jewish King Lear in Pensa; Klezmer songs; three loves — Negro, American, Hasidic; street songs from Vilna; Hasidic songs and dances; "Matchmaking" — an unusual operetta; American songs in Jewish style; six Jewish acrobats; the Marseillaise.

What the Jewish comedians knew of "Negro love" and "Java Celebes" is hard to imagine; and the Marseillaise is a rather comic end to a Jewish folk carnival.

83. S. Mikhoels, "Mikhoels Vofsi On the Theater," interview, *Literarishe bleter*, April 27, 1928.

84. Ibid.

85. Andre van Gyseghem, *Theatre in Soviet Russia* (London: Faber and Faber, 1943), p. 174.

86. In the "war of the languages," Ben-Gurion came down on the side of the Hebrew HaBima rather than this Yiddish "leftist" acting.

87. Max Osborn, "Marc Chagall," *Zhar-ptitsa*, no. 11 (1923), p. 13.

88. Kultur-Lige's programmatic brochure exemplifies the conflict. It attacks the parallel Hebrew school organization Tarbut as being "Zionist-Rabbinical" and promoting Eretz-Israel, "A land where Jews don't live they call our land, a language Jews don't speak they call our language."

89. In *The New York Times*, Dec. 14, 1926, critic J. Brooks Atkinson wrote, "The effect is astonishing, as unreal as the mystic legend of the play."

90. *Das Moskauer jüdische akademische Theater.*

91. Faina Burko, *The Soviet Yiddish Theatre in the Twenties* (Ph.D. diss., Southern Illinois University, Carbondale, 1978), p. 81.

92. Yosef Schein, *Arum moskver yidishn teater* (Around the Moscow Yiddish Theater) (Paris: Les éditions polyglottes, 1964).

93. See p. 151.

Notes to Chapter 4

94. Chagall began *My Life* just before he left Russia in 1922, probably for publication there, and finished it in Berlin in 1923. Written in Russian (not his native tongue), it reinforces the public image the famous painter had by then acquired. Its writing is colorful (e.g., "Lenin turned it [Russia] upside down the way I turn my pictures"), and provides occasional explanations of the oddities in his paintings, but the text is problematic. As André Salmon indicated in the French edition, it was written in an impossible and untranslatable Russian. (The Berlin publisher Cassirer addressed this problem by publishing the drawings of *My Life* without the text.) Clearly, it conveyed Chagall's associative, disheveled Yiddish in Russian words. Bella Chagall, a newcomer to France, translated the text into French with the aid of her French teacher; it was then patched up again and published only in 1932, by which time many specific details were lost or distorted (other details were added or changed). The English and German editions were translated from that French version and contain many puzzling things. For example, one finds in the English version: "However, to live in Petersburg, one needs not only money, but also a special authorization. I am a Jew. And the czar had set aside a certain residential zone in which the Jews were obliged to stay." Surely, Chagall meant the Pale of Settlement, hundreds of kilometers from the capital. Elsewhere, the changes may reflect Bella's censorship or "adaptation" for a non-Jewish audience. For example, Chagall's plea to his presumed ancestor, the synagogue painter Hayim Segal, to come out of the grave and "blow into me, my bearded grandfather, a few drops of *Jewish* truth!" (i.e., teach me the Jewish tradition of folk art) in the English edition became, "distill in me one or two drops of *eternal* truth."

The Russian original, however, was translated into Yiddish in 1924 by two major Yiddish Expressionist writers who knew both Russian and Yiddish well, Peretz Markish and Oyzer Varshavsky; both were friends of Chagall, who illustrated the two journals they edited in Paris, where they all resided at the time. Chagall edited the translation and published it himself in his own name in several Yiddish journals around the globe, notably in the prestigious literary journals *Literarishe bleter* (Warsaw) and *Di Tsukunft* (New York); Chagall's memoirs appeared in several installments in *Tsukunft* in 1925, seven years before the French edition. Chagall intended to publish the Yiddish autobiography in book form before any other language (as he wrote to the New York literary critic Sh. Nigger), but it never materialized. The manuscript, including corrections, is preserved in the YIVO archives (New York). See the discussion of this issue by the YIVO Librarian, Dina Abramovitsh, in

"Marc Chagall's Memoirs of his Youth in *Tsukunft* and his Letters to A. Lyesin," *Tsukunft*, vol. 95 (1988), nos. 5–8.

95. Unfortunately, Chagall criticism and biographies are written mostly by authors, Jews and non-Jews, who no longer know the languages and situations of that lost world; mistakes in reading the Yiddish and Hebrew texts and subtexts abound.

96. See Chagall's "Leaves from My Notebook," translated in this book, pp. 173–74.

97. We have detailed statistics from the census of 1897. The figures here are based on the relevant entries in the Russian *Evreiskaia entsiklopediia* (Jewish encyclopedia) (St. Petersburg: Brockhaus and Ephron, 1915), and Ch. Shmeruk's dissertation (1961).

98. *Shtetl* was derived from the Polish *mjasteczko*, small city (from *mjasto*, city), then adopted in Russian as *mestechko*. In many English books, including autobiographies and translations, "shtetl" is misleadingly translated as "village." In some English titles given to Chagall's paintings, we find the same confusion.

99. In a lecture in New York in 1943, praising what the Russian Revolution did for the Jews, Chagall told how, as a child, he would hide under the bed when he saw a *gorodovoy* through the window.

100. On the philosopher Levinas and other Litvak Jewish intellectuals in France, see Judith Friedlander, *Vilna on the Seine* (New Haven and London: Yale University Press).

101. Abram Efros, *Profili* (Profiles) (Moscow: Federatsiia, 1930).

102. An example is *eretz* (land) with a Yiddish *ayin* instead of the Hebrew *alef*, on the gate of his *The Cemetery Gates* (1917).

103. We don't know how long he attended the Russian school; he was not a great student and had to repeat at least one grade.

104. Chagall was uncertain about his dialectal spelling and changed every *ey* into *oy*; for example: he writes *hoym* (home) instead of *heym*, and even *Roynhart* for [Max] Reinhardt. This is how his son-in-law Franz Meyer and all who followed him invented a new Jewish name for his beloved uncle, spelled in German: *Neuch* (which in Lithuanian Yiddish is pronounced *Neyakh*) instead of *Noah*.

105. See Appendix A, "Why Marc Chagall?" p. 61.

106. Virginia Haggard, *My Life with Marc Chagall* (New York: Donald I. Fine, 1986), p. 14.

107. Late in life, he hinted that his father may have registered his birth two or three years earlier than the actual date, to protect him from being conscripted into the army or, according to Bella, to protect his younger brother David (the exemption was based on a considerable distance in age between the two). That would take two or three years off his old age! However, his son-in-law Franz Meyer demonstrated that this was implausible, for Chagall's younger sister was born in 1889 and they were not twins. See Meyer, *Marc Chagall: Life and Work* (New York: Harry N. Abrams, 1963), p. 11.

108. Also called in Russian *Lioznii*, in Yiddish *Lyezne*, and in Polish *Lozniany*.

109. Shatskikh found that Vitebsk did indeed burn down on August 7, 1887 (7/7/87), confirming Chagall's story that, when his mother gave birth, both mother and baby had to be dragged to the other side of town — a story that became the source of his frightening flaming-red colors. See her "When and Where was Marc Chagall Born?" in Vitali, *Marc Chagall: The Russian Years 1906–1922*.

110. In a letter to Opatoshu, he wrote that he felt at home in Vitebsk only in "my own few streets," and in another, "Do I know Russia? I know just a few streets in Vitebsk, and some of Petersburg and Moscow."

111. See p. 143.

112. Chagall reached some of the highest levels of St. Petersburg Jewish intelligentsia. And a strange sight he must have been! His friend of those years, Aleksandr Romm, an aspiring artist and son of a St. Petersburg surgeon (who later quarreled with Chagall in Vitebsk and is, admittedly, a hostile though admiring witness) described "Moysey" as seen with the eyes of his social class: "A provincial with bad manners, a not quite correct Russian language, and rumpled clothes." In Aleksandr Romm, "Marc Chagall," unpublished manuscript.

113. He made the same boast in a letter to the Yiddish writer and activist Daniel Charney.

114. In 1928, his friend Opatoshu sent him the first two books of the Pentateuch in the spectacular, poetic translation by the American Yiddish poet Yehoash — and Yiddish was a language Chagall truly understood. Chagall thanked him profusely and explained how he needed it for his work for Ambroise Vollard.

115. In the catalogue of the Musée national message biblique Marc Chagall, Nice, we find: a) gouaches and drawings of 1930–32: 23 from Genesis, 14 Exodus, 1 (nonspecific) from each, Numbers and Joshua; b) engravings of 1931–34: 35 Genesis, 14 Exodus; while the engravings of 1952–56 include works from Leviticus, Deuteronomy, Joshua, Judges, Samuel, Kings, Isaiah, Jeremiah, Lamentations, Ezechiel. The lithographs of 1952–68 are again mostly from his beloved Pentateuch, as well as the "simple" and popular books of Ruth and Esther.

Why Marc Chagall?
The artist claimed that his family's name was Segal and that his father changed it to Shagal. How did it happen? Why should a simple herring trader change his name? And was it easy to change a name in tsarist Russia?

The name Segal (accented on the first syllable, Ségal) is spelled SGL in Hebrew, that is, with no written vowels (because it is an acronym for the Hebrew designation Sgan Levia ["Attendant to Levites"]). But Lithuanian Yiddish speakers confused "S" and "Sh," never knowing which to use where. In western Lithuania, every "Sh" was pronounced "S," while in eastern Byelorussia, the contrary was true: people said *tshvantshik* instead of *tsvantsik* (twenty), *zhibn* instead of *zibn* (seven); Chagall himself, in his published Yiddish autobiography, called his hometown Lyezhne instead of Lyezne (Lyozno). As Marvin Herzog, the specialist on Yiddish dialectology, tells me, this tendency was especially strong in eastern Byelorussia. (See the recordings of pronounciation in Mohilev, Lyozno, Vitebsk, and the former Vitebsk Gubernaia, in Mordekhai Venger, "Vegn Yidishe dialektn," in *Tsaytshrift*, vol. 1 [1926], and vols. 2–3 [1928]. Chagall himself rhymed "S" and "Sh" in his Yiddish poems.)

Thus the name SGL was pronounced ShGL. Shifting the accent to the last syllable, it became Shagál. This stress on the last syllable and the resulting vowel pattern is used in other family names made of Hebrew acronyms: ShaBáD, ChaBáD, ShaDáL, YaLáG (spelled ShBD, ChBD, etc.); the person who registered the name in Russian must have been proud of the fact that it was an honorable, Hebrew name. It was probably Marc's paternal grandfather, a Hebrew teacher, who did so. It could not have been Marc's father, for Uncle Zusia in Lyozno was also a Shagal, as the artist indicated in the painting *Uncle's Shop in Lyozno* (1914–15), in which his uncle's barbershop is depicted with a sign, in Russian, bearing that name.

Later, when Chagall moved from writing in Cyrillic to Latin letters, he Frenchified the spelling to Chagall. (One wonders if his fame would have been the same had he been called Segal, rather than the interesting, ultimately stressed, and French-sounding Chagall?) Yet he still claimed that Hayim Segal, the eighteenth-century painter of the Mohilev Synagogue, was his great-grandfather (this is possible, for Lyozno was in Mohilev Province). Indeed, in the two versions of *The Pinch of Snuff* (1912), he included, inside the book read by the pious Jew, in Hebrew, SGL MShH (read as Segal Moyshe, in roll-call order). The same name, MShH SGL, is inserted in the Biblical quotations in *The Red Jew* (also known as *Jew in Bright Red*; 1915) and *The Green Jew* (1914).

"Marc" seems easy, but it is not clear when exactly he acquired it. His Jewish name was "Moyshe"; his parents Russified it in daily use, as they did with the names of most of their children, and called him "Moshka." In his Yiddish autobiography, he refers to himself in Vitebsk as "Moshke from Pokrove Street," yet his "aristocratic" friend (as Chagall dubbed him) called him "Marc." His friends in St. Petersburg used his full name in Russian — without the childish diminutive Moysey — but in France he became Marc. The name came perhaps in imitation of the Jewish sculptor Marc Antokolski from Vilna, who lived in St. Petersburg and was famous in Russia in the previous generation. In his Paris years, Chagall often did not sign his work at all, or signed without his first name; his Russian paintings are signed in Russian or, later, in French. Yet, he sometimes returned to signing MShH SGL (as in the *The Red Jew* and *The Pinch of Snuff*).

Appendix B

Misinterpretations of the murals

Many critics and scholars have commented on Chagall's murals for the Yiddish Theater. The problems the works pose are not easy to resolve, for, on the one hand, they seem to contain allusions to cultural stereotypes and to Chagall's biography, fictional world, and paintings, while, on the other, it is easy to fall into the trap of allegorizing, reading the paintings simply as an encoded personal message. No doubt, much of the contemporary evidence is lost, and the identities of various actors presumably represented in the *Introduction* cannot be established. It is not even clear that, in fact, Chagall represented particular persons in all cases; the figures are quite schematized, and critics differ over even the identification of Mikhoels (presumably painted two or three times in the *Introduction*).

The most inventive interpretation so far has been written by Ziva Amishai-Maisels ("Chagall's Murals for the State Jewish Chamber Theatre," in Christoph Vitali, ed., *Marc Chagall: The Russian Years 1906–1922* [Frankfurt: Schirn Kunsthalle, 1991], pp. 107–27). The wide availability of that essay, however, requires a critical response. To this reader, Amishai-Maisels's daring interpretations are farfetched and based on absurd logical leaps, faulty Yiddish, and an assumption that Chagall was a painter with a precisely encoded message who could inscribe all his personal grudges in the paintings without any of his peers in the theater noticing it. The basic assumption — that Chagall "used the facade of poetic images which he refused to explain to hide secret messages" — is questionable. The claim that "this approach derived from his Jewish upbringing which had taught him to interpret the Bible on four levels" — i.e., that in the *heder* he could have studied the difficult kabbalistic theory of four levels of meaning — is highly doubtful, as is the possibility of identifying four levels of meaning in each Chagallian image.

That author also claims that Chagall "believed that anyone interested in his work would study it closely, and that as long as the in-group he worked with — in this case, the director and the actors — were aware of the meanings he has added, that was enough" (p. 110). Yet soon after, she claims that Chagall attacked Granovskii in this very painting: "Chagall indicates his scorn for Granovsky's scant knowledge of Jewish traditions" (p. 113). Did Granovskii understand and condone the attack? Why do we find no trace of these interpretations in the memoirs of Efros, who lectured about the paintings in the theater itself?

Let us analyze several specific claims of this interpretation. In her reading of the *Introduction*, through some leaps of logic, the author identifies the green Chagallian animal at the left as "Malevich's cow," because in 1913 Kazimir Malevich made a painting with a cow and a violin (along with some other things, we may add). But Malevich's cow was a postcard brown cow (as on Swiss chocolate bars), while this animal is green, which is interpreted thus: "Moreover, the color indicates that Malevich's new style is a 'griner,' an inexperienced style which has not stood the test of time" (p. 111).

Green, however, was one of Chagall's favorite colors: the face of *The Green Jew* (1914) has certainly withstood "the test of time"; the green-clad Jew in *The Spoonful of Milk* (1912), the green face of Chagall himself in *I and the Village* (1911), and the green face of the fiddler in the panel *Music* from the Yiddish Theater suite are other examples; and in his first theater production, for the Comedians' Resting Place in St. Petersburg, Chagall painted the faces of all the actors green. But Amishai-Maisels offers another explanation for the green cow as well: "In the mural, Malevich's cow is ironically painted green and set in the air in memory of the criticism launched against the works with which Chagall had decorated Vitebsk: 'Why is the cow green and why is the horse flying in the sky?' Thus Malevich is taken to task for mocking the irrationality of Chagall's art" (p. 110). Is the cow then Malevich's or Chagall's? Is the green Malevich's or Chagall's? And who was mocking here?

On the page in *My Life* to which we are directed, Chagall is unequivocal about it: "All the house-painters . . . as well as their apprentices, began to copy my cows and my horses. . . . My multicolored animals swung back and forth, swollen with revolution. The workers marched forward singing the International. . . . Their Communist leaders appeared to be less satisfied[:] Why is the cow green and why is the horse flying in the sky?" (Chagall, *My Life* [New York: Orion Press, 1960], p. 139).

Did the Communist leaders represent Malevich? And if so, did they mock Malevich's cow, or, rather, Chagall's unrealistic color? All this overinterpretation is accompanied by a declaration that "these fantastic images become understandable through an analysis of the idioms Chagall used and a knowledge of his experiences and the art of those involved in them" (p. 110). Is the whole theater mural really a manifesto against Malevich's Suprematism — "a 'griner,' an inexperienced style"? The figure welcoming the cow is described as "a Jewish folk musician/artist with a stringless broken violin," yet in the next sentence he becomes a peasant; a few lines later, the peasant is transformed into El Lissitzky! This is supported by an invented Yiddish: the fiddler does a split, and our author fantasizes that an acrobatic "split" in Yiddish is *shpaltung*, therefore indicating the "rift in the Vitebsk school." But there is no such word in Yiddish; in Chagall's time, there probably was no word in Yiddish for such coarse acrobatics, though later it was called a *shpagat*.

That Malevich and Lissitzky should become heroes of Chagall's *Introduction* is at least strange; most arguments supporting it are as absurd as the above. Amishai-Maisels associates the fiddler on the right with Lissitzky, but the identification of this fiddler as Mikhoels (by Franz Meyer and Aleksandra Shatskikh) is more logical and in accord with Chagall's stories about his influence on Mikhoels. This can be supported by a more important Yiddish expression: *shpiln* means both to play music and to act in a play, hence playing the fiddle is an obvious metaphor for acting. Thus, the green cow, representing Chagall's unrealistic art (just executed in Vitebsk), charges into the situation, and Mikhoels, not knowing how to play [i.e., perform a play], comes to Chagall for advice.

In her interpretation of the murals, the same author misreads the Yiddish inscription **IKTIKT** as Mkit; from this, she extrapolates that it "suggest[s] the name 'Mikita,' a Ukrainian version of 'Nikita,' which was used by Jews in Vitebsk to represent the typical non-Jew" (p. 113). Where is the evidence? Why would the northernmost city in Byelorussia use a Ukrainian name? (Chagall's Slavic language was Russian, in which the name is pronounced *Nikita*.) And why would this name, rather than Ivan, represent the "non-Jew"? And yet, based on this invented word, a figure "Mikita" is found in the painting and becomes the focus of a whole Christian-Jewish antagonism, including a criticism of Granovskii himself!

Amishai-Maisels writes, "Granovsky has no arms. He is another 'kalike,' even worse off than Lissitzky. But being without hands entirely not only means that he is unsuccessful, but that he is a 'goylem,' a dummy. His lack of hands makes him unable to accept the gift of Chagall's talent, proffered to him as a palette, and the way he turns away and kicks back at Chagall reflects his disdain" (p. 113). True, a *kalike* (cripple,

6
Drama
1920
Tempera and gouache on canvas
212.7 x 107.3 cm
(83 ¾ x 42 ¼ inches)
State Tret'iakov Gallery, Moscow

7
Literature
1920
Tempera and gouache on canvas
215.9 x 81.3 cm
(85 x 32 inches)
State Tret'iakov Gallery, Moscow

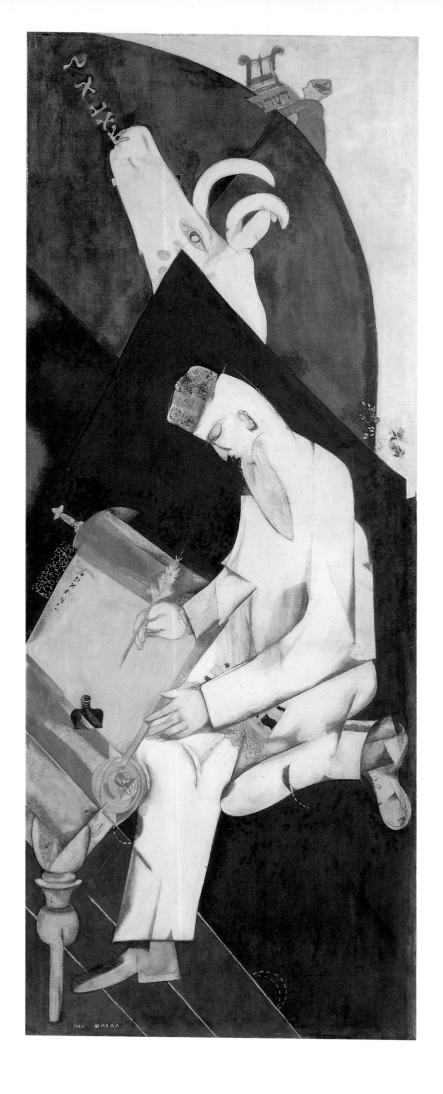

8
**Study for
Introduction to the
Jewish Theater**
1920
*Pencil, ink, gouache, and watercolor on
paper, mounted on board*
17.3 x 49 cm
(6 ¾ x 19 ¼ inches)
*Musée national d'art moderne,
Centre Georges Pompidou, Paris*

9
Study for the Jewish Theater

1920
Pencil and watercolor on paper (verso)
11.5 x 26.8 cm
(4 ½ x 10 ½ inches)
Musée national d'art moderne,
Centre Georges Pompidou, Paris

10
The Green Violinist

ca. 1920
Pencil and watercolor on paper
32 x 22 cm
(12 ⅛ x 8 ⅝ inches)
Collection Ida Chagall, Paris

11
The Green Violinist
(study for Music)
1920
Pencil, gouache, and watercolor
on brown paper
24.7 x 13.3 cm
(9 ¾ x 5 ¼ inches)
Musée national d'art moderne,
Centre Georges Pompidou, Paris

1920
Ink and watercolor on paper
24.1 x 12.7 cm
(9 ½ x 5 inches)
Collection Ida Chagall, Paris

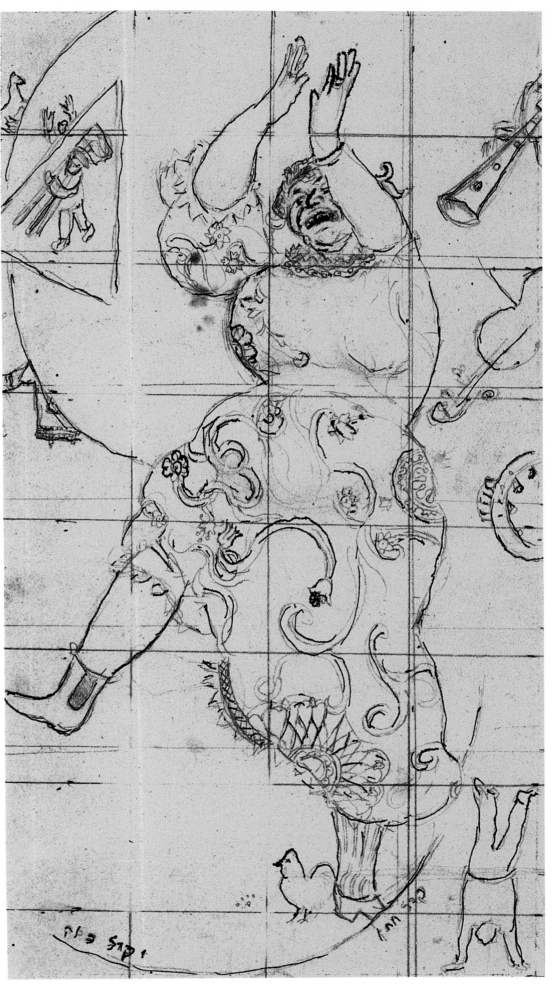

13
Study for Dance
1920
Pencil and ink on paper
24.8 x 13.4 cm
(9 ¾ x 5 ¼ inches)
Collection Ida Chagall, Paris

14
Study for Literature
1920
Pencil, ink, and gouache on paper (recto)
26.8 x 11.5 cm
(10 ½ x 4 ½ inches)
Musée national d'art moderne,
Centre Georges Pompidou, Paris

14
Study for Literature
1920
Pencil, ink, and gouache on paper (recto)
26.8 x 11.5 cm
(10 ½ x 4 ½ inches)
Musée national d'art moderne,
Centre Georges Pompidou, Paris

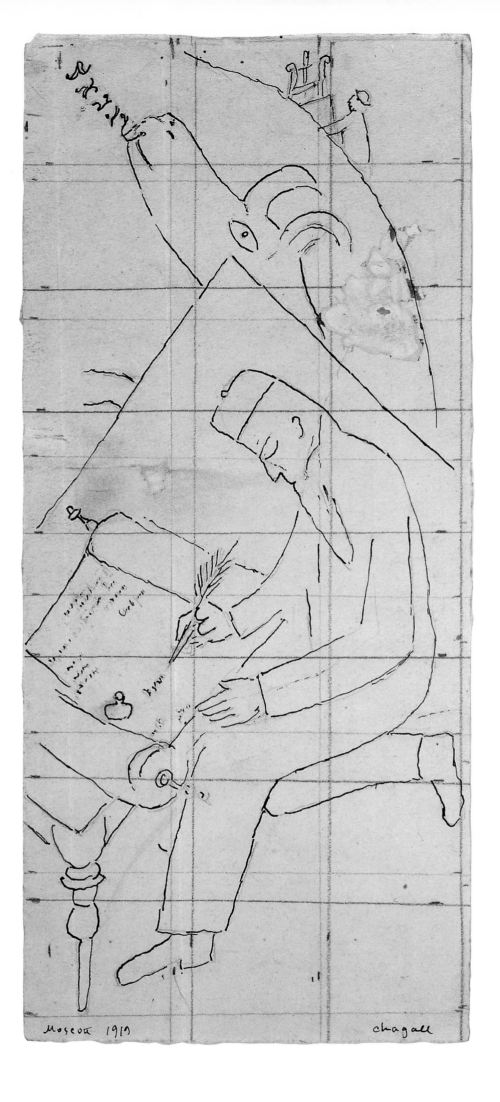

Moscou 1919   chagall

15
Set design for Mazel Tov
1920
Pencil and gouache on brown paper
on board
47.5 x 63.5 cm
(18 3/4 x 25 inches)
Collection Ida Chagall, Paris

16
Set design for Mazel Tov
1920
Pencil and watercolor on paper
25.5 x 34.5 cm
(10 x 14 inches)
Collection Ida Chagall, Paris

17
Set design for It's a Lie
1920
Pencil and gouache on paper
22.5 x 30 cm
(8 ⅞ x 11 ¾ inches)
Collection Ida Chagall, Paris

17
Set design for It's a Lie
1920
Pencil and gouache on paper
22.5 x 30 cm
(8 ⅞ x 11 ¾ inches)
Collection Ida Chagall, Paris

הגש אלי[?] [?]לי[?]

Декорац для Шол. Алейхема

Marc Chagall
1920

18
**Costume design for
Mikhoels**
1920
Pencil and watercolor on paper
27 x 27 cm
(10 ⅝ x 10 ⅝ inches)
Collection Ida Chagall, Paris

Michoels 1919 Marc Chagall

19
Man with Long Nose
(*costume design for* Sholem
Aleichem Evening)
1920
Pencil and watercolor on paper
27 x 19.5 cm
(10 ⅝ x 7 ⅛ inches)
Collection Ida Chagall, Paris

20

Woman with Child
(costume design for Sholem
Aleichem Evening *)*
1920
Pencil and gouache on paper
27.7 x 20.3 cm
(10 ⅞ x 8 inches)
Collection Ida Chagall, Paris

21
**Portrait of the Artist's
Sister Aniuta**
1910
Oil on canvas
92.3 x 70.3 cm
(36 ¼ x 27 ⅝ inches)
Solomon R. Guggenheim Museum
48.1172 x 91

*Portrait of the Artist's
Sister Aniuta*
1910
Oil on canvas
92.3 x 70.3 cm
(36 ¼ x 27 ⅝ inches)
Solomon R. Guggenheim Museum
48.1172 x 91

22
The Soldier Drinks

1911 – 12
Oil on canvas
109.1 x 94.5 cm
(43 x 37 ¼ inches)
Solomon R. Guggenheim Museum
49.1211

23
Paris Through the Window
1913
Oil on canvas
135.8 x 141.4 cm
(53 ½ x 55 ¾ inches)
Solomon R. Guggenheim Museum,
Gift, Solomon R. Guggenheim 37.438

24
The Flying Carriage
1913
Oil on canvas
106.7 x 120.1 cm
(42 x 47 ¼ inches)
Solomon R. Guggenheim Museum
49.1212

25
Quarrel
ca. 1914
Gouache and pencil on cream
wove paper
28.5 x 24.1 cm
(11 ¼ x 9 ½ inches)
Solomon R. Guggenheim Museum,
Gift, Solomon R. Guggenheim 41.436

26
Remembrance
ca. 1918
Gouache, india ink, and
pencil on paper
31.7 x 22.3 cm
(12 ½ x 8 ⅝ inches)
Solomon R. Guggenheim Museum,
Gift, Solomon R. Guggenheim 41.440

Erinnerung
1914   Chagall
              914

27
The Dream
1920
Gouache, pencil, ink, and bronze
paint on paper
32.1 x 43.2 cm
(12 ¾ x 17 inches)
Solomon R. Guggenheim Museum,
Gift, Solomon R. Guggenheim 41.447

"La rêve"   Marc Chagall 920

28
In the Snow
1922/ca. 1930
Gouache and ink on paper
23.6 x 31.4 cm
(9 3/8 x 12 3/8 inches)
Solomon R. Guggenheim Museum,
Gift, Solomon R. Guggenheim 41.453

Marc Chagall   1922   "Dans la neige"

**29
Musician**

1922
Supplementary sheet to
Mein Leben (My Life), *30 / 110*
Etching and drypoint on paper
Paper: 44.1 x 34.9 cm
(17 ⅜ x 13 ¾ inches);
plate: 44.5 x 34.9 cm
(10 ⅞ x 8 ⅜ inches)
Solomon R. Guggenheim Museum 38.757

**29
Musician**

1922
Supplementary sheet to
Mein Leben (My Life), *30 / 110*
Etching and drypoint on paper
Paper: 44.1 x 34.9 cm
(17 ⅜ x 13 ¾ inches);
plate: 44.5 x 34.9 cm
(10 ⅞ x 8 ⅜ inches)
Solomon R. Guggenheim Museum 38.757

Marc Chagall

30
Green Violinist
1923 – 24
Oil on canvas
198 x 108.6 cm
(78 x 42 ¾ inches)
Solomon R. Guggenheim Museum,
Gift, Solomon R. Guggenheim 37.446

30
Green Violinist
1923 – 24
Oil on canvas
198 x 108.6 cm
(78 x 42 ¾ inches)
Solomon R. Guggenheim Museum,
Gift, Solomon R. Guggenheim 37.446

31
I and the Village
ca. 1923 – 24?
Gouache, watercolor, and
pencil on paper
39 x 30 cm
(15 ⅜ x 11 ⅞ inches)
Solomon R. Guggenheim Museum,
Gift, Solomon R. Guggenheim 41.435

31
I and the Village
ca. 1923 – 24?
Gouache, watercolor, and
pencil on paper
39 x 30 cm
(15 ⅜ x 11 ⅞ inches)
Solomon R. Guggenheim Museum,
Gift, Solomon R. Guggenheim 41.435

A Hilla Rebay

Marc Chagall

A Madame Hilla Rebay sympathiquement.

Marc Chagall

Paris. 1934.

32
The Soldier Drinks

ca. 1923 – 24
Gouache on paper
63.3 x 48.3 cm
(25 x 19 inches)
Solomon R. Guggenheim Museum,
Gift, Solomon R. Guggenheim 41.459

Texts and Documents

Edited by Benjamin Harshav
Translated by Benjamin and Barbara Harshav

Edited by Benjamin Harshav
Translated by Benjamin and Barbara Harshav

The Art of Marc Chagall

This first book on Marc Chagall, written in Russian by Abram Efros and Iakov Tugendhol'd, was published in Moscow by Helicon in 1918. It includes two contributions by Efros and one by Tugendhol'd as well as thirty reproductions of the artist's paintings and graphics. The book bears the inscription, "composed with the help of the Circle for Jewish National Aesthetics 'Schomir.'"

The Emperor's Clothes *Abram Efros*

Here is a book about an artist — young but already famous — perhaps the most brilliant of our *hommes d'aujourd'hui*, but one who has experienced a hard lot: to be recognized without being understood. Marc Chagall fell under the wheel of one of those quiet artistic revolutions that seem to occur unnoticed and coincidentally, but whose victims include the most unusual talents.

What happened? What happened is the deepest rupture, still unnoticed and unaccounted for, of the most solid relationships between traditional antagonists — the artist and the masses. Oh, the roles have changed in an amazing way! The imperially conservative masses — Her Highness the Masses, the masses, slandered and adored, whom all revolutionaries of art have cursed and yet tried to captivate; the masses surrounding the artist like guards around Saint Sebastian, the masses marching over the corpses of innovators, the implacable, stubborn, pursuing, stinging, branding masses — what has happened to her in our time?

We see before us those strange idyllic years when the masses began, obsequiously, to accept everything the creative caprice of the artist offered her. She became his searching slave. She agreed to everything. She blessed everything with her thousand-mouth blessing: nothing appalled her — and nothing surprised her! The grief of many young artists who wished, in vain, to have their own period of rejection is understandable and legitimate: the masses really violated the good canons of rejection, established by the experience of so many heralds of new values in art.

Poor Chagall! He too experienced the meaning of this popular complacency, the worrying smile of devotion, and the frowning brows of attention. He too knew that if they hail a recognized writer so as not to read him, they hail a recognized artist so as not to look. Shuffling through an exhibition, one figure throws to another, hurrying to sneak by Chagall: "Ach, Chagall . . . He is very talented . . . " — "Yes-yes . . . Very-very . . . ," — and, relieved, they vanish into the next gallery, where they regain human language and, with a profusion of words, they burst into excitement before the *comme il faut* canvases of some Excellency.

The Emperor's clothes . . . Andersen's tale . . . till the first fool screams: "The Emperor is naked. . . ." Well, this is so understandable! Art blinds like Lady Godiva with her nakedness. That's why experienced viewers and true appreciators, art historians and art critics — all wear glasses and increase their size every year. But the masses can glue her eyes to the forbidden crack without fear: she won't go blind because she doesn't see anything anyway.

Art criticism is often an act of grace in relation to the profane, and an act of justice in relation to the artist; it teaches the former to see and gives the latter an opportunity to be understood. Must it linger at the deaf lawsuit between Chagall and his viewers? It seems that the time has come to stand up between them, especially since the artist is right and, this time, the viewers are not so guilty — for Marc Chagall put before them truly the most difficult problem: about the boundaries of what is permitted in art.

Chagall *Abram Efros*

I. The Nature of His Art

1. He enters the room the way practical people walk in, with confidence and precision, overcoming space, striding forcefully, testifying to a consciousness that the earth is earth and only earth. But look: at a certain step, his body totters and snaps drolly; like Pierrot collapsing in half in a puppet theater, fatally stung by betrayal and bending slightly sideways, cracked, with an expression apologizing for some guilt unknown to us, Chagall approaches, shakes hands — and sits down obliquely, as if falling into the chair. Chagall has the beaming face of a young fawn; but in conversation, the kindly softness sometimes evaporates like a mask, and then we think that the corners of his lips are too sharp, like arrows, and he bares his teeth tenaciously, like an animal, and the gray-blue kindness of his eyes too often shines with the fury of strange explosions, perspicacious and blind at the same time, making his interlocutor think he is probably reflected in some fantastic manner in the mirrors of Chagall's eyes, and perhaps will later recognize himself in one of those green, blue, red, flying, dishevelled, folded-over, twisted people — in Chagall's future paintings. And when hours pass in conversation, talking about the dear mundane world, work, his wife, his child, Chagall suddenly boils over with some prophetic phrase like: "We talk only as if before God, our way is faultless because it is God's way . . . " — we are no longer amazed; we even understand Chagall, we can see what strong but rational-intangible threads link Chagall's phantasmagoric expressions with his stories about dear daily life, illuminating it and permeating it with light, and opening, behind the first plane of his words, a second, third, fourth, and more planes — the planes of his soul. They are as inevitable in Chagall and as essential to his flesh and blood as those unexpected gray strands cutting through the bright curling hair of the not-yet-thirty-year-old artist.

2. His art is as difficult as Chagall himself: to love him, you have to get close to him, and to get close, you have to go through the slow and insistent temptation of penetrating his shell. Because the first impression gets helplessly entangled in the contradictions and idiosyncracies of Chagall's art.

That Chagall is very talented can be seen right away; but why does he do all those strange things? Why is this marvelously painted old Jew green? And another have red and green hands? And a third have an identical miniature Jew standing on his head, just turning to the other side? In the belly of a horse we see an unborn colt, and two human figures protrude from under his hooves. The head of an old woman has leaped off and is flying upward, and the headless body swiftly sinks down to a cow standing on the roof of a house. And the girl with a bouquet — a boy glued to her lips, folded up in the air, around her head, like a cat hurled upward; an ox has a man's jacket and human hands, and sits pensively leaning on his elbow, between two bare feet dangling from his shoulders, which probably belong to that feminine head covered with a kerchief, the nape of her neck hanging down, who spits into his mouth. And the man looking through a window at Paris has a Janus-head — one face forward, one face backward; and the cat with a girl's face looks from the windowsill at two people lying with their heads end to end at the foot of the Eiffel Tower and as tall as the tilted multistoried buildings all around. . . .

What is it — disease or mischief, that particular aesthetic mischief of the young, with which so many great artists begin their creative path?

Perhaps all we now need to do in relation to Chagall is just to forgive his present boldness for his great future. Or is there some third point of view from which another "angle on Chagall" opens up, in which his present creation is no longer a madness or throwing dust in your eyes, but is artistically justified and psychologically convincing in its mundane absurdities, and where the questions of inexperienced people — "why does he do it?" — will be met by us, the viewers "who came to Chagall," with the same astonishment with which Chagall himself meets the visitors to his exhibition who pour onto his pictures their "why?" and "what for?"— Yes, exactly.

3. It is hard to get close to Chagall because you have to overcome his contradictions, to be able to synthesize them. Behind the elements of his art thrusting out in all directions, you have to find one axis and a general guiding force dominating the multitude of colorful parts.

Chagall — a master of mundane life, but also Chagall — a visionary; Chagall — a storyteller, but also Chagall — a philosopher; a Russian Jew, a Hasid — but also a pupil of French Modernism; but also, in general, a cosmopolitan fantasist, soaring like a witch on a broomstick above the globe and in his swooping flight carrying behind him a multitude of various particles from a multitude of various lives that descend in a swarm on his canvases when times of meditation and creativity emerge, and the flowing and roiling elemental force of Chagall's visions is graphically transformed into images and colors.

Were Chagall only a visionary, it would not be difficult to accept him, as it was not difficult to accept the visions of Curlanis. It would be even easier were Chagall a pure depicter of mundane life, even if he were the most left and radical among the artists creating forms of new realist painting today: we are already experienced enough with various "deformations" not to be scared of them, and perhaps even to find some charm in them. Finally, it would not be difficult to be tempted by the possibility of deciphering a convoluted and complex allegory if Chagall's headless and green people were only allegories that could be changed into a simple and easily understood parable, like the monsters, scarecrows, and cripples in Goya's etchings.

But Chagall is neither this nor that nor the other. His visions live entirely in the confines of the simplest mundane life, while his mundane life is entirely visionary. The people and objects of daily life are permeated with the nature of specters, but these Chagallian specters are by no means shadows with no mass or circumference or hue, and whom chopping or stabbing is as senseless as chopping or stabbing the air. Chagall's spectral daily life has all the palpability and weight of normal objects and bodies. And if, nevertheless, he is governed by some law that tears him apart and brushes people, animals, and objects around the air, confounds all logic and sense of earthly proportions and interrelations, the poor law of allegory or the low law of a crossword puzzle is least guilty in it; we face here not a logical game, but an authentic, unconditional seeing of an immense internal saturation.

4. You can understand Chagall only through empathy, not through comprehension. The law of deformation, which gives such a strange countenance to Chagall's works — that law, which moves the absurdities and strangenesses of children's stories, inventions, and fears — is the same law that creates the phantasmagoric world of Jewish national mysticism, which endeavored in the great movement of Hasidism miraculously to transform the mundane life of poverty and suffering of shtetl existence.

The favorite and primary link between events in stories

children tell is the word "suddenly," which is not at all mechanical or external — otherwise the pure truthfulness of childish fantasy would have brushed it aside; on the contrary, the word "suddenly" expresses the very essence and intimate nature of that elemental force of unlimited possibilities, which, in the child's eye, abound in the world; the word "suddenly" merely warns the listener that this omnipotent, elemental force will splash one of its caprices on him. If we translate this "suddenly" into adult language, we get "miracle." But not "miracle" in the sense of an unusual and rare exception violating the laws of nature, but "miracle" as a habitual element of daily life, a "miracle" that denies the very possibility of "life without miracle," and asserts that "anything may happen and does"; and this is precisely the world perception that has created the practical miracle-making of Hasidism in the modern history of the Jews.

Such an internal belief that "anything may happen" speaks in Chagall's work. Therefore, you can penetrate his art without breaking the shell only if you rouse in yourself the vestiges of childhood dreams, reviving in your soul those forgotten sensations, when the fear of a dark room lived in us, for we knew that the hairy hands of some monster may penetrate the desolate and black walls and drag us off, and the old chair may suddenly bare its teeth and pounce on us.

What's the difference between the demands offered the reader by Hoffmann's fantastic world and the fantastic world of Baron Münchhausen? Isn't it that Hoffmann requires belief in his unrealities, and Münchhausen demands disbelief? Isn't this the foundation on which they build their respective effects? Like Hoffmann, Chagall needs a spectator who believes in him; his spectator must be able to succumb to the unrealities of his paintings and visions, to entrust himself to their special logic just as he can abandon himself to the flow of Hoffmann's inventions. That is why, when a naïve spectator approaches Chagall with his naturalistic criteria and angrily points out "Chagall's absurdities," the artist can only wonder bitterly: he truly understands nothing in his spectators' indignation, for they do not measure his art with the same yardstick as he. An axiom in the cognition of art states that the art of every master is a country with its own special laws; to understand an artist in this sense implies succumbing to those laws and approaching the external manifestations of his work — paintings and statues — from the inside, from the creative will of the artist. That is why, if Chagall's art is invincibly chaotic and hopelessly senseless when approached from the outside and measured with the illegitimate yardstick of realistic-mundane painting, it is, nonetheless, clear and opens up to you almost schematically if you follow its own internal logic.

5. In the development of Chagall's art so far, three periods clearly emerge. External boundaries determine the first as a preparatory, provincial-Petersburg period, when Chagall came from his Vitebsk Province to St. Petersburg to study painting, attended Bakst's school, and worked on his first independent paintings. The second period — abroad; Chagall left for Paris, where he became "Chagall," impressing the turbulent Bohemia of La Ruche with his unusual canvases, which promoted him to the ranks of the most interesting "masters of tomorrow," and which were taken triumphantly to exhibitions of the new art in Berlin and Amsterdam. In this period such chimerical canvases were created as *Paris Through the Window*, *The Carter*, *The Calf Seller*, *The Brides*, and so on, with their headless bodies, two-faced heads, and flying cows. Finally, the current period — the period of his return to Russia at the outbreak of the Great War, when Chagall created his Vitebsk cycle: *The Barbershop*, *The Shtetl Lyozno*, *In the Provinces*, *On the Outskirts of Vitebsk*, *The Praying Jew*, *The Birthday*, *The Guitarist*, and others.

The internal line of his creative work passed through those chronological boundaries amazingly whole. Chagall had no interruptions, no treading water, no deviations. The originality of Chagall's art was evident from the beginning and it always went its own way; the boundaries of the above-mentioned external periods of development indicated only turning points and the interrelations of the two major elements of his work. These elements, inseparably linked to each other from Chagall's first steps, are the genre of mundane life and visionary mysticism. Chagall's earliest paintings created the basic "Chagallian" impression: the unreal countenance of real life. The Chagall of those works is a dreamy child who grew up in a Hasidic family in a Jewish shtetl. But childhood and Hasidism mean a dream multiplied by a dream; this is the source of the boundless ore of Chagall's fantasy. And the mundane life around him is the life of a small Vitebsk town; that is, the very quintessence of everyday life, the very thick of the most pitiful poverty and opaque existence.

Chagall's dream and the shtetl existence had either to break each other or find a higher and integral unity. Art gave Chagall the redeeming synthesis. Chagall's painting showed the light in the humble poverty of the people, streets, cattle, and huts of his little Lyozno, which he depicted with all the acuity of love for his hometown. Chagall's childish vision and Hasidic mysticism discovered a world of miracle in the daily round.

There are two paintings, *The Wedding* of 1908, and *The Funeral* of 1909, where we can observe precisely and profoundly how his hometown existence is transformed in the young Chagall, and how he constructs his canvases. First of all, there is a simple story about a simple event from simple life. A story with no details and no makeup, laconic and clear. *The Wedding*: two musicians walk in the street, behind them come the bridegroom and bride, followed by an old man and woman and two children, and three more relatives bring up the rear; a water-carrier and a merchant, a woman and a couple of kids have stopped in the middle of the street and are watching the procession, and in back, a Jew with long coattails excitedly shakes his hands in the air.

The protocol of daily life! But what a remarkable face it all has: as in children's drawings, people are higher than the buildings because people are more important than buildings, and the perspective of the street is sharply reared up for, otherwise, not everybody would be seen, and not everything would be clear to us spectators — and is it possible not to show us anything in this Lyozno heaven, including the streetlamp, raised like a torch above the procession? As in Hasidic legends, the figures of the Jews in Chagall's country are unusual and transformed: yes, those are shtetl Jews, but they are apparently made of some special material, and we won't be astonished if the whole procession suddenly rises up into the air, where the fiddler will go on chirping and the bridegroom will take the bride — we shall not be astonished because what we see is "life inside a miracle," and perhaps the Jew with long coattails, shaking his hand, is prophesying about this miracle, the birth of the Messiah out of this new couple, for believers expect the Messiah from every wedding.

In *The Funeral*, Lyozno existence reveals its mystical nature even more clearly: again everything is simple and everything is chimerical, but too simple and too chimerical. In the middle of the reared-up street, between the huts, lies the corpse in a shroud, surrounded by burning candles; a giant gravedigger raises his shovel; a woman spreads her hands high; and above them all, astride the roof of a house, a strange Jew, bent over his violin, draws a melody — in harmony with the wind howling under the glowering sky, tearing up the clouds, and shaking the eaves, while over the huts a shoe and sock hang instead of signs.

It is amazing that, even in those early years, Chagall uses color and hue as means of characterizing and influencing the psyche of the viewer, and not just for conveying the realistic-existential coloring of the objects. Chagall goes hand in hand here with the most progressive and sensitive masters of our art. The painting of our days consciously uses the influence of color not only on the eye, but also on the spiritual world: the painterly texture of the picture is assigned the task of evoking a direct reaction in the internal world of the spectator by circumventing the plastic image, playing on the spectator as on a keyboard with color, line, layering of paint, and curve of the line; sometimes the artist even tries to characterize an object by the very selection of colors. Chagall promoted this "psychic value of color" from the start — subtly and freely. And perhaps it is because of its "color mystique" more than anything else that the realistic life in his pictures is permeated with the order of a different, miraculous existence.

6. When Chagall turned up in Paris and had a chance to get close to the very center of world art, the balance between the everyday-life and the visionary elements of his art was deeply disturbed. Above the little world of Lyozno, with its small dimensions and domestic density, hovered the monstrosities and spaces of a Cyclopean city. What Chagall encountered in the art world of Paris shattered all the clamps of his everyday images and themes. Chagall's mysticism, in its very essence, in its striving to transform the countenance of daily life, carried a centrifugal force striving to rend the frozen forms of observable existence. However, that early Chagall was still too attached to "the earth," to "his Lyozno," not to hold the destructive impulses of his fantasy in check. But now, Paris removed all his shackles, and his Lyozno daily life was literally torn to pieces by the unlimited explosion.

Chagall landed in Paris at the moment when Cubism was at the zenith of its triumph and influence. That is, from the outside, in the form of a mandatory aesthetic program, Chagall confronted those aspects of Cubism to which his own art strove from inside him. Cubism splintered the whole visual world into pieces and parts in the name of an abstract aesthetic principle; but the mysticism of Chagall's creation, albeit by different laws, also attempted to tear up the cover of daily life. If, by its nature, the cold, heady force of Cubism was strange to Chagall's fiery immediacy, in its results, the triumphant Cubism gave it exactly what it needed. Most important, in the eyes of the masters of the new art, Cubism destroyed the value of any re-creation of objects in their normal, "everyday" aspect; the mandatory, essential "deformation" of objects was pronounced as the basic principle of art. Thus, the doors were wide open for Chagall's fantasy. The raging force erupted. Some terrible cataclysm crumbled Chagall's native world of shtetl Judaism. That cycle of chimerical canvases, described above, which created Chagall's resounding fame among the innovators and their adherents, and evoked a similar rage in the philistines and Naturalists — that cycle is a truly shattering confession, a stunning story of a fiery storm which gusted over Chagall's art in Paris. "Foil . . . Clowning . . . " — but I don't know anything more palpable and visual in its power of persuasion and sincerity than those extraordinary paintings. It truly took a lot of internal courage and artistic talent to imprint the rage of the storming force so directly and plastically. Perhaps those who value this cycle above anything else in Chagall are not so wrong, for such a conjunction of tense depth and artistic significance did not recur in him later on. Incidentally, this assessment would be true only if what Chagall told us here did not have such an exclusively narrow, personal character, if that broad, generally significant value of the internal experience that marks his creativity in the two

other periods were expressed here.

Be that as it may, in any case, the purely artistic organization of those Paris compositions is no doubt remarkable. Channeling the minute chaos of formless visions into a plastic frame, it was possible only by a strong artistic welding of all parts of the picture. Cubism helped Chagall here too, for if Cubism is especially strong in anything, it is in the iron functionality of its artistic constructs, in that utterly granite solidity that characterizes the constructions Cubism erects from parts of objects that had disintegrated into their components. Chagall knew how to achieve the same thing — he channeled the flood of his anarchic force into the sturdiest artistic shores. The raging colors and precise rhythms of the Paris canvases bound them as with a steel hoop, and their magnificent organization calmed the viewer's eye, excited by the internal chaos of the picture.

7. Chagall was faced with a choice: either return his art to the forms of the real world or stop being an artist. You cannot float in the melted stream of fuzzy mystical visions for years, for this fire not only illuminates but also consumes. A third solution is possible: mannerism, when, with a gelid hand and ashen heart, the artist produces imitations of himself and offers false visions as true. But of course, Chagall, with his unusual ultimate sincerity, could not become his own follower.

His return to Russia at the start of the war was a cure for Chagall. Like a prodigal son returning to his father's home, he returned to his Jewish shtetl world. He attached himself to it with the same zeal and fervor of spirit with which, in Paris, he crumbled and eroded its poor forms. The Vitebsk cycle of Chagall's paintings emerged in a feverish and whining sweep and Chagall's devotion to work, always great, here knew no bounds. Chagall created dozens of canvases, each a precise embrace, arms stretched out to everything Chagall saw again in his homeland. He cultivated and lavished all the subtlety and delicacy of his amazing palette and the nobility of a refined painting to record respectfully the face of his reacquired homeland.

The tattered parts of Lyozno daily life are reunited; and "the soul of things" that stormed in the general stream return to their objects; and in Chagall's painting, the previous Jewish world reappears. Chagall paints every alley, every person, every house of his home places. In the Vitebsk cycle, his whole family parades before us, young and old, childhood friends, neighbors, street urchins, beggars, houses, huts, trees, grass, cattle — Chagall even paints the forbidden pig affectionately, for truly everything is blessed and holy in this reacquired daily life. And at the same time, what a difference from the daily life of his first, pre-Paris period! If there Chagall's mystical force strove to break out of objects, here it strives from the outside to get into things. In *The Wedding* of 1908, people still walk on the earth and we only feel that, at any minute, they may leave it and soar in the air, where the true nature of their being draws them; whereas in the paintings of the Vitebsk cycle, these people, on the contrary, are still soaring in the air, as in the paintings of the Paris period, but they are already descending to the earth and soon will have to land finally and stand on their feet. Thus a young couple hovers over the shtetl in the painting *To My Wife*; thus an old Jew with a sack soars over the town in *On the Outskirts of Vitebsk*; thus above the girl with a bouquet in *The Birthday* a young man has frozen in the air kissing her lips. Even whatever has landed on the earth still has some instability in these paintings, a lack of firmness like the first touching of the earth after a long flight, as if the earth's gravity had not yet fully embraced this new Chagallian daily life. In this sense, we must note with what fragility and lightness people and things stand on the Vitebsk canvases, and how even houses and rooms are still unstably attached to the earth. That is the source of the strange coloring of objects, the green, violet, red bodies and faces of people; this is the heritage of the Paris whirlwind, its mystical colorfulness, the glow of its colorful fires.

8. Today, Chagall stands in the very heat of his Vitebsk period — what the results will be we can only vaguely guess. There are reasons to think that Chagall's present road leads him to that "grand art" of transformed daily life indicated in several of his recent big works — in the magnificent *The Praying Jew*, in *The Green Old Man*, and such; here the shtetl Jews have grown into enormous national figures, deeply rooted in their mundane typicality and, at the same time, endowed with all the internal significance of a symbol.

However, new traits have recently begun to break through in Chagall's works, traits of an even denser, hotter, hastier, voluntarily obsequious submission to "the tyranny of small things," the rule of dear daily life. I saw a new series by Chagall: his dacha cycle. A man lives in a dacha with a front yard with green trees, on the balcony hang red dotted curtains, on the table sits a golden samovar, and, in a wicker basket, scarlet and blue berries — here he is, man in Paradise, as if, after a hard earthly road, he now abides "in a place of light, a place of grains, a place of peace. . . ."

Is it a final reconciliation with everydayness that the subdued artist has to go through? But what will then link his "grand art" with the "apology for a dacha"?

How can we know? . . . Except for guesses, what does Chagall leave us? We must admit courageously that there is nothing more hopeless than predicting his future, for among our artists, there is no spirit more free and unexpected in his creative ideas than this God-intoxicated Chagall. . . .

II. The Palette. Graphics.

1. Russian art may be called art in makeup. You must not get too close to it; otherwise, instead of a hero, you will face XY in makeup. Russian artists are charming storytellers, clever stage directors, and sensitive psychologists. But how many of them can also be called masters? In Russian painting, you enjoy the insightful vivacity of portrait characteristics as much as the accuracy of scenes from everyday life and the almost frightening prescience of historical resurrections; Russian paintings can be read inexhaustibly. But do not get close to their canvases! Beyond the figures and objects, when your eye detects the rough surface of a hastily painted canvas and your gaze follows the clods and ruts of the daubs — what despondency overcomes you among this swampy overflow of paint! With fatal clarity, you will distinguish that the traits that captivated you are not art, but only the makeup of art, in which all effects are calculated on "looking from afar," "looking from a distance," "looking from an auditorium," through the deluding prism of the footlights. The unstable layers of paint hold shakily onto the canvas, the color is exaggerated, the tone is approximate, the contour is dangling.

Art in makeup. . . . I remember Verhaarn in the Tret'iakov Gallery seeking masters of the brush and finding only makeup artists. We had no way to respond to him when he filtered our painters through the golden sieve of the French palette — a palette of masters and mastery — and hall after hall and artist after artist flew somewhere into non-being. We ourselves often called our art provincial, but we believed that a provincial aware of his provinciality was not hopeless. Yet nevertheless we did not value our art so poorly.

Verhaarn's judgment was the judgment of the metropolis of art on a provincial school; and when, stooped and pulling the hanging threads of his endless moustache and dropping precise evaluations, the poet ran from an ancient icon to Shchukin's *Lady in a Cap*, and drew in the air with his long fingers before Levitskii's *Anna Davia*; when, throwing his glasses on his nose before Sylvester Shchedrin, Fedotov, or Ivanov, he pronounced ambiguous aphorisms about Cézanne, Corot, and the Dutch; and later, without stopping, slowing down pensively only before the bursts of snow in Surikov's *Morozova*, swept by even Repin, Levitan, and Serov, to nod affirmatively before Vrubel's *Portrait of My Wife*, and to finish with a deeply satisfied "Voila!" . . . before Somov's *Lady in Blue* — the circle of art was drawn by him with authority and conviction.

Should we reconcile ourselves to that? But what can we do? That's how it is, you cannot circumvent or get around it; our art is the art of painters but not of masters; it has no taste for *métier*; and every name that augments the short dynasty of Russian masters of the brush is a true event.

2. How did the provincial Chagall turn out to have that rarest of gifts denied so many great and praised talents? An accidental caprice of fate? Or the buds of a French seed falling on the sickly sharpened sensibility of Chagall's talent? Be that as it may, the large pleiade of the young generation of our artists counts only one master, and this master is Chagall.

A skillful and excellently precise brush; now fondly licking, now scratching; now bathing in the even ripple of the daubs, now scattering marvelous "Chagallian" little dots, drops and patterns, joyful and resounding, scarlet, green, yellow, leaping and coiling, like deposits of posies and Chinamen on the joyous wallpaper of our half-forgotten nursery; the surface — exquisitely worked — now rough, sometimes protruding with the bald spots of the background, sometimes swelling with layered hills of paint; an even and smooth growing and waning of the tone, precise and finished, reminiscent of the growth of a range of sounds under the fingers of a flawless pianist; and a special soft film of velvet, or even the delicate down of a peach, lying over everything and evoking in the spectator a wish to touch and caress the painting, to feel its grain with his fingertips — this is Chagall's palette, transforming the colorful cover of his paintings into a kind of geographical relief map, where you can travel long and fruitfully, conscious that the irregularities, convexities, and concavities of every centimeter are utterly justified.

A magician among the images and visions of his paintings, among his tubes of paint, ringing his brushes and knocking his easel, he also conjures up the image of a veritable alchemist in a pointed hat knocking his retorts and test tubes, where the philosopher's stone crystallizes in smoke and flame. What a stew of spices had to be activated to create the painting of *The Green Lovers, Mariasenka with a Dog, The Sweeper, The Praying Jew*! Only such an elasticity of artistic means of depiction, operating with "infinitely small" units of painterly elements, allowed Chagall not to get lost in the whirlwind fogs of his spectral existence, to fill the skin and bones of the simplest beings and objects with the movement of some flaming and tenuous matter, and force us spectators to believe that the axioms of the regular painterly experience — that presumably a body has "body color," a large object is larger than a small one, things are not but seem to be, etc., etc. — are just a boring delusion of a tired routine that he, Marc Chagall, has the authority and power to waive.

3. We are talking about Chagall's painterly art at its peaks and in a static perspective, relying on the best of his recent experiments. Obviously the history of the development of Chagall's mastery would have brought some qualifications into our description. However, even in this most recent and accomplished stage, in one respect Chagall is not without fault: He cannot be coarse. He is not sufficiently courageous. Like an adolescent boy, he hasn't yet emerged from the immature plumpness of his limbs. He cannot force his brush to scream and shock. He does not command resounding and terrifying tones. He may be angry, raging, sometimes even furious, but not fearsome. Like the youth Jeremiah, summoned by God to serve a prophet, he could have repeated, "Oh, Lord Yahweh, look: I cannot prophesy for I am still a youth." Blessed be he, that his current period of reconciliation with mundane life requires only an elegiac tenderness and a calm joy, and there is room and order for all the delicate and skillful devices of his palette. But let us recall his Paris cycle — a cycle of storm, shock, and chaos. So what? So, our reproach relates primarily to this period. For his is not the roar of apocalyptic storms; Chagall whistles on a lyrical pipe, he found sharp, confused, and penetrating tones, for let us not forget that he is a master; and with the ebb and flow of rage and passion, he hurls at us with a wind-up of the whole great force of his clairvoyance and talent. But it is not the same brush with which the artist, engulfed in the horror of a cataclysm and torn by his spiritual pain, hits the trembling and sighing canvas with both hands. There is some discrepancy between the tossed-about, torn parts of objects hanging in the voids of the canvas, and the insufficiently simple and rigorous, over-subtle and aristocratic texture of his painterly script. When even the air cracks and shrinks and settles in Cubistic folds and edges, as in his Paris works, then Chagallian anxiety and confusion is not enough.

One thing we don't yet know: is this softness and lack of courage in Chagall's nature, and will lyricism forever be the primary force of his creativity? Or, forged and reinforced with time, will Chagall find another language for fiery and fateful visions of his creation? If that happens, and if the boundaries of his ability and powers thus expand, then Chagall will appear before us as one of the most accomplished talents of our art.

4. A painter turning to graphics becomes a philosopher of his own work.

This will be recognized when we recall that graphics are the most abstract and generalizing kind of art. They are more calculation than impulse, more thought than feeling, more prose than poetry. Therefore, painting is always more mysterious than graphics; and an artist, shifting from the palette to the pen, exposes himself and carries his true face out of the dusk into the light. Perhaps we must even say that the graphics of a painter are only the formulas of his painting — condensations composed of the main features of his art.

Chagall turns to graphics suddenly, often, and in a storm. The painterly series and the graphic series intersect and interact. In their parts, motifs, and topics, they are amazingly close. There are graphic themes that later became paintings; there are paintings that were eventually transposed into paper and ink. Chagall is a graphic artist as much as he is a painter. Therefore, his graphics are not a peripheral branch of his art. They leave no room for the accidental. These are not fruits of creative pauses or fuzzy ruminations, drawn on pieces of paper as most artists draw them if they are not masters of graphics by profession. Chagall's graphic works are even denser, fuller, and more saturated than his paintings. This is how they should be, for if, on canvas, Chagall creates his images, on paper he thinks about them, investigates their nature. In this sense, it is significant that Chagall is now especially and eagerly absorbed in graphics. Sometimes it seems that this profusion of graphic material indicates that Chagall faces the closure of the current period of his painting, for the artist is too cognizant of his work to be able to stay long enough with the current themes and devices. However, it would be most incautious to exaggerate the meaning of this. Chagall never becomes analytical, classifying, cerebral. He is always ardent; and, even if his works on paper are just a philosophy of his art, it is cognate to that fiery philosophy with which the Kabala seared the thought and heart of Judaism, running God's chariot, the Merkava, through the spheres of the universe; it is cognate to the ecstatic world view of Hasidism — and, in the Christian domain, to the systems of the Church mystics.

Therefore, Chagall meditating on his visions, Chagall the draftsman, is perceived even more sharply than Chagall the painter. Reading Chagall's graphic "book," you read a master's compendium of his art — precise, laconic, and lucid: about the world of spirit gliding through the world of matter, about the disintegration of daily life exploded by the raging of hidden forces, about the delicate and intimate earth gathering and coalescing the scattered parts of beings and things. But here everything is exposed, here there are no unfinished words; this is Chagall as he is.

In his painting, the color and tone of the paints, the lightness and accuracy of his brushstrokes, the clever network of daubs obstruct and skim the rage of his spirit that fills the canvas; they seduce with their own soft beauty. In his graphics, however, the furious dynamism of his art appears before us entirely bare. Black clods, black grains of dust, black ornaments, black nets, black pieces of figures and objects, tense as if screwed to the utmost — they truly jump onto the spectator, sweep him into their whirlpool, and carry him off. In the images of his painting, Chagall is often uncertain. Even more often, we perceive him with uncertainty; parts of the painting seem to us overly vague, the visions caught in mid-flight by one wing. Chagall's graphic solutions are crystallized to the highest degree, absolute and final. We think about it first of all when, using Hugo's definition, we say that Chagall created in art a new tremor.

5. Painting and graphics are, in principle, mutually opposed

and hostile; but in the work of one artist, such a relation between them cannot exist because the living personality of the master reconciles them. In this case, they sometimes even color each other. Traits of graphic schematization and sharpness appear in the painting; while, in the graphics, we may observe a certain painterly gamut of tones and glimpses of chiaroscuro. Such is the case with Chagall. For his painting *The Birthday* may serve as a telling example of this kind, which emerged in the very heat of his latest graphic "Chagallesques" and obviously bears the imprint of graphic art. But Chagall's graphics, too, are the graphics of a painter, even by virtue of the fact that typically they lack contours and one continuous blot.

Chagall has a device that became famous and evoked imitations by his friends and foes, and which constitutes the axis of his graphic technique; thanks to it, the appearance of an image on paper has the following visibility: from the paper, separate black threads of lines of various degrees of force and delicacy begin to emerge; moving toward the center, they grow denser, tighter, harder, shift into spilling blots, form with them the supporting parts of the image, endow them with a final finish; then they flow onward, again lose density and mass, splay out, become more transparent, thinner, gossamer, again shift into bundles of strings, and, in separate threads, disappear altogether in the surface of the page.

Needless to say, how painterly in its essence is this device, which Chagall uses with amazing, unparalleled mastery. It predetermines both the lack of a counter-line and the possibility of a timely use of graphic chiaroscuro. Thanks to this device, the line of the contour in Chagall becomes really only "implied." Between one part of the image and another there is no direct link. Only in his mind and involuntarily, through the white blanks of the page, from one net of threads to another, does the spectator carry the line boundary and define the image. For such an image — and this is the second-most-important result — the white blank of the paper in Chagall's graphics is not a background for the image but its part, a living, active substance that forms and individualizes it. Hence, also, the characteristics typical of Chagall: the torn and splayed edges of his figures, the tone of dense and rarified dots/grains of dust around his objects, the rhythmical series of flowers, circles, diamonds, with which he floods the costumes of his graphic heroes; all these are variants of the basic order as well as echoes of a "Rembrandtian" chiaroscuro of strokes and nets that, here and there, runs through Chagall's page.

Today, Chagall has moved into illustrations. He has made a delightful pictorial setting for children's stories. Such a Chagall we didn't know before. The page seems to have swallowed the thick and restless lava of his regular black masses. The boundaries and blots are scattered accurately and even niggardly, reminiscent of the dry pattern of branches in the evening sky. Chagall's pen has become laconic and lucid, he has subordinated it to himself, for he himself succumbed to the text of the stories. His painting attained transparency in its obedience to daily life — it seems that the burden of illustration will supply a purifying simplicity to his graphics.

The Artist Marc Chagall   Iakov Tugendhol'd

> Sasha is three years old — three thousand,
> and perhaps three times three thousand,
> Sasha doesn't measure his age in years.
>
> Remizov, *Maka*

1. In French exhibitions of recent years, the works of the young artist from Vitebsk, Marc Chagall, attracted my attention. Fiery-colored like Russian *lubok*, expressive to the point of grotesque, fantastic to the point of irrationality, they stood out not only among the works of Russian painters, but also against the background of the young French painting. I remember the impact they made in the Autumn Salon among the "Cubist" canvases of Le Fauconnier and Delaunay, those Fauvist innovators. While the mind-boggling brick structures of the Frenchmen exuded cold intellectualism and the logic of analytical thought, what was astonishing in Chagall's paintings was some childish inspiration, something subconscious, instinctive, unbridled, and colorful. As if by mistake, next to the adult, too-adult, works, works of some child, truly fresh, "barbaric," and fantastic had landed here. Those multicolored crooked huts with graves in the middle of the street and a fiddler chirping on the roof, that fiery-bloody Golgotha with Judas removing the ladder, could have repelled with their coarse expression, their savagery of theme, the loudness of their colors. But it was impossible not to see them or not to absorb their sharp aroma, because, behind them, you felt the all-conquering force of a great talent, and a foreign talent at that. *"Tiens, il y a quelque chose — c'est très curieux!"* — said the Frenchmen, and indeed, in Chagall, you guessed something inexplicable in European terms, and therefore "curious," as many things in the "barbaric" polychrome music of the Russian ballet seemed curious.

At another exhibition, Chagall showed works refined in their polychromy and ornamentation. Headless flying people, sentimentally inspired animals, houses outside of time and space as in a sweet and wild childish dream, were painted in black and white, gold and silver, scarlet, cerise, and other unusual and subtle shades. Chagall's fantastics and palette seemed overly tense, unhealthy, and delirious, but you couldn't doubt their sincerity — could such phantoms and such outbursts of painterly heat be invented on purpose?

Chagall roused interest; merely condescendingly approved and almost boycotted by the powerful in Russia — he was accepted in the bosom of Paris bohemia, invited to exhibit in Amsterdam, Brussels, Berlin. But the war stopped his rapid rise — Chagall found himself where he came from: in the godforsaken Russian province, in his native Vitebsk. The result of his return to his native and familiar places was a series of studies of mundane life, surprisingly realistic, strong and calm, but quite varied. Chagall is still steeped in searching, in frenetic pluralism, at the junction of many roads — like a child who has before him an infinity of influences, wishes, and opportunities. But even what he has accomplished so far allows us to talk about him as an artistic phenomenon, as something authentic and original, which has already come to light and begun glittering fantastically.

2. Can one "explain" an artist? Doesn't the creative spirit blow wherever and however it wishes? I think, however, that one not only can but must knock at the promising door and inquisitively seek keys to it. To say that an artist is simply what he is, as he is "made," is to say nothing. Perhaps even the genius of Dostoevskii's psychologism is related causally to that minute he experienced on the gallows.

The attempt of a "literary" explanation does not diminish the artist. On the contrary, his artistic merits are diminished when he himself is so "anecdotal" that such an explanation is superfluous. One can explain Chagall in a literary manner, but he himself is not a storyteller, not an illustrator, but first of all *a painter*.

Chagall was born a Jew, grew up in a Lithuanian province, matured in Paris. Those are three biographical moments we can account for in such a seemingly irregular phenomenon as Chagall's drolleries. Let us dwell on each of them.

Much that would seem "strange" in another perspective is explained by Chagall's national Semitic origin. I don't mean simply the proximate meaning of this origin, not just that Chagall grew up in a Jewish milieu. Marc Antokolskii, to the end of his life, never learned to express himself correctly in Russian; nevertheless Stasov Stasov — the major Russian critic who originated the interest in and collection of Jewish folk art — was utterly justified, specifically *à propos* Antokolskii, in regretting the lack of a national element in the work of "Europeanized" Jews. Stasov wrote, "How much they could have presented to the rest of the world: original melodies, unique rhythms, characteristic expressions, and pristine tones of the soul!" Isaac Levitan had a lot of soft Jewish melancholy, but essentially represented a different strain of the Semitic soul — its ability to transform, to resonate with its surroundings: in Levitan's landscapes, the objective melancholy of Russian nature, sung in the poetry of Tiuchev and Balmont, found its highest affirmation. Similarly, we can call Israels and Pissarro Jewish artists only insofar as the former sounded a note of sorrowful intimacy; and in the plein air of the latter, there nestled something soulful, unlike the positive impassivity of his fellow Impressionists. But this "soulfulness" is in any case not a primary but a secondary phenomenon of the Jewish soul. This sadness is acquired historically, yet not it, but the joy of the *Song of Songs*, lies at the source of Jewish culture. However, could one talk in general about a national substance of the Jews in the sphere of art? Isn't it well known that there is no Jewish art because the biblical religion forbade the creation of "graven images," and the historical conditions of an ever-worrying life could not be conducive to the flourishing and consolidation of beauty? But first of all, as Stasov once observed, the accepted view of Jewish art as an empty place does not correspond with reality. From Stasov's time on, the collection and study of Jewish antiques has been well advanced and it has become clear that, if the creative talents of biblical artists did not materialize or did not survive to our day in the domain of grand art, they did find their application in small art — in synagogue art and domestic utensils, in embroideries of the curtains and coverings of Torah scrolls, in golden, silver, wooden, filigree, and enamel objects, in miniature manuscripts. Religion forbade the representation of man — the artists depicted domestic animals (beginning with the frieze of the palace of Hyrkanos). Religion forbade the convex depiction of animals to avoid the temptation of idolatry — the artists painted them in colors or concave. It was precisely in the flora and fauna ornaments that the decorative talents of Jewish art were expressed — decorative because another, three-dimensional, relation to the world was forbidden. Hence, its supernatural character, fully corresponding to the metaphysics that grew from the biblical consciousness. On the other hand, Jewish art had to develop abilities to transform alien beauty: nomadic in its history, it absorbed elements of Phoenician, Assyrian, Hellenistic, and Arabic culture. Hence its "national" weakness and racial, ancient refinement.

In this sense, Bakst's art is undoubtedly "national." Decorative in its nature, eclectic, and penetrating all cultures. I remember what Bakst told me, "I always set myself the goal of conveying the music of what is depicted (*l'ambience de l'oeuvre*), having liberated myself from the bounds of archeology and chronology of mundane life." This colorful-musical empathy for the depicted epoch is first of all a sensuous perception, perception-as-assimilation — not archeologically, but with its sensibility, Eastern-spicy in its coloring and classically refined in its linear content — it is the product of some ancient, millennia-old preparation, perhaps a reflection of that Hellenistic Judaism that covered the Jerusalem of Herod's time in glorious garb of the beauties of Japheth. In his beautiful essay, "*Terror antiquus*," Viacheslav Ivanov observed this *ancient memory* in Bakst's mien, though he glossed over his racial antiquity.

The same, it seems, should be said about Chagall. No matter how young he is, the heritage of the ages weighs on him. Just that: "weighs"; the excessive weight of this burden explains his hypertrophical nervousness. This does not in the least contradict Chagall's childishness, which I mentioned at the beginning of this essay: when a child paints eyes not in profile but *en face*, he repeats an ancient experience of archaic wisdom. And isn't a wunderkind just this spontaneous and mysterious manifestation of an alien experience, accumulated by inheritance, that dwells in him and plays with his childish fingers? Every one of us is farsighted and fantasizes in sleep; but in the sober morning, we catch at the escaping dream in vain! Chagall's art is of the night: he knows how to remember dreams; and in the dreams the present is entangled with the past.

The roots of Chagall's painting go into distant depths and its buds are swathed (and poisoned) by the present. In his pointed huts and even in the swirling clouds there are echoes of Egyptian pyramids; in his palette, which I earlier mentioned as influenced by the Russian *lubok*, there is something more ancient and stronger than the *lubok* — some exotic colorfulness, as if the gamut of antimony, scarlet, fresh flowers, and even the very texture of his painting seems to be color-dense, cosmetically sensitive. In his paintings, there is no Man, forbidden image, or the likeness of God (he does not paint individual portraits), but there are people and animals. People — poor, oppressed by Orthodox commandments, apochryphal fears, stringent religious observance. Animals — meek, sentimental, like gazelles, or, on the contrary, with the look of a predator. Like the pig muzzles in Gogol', curious "muzzles" of bulls and calves peep into his interiors, and then appear as demonic symbols of the sinful temptation that led Aaron to cast an idol of the golden calf at Mt. Sinai. There is something erotic from Sodom, reminiscent of Bosch and Goya, in those Chagallian animal faces.

Chagall's fantastics is saturated with the fears and superstitions of Lithuanian Jewry, who experienced the horrors of Chmielnitskii's pogroms and the Polish-Russian wars, and lives with the prayer-mysticism of Hasidism. Much in its fantastics is dark and enigmatic for me, as in the Kabbala. But I feel in it, in those homeless and flying people, a burning thirst for the mysterious, a tortured renunciation of the life of the contemporary ghetto, "rancid, swampy, and dirty" (Bialik). Of course, the roots of Jewish mysticism go back to the depth of Eastern religion, but it flourished along with the persecutions of Judaism — in the discrepancy between the bitter reality and the flights of dreaming. In Wyspianski's tragedy *Wesele* (*The Wedding*), it is not the funny invitation of a healthy girl, but the magic oath of the darkly exalted Rachel, daughter of the innkeeper, that summons the ghosts to the wedding. She came to the wedding precisely because she sensed the mysticism of the events in this nuptial "singing hut." *Ach ta chata rozspiewana*! (Oh, this singing hut!) she says to the poet and is the first to throw out the window the invitation of the

autumn night, calling "everybody who suffers, who is tortured by fear, whose spirit strives toward freedom" to appear at the wedding. Because Rachel's soul, fettered by the mundane life of the inn, in her passionate ecstasy longs for a shining miracle.

This black night, the night of oaths and miracles, peers through the window of Chagall's study *The Clock*. The heavy pendulum counts the centuries-minutes of monotonous life, and tiny cumbersome figures seek something in the uncanny nocturnal void. . . .

In another study, two Jews, an old man and a boy, sit at a table dreaming in the rainbow, green-orange circle of a lamp. The cheap lamp, smoking like ancient incense, is flaming with the gold of a fire (in which the biblical Jews saw the emanation of God), and the gaze of the Jewish boy, drawn to it, is enflamed ecstatically: perhaps he sees the redeemer messiah, the promised land. . . . Chagall's work has neither literariness nor "civil grief," but does have some ardent and sorrowful *thirst for myth*.

3. But Chagall's fantastics would not be national if it cut off its ties with its soil, the mundane life. There is in it the same note of strong realism approaching the grotesque, and abandoned irony approaching self-mockery, that had to lurk in the Jewish soul as a natural self-defense of life, as the instinct of historical self-preservation. Medieval miniatures of Jewish artists are full of humorous grotesques; humor fills the parables, fables, proverbs even now inseparable from Jewish speech. In Bialik's poem describing the passionate waiting for the Messiah, he didn't forget the details of the coarsely realistic, clumsily funny life.

That is not the way the Poles in Wyspianski's play wait for the galloping of the Archangel. Waiting for centuries in vain did not teach the Jews to combine humor with the pathos of tragedy. The eternal wanderer, Ahasverus, whom Chagall liked to depict wandering over the blue cupolas and roofs of a Russian province, saw so much in his historical age and got so used to everything that nothing will crush his eternal passage:

Toujours le soleil se lève,
Toujours, toujours
Tourne la terre où moi je cours
Toujours, toujours.
— Béranger, *Le juif errant*

This is the world irony, I would say, and the premature old man's wisdom that erupts in Chagall. And everywhere, at the thresholds of houses, under snowflakes, and even on the roofs, his old fiddler, the eternal accompaniment of weddings and funerals, plays a melody, old as the world and monotonous, with a recitative. . . . I remember my amazement at a study of Chagall's showing a pregnant woman and a pregnant horse. "Is it my fault it always happens like that?" answered the artist. I also recall another work named "What Happens at Home" — a crowded Jewish interior where people eat, pray, and give birth, and above it all, as in a dream, phantoms of people are flying as if falling from the opened sky. Rozanov, who attached himself so one-sidedly to the "wedding" essence of the biblical soul, would have seen in this painting by Chagall a synthesis of "all of Israel," a bedroom of world history with its "womb" and "offspring bearing." But this is something else; this is the synthesis of the eternally living mundane life and the fantastics hovering above it. Chagall's interior where people eat, pray, and give birth and where, instead of a ceiling, there is a thick blue sky — it is the same "singing hut," the singing hut of the homeless-fantastic mundane life, by some miracle existing between sky and earth. . . .

Here we approach the very essence of Chagall's talent; he

sees the real world sharply and senses another world beyond it. In the cynical grotesques of Chagall there is the fairytale quality of capriccio; in the small provincial mundane life, he grasps some great being. . . . In this sense, Rozanov's retrospective formula "Zion, Babylon, and Vilna" is really applicable to Chagall if we substitute Vitebsk for Vilna. Chagall grew up in a crowded provincial ghetto and the images of mundane life pursue him obsessively, even when he describes the subtle and lyrical aloofness of the loving Pierrot and Colombine. But apparently there is some clearing in "provincialism," at *his* street, *his* home — into the boundless mystical. The dirty girl Aldonza is no less inspiring than the beautiful Dulcinea because she leaves room for a dream. Hoffmann, who grew up among philistines, apple-sellers, and the Tomcat Murr, was a bright storyteller; and Gogol' found fantastic curios in the stupidity of Russian mundane life. Chagall senses the supernatural, the mysterious, not only in Jewish life, but in mundane life in general. He is a student of Bakst and Dobuzhinskii, but in the *authenticity* of his provincial observations, no doubt, the student surpassed his teachers. For in Chagall's "provincialism" you don't find Dobuzhinskii's graphic precision, his metropolitan mockery of the provinces, but there is some spiritual participation in the described milieu, an artless naïveté of observing. Dobuzhinskii senses the mysticism of the big city, whereas in the province he is captivated by the funny and old-fashioned. Chagall senses the mysticism of the provincial even in the funny and contemporary. His province is a fairy tale, sentimental and cynical at the same time, boring and mediocre, and yet fantastically bright. He has holidays when dancing grass grows green in the sky and huts sway upside down, and funerals where the sky is covered with a black crepe.

His churches, mills, market-fair showbooths, many-colored hats are like children's toys; his clumsy little humans at weddings and funerals are like marionettes; and even inanimate objects, lamps and tables, seem in his paintings to be mysteriously alive. Chagall could realize on stage what the contemporary theater needs more than anything — *psychological decoration*, in which mundane life-style would seem real and inspired from within, like things in Remizov's world, through the prism of the girl Sasha, who is "three years old — three thousand, and perhaps three times three thousand" *(Maka)*. For Hoffmann was right: only *"childish poetic sensibility"* can introduce us into the true world. But, in Chagall's early work, there was an unhealthy childishness — a hypertrophy of "three thousand" years, and a tense worry of the contemporary Jewish Pale. As if some bloody, pogrom fears poisoned his childhood, and his fantastics often seemed like a feverish delirium of a sick child. . . .

4. Paris exerted a positive influence on Chagall. He remained himself, but acquired what he lacked — form. From childhood on, he had a sensibility for color and linear patterns, but in his images, there was none of the "plasticity" that brings images closer to semblances, which religion had forbidden since ancient times. In his works, there was no flesh, and his decorative mysticism was not sufficiently convincing. He was in danger of remaining a "wunderkind" in short pants. His stay in Paris brought him close to Aryan idolatry without depriving him of the national-eastern qualities (color and ornament); it made his work more condensed by acquiring a sense for *volume*. The stone-gray landscape of Paris taught him to feel the borders of objects to a much greater extent than the crooked walls of the provincial, colorful houses.

Chagall passed through the school of Cubism, but he did just that: he passed through it without getting fossilized spiritually as did many others; for him, form didn't become a

sovereign fetish. A good example of this influence is the outstanding study *The Sweeper* — a hard, metal-formed figure among heavily swirling provincial dust. Only now, having seen Cézanne and El Greco, was Chagall able to paint such architecturally ornamented, compositionally solid, and truly monumental biblical images as his dour religious Jew in a black-and-white tallis, resembling a biblical prophet, or some other artisan on the background of a pyramid of heaped-up huts.

But this, of course, doesn't mean that Chagall began painting à la Cézanne or Picasso — his mode of observation emerged from the Paris crucible with all its erstwhile originality. The black-and-white harmony of *The Praying Jew* perhaps reflected the beauty of black-and-white velvet of the synagogue seen in childhood. The influence of Paris was manifest precisely when Chagall returned to his home province. He painted the same motifs that had earlier captivated him, only now they reflected not just a "childish poetic sensibility," but also the mastery of a mature artist. In the blue domed temple and little houses covered with snow of his *Eternal Jew* there is a beautiful, sharp hewing of surfaces. The dark, dirty smocks of his Jews became formed and articulated in hard, sculpted folds with rusty blue shades. Without losing any of its mysticism, the whole Chagallian world became materially tangible: Chagall learned to see dreams while awake, in the middle of the sober day.

But his return to his homeland also brought some humility to his observation, softened his satirical edginess and screaming colorfulness. Such are his Vitebsk sketches of 1914. In those provincial streets, under a somber gray sky, with the heaped-up wooden houses, delicately puffed-up trees, naïve shop signs, and poor thin horses, you no longer hear the anguished scream. You sense in them some subdued, humble love. His *Barbershop* is veiled in calm — one of the best interiors I have seen in exhibitions of recent years, and I.A. Morosov did well to buy it — a provincial barbershop filled with a meek sun, dusty air, and the pitiful smile of cheap wallpaper. . . .

The ennobling of Chagall's colors was especially reflected in the sketches of Vitebsk women. Here is a woman in a yellowish coat, pale pink skirt, against the background of a gray wall and black rags; from this coarse and poor piece of life, Chagall created a refined "legend" of cool harmony. And here is a woman ironing with a black ornamented iron, among the decorations of the wallpaper and the green-scarlet curtain — a work of subtle Degas-like beauty. The stamp of a master lies on many other studies — soldiers with bread, painted with an amazing confidence, guitarists substituting for the former fiddlers, and even on the series of provincial Pierrots and Columbines. Somebody said that you can recognize a colorist in the gray tone, indeed Chagall's gray-black gamuts testify to his coloristic taste.

Chagall remained the same decorator and ornamentalist his race made him. But his work began to liberate itself from the flood; his people stopped flying in the rooms. In reality itself, in the truth of three dimensions, he began to guess the mystical life of colors and lines. The young and homeless Ahasverus stood with both feet on the ground — wet, warm, fruitful. And though, as before, he is different in every painting, still this nestling to mother earth is a hopeful sign of Chagall's creative blossoming.

He has to preserve his Hoffmannesque "childish poetic sensibility," so rare in our adult, too adult, time, and his sharpness and fantastics. But he will finally have to overcome his nervousness, his anguish. When the legacy of "three thousand" years stops burdening him, and becomes instead his epical tradition, his wonderful art will become religiously pacified and luminous, and, therefore, also objectively valuable.

The New Yiddish Theater

The Jewish Theater Society and the Chamber Theater

Lev Levidov

This text and the two that follow were included in a programmatic brochure published by the Jewish Theater Society in Petrograd, in Yiddish, with the title The Yiddish Chamber Theater: On Its Opening in July 1919.

"Let there be light" — and the Yiddish Chamber Theater appeared in the white world. . . . Dreams came true, all our wishes were fulfilled.

I remember it was on November 9, 1916, that the Jewish Theater Society was opened. A joyful, festive day. The auditorium was packed, excited faces, solemn speeches, an enormous elation of the soul. A new society was born and it called aloud: "Come work for a Yiddish, national, painterly theater!" . . . The congratulations, the speeches, the telegrams flowed together, as in a chorus. . . .

Isn't it strange, frightening? Jews, who have contributed the best artists, who have given the most splendid flowers to the universal altar of art, don't have their own theater to speak Yiddish with them? . . . No! Such a theater must be. This is demanded by the honor and dignity of the Jewish people, this is demanded by our national culture. . . . The new Yiddish Theater Society promised to create such a theater, a theater for us. They swore to devote all their strength to carry out that assignment. And with excitement, with love, they set to work.

It was a hard time. The old regime lay dying and, as it died, as always, bloodthirsty and mercilessly, it persecuted the exhausted Jewish people.

A Yiddish theater. . . . What had borne such a name in the Jewish street was not a theater: the Yiddish actors had no right of sojourn, no place to rest; the Yiddish language was persecuted and derided; the surrogate theater that existed was not cultural and was benighted. The whole being of Yiddish theater was like a stupid, invented tale. . . .

Meetings of the new society began — raging, passionate, long. No one knew what they should begin to do. What to do first, how to build the new building? . . . Hadn't all previous attempts come to nothing? . . . There was no clay, no bricks for the building. . . . At the first meetings, the word was spoken for the first time: "A Yiddish studio," a Yiddish theater school. And that word was soon accepted, found a warm resonance in all hearts. Yes, we really should have one, we really should begin here. Three long meetings were devoted to the single question of whether to create a school-studio or a studio-school. . . . How many arguments were poured out, how much excitement. . . . They discussed programs, they prepared a repertoire, they listed the teachers and actors by name, they wrote estimates . . . and then . . . the Revolution blazed up, and the light of our work disappeared in the glow of Revolutionary sun. A series of meetings and assemblies began, political arguments took over. The issue of the theater was left by the wayside. In vain did some try to go back to work — no one thought about theater any longer. The convention of Yiddish actors in Moscow did no more than force some to think again about beginning the halted work. That was hard to do. The political sea was too flamboyant, the world order had moved too much for people calmly to be able to begin again to build the national, cultural life. But it seems that culture is stronger than the transient phenomena of life. New times came, new songs, new faces. And among the new, also old and good friends. Why not? . . . Welcome. . . . Let us now begin our work for the community again. The thought has again appeared that excited us and made us all happy. Out of the chaos, our idea is born again, the idea of the studio. The studio is our own child, our only child, the holy dream that was dreamed by the Yiddish Theater Society. And now the dream is realized. The studio began to live, not only in words, but in action. And it lives, and works, and gets out into the wide world. The Yiddish Chamber Theater is yet a second step from our studio. And the current performances of the Yiddish Chamber Theater are the beginning of a new period, of a new life in the Yiddish theater. What kind of spectacles these will be we shall see later — we shall see what they will give the Jewish people. But, on the other hand, we see here young, capable people, who love with body and soul their theater, their language, the idea of our own national theater, and they work hard, very hard. And that says everything.

The new word has already been said, the new word has been turned into new action. . . . New Theater, you have our best wishes. The Jewish Theater Society sends you its blessing.

Lev Levidov
Chairman of the Jewish Theater Society

Our Goals and Objectives *Aleksei Granovskii*

A hundred and fifty days ago, we opened the doors of our studio and beckoned to those who wanted to work and lend a hand to build the Yiddish theater.

A hundred and fifty days — in such a short time, one normally cannot speak of achievements and realization.

And if, today, we raise the curtain, we won't and can't say: See, this is what we have accomplished. No, we just want to say: Look, this is the path we want to take.

Do not be concerned about the technical roughness of our first performances. We are still young: we have been alive for only five months. . . . We invited no professional artists, no experienced stage workers; not only did we not invite them, we didn't let them in, because more than anything we hate in art the artisan smugness of the "professionals," their artisan approach to "play" and "performance," their inability to abandon themselves to the joy of creation.

On our path we took along no artisans; but we ourselves, obviously, had no time in 150 days to become masters. And what we show you, raising our theater curtain for the first time, is just a vague hint of the path we tread.

Yiddish theater. . . . It never existed, and the mess that dominated the Yiddish stage was an eternal reminder to build the Yiddish theater! And our task, our goal, is to create something we never had and always strove for — the Yiddish theater.

We do not agree with those who assume that Yiddish theater has its own special laws, must feed on a specific repertoire, and must not depart from daily life, or, what is called in Russian, *byt*.

We say: Yiddish theater is first of all a theater in general, a temple of shining art and joyous creation — a temple where the prayer is chanted in the Yiddish language. We say: the tasks of world theater serve us as the tasks of our theater, and only language distinguishes us from others.

How and what will our theater be? What gods will it serve?

We cannot answer these questions. We don't know our gods. . . . We seek them. . . .

Seeking — this is the word we put at the head of our program. . . . We shall seek roads for the actors, as for the director, the painter, and the playwright.

We shall not stand still for a moment. And, perhaps, in seeking a path, we will have to stray, perhaps we will make gods for ourselves whom we will later topple from their thrones. . . .

Perhaps. . . . But one thing will serve as our justification — our will to find the right path to the true gods.

I have the great honor to be a leader of the first Yiddish theater. And today, with the serious feeling of the responsibility I assumed, opening the doors of the theater to the general audience for the first time, I beg everyone who has come to our little lights to transfer the whole weight of criticism and carping to us, the leaders, and not to touch the studio workers — because none of them thinks he is ripe enough to appear before your observing and serious eyes, for each of them treats reverently the task he has set himself — to become an actor of the Yiddish theater. And if, today, they stand face to face with you, it is only because they fulfill the disciplinary requirements of their leaders.

We found it necessary to open our doors so early to the general audience in order to proclaim to everyone, to all who cherish Jewish art, Jewish culture, Jewish theater; to all who are willing to take pains, seek, struggle and achieve: "Come to us!"

Using the kind proposal of the Yiddish Theater Society to write a few lines for the opening of the Yiddish theater, I cannot refrain from expressing my profound gratitude to all my colleagues in our work, for finding a way to devote themselves entirely to the work, for their extraordinary attitude toward the goals and objectives of our studio, for their ability to forget personal interests in the name and for the sake of the common work.

Aleksei Granovskii
Artistic Director of the Yiddish Chamber Theater

The Past and the Future of Yiddish Theater
M. Rivesman

The sad, almost hopeless situation of Yiddish theater is known to everyone who was ever more or less interested in it. We can say that in no area of Jewish art has the Jewish people been so frozen as in the area of theater art. Before our eyes lies a desert with no hint of an oasis. In that desert, no Moses ever appeared, no Pillar of Fire ever arose to eject even for a moment the darkness, the chaos of Yiddish theater. And saddest of all is that those who strayed in the gloomy and broad desert, the Yiddish actors, could not say, "We want to return to Egypt to the fleshpot." . . . No! The Yiddish actor never had a good, satiated day; never has his pharoah, his bitter lot, shown him a ray of happiness.

If we want to find out why it happened, if we want to ascertain the reasons for the harsh, almost fatal, illness, to investigate the source of this poverty and, let us say it openly, this shameful weakness of Yiddish theater art, we have to admit that the whole responsibility falls on the cultural elements of the Jewish people.

Until the 1870s, no one even knew or talked about a Yiddish theater. The *Haskala* people with their conspicuous tendency to quote the "Holy Tongue," on the one hand, and the assimilationist elements of the Jewish people, on the other, were both hostile to the so-called "jargon," and contemptuously put a black seal on the "mother tongue," called it "maidservant." And only such true friends of the Jew as Sh. Abramovich [Mendele Moykher Sforim] had the boldness and courage to write in Yiddish.

If the Yiddish language was a maidservant, the Yiddish theater was her brother. Forty years passed and throughout that long period, the Yiddish language triumphantly showed it was not a maidservant at all, though it does faithfully and honestly serve the Jewish people. Mendele Moykher Sforim, Sholem Aleichem, Peretz, Sholem Asch, Frug, Morris Rosenfeld, Yehoash — such names than can adorn the finest European literature, and they have indeed crowned the "jargon" with an enduring crown studded with the most precious diamonds. And still the Yiddish stage remained poor, neglected and debased, morally and artistically downtrodden, almost as forty years ago.

The Jewish intelligentsia, the Jewish art patrons showed no sign of attention to Yiddish theater. A sickly weakling, it was born in southern Russia forty years ago, and has remained anemic and weak to this day. The pioneer of Yiddish theater, Avrom Goldfaden, may have been cultural and talented, to a certain extent; but he had absolutely no idea of theater art in the European sense of the word. With no plan, no view toward the future of Yiddish theater art, he laid the first weak stone for the Yiddish theater building, and the material, the bricks he took for this building were so weak the building was shaky from the very first day. Its architecture was far from an aesthetic taste, from what is called art. The first Yiddish actors were ignorant artisans, often people who left their workshops looking for an easier piece of bread, mostly promiscuous young people for whom acting on the stage was the same as a "Purim-shpil." With no literary taste, no sign of intellectual development, they played, sang, and danced, and were happy when the rich contractors in Romania burst out laughing at their "Purim-shpil" barbs. Today a lover, the next day a "Kuni-Lemel" [shlemiel], tomorrow a witch, the Yiddish actors, as it were, did not feel their shame and "thundered" — as they put it — in the same manner wherever the police allowed them. The Jewish cultural elements stood at a distance, criticized, mocked, but did not dip a finger in cold water to remove all ugliness and clumsiness from the Yiddish theater. Chaos reigned: you will find no art, no direction on the Yiddish stage. And if you recall such talented Yiddish actors as, for example, Kaminskaya, Edelman, Zhelyazo, Libert, and others, you must admit with deep grief and despair that those talented actors, too, were content with the heavy atmosphere prevailing on the Yiddish stage; that they, too, never protested the contemptuous order, never strove to progress; and for that very reason, they regressed. Their god was Gordin, to him they bowed and knelt and brought offerings. But those offerings had no sweet smell of art either, for the altar, the Yiddish stage, remained dirty, desecrated by ignorance and frivolity.

Yes, there were moments when rays seemed to appear, which were supposed to illuminate the darkness of Yiddish theater art, the mundane dusk in which it was covered like a mourner: the immortal Peretz wanted to be Samson and rip the chain binding Yiddish theater art. He traveled through cities and towns, screamed "Save us!," rattled an alms box inscribed with the terrible words, "Charity saves from death." But it didn't help. "Kuni-Lemel" and the Witch Yakhne screamed louder, the Jewish intelligentsia didn't respond, the portly Jewish patron carefully hid his wallet, and the Yiddish stage remained a dirty, promiscuous maidservant, laughing wildly, dancing, making ugly grimaces, here, in Russia, and overseas — in America. The same lot fell to the poor, sickly, and talented Peretz Hirshbeyn, who tried to start a new page in the Book of Lamentations of the Yiddish theater. Neglected, rejected, despairing, filled with grief and rage, he had to fall like a scorned Don Quixote and buried all his hopes. Swindlers, speculators, dead souls, good-for-nothings, ignoramuses governed the Yiddish stage, and *Holy Sabbath* gave way to the play *To Be a Jew*; *The Jewish Core* irritated along with *The Soul of My People* and other trash.

And only a year ago a mournful shout was heard: "How long?" Till when will the immortal "Kuni-Lemel" and the screaming "Witch Yakhne" dominate? The shout was issued by the newborn Yiddish Theater Society.

Of course, from shouting to doing is a long way. We must however admit that the shout resonated among a small group of people, and the "dry bones" of the Yiddish theater art called the attention of several social activists. The positive result was that, for the first time, not a dilettante but a professional, A. M. Azarkh [Granovskii], became interested in the Yiddish theater. He gave a lecture to the Drama Section, where he developed a plan to create a theater studio, modeled on European theater studios. With a courageous energy, he strove to realize his plan, and — let there be light — the doors of the Yiddish theater were opened.

The first Yiddish theater studio set serious objectives for itself. It encountered great difficulties on its path. It experienced grave doubts, moments of groping and of despair. But it has come to life — it demands existence. It wants to produce the kernel from which a normal Yiddish theater, Yiddish theater art in a European sense, will develop. It wants the future Yiddish actor to be first of all a true professional, to respect the art he wants to serve. It wants the Yiddish stage to become a "Holy Place," the Yiddish actor to feel responsibility for his work; though a son of his people, he will, at the same time, be a faithful son of art in the highest and finest sense of the word. It wants the most talented Yiddish writers to create for the Yiddish stage, aware that their work will not be profaned, that the Yiddish actor and the Yiddish audience will respect the place that holds up a mirror to Jewish life. It wants to refresh the dirty, moldy Yiddish repertoire and illuminate it with masterful translations and truly literary, original dramatic works. In short — it strives, and the striving is, in itself, a great achievement. The will to create something better and more serious will be its advocate; the call, the waking must

attract the attention of the best Jewish cultural forces.

We believe we are standing on the threshhold of a new Yiddish theatrical age. We believe the revolution that wants to destroy the old, sick building of the former Yiddish theater will bring its good fruits. We believe the activity of the young Yiddish "Chamber Theater" will be treated not with disparaging criticism, a suspicious smile, a shrug — but with empathy, with seriousness of word and deed. We believe those who will criticize will honestly admit that every beginning is hard, that only he who does nothing makes no mistakes.

The situation of Yiddish theater today is harsh and bitter. But even harsher are the conditions, the hostile atmosphere in which one has to work, which can be defined as "Plenty of critics and few doers." . . .

So come, writers, experienced professionals, musicians, painters! Answer our call and courageously help build a beautiful, strong, and truly Yiddish-European theater building! Don't stand aside, bring bricks and clay — and let the language of the builders not be confounded. Let us understand and empathize with each other. Let us strive to the sun with the tower we are building, and let us remember that only in unity, in a united striving and will, lies the future of the new Yiddish theater.

M. Rivesman
Literary Director of the Yiddish Chamber Theater

The Historical Path of the Yiddish Theater

Abram Efros

From "Before the Opening Curtain: On the Opening of the Season in the Yiddish Theater" (in Russian). In Teatr i muzyka *(Theater and music), Moscow, no. 9 (1922), pp. 110–11. After leaving the theater for several months, Efros wrote this article à propos the dress rehearsals for Granovskii's staging of Goldfaden's* The Sorceress. *The first part of the article is omitted.*

. . . I sat in the empty hall at night, not used to being a stranger, watching Granovskii knock on the bannister, interrupting the rehearsal and changing the complex pattern of movement for the hundredth time; the mass body of the troupe, when stopped, scatters immediately, softens, rearranges itself on the stage, only to reassemble obediently, fuse, freeze, and dart ahead — pattering, leaping, and somersaulting — over the surfaces, roofs, ladders of a fantastic Jewish *shtetl*, invented and populated by the generous talent of [the artist Isaak] Rabinovich. Sensing in myself a growing joy in this unfolding "Jewish game," in these sayings, songs, purely national intonations that suddenly became theatrical, in the beautiful subtlety with which Mikhoels serves them up, in the freshness of young Zuskin's talent (an undoubted discovery of the theater), I felt clearly one thing which I had never felt before and which suddenly explained to me why — in spite of all our disagreements and distancing, in spite of my skepticism and negation, the failures, clumsiness, artificiality, unjustified elements in the performances — I nevertheless am drawn, I would say hypnotically, to the stream of GOSEKT, as to the riverbed of the imperative, unavoidable, historically unique path of the Yiddish theater.

Oh, that Yiddish theater! — Without a foundation or a roof, without borders to its domain or any blueprint! A theater that is its own grandfather, father, and son. A theater that has not yet any past, present, or future, and that must create for itself a past, a present, and a future. A theater that has to live simultaneously in three dimensions of time. A theater with no tradition, but which has to invent for itself a historical line; a theater without a present, but that has to be at the cutting edge of contemporary theater art; a theater without perspectives, but that has to mold the form of what is to come. That is why we have no choice here. Here we cannot prefer one thing to another. Here talk about trends is more negligible than anywhere else. Here you can either be in the center of the Jewish "stage" — or be entirely outside it. Coexistence is impossible here; there is room here for only one thing, and one yardstick: what stands before us? A theater of all dimensions of time? "A theater of three times," creating of its "now" both a forward and a backward? Speaking simultaneously with the triple voice of history, reality, and future? If so, then *no matter what it is* in its composition, quality, magnitude, it is the center, the regulator, the lawgiver; it is history, no matter how little the tribal philistine recognizes it, no matter what fashionable or approachable admirers it has gained for itself on the side, and no matter where it may be drawn by alien pointing fingers.

In its national sphere, the Yiddish Chamber Theater is such a historical center, dominating the situation, directing the evolution, although alongside it there is the very good HaBima and the very bad Brandesco or Zhitomirskii (I have little orientation in those pseudonyms, for which I apologize). And though in HaBima, my dear fellow tribalists are so enthusiastic they come down with hiccups, and in Brandesco-Zhitomirskii they fill the auditorium till they faint, nevertheless, in spite of it all, both HaBima and Brandesco and many other things around are a mere mirage, fiction, while the Chamber Theater is a historical reality.

In this sense, its role is like Chagall's role in plastic art, in spite of the absolute polarity of artistic temperaments, Chagall the ecstatic and Granovskii the intellectual. And so not in vain did Chagall enter the stage for the first time in the Yiddish theater, not in vain did he spread his theatrical forms precisely from this stage. These forms, like everything else in his art, became kinds of obligatory models essentially influencing the formation of characters in *The Sorceress* of Rabinovich, who created brilliant "variations on Chagallian themes" in his costumes.

Looking back, we may say that Chagall is "an artist of three times," as GOSEKT is "a theater of three times." Chagall, too, has absorbed in his art the traditions of the national past, the modernism of today, and the buds of the future. He drew threads back, in depth, to the past — close to the rooted, authentic, living faces of old Jewish life — and brought them to his paintings with all their living and dead inventory, with all their long coattails and long beards, canonicity and peculiarity, everydayness and fantasy, as GOSEKT brought them in *The Sorceress* onto the theatrical boards. But in the language of his paintings, Chagall is so contemporary that he marches in the front row of the European masters of leftist art, while his relation to the future is determined by the stamp he has placed on a huge contingent of young artists, including many who are now eager to dissociate themselves from him.

Chagall's so-called "Vitebsk period" was in this sense crucial for the work of the young generation of Jewish artists. For the first time on the Yiddish stage, Granovskii's *Sorceress* succeeded in finding adequate theatrical solutions for the same age-old life in the forms of contemporary leftist art, and, with that precision that sets landmarks for the future, for the work to come. The solutions of *The Sorceress* have general significance and it seems that *The Sorceress* is the first step of a "Vitebsk period" in the emergence of the Yiddish Chamber Theater as an important and influential force.

Our Theater *Aleksei Granovskii*

Published, in Yiddish, in Literarishe Bleter, *Warsaw, vol. 5, no. 17 (April 27, 1928).*

In 1919, I was given the task of creating a Yiddish theater school; the school was opened the same year in Leningrad, and then numbered thirty-some students. In 1920, the first graduation and simultaneously the first theater performance took place. Since we felt it necessary, considering our teaching methods, to produce a unified whole, we doubted if we should accept students from other dramatic schools or actors from different theaters. All the human material of our theater came to us as "raw material," and only after they had been processed in our workshops were they to appear on our stage. For us, the foundation of artistic education was that the actor himself must be in control of his own emotional apparatus; he then trains his own capabilities, his body, and all his feelings to be subordinate to his will, his controlling reason, and that precise rhythm on which we build all our productions. In other words, the basis of artistic education is to train the actor's capability to become a part of the organic whole of the performance.

I consider stage art an independent and sovereign domain. Therefore, all elements constituting a finished performance — the man, the script, the music, the sets, and the light — must be subordinate to a single, steadfast thought and the completed score of the production. I don't mean that I want to bind the actor and deprive him of the possibility of being creative — on the contrary, he is given the greatest opportunity to express himself. But since he is educated in the sharp consciousness of our task and feels that he is a responsible part of a monolithic whole, he is capable of subordinating himself to the primary task and of being creative within its framework.

For us, dramatic literature is also only one element of a harmonious whole and does not retain any independent meaning. We calculate precisely (or strive to) the rule-governed mutual relationships of all elements, and subordinate them to the main thought that is our sole task and sole purpose. When I approach the production of a work, my major task is to show the spectator how we perceive and understand this work, the whole atmosphere and the whole world in which our heroes live. Therefore, it is fully justified, when the author does not show his milieu (as for example, in Jules Romain's *Truadec*), that I create the milieu, that is, I create variations on Romain's theme. I do it because I believe that a work for the stage that does not show the "air" in which the acting figures live is superfluous and does not exist at all for the theater.

For the performances I select all kinds of dramatic means of expression (drama, comedy, operetta) according to what each stage moment foregrounds. Practically, we carry out this task in the following manner: when we agree on a specific play, I propose the script on the basis of which I create, together with my dramaturgical assistants, the text for the actor. Then I make a sketch of the actor's score, and everyone who participates in the staging — the composer, the painter, the technician — gets his precisely drawn task. As for the rehearsals, the work is conducted in the following manner: first of all, the actor has to master the text and the melodies, he must perceive the main rhythm of the performance; and only then is he set in motion. On average, every play is rehearsed 150 times, but never more than 250. That depends on how complicated the task is and how fast the actors master the image and the relations between all the parts.

Such are the principles according to which we work and on which the theater has been built for the last ten years; and with this theater, we are launching a lengthy worldwide tour.

Berlin

My Work in the Moscow Yiddish Chamber Theater
Marc Chagall

Published, in Yiddish, in Di Yidishe Velt: Monthly for Literature, Criticism, Art, and Culture, *Vilna (Kletskin), no. 2 (May 1928). A shorter version of this chapter, translated from a translation, can be found in Chagall's* My Life.

"Here are the walls," said Efros, "do what you want with them." It was an apartment, run-down, its tenants had fled. "See, here we will have benches for the audience, and over there, the stage."

To tell you the truth, "over there," I didn't see anything but a vestige of a kitchen, and "here"?

I shouted, "Down with the old theater that smells of garlic and sweat! Long live . . . " And I dashed to the walls. On the ground lay sheets; workers and actors were crawling over them, through the renovated halls and corridors, among slivers, chisels, paints, sketches.

Torn tatters of the Civil War — ration cards, various "queue-numbers" — lay around. I too wallowed on the ground. At moments, I enjoyed lying like this. At home they lay the dead on the ground. Often, people lie at their heads and cry. I too love, finally, to lie on the ground, to whisper into it my sorrow, my prayer. . . .

I recalled my great-grandfather, who painted the synagogue in Mohilev, and I wept: why didn't he take me a hundred years ago at least as an apprentice? Isn't it a pity for him to lie in the Mohilev earth and be an advocate for me [in the World to Come]? Let him tell with what miracles he daubed with his brush in the shtetl Lyozne. Blow into me, my bearded grandfather, a few drops of Jewish truth!

To have a bite, I sent the janitor Ephraim for milk and bread. The milk is no milk, the bread is no bread. The milk has water and starch; the bread has oats and tobacco-colored straw. Maybe it is real milk, or maybe — fresh from a revolutionary cow. Maybe Ephraim poured water into the jar, the bastard, he mixed something in and served it to me. Maybe somebody's white blood. . . . I ate, drank, came to life. Ephraim, the representative of the workers and peasants, inspired me. If not for him, what would have happened? His nose, his poverty, his stupidity, his lice crawled from him to me — and back. He stood like this, smiling feverishly. He didn't know what to observe first, me or the paintings. Both of us looked ridiculous. Ephraim, where are you? Who will ever remember me? Maybe you are no more than a janitor, but sometimes by chance you stood at the box office and checked the tickets. Often I thought: they should have taken him on stage; didn't they take janitor Katz's wife? Her figure looked like a square yard of wet wood covered with snow. Carry the wood to the fifth floor and put it in your room. The water streams. . . . She screamed, protested during rehearsals like a pregnant mare. I don't wish on my enemies a glance at her breasts. Scary!

Right behind the door — Granovskii's office. Before the theater is done, there is little work. The room is crowded. He lies in bed, under the bed wood shavings, he planes his body. Those days he was sick.

"How is your health, Aleksei Mikhaylovich?"

So he lies and smiles or scowls or curses. Often acrid words, of the male or female gender, fell on me or on the first comer. I don't know if Granovskii smiles now, but just like Ephraim's milk, his futile smiles console me. True, sometimes, I felt like tickling him, but I never dared to ask, "Do you love me?"

I left Russia without it.

For a long time, I had dreamed of work in the theater. Back in 1911, Tugendhol'd wrote somewhere that my objects are alive. I could, he said, paint psychological sets. I thought about it. Indeed, in 1914, Tugenhol'd recommended to Tairov, the director of the Moscow Chamber Theater, that he invite me to paint Shakespeare's *Merry Wives of Windsor.* We met and parted in peace. The goblet was overflowing. Sitting in Vitebsk — commissaring away, planting art all over the province, multiplying student-enemies — I was overjoyed to get Granovskii's and Efros's invitation in 1918 to work in the newly opened Yiddish theater. Shall I introduce Efros to you? All of him legs. Neither noisy nor quiet, he is alive. Moving from right to left, up and down, always beaming with his eyeglasses and his beard, he is here and he is there, Efros is everywhere. We are bosom buddies and we see each other once every five years. I heard about Granovskii for the first time in Petrograd during the war. From time to time, as a pupil of Reinhardt, he produced spectacles with mass scenes. After Reinhardt's visit to Russia with *Oedipus Rex,* those mass scenes created a certain impression. At the same time, Granovskii produced spectacles using Jews of all kinds of professions whom he assembled from everywhere. They were the ones who later created the studio of the Yiddish theater.

Once I saw those plays, performed in Stanislavskii's realistic style. As I came to Moscow, I was agitated. I felt that, at least in the beginning, the love affair between me and Granovskii would not settle down so fast. I am a person who doubts everything under the sun, whereas Granovskii is sure of himself, and a bit ironic. But the main thing is that, so far, he is absolutely no Chagall.

They suggested I do the wall paintings and the first production for the opening of the theater. Wow, I thought, here is an opportunity to turn the old Yiddish theater upside down — the Realism, Naturalism, Psychologism, and the pasted-on beards. I set to work. I hoped that at least a few of the actors of the Yiddish Chamber Theater and of HaBima, where I was invited to do *The Dybbuk,* would absorb the new art and would abandon the old ways. I made a sketch. On one wall, I intended to give a general direction introducing the audience to the new Yiddish People's Theater. The other walls and the ceiling represented klezmers, a wedding jester, women dancers, a Torah scribe, and a couple of lovers hovering over the scene, not far from various foods, bagels and fruit, set tables, all painted on friezes. Facing them — the stage with the actors. The work was hard; my contact with the work was settling down. Granovskii apparently lived slowly through a process of transformation from Reinhardt and Stanislavskii to something else. In my presence, Granovskii seemed to hover in other worlds. Sometimes, it seemed to me that I was disturbing him. Was it true? I don't know why he did not confide in me. And I myself didn't dare to open serious discussions with him. The wall was breached by the actor Mikhoels, who was starving just like me. He would often come to me with bulging eyes and forehead, hair standing on end, a pug nose and thick lips — entirely majestic.

He follows my thought, he warns me, and with the sharp edges of his hands and body he tries to grasp. It is hard to forget him. He watched my work, he begged to let him take the sketches home, he wanted to get into them, to get used to them, to understand. Some time later, Mikhoels joyfully announced to me, "You know, I studied your sketches, I understood. I changed my role entirely. Everybody looks at me and cannot understand what happened."

I smiled. He smiled. Other actors quietly and carefully snuck up to me, to my canvases, began observing, finding out what kind of thing this is. Couldn't they also change? There was little material for costumes and decorations. The last day before the opening of the theater, they collected heaps of truly old, worn-out clothes for me. In the pockets, I found cigarette butts, dry bread crumbs. I painted the costumes fast. I couldn't

even get out into the hall that evening for the first performance. I was all smeared with paint. A few minutes before the curtain rose, I ran onto the stage to patch up the color of several costumes, for I couldn't stand the "Realism." And suddenly a clash: Granovskii hangs up a plain, real towel! I sigh and scream, "A plain towel?!"

"Who is the director here, me or you?" he answers.

Oh, my poor heart, oh sweet father!

I was invited to do the stage for *The Dybbuk* in HaBima. I didn't know what to do. Those two theaters were at war with each other. But I couldn't not go to HaBima, where the actors didn't act but prayed and, poor souls, still idolized Stanislavskii's theater.

If between me and Granovskii — as he himself put it — the love affair didn't work out, Vakhtangov (who had then directed only *The Cricket on the Hearth*) was a stranger to me. It will be very hard, I thought, to find a common language between the two of us. To an open declaration of love, I respond with love; but from hesitations and doubts, I walk away.

For example, in 1922, they invited me lovingly to Stanislavskii's second art theater to stage together with the director Diky Synge's *Playboy of the Western World.* . . .

I plunged into it body and soul, but the whole troupe declared a strike, "Incomprehensible."

Then they invited somebody else and the play was a flop. Isn't it true?

At the first rehearsal of *The Dybbuk* in HaBima, watching the troupe with Vakhtangov, I thought, "He is a Russian, a Georgian; we see each other for the first time. Embarrassed, we observe one another. Perhaps he sees in my eyes the chaos and confusion of the Orient. A hasty people, its art is incomprehensible, strange. . . . Why do I get upset, blush, and pierce him with my eyes?"

I will pour into him a drop of poison; later he will recall it with me or behind my back. Others will come after me, who will repeat my words and sighs in a more accessible, smoother and clearer way.

At the end, I ask Vakhtangov how he intends to conceive of *The Dybbuk.* He answers slowly that the only correct line is Stanislavskii's.

"I don't know," said I, "of such a direction for the reborn Yiddish theater." Our ways part.

And to Zemakh, "Even without me, you will stage my way. There is no other way." I went out into into the street.

Back home in the children's colony in Malakhovka, I remembered my last meeting with An-ski,[1] at a soirée in 1915 at "Kalashnikov's Stock Market." He shook his gray head, kissed me, and said, "I have a play, *The Dybbuk,* and you're the only one who can carry it out. I thought of you."

Ba'al-Makhshoves, who stood nearby, blazed agreement with his eyeglasses and nodded his head.

"So what shall I do? . . . What shall I do?"

Anyway, I was told that a year later Vakhtangov sat for many hours at my projects, when he prepared *The Dybbuk.* And they invited someone else, as Zemakh told me, to make projects à la Chagall. And at Granovskii's, I hear, they over-Chagalled twentyfold.

Thank God for that.

Malakhovka 1921 — Paris 1928

P .S. I just heard that the Muscovites are abroad. Regards to them!

1. An-ski (S. Rapoport, 1863–1920), scholar, folklorist, and writer, was author of the play *The Dybbuk.*

My First Meeting with Solomon Mikhoels

Marc Chagall

Published, in Yiddish, in Yidishe Kultur: Monthly of the Jewish World Culture Union, *New York, vol. 6, no. 1 (January 1944).*

My destiny brought me here to America; and, suddenly, after so many years, I see here my old friend Shloyme Mikhoels. He arrived with my new friend, the poet Itsik Fefer, bringing regards from our homeland.

Since you have asked me to write something about Mikhoels, who is now celebrating his twenty-fifth year in the Yiddish theater, I remember with pleasure my first meeting with him.

Those years when I first started working in the Yiddish theater rise up in my memory.

In my dreams . . . I transpose myself to my city. Thin young trees, bent, sighing as on a day of *Tashlikh*.

In my youth, I walked like this through streets searching. . . . For what?

Among my holidays, once upon a time, there was one great one: Sholem Aleichem came to read his writings in my city. I had no money for a ticket, but anyway I was angry at the small town guys who read Sholem Aleichem and laughed all the time just for the sake of laughing. I, on the contrary, didn't laugh so much and thought that Sholem Aleichem was a "Modernist" in art. Someday, I would show them.

Some twelve years later (around 1919), a Yiddish theater studio from Petrograd, with an unknown director, arrived in our city. The director surely came to our city because his wife was from Vitebsk. The "studio" was a conglomeration of young and old amateurs. After the performance, I walked around glumly in the lobby of the city theater accompanied by my old teacher, the artist Yehuda Pen, who teased me with his *misnaged* smile — you don't know why or wherefore. . . . Finally I ran into the director himself.

Aleksei Granovskii — tall, supple, blond. He looked a bit like a Christian. He would rarely open his mouth — maybe because of his bad teeth. He could speak with his mouth shut. His eyes smiled from an accidental, unknown pleasure that would alight on him like a fly. And he would look both at you and at somebody else on the side. . . .

"I really need you, Chagall!" he says suddenly. "You know, I have a play . . . just for you. . . ."

For quite a while, I had thought it was time for me to get into Yiddish theater. Something had to "burst," to open up in me. But why wasn't I drawn to Granovskii as to somebody else? To whom? What for? Meanwhile, my friend Efros called me from Moscow to come paint the walls of the new Yiddish theater and design the sets for the first production of the theater to be founded there.

I came to Moscow and found the producer and director Granovskii in bed. He was coquettishly playing sick and indulging himself in bed. He conducted conversations from his bed. I showed him the finished sketches I had brought from Vitebsk. As we talked, Mikhoels entered the room. Delicately, carefully. He said something very respectfully, listened attentively, and exited confidently, as the future theater soldier and general.

Granovskii would make short, smiling remarks, which would be snatched up by the actors all around like a treasure and later lapped up in the long corridors.

"You hear? — Granovskii said — You hear? — Granovskii laughs! Hush — Granovskii sleeps! A man sits in his room! He declares his love." . . .

But my "affair" with him — he said — somehow doesn't hold together . . . !

Why?

I really didn't have much luck with directors. Not with Vakhtangov, who at first empathized neither with my art nor with my sketches for *The Dybbuk* in HaBima, and yet later asked to make it à la Chagall without me; nor with Tairov, who was still sick with Constructivism; nor with the Second Studio of the Moscow Art Theater, which was still drowning in psychological realism. . . . All of them, as well as others, asked me to make sketches, and later got scared of them.

And here was Granovskii. Truly a seeker. He spoke only Russian in the Yiddish theater. He really did have talent, perhaps eclectic yet gracious; but he was straying on the paths of his German teacher Max Reinhardt with his theories of mass scenes, which were then in fashion. Granovskii searched gradually, not so much with the fervor of a Jewish soul, but as if through books. He wanted to liberate himself from the decorative German path, and kept looking for new Jewish forms, which began appearing here and there in the Jewish plastic world.

It fell to me to be the first painter in the new Yiddish theater, but Granovskii didn't talk to me and got away with just a smile; I with my "character" was also silent.

The rehearsals of Sholem Aleichem pieces, which were to open the new theater, were conducted on one side, and I was steeped in my work on the other side.

But I harbored a very special hope for the magical Mikhoels. He didn't get underfoot like the others, walking back and forth in the long corridors of the small theater, which had just been rebuilt for a private home (later it moved to a bigger house). Everywhere pieces of wood, old newspapers, boards, sticks, and other rags were lying around. One actor carried a ration of black bread and another carried a bottle of bluish milk mixed with water into his room. And I sat on the ladder, painting the murals. The janitor Ephraim, a young wild animal, would bring me my ration of bread and milk and meanwhile laugh his fill over my paintings. So I would sit like this on the ladder, painting the wall. I wanted to paint myself into it, you, my own cities and towns. My Bella would come to "console" me with the little angel — Idochka — hardly two feet high. She would wander around below and look at Papa above — it's too high for her. Meanwhile, Mama would go learn Yiddish performance from her teacher Mikhoels. From afar I would hear her voice, "Bells are ringing. . . ." [From a poem by Peretz Markish.] And I would sit and think about the new art in the new theater, with no pasted-on beards scaring me like ghosts. I would think about those Purim-players, about that beggar with the green face and the sack on his back where he hides a Siddur, a herring, a piece of bread, and now I would see him at night, in the moonlight with his beard swinging like a tree in the city park. I wanted to paint him and take him to the stage. . . .

When I let myself "think" like that, I was liable to lose my balance and fall from the ladder on top of my Idochka below. Silently I begged my distant dead relative — who, once upon a time painted, to his good fortune, the walls of a synagogue — to help me. I felt that, nearby, a young Jew was sitting and walking around — he could help me if he wanted to approach me first, open his mouth — perhaps he himself would become a different person. . . .

That was young Mikhoels — strong though short, thin but sturdy, practical and dreamy; his logic merged with feeling, his Yiddish language sounded as if it came from Yiddish books. He could help, he would pull himself out and pull other actors, even the director himself along.

Right at my first meeting with Mikhoels, I was amazed by that rare though still vague artistic striving and force, which one day will stumble onto logic and form, which — if you find them — take on various sounds, rhythms, and colors, although it all may look both illogical and unreal. Those are forms that break old artistic conventions and promise something important in life. . . .

I sat on the ladder in the auditorium for a long time surrounded by my murals and sketches for the Sholem Aleichem pieces.

I locked the doors. Only rarely did Granovskii himself come in to discuss art and theater, and the forthcoming production. Once Mikhoels approached me with his mincing steps and said in measured, clearly-veiled words, "Mark Zakharovich, lend me your sketches. I want to study them. We cannot continue like this — you here and we there, everyone separate!"

But indeed, I could sit like this for a long time, do my work, gather up my bundles and disappear.

Mikhoels's open and friendly approach was symbolic of a new type of Jewish man and artist at the beginning of the great Revolution.

Therefore, I cannot forget how, a few months later, I heard Mikhoels's long call from his distant room in the corridor, "Chagall, I un—der—stood! . . . Where are you? I understood. . . . "

And he came up to my ladder holding the sketches.

"See, Chagall!" With joy in his eyes, covered with a smile reaching to his feet, he stood and moved with Sholem Aleichem's text beaming from his mouth. There was no doubt: Mikhoels had found something, found the true nuance and rhythm — that is, the form, the content, the new spirit, the new actor. It was a new world.

I was happy and continued my work, which had to be finished, for soon the theater was to be opened. Jokingly, Granovskii said they would take me off the ladder and call two doctors to pacify me when they hung my big canvases on the walls.

I was waiting — what would happen? The rehearsals of Sholem Aleichem's pieces continued in the old style. The familiar psychological realism. I imagined that Mikhoels alone would stand out from the whole troupe, and the other actors along with Granovskii would be puzzled: what happened? they would ask themselves. How did Mikhoels suddenly break loose from the chain while we can't adapt to it? Once, I was sitting on my ladder, listening. I heard feet tramping on the other side of the wall. . . . Hands opened my door and all the actors suddenly entered the auditorium and said in chorus, "Chagall, Mikhoels has sent us to you. He has changed his role entirely. We asked him, 'What is this?' He says, 'I don't know, go to Chagall, he will explain.' So we came to you, tell us how and what to do, to be like Mikhoels." . . .

I listened to them and grew sad. I jokingly wanted to sick my painted animals on the walls on them; let the klezmers "scare" them with a sudden playing and let them go back. I was "ashamed" of myself — look, I had been hanging before their eyes for a long time; but when Mikhoels changed his art, they came to me. Isn't there a director?

I answered, "Mikhoels himself can explain a lot to you, much better than I can."

What kind of art is it — Mikhoels's art?

It is almost the same question that could have been asked in the past about the objectives and dreams of the new Jewish plastic art.

Goldfaden, Peretz, Sholem Aleichem, and others are for the actor what "nature" is for the artist.

For the artist does not copy nature, but creates it facing it. Thus, both the artist and the actor create a new kind of nature. And only this means to have "respect" for the playwright as for nature. Otherwise, the artist creates mere photography, copy illustration, and not art. And if, at a certain moment, the theater merged its soul with Jewish plastic art, it would come

to life, and show the world its soul. But if, however, the theater kept itself distant, it would remain "local," with its accidental actors' talents. I don't mean the accidental, "decorative" help of the invited artists. This is often a triviality.

It's not enough to speak about the history of Yiddish theater from the point of view of worn-out literary psychological plays for reading and roles confined to their time. Of course we had this and still do have a dozen fine and great Yiddish actors — born talents. Fortunately, I have seen some of them at different times. Just as the history of art has had several fine greater and lesser artists. Yet those who perceived and merged with the whole period in art have had a deeper significance. Just as, recently, the French trends in plastic art; and as, among us Jews, the classics of the new Yiddish literature which created style — so is the new Yiddish actor in the theater. In the same way, Mikhoels strove to create a new Yiddish actor in the new Yiddish theater and a new theater style. And when you discover inside yourself the important meaning of the technical material, you also see the whole human being inside you.

Thus Mikhoels opened the wide road on which he can deepen and broaden his theater art with his own power. Mikhoels is one of the rare happy people who arrived on such a road of art, understood it, and discovered himself.

Later I saw other actors of the Moscow Yiddish Theater, especially Zuskin, with a melody on his thick lips, walk the same road.

Later I saw the director Vakhtangov sitting in the auditorium before my murals and, like one set ablaze, leading the troupe of HaBima with Rowina and others in *The Dybbuk* on the same road, though earlier he had been opposed.

Studying art in such a way, Mikhoels grasped life. And, just as on the theater stage, so on the stage of life, he transferred an understanding and analysis of the problems of our life in that tragic and great time. For our time, too, is our material, we work and breathe with it in our art.

This shows the absurdity of the opinion that there is a "pure" art, art for art's sake. On the contrary, art that is ostensibly called "pure" is very often dirty.

And if Mikhoels, as he said, once learned from me, perhaps I must now learn from him.

Then I myself wouldn't have been drowned in my doubt as in a pot of paint that paints the Jewish face and soul in a hue of mystery and sadness.

Mikhoels and Chagall *Yosef Schein*
Published in Y. Schein, Around the Moscow Yiddish Theater *(in French). Paris: Les Editions Polyglottes, 1964.*

Mikhoels's success in the role of Menakhem-Mendel Yakenhoz was greatly due to the painter Marc Chagall. Mikhoels used to tell of this collaboration with a wise, good-natured smile, "On the day of the premiere, Chagall walked into my dressing room. After preparing his colors, he set to work. He divided my face into two parts. One he painted green, the other yellow (as they say, 'green and yellow' [pale, downcast]). Chagall lifted my right eyebrow two centimeters higher than the left. The wrinkles around my nose and lips spread all over my face. These wrinkle lines highlighted Menakhem-Mendel's tragic lot.

"I looked in the mirror and was convinced that the makeup created the dynamism and expressivity of the character. The artist continued working diligently. Suddenly his fingers remained hanging over my face with a question mark. Something bothered him. He put a finger to my eye, took it back, and taking several steps back, observed me and added regretfully, 'Oh, Solomon, Solomon, if you didn't have your right eye, I could have done so much.'"

Mikhoels laughed but soon became pensive and serious.

"My living eye, my Mikhoels eye, hindered Chagall from bringing Menakhem-Mendel's eye, which he saw and sensed so vividly. The reason apparently was in me."

The Artists of Granovskii's Theater *Abram Efros*
Excerpted from an essay originally published, in Russian, by Iskusstvo, Moscow, *vol. 4 (1928).*

I. The years of war and the years of revolution occurred at a period of crisis for the Russian theater. Its development in those fifteen years was not organic, but indeed, at times, paradoxical; secondary elements played a greater role in it than basic ones. Its history is one of scenic accessories rather than of theatrical art, a history of the external formation of the stage; in many ways, it is just a history of stage designers.

This is not contradicted at all by the fact that the Russian theater has now achieved a world name. In some European centers, it has even had a transforming influence. But should we console ourselves with the fact that the situation there was even worse? Western criticism, having recovered from the earlier excitement, now claims in revenge that we were only an exotic episode. As proof, they add that we were succeeded by a fashion for Negroes. This would have sounded devastating had we pronounced the word "Negroes" with the same accent. But you don't have to live through the Russian Revolution to give such words their true significance. For that, it is enough to be a hero of His Highness Vulgarity. We, however, are prepared to say this: Russian and Negro art were a fresh wind for the West.

This does not change anything in the internal processes of our theater. I could have described the striking aspect of their appearance as the blush of the crisis. In the beginning, Russian theater was in a fever of decorationism, the role of the artist made disproportionately large. I am not afraid to assert (as my professional memory reminds me) that the premieres of 1912–17 were impressive mostly for the triumphs of their design rather than their actors. Later, after the October upheaval, came the era of Futurism. This happened not because Russian Futurism was belated, as the innovations of Western culture were usually late penetrating Russia. This time, Europe was hasty and we were very complacent. But in 1917, due to one of the most brilliant paradoxes of the Revolution, the Futurists became the power in art. They were part of the new government, delegated to the domain of art. Incidentally, there was no equality in the use of time. The Futurists did not fill their five years. The rage of their abstractions, shifts, and breaks evoked a reaction as early as 1920, which soon assumed the character of a violent outburst of simplification. The theater was, in Tolstoi's words, attracted to "gruel." Even the nihilism about decorations now saw its hour of triumph, only appeared on the stage under another name — common in theatrical practice! Such is the "Constructivism" of Meierkhol'd and his group: The stage was shamelessly bare, with only cranes, ropes, traps, hatchways, back walls, workers. It was pretty cynical, and enough to become fashionable and infect the theaters with pandemonium. Though it was soon over, Russian theater emerged exhausted: its decorations are now withered and melancholy. There is an artist on stage, but in essence there isn't. He is hardly active and almost invisible. In the best case he imitates himself. He is a veteran member of the staff and not a leader of the theater as he was in that decade between 1910 and 1920. The artist has reverted to the status of non-entity, while the actor, the ensemble, the acting, again stand on the first plane. I would be willing to consider this a sign of healthy growth were I not afraid that today's indifference to the artist would deteriorate to apathy.

The artist, however, has his place in the scenic system of elements. It is not dominant, but it is not third-rate, and so our stage is still unbalanced. We now have much experience, but little tact. And in art, it seems that there is no greater sin. We have not recovered a sense of measure. The Russian stage of the period 1925–30 is still sick with disharmony.

II. Granovskii began building his theater in the heat of the Revolution. This is natural, for there is no time more favorable for both creators and adventurers. The year 1919 was terrible. The period of Military Communism was at the zenith of crisis. Lenin's strategic genius was already looking for a detour. The Revolution exploded all possiblites. Russian culture swelled and burst in geysers of projects and schemes. In the theater, Meierkhol'd proclaimed his "October." Vakhtangov led the Third Studio onto twisting rails. Granovskii founded the Yiddish theater.

To do so he couldn't simply put up minus signs and work with the method of negation, as did Meierkhol'd. Nor was Vakhtangov's complex strategem available to him. Either solution presupposed the existence of a highly developed theatrical culture which had already exhausted its straight paths. Granovskii had to build on an empty space. He was his own ancestor. There was nothing behind his back. From time to time, itinerant theatrical groups of Jewish ne'er-do-wells, unfit for any other profession, had crisscrossed the Pale of Settlement. And in the 1910s, a sad shtetl symbolist, the Vilna Maeterlinckoid Peretz Hirshbeyn, had pulled before the puzzled Jewish petite bourgeoisie his infinite nose, his meager possessions, and his loving, naïve, and unwitting parodies of the dramaturgy of European modernism.

True, along with Granovskii there was HaBima, which radiated well-being. All the good fairies of aid and publicity surrounded it. It was supported by an amazing amalgam of Zionists, the Rabbinate, parts of the Communist Party, and those liberal anti-Semites who considered the language of the Bible the only thing bearable about the Jews. One of the first proofs of Granovskii's real talent was that he circumvented HaBima, recognizing with some higher sense the parasitism of that phenomenon. HaBima lived with an alien mind, claiming for itself the wages of others. It cloaked the devices of Russian directors and the conventions of the Russian stage in a cover of the modernized ancient Hebrew speech. It was Stanislavskii's bastard child by an accidental Jewish mother. I remember one skit staged by HaBima in which one character addressed another character with the words, *"Adoni ha-student"* — "Mr. Student!" Then and there, at the premiere, I thought that the whole nature of an obedient little theater was reflected in this Esperanto. Not in vain did it fear Jewish artists, who were young and entailed risk. HaBima instead preferred either to have a nameless nobody or to invite the experienced conventionality of Eastern decorations by Yakulov and even Miganajan. Only when the pleiade of Jewish artists, roaring and shimmering, went through Granovskii's stage, did HaBima stretch out its hand to them. Had I written memoirs, I could have told about my meeting with Zemakh, who tried to persuade me to influence Chagall, Al'tman, and Rabinovich to work for HaBima. It became dangerous to ignore them and they themselves did not show any desire to offer themselves. Incidentally, even for that step, an instruction from the side was necessary, which appeared in the person and authority of Vakhtangov, who came to HaBima to stage *The Dybbuk*.

Granovskii did not find his course from the start. Like a thoroughbred puppy beginning to walk, he at first stumbled comically in various corners. Now it is funny to read his pathetic declarations of 1919. The brochure proclaiming them has long since become a bibliographical rarity. For Granovskii, it is no longer dangerous. It contains many nouns written with capital letters and even more exclamation marks. In essence, the most important thing in it is the will to exist; the least significant are its theatrical dogmas. This was confirmed by the early productions, in which Granovskii stood shakily on his legs and often groped in a vacuum. The Prologue [by Mikhoels] worked with harlequins and colombines. *Amnon and*

Tamar by Sholem Asch retailored the Bible for the nth time. *The Blind* by Maeterlinck came late by an immense decade. If that were to become the predominant direction, Granovskii's theater would merely have produced a more complicated variant of HaBima. But in fact, the change of formal elements was significant, and it became the foundation of Granovskii's further work. Jewish folk speech supplanted the bookish Hebraism; German theatrical methods deformed the Russian stage tradition.

This, however, did not resolve the problem, did not yet create a Jewish theater. The essence was not here. These were only separate levers. An Archimedean point was needed.

III. Granovskii selected his first designer in a manner typical of other Russian theaters at the time, not forseeing the role the artist would later play in realizing his projects. Furthermore, he apparently did not notice what was happening with artists on the Russian stage, where the exacerbated dialectics of their interrelationships took a tragic turn. In the decorational systems, entire historical layers were being shaken out in the open; yet Granovskii remained unconcerned. *The Prologue* was concocted with homemade means, which seemed simple as long as, for the protagonists — Harlequin, Pierrot and Colombine — there were uniforms granted them once and for all; and accordingly, the curtain was of course made like a chessboard — white and black squares. For *Amnon and Tamar*, he invited the assistant of a famous master, and for *The Blind*, simply the daughter of a famous father. Granovskii warmed his hands in the slanted rays of someone else's fame. When he decided finally to approach great people, he unexpectedly selected Dobuzhinskii.

What charms did he find in this master? Did he himself find him, or was he given him? I don't know; I think it was by accident. I don't believe Granovskii when he says that Dobuzhinskii understood him, because Granovskii didn't understand himself; more precisely, neither of them knew what Granovskii needed. It's not worth seeking lofty motives; in retrospect, all the reasons for historical events look very important; Stendhal and Tolstoi unmasked the writing of history. Be that as it may, Dobuzhinskii was accepted, and Granovskii was happy. But that meant handing over a matter requiring young inventiveness and fresh devices to a brittle second generation of "The World of Art." Thus, naïvely, on the way to his room, Granovskii stumbled into another. He regressed to the decorational experiments of the 1910s.

Of that pleiade, Dobuzhinskii was not the most interesting; and, besides, his best days were far behind him. In 1919, when Granovskii suddenly offered him the chance to speak Yiddish, he was already in deep obscurity. He didn't know what to do with himself as his contemporaries didn't know what task to give him. He still wore the popularity he had once achieved through the productions of the Moscow Art Theater, but he was exhausted and couldn't always repeat himself faithfully. He only tried to preserve his clichés, but with worried jealousy, as one guards a hard-earned, yet insufficiently large property. Here his nature as a follower, not a leader, was evident. The elders of "The World of Art," who raised and influenced him were different — they lasted longer and risked more.

Dobuzhinskii brought to Granovskii's stage his old-fashioned aestheticism, his love for the beauty of costumes, a subdued nostalgia for things and architectural forms, and the worn-out clichés of emblems and accessories — from the logo of the theater, with its stylized Hebrew letters and black-and-white contrasts of surfaces, to the stylized interiors and human figures used for Asch's *Winter*. His sketches have been preserved; you can see them at Granovskii's even now. But Dobuzhinskii didn't make any special effort, and the handwriting of an artist betrays him as much as does the handwriting of a writer. Dobuzhinskii didn't take pains; his hand was guided by condescension. From this work, he expected "neither loud fame, nor persecutions" [Pushkin]. It was with only slight interest in Granovskii's project that he just as slightly helped his "young friend."

I met him casually in the auditorium of the Yiddish Theater in Moscow, already at the time of Granovskii's brilliant success. I think they were performing *The Sorceress*. He was agitated, distributed compliments, and occasionally, as if unwittingly, dropped phrases about how good it was to work on such young stages. He was clearly waiting for an invitation. Obviously, he assumed that he, the godfather of the theater, could expect this as a matter of course. We made believe we didn't understand. All roads to artists of his type were taboo. He departed, tense, officious, and angry. He didn't understand a thing about what took place in those years.

IV. The theater moved to Moscow in the spring of 1920, which became the date of its second birth. The real history of the Yiddish theater begins here. Feverish, raging, roiling Moscow, headquarters of the revolutionary state, potential capital of the world, shaken daily, hourly, by the thrusts and explosions of events, the turns of the wheel, the breakdowns of the machinery, engulfed with typhus, covered with rumors, starving on rations, heating its ovens with fences and furniture — but constantly seething with a triumphant, historical effort of will, crystalizing the dim movements of the masses; emitting — "To everyone! Everyone! Everyone!" — protests, appeals, orders, slogans; thundering with the triumphant copper of hundreds of orchestras; in the weekdays of its new calendar, pouring the scarlet of its red banners over dense crowds marching through the streets; turning into reality the creative chimerae of dozens of directors, hundreds of artists, thousands of actors, bare-legged dancers, circus performers, dilettantes and adventurers; generously giving them money (though devalued), buildings (though falling apart), materials (though disintegrating) — Soviet Moscow ignited in Granovskii a decisive spark. He became himself. He found the Archimedean point of the Yiddish theater.

I am slightly afraid of the term I would use to characterize it, a term brown with the clotted mud of centuries, which you won't find in any other language but Russian. But it expresses what I need and I shall utter it. This word is — "Jewness" [*Zhidovstvo*]. I am prepared to explain: is it a metaphor? Yes and no. The Russian Revolution accustomed us to posing a question about the social meaning of every artistic phenomenon. The Revolution has the right to demand it, for under the conditions of a social cataclysm, there are no neutral forces; art becomes the same accomplice or enemy as anything else. My term means that Granovskii's theater, like a screen blown up by light, reflected the appearance of the awakened and agitated masses of the Jewish people on the stage of revolution. The upturned daily life of shtetls and cities, with all their people and smells, flooded onto the stage. This was both the strength and the weakness of the theater. The old world was broken down, and Granovskii showed it with an immense expressiveness; but the new had not yet been found, and Granovskii didn't know how to anticipate it and present it prematurely. His theater was passive. This is not a reproach. Show me if it was different anywhere else! All other theaters of Soviet Russia were like this.

But my word loses its metaphorical arbitrariness in the artistic-theatrical sense. Here it is literal. Granovskii accomplished an immense and positive revolution. Political radicalism is often combined with aesthetic reaction. The power of taste is protected more securely than the power of

classes. Granovskii was one of the few who not only dared but could perform the upheaval. This "Jewyness," which the anti-Semitism of the pogroms mocked and tormented, which the Russified Jewish intelligentsia hushed up in confusion, which the Europeanizing progressives of university chairs haughtily suggested eliminating, which offended the ear, and stung the eye — in a word (here at last is a fitting case for a theological quotation!), "The stone that the builders refused is become the headstone of the corner."

People should have howled with indignation. They didn't dare because, in the yard and at home, the Revolution performed. Visiting Granovskii, to the sacramental formula of petit bourgeois opposition of "What a country, what a government!" They added, "What licentiousness!" Afterward, they went to HaBima to view an aristocratic Jew, with biblical speech, pathetic gestures, and exotic costumes. Incidentally, some higher echelons of the Revolution preferred the same comeliness. Negatively, this was expressed in the fact that the people didn't go to Granovskii; positively, at the premieres of HaBima, you could see the Moscow Chief Rabbi Mazeh next to Politburo member Kamenev, nodding to each other in satisfaction.

V. Granovskii really unfurled the "Yid" on the stage. He threw his audience the forms, rhythms, sounds, colors of the phenomenon which bore this nickname. Had it only been by imitation of shtetl daily life, by a naturalistic counterfeit of the countenance and life of the everyday Jew, even with a light admixture of a Jewish anecdote, that traditional consolation of both the friendly and hostile citizen — so be it! Ultimately, it would have been acceptable to everyone, and you could have pitied them, "Poor people. . . . How good it is that history, nevertheless, moves!" But Granovskii demanded something entirely different of the auditorium. He wanted the filth he unfolded to be accepted as an immense, self-sufficient value. Granovskii deepened its theatrical and artistic features to the level of an all-encompassing imperative, a universal generalization. From dross he made gold. On an evening of self-parody at the theater, the young actor Zuskin masterfully portrayed "a series of magical transformations" of a dignified Jew who found himself at Granovskii's and, at first, couldn't believe his ears, then turned scarlet, and finally dashed out of the auditorium screaming, "Ay, ay — what an anti-Semite!" As a matter of fact, the long hems of the *capotas* and fringed undergarments, the curls of beards and hair, the curves of noses and backs hovered over the space of the stage in Granovskii's theater, if one can say so, as absolutes. The singsong, gutteral speech, squeaking at the ends of sentences, entered the ear like a molded, finished, self-sufficient system. The scattered, hurried movements and gestures, interrupting each other, ran like a counterpoint of beads. Granovskii turned the features of small daily life into a theatrical *device* and a stage *form*. From this moment, the Yiddish theater came into being.

But the key to the problem was not with the director but with the artists. Granovskii had to borrow. He didn't hesitate for he never suffered from stupidity. He caught the artist by the lapels and didn't let go of him until he attained his objective. The artist gave him the basic formulas for the images he sought, the first devices for their embodiment, and the initial stages of their development. And it was this that formed the contrast between the role of a designer on the general Russian stage and his later significance for the Yiddish stage. In the 1920s, when the masters of theater painting were only allowed into the auditorium condescendingly, as traditional guests at the premiere — and were, as much as possible, prevented from working on the stage as executors of the decorations — it was precisely then that the Jewish artist played a primary role in creating his national theater. This assertion will not surprise anyone; I mention the well-known phenomenon only in passing.

Among the components that went into the construction of the Yiddish theater, painting was the most mature in its development and the most specific in its manifestations. It did not get entangled in elementary searches for its own artistic form the way that the tongue of Yiddish writers tripped over itself and formulated more jargon than Yiddish. Neither did it have such quantities of raw ethnographic slang as did the works of Jewish composers, who were satisfied with copying folksongs and melodies that they peppered only lightly with modernism. Painting and graphics gave Granovskii a ready-made solution for conquering the auditorium. The entire group of Jewish painters worked dynamically and triumphantly, creating work that was saturated with personalities, rich in nuances, and unquestionably contemporary in its formal expressiveness. In every trend of European and Russian art, in every school, it had leading representatives.

True, this diapason was too broad. Danger was inherent in it. You had to select correctly. The story of Dobuzhinskii might have been repeated. There were all sorts of people and programs. Granovskii had to understand that in the artistic revolution, as in the social revolution, you always have to steer the most extreme course; the resultant force of intentions and possibilities will sort itself out. The Yiddish stage needed the most "Jewy," the most contemporary, the most unusual, the most difficult of all artists. And so I mentioned Chagall's name to Granovskii. Granovskii's always-sleepy eyes opened with a start and rounded like the eyes of an owl at the sight of meat. Next morning, Chagall was summoned and invited to work on Sholem Aleichem's miniatures. This was the first production of the Moscow period. Chagall began a dynasty of artist-designers.

VI. He had just returned from Vitebsk, where he had been Commissar of Art, but, fed up with power, had abdicated this lofty title. At least, that's his story. The truth was that he was deposed by the Suprematist Malevich, who took over Chagall's students and usurped the art school. He accused Chagall of being moderate, and of being just a neo-realist, still entangled in depicting some objects and figures, when truly revolutionary art is objectless. The students believed in revolution and found artistic moderation insufferable. Chagall tried to make some speeches in his own defence, but they were confused and almost inarticulate. Malevich answered with heavy, strong, and crushing words. Suprematism was pronounced the heresy of revolution. Chagall had to leave for (I almost wrote "flee to") Moscow. He didn't know what to do and spent the time telling stories about his experience as commissar in Vitebsk and about the intrigues of the Suprematists. He loved to recollect the time when, on revolutionary holidays, a banner waved above the school depicting a man on a green horse and the inscription, "Chagall — to Vitebsk." The students still admired him and covered all fences and street signs that had survived the Revolution with Chagallian cows and pigs, legs turned down and legs turned up. Malevich, after all, was just a dishonorable intrigant, whereas he, Chagall, was born in Vitebsk, and knew well what kind of art Vitebsk and the Russian Revolution needed.

Meanwhile, he quickly consoled himself with work in the Yiddish theater. He set us no conditions, but also stubbornly refused to accept any instructions. We abandoned ourselves to God's will. Chagall never left the small auditorium on Chernyshevskii Lane. He locked all doors; Granovskii and I were the only ones allowed in, after a carping and suspicious

interrogation from inside as from the guard of a gunpowder cellar; in addition, at fixed hours, he was served food through a crack in the half-open door. This was not simple intoxication with work; he was truly possessed. Joyfully and boundlessly, he bled paintings, images, and forms. Immediately he felt crowded on the few meters of our stage. He announced that, along with the decorations, he would paint "a Jewish panel" on the big wall of the auditorium; then he moved over to the small wall, then to the spaces between the windows, and finally to the ceiling. The whole hall was Chagallized. The audience came as much to be perplexed by this amazing cycle of Jewish frescoes as to see Sholem Aleichem's skits. They were truly shaken. I often had to appear prior to the performance with some introductory remarks, explaining what kind of thing it was and why it was needed.

I talked a lot about leftist art and Chagall, and little about the theater. That was natural. Today we can admit that Chagall forced us to buy the Jewish form of scenic imagery at a high price. He had no theatrical blood in him. He continued doing his own drawings and paintings, not drafts of decoration and costume designs. On the contrary, he turned the actors and the production into categories of plastic art. He did not do actual sets, but simply panels, processing them with various textures, meticulously and in detail, as if the spectator would stand before them at a distance of several feet, as he stands in an exhibition, and appreciate, almost touching, the beauty and subtlety of this colorful field plowed up by Chagall. He did not want to hear about a third dimension, about the depth of the stage. Instead, he positioned all his decorations in parallel planes, along the apron, as he was accustomed to placing his paintings on walls or easels. The objects were painted with Chagallian foreshortening, with his own perspective, which did not consider any perspective of the stage. The spectators saw many perspectives; painted objects were contrasted with real objects; Chagall hated real objects as illegitimate disturbers of his cosmos and furiously hurled them off the stage; with the same rage, he painted over — one might say plastered with color — that indispensable minimum of objects. With his own hands, he painted every costume, turning it into a complex combination of blots, stripes, dots, and scattering over them various muzzles, animals, and doodles. He obviously considered the spectator a fly, which would soar out of its chair, sit on Mikhoels's hat [of Reb Alter] and observe with the thousand tiny crystals of its fly's eye what he, Chagall, had conjured up there. He did not look for types or images — he simply took them from his paintings.

Of course, under these conditions, the wholeness of the spectator's impression was complete. When the curtain rose, Chagall's wall panels and the decorations with the actors on the stage simply mirrored each other. But the nature of this ensemble was so untheatrical that one might have asked, why turn off the light in the auditorium, and why do these Chagallian beings move and speak on the stage rather than stand unmoving and silent as on his canvases?

Ultimately, the *Sholem Aleichem Evening* was conducted, as it were, in the form of Chagall paintings come to life. The best places were those in which Granovskii executed his system of "dots" and the actors froze in mid-movement and gesture, from one moment to the next. The narrative line was turned into an assembly of dots. One needed a marvelous finesse, with which Mikhoels was endowed, to unify in the role of Reb Alter Chagall's static costumes and images with the unfolding of speech and action. The spectacle was built on compromise and tottered from side to side. The thick, invincible Chagallian Jewishness conquered the stage, but the stage was enslaved and not engaged in participation.

We had to break through to the spectacle over Chagall's

dead body, as it were. He was upset by everything that was done to make the theater a theater. He cried real, hot, childish tears when rows of chairs were placed in the hall with his frescoes. He claimed, "These heathen Jews will obstruct my art, they will rub their thick backs and greasy hair on it." To no avail did Granovskii and I, as friends, curse him as an idiot; he continued wailing and whining. He attacked workers who carried his handmade sets, claiming that they deliberately scratched them. On the day of the premiere, just before Mikhoels's entrance on the stage, he clutched the actor's shoulder and frenziedly thrust his brush at him as at a mannequin, daubing dots on his costume and painting tiny birds and pigs no opera glass could observe on his vizored cap, despite repeated, anxious summonses to the stage and Mikhoels's curt pleas — and again Chagall cried and lamented when we ripped the actor out of his hands by force and shoved him onto the stage.

Poor, dear Chagall! He, of course, considered us tyrants and himself a martyr. He was so deeply convinced of it that, ever since, for eight years, he never touched the theater again. He never understood that he was the clear and indisputable victor, and that, in the end, the young Yiddish theater had stuggled because of this victory.

May 1928

The Moscow State Yiddish Theater

Osip Mandelshtam
Originally published, in Russian, in Vechernaia Krasnaia Gazeta, *Leningrad, August 10, 1926. The review was included in Mandelshtam's posthumously published* Collected Works *(vol. 3) with the title "Mikhoels."*

On the wooden walkways of an unsightly Byelorussian shtetl — a big village with a brick factory, a beer hall, front yards, and cranes — shuffled a strange figure with long hems, made of an entirely different dough from the whole landscape. Through the window of a train, I watched that solitary pedestrian move like a black cockroach between the little houses, among the splashing mud, with splayed arms; and golden yellow glimmered the black hems of his coat. In his movements, there was such an estrangement from the whole situation and, at the same time, such knowledge of the road, as if he had to run and to and fro, like a wind-up toy.

Sure, big deal, never seen: a Jew with long hems on a village street. However, I remember well the figure of the running Rebbe because, without him, that whole modest landscape lacked justification. The coincidence which that very moment pushed into the street this crazy, charmingly absurd, endlessly refined, porcelain pedestrian helped me understand the impression of the State Jewish Theater, which I recently saw for the first time.

Yes, a short while before that, on a Kiev street, I was ready to approach a similar respectable bearded man and ask him, "Didn't Al'tman do your costume?" I would have asked just like that, with no mockery, quite sincerely: in my head, the realms grew confused. . . .

How fortunate is Granovskii! It's enough for him to assemble two or three synagogue beadles with a cantor, summon a matchmaker-Shadkhan, catch in the street an elderly salesman, and a spectacle is ready and, in essence, even Al'tman is superfluous.

This paradoxical theater, which, according to some critics as profound as Dobrolubov, declared war on the Jewish petite bourgeoisie, and which exists only to eradicate prejudices and superstitions, loses its head, gets drunk like a woman when it sees a Jew, and immediately pulls him into its workshop, to the porcelain factory, scalds and tempers him into a marvelous biscuit, a painted statuette, a green *shadkhan*-grasshopper, brown musicians of Rabichev's Jewish wedding, bankers with shaved layered pates, dancing like virtuous girls, holding hands, in a circle.

The plastic fame and force of the Jews consist of having worked out and borne through the centuries a sense of form and movement, which has all the traits of a fashion immutable for millennia. I am speaking not of the cut of their clothes, which changes, and which we need not value (it doesn't even occur to me to justify the ghetto or the shtetl style aesthetically); I'm talking of the internal plasticity of the ghetto, of that immense artistic force which outlives its destruction, and will finally flourish only when the ghetto is destroyed.

Violins accompany the wedding dance. Mikhoels approaches the footlights and, stealthily, with the careful movements of a fawn, listens to the music in a minor key. This is a fawn who has found himself at a Jewish wedding, hesitant, not yet drunk, but already stimulated by the cat-music of a Jewish minuet. This moment of hesitation is perhaps more expressive than the whole subsequent dance. Tapping on the spot, intoxication comes, a light intoxication from two or three drinks of grape wine, but this is enough to turn the head of a Jew: the Jewish Dionysius is undemanding and immediately produces joy.

During the dance, Mikhoels's face assumes an expression of wise weariness and sad exaltation, as if the mask of the Jewish people, approaching antiquity, is almost identical with it.

Here the dancing Jew is like the leader of an ancient chorus. The whole force of Judaism, the rhythm of the abstract, dancing thought, the whole dignity of the dance, whose only impetus is ultimately empathy with the earth — all this is absorbed in the trembling hands, the vibration of his thinking fingers, inspired like articulated speech.

Mikhoels is the epitome of national Jewish dandyism — the dancing Mikhoels, the tailor Soroker, a forty-year-old child, a blessed *shlimazel*, a wise and gentle tailor. And yesterday, on the same stage, Anglicized jockey ragamuffins, on tall girl-dancers, patriarchs drinking tea in the clouds, like elders on a porch in Homel.

Jewish Luck *Viktor Shklovsky*
This review of the 1925 film Jewish Luck (Menakhem-Mendel), *which was directed by Granovskii and used the sets and actors of the Yiddish Theater, was published, in Russian, in* Evreiskoe Schast'e. *Moscow: Kino-petshat' (Kino-Izdatelstvo RSFSR), 1925.*

What does a Jew do? He spins around. — This is from *Jewish Luck*. It was very hard for Jews to spin around. Small towns, filled with houses and children. Huts with dilapidated roofs. Their own soil only in the cemetery. And that's where they grazed their goats. They lived on air, and that wasn't fresh either. Jews, separated from productive work, from land and factories, a whole nation living in the cracks and interstices of life. Petty buying and selling, shaving, mending dresses. The lowest wages in the world. So dense that new buildings weren't constructed because there was nowhere to go during the construction. On the old house they patched up a new one, a wall on top of a wall, a roof above a roof. — Mice have such a disease when their tails grow into each other in the cellar. Thus houses and people grow into each other in Jewish shtetls. Stifling, closed everyday life, and on the Sabbath, wires encircle the whole town. All around alien fields and alien, hostile people. People in a prison create their own language. The downtrodden are sharp-witted. The best Jewish anecdotes are created by Jews about themselves. One of those anecdotes is Sholem Aleichem's story about a man of air, a destitute pauper, a failing and indefatigable tradesman, insurance agent and — finally — matchmaker. Jews say of such people, "He doesn't walk by himself — his guts carry him." — For us, *Jewish Luck* is almost a historical film. Such Jewish life no longer exists. The Civil War hit them hard. Pogroms rolled through the shtetl. The very places where the pasted-together huts stood were plowed up. Hunger came in the wake of the pogroms. In Kherson, orthodox Jews, fearing they would die in the general devastation and not be buried by the rules, came to the cemetery and lined up for death. The Revolution was a hulling mill for the Jews. The old closed world was shattered. Everyday life is finished. Small trade, middleman trade, was crushed under the pressure of state capitalism and cooperatives. In the new tight life there was no room to spin around. But the Revolution removed all limitations from the Jews and destroyed the most essential trait of the Jews — the Pale of Settlement. The plants and factories were opened for Jewish workers. The proletarian supplanted the artisan. And instead of the right to graze a goat in a cemetery, Jews got the right to the land. Now, in Byelorussia and at the Azov Sea, an immense work to grant land to the Jews is proceeding. Kolkhozes emerge, the soil is irrigated. Now it is clear that Zionism, a Jewish state in Palestine, will produce only a southern resort for rich Jews. A patriotic resort with oranges. The Jewish colonies at the Azov Sea get 1,620,000 acres. In the Soviet state, a new autonomous district will be added, perhaps a new republic. — No need to pity the torn umbrella of Menakhem-Mendel, no need to look for romanticism in the past, in the grown-together tails of a mouse cellar. But we need to know the old daily life. Director Granovskii has succeeded in reconstructing much of the past in his film. The film is theatrical. Granovskii doesn't want to sell his "theatrical sword." But in film, you don't need swords, you need to know the technique. Therefore, the film has a new handwriting for the cinema. There is real everyday life. The artist Natan Al'tman has treated his task very carefully. Natan Al'tman is a person with great national culture, a person with his own face. But the film, as I said, is a historical work, in it "thus it was" is more important than "thus I want it to be." Al'tman constructed the Jewish rooms well; he did not overburden them with details, he hid his work in the film as the illuminator hides his work. Light in a film should shed light and not appear as a separate item in the program. The titles in the film are made by Isaac Babel. They exploit the material of the film well and are closely connected with the actors. They are not titles but conversations. They are speech. They endow the film with the charm of the human voice.

Five Years of the State Yiddish Chamber Theater (1919–1924) *M. Litvakov*

Excerpted from an essay, in Russian, published in Moscow in 1924 by Shul un bukh.

1. Theater and Revolution.

In quiet epochs all arts, including art of the theater, lead a quiet life. They digest and transform the achievements of the past epoch of *Sturm und Drang* into facts of daily life. They express the tempos and rhythms of the inertia that has set in. But revolutionary epochs, toppling all previous foundations of life, also shake up the arts. And what art is as sensitive to social upheavals as the art of the theater? For theater is the most social of all arts; theater lives only in an audience, and not only does the actor infect the auditorium, but the auditorium also has a powerful impact on the actor and on the spectacle as a whole.

Why is it that, in Moscow, this center of world revolution, we feel such an indescribable theatrical chaos, a real world-confusion, a noisy brouhaha? The continuous destruction of old theater foundations and the painful search for new ones, the feverish toppling of old gods and the wild pursuit of new idols? Where does it come from?

If it had remained in the hands of the famous caste of art-priests, everything would have stayed as it was, with no changes. Because there is no more moldy, organically conservative social stratum than this stratum of narcissistic Dalai Lamas. But the spectator has changed. The spectator, the audience — with no distinction of class or social group — that emerged from the mangle of the great imperialist war and that, to this day, lives under the pressure of the workers' revolution — in short, the public of the epoch of the October Revolution and the Comintern — conceals in its soul, consciously or not, powderkegs of storm-alarms and dynamic unrest. Bourgeois idylls à la *The Cricket on the Hearth* don't get into their heads, and the boring sighs of pre-Revolutionary petit bourgeois in various "cherry orchards" cannot calm their firestorm yearning.

But a completely unexpected bankruptcy occurred, not only with respect to the content of the theatrical spectacle, but also with respect to form. This creeping realistic description of daily life we are sick of, this antiquated loyalty to forgotten details — all this smacks of a museum of antiquities and not of the burgeoning art of throbbing contemporaneity. Naturally, to the extent that, in such a theater, we feel vigorous mastery, even of the old style, we may watch the spectacle with some enjoyment: dear past. And those social groups who look in various ways for such sanctuaries where the thunder of the impetuous revolution cannot reach would give such theaters top priority.

But here art absolutely ceases being a moving force of the cultural development of the masses; it is transformed into a store of "sublime swindle" (Pushkin), which is dearer to some than a "wealth of mundane truths."

Other theaters, the theaters of today, which strive to keep pace with the Revolution and consider themselves only a segment of its immense front, strive to expose this "wealth of mundane truths." They aim at exploding the hidden powderkegs of unrest in the soul of the spectator, they lift him forcibly on the waves of dynamic tempos, leaping rhythms, dazzling colors, and dizzying movements.

One of the most conspicuous theaters of this type — and such theaters are scarce even in the Soviet Union — is the State Yiddish Chamber Theater.

2. Theater and Comedians of Revolutionary Joy.

For many years, pious intellectuals and anxious caretakers of the spirit have been preparing to build a "serious" Yiddish theater. What did they mean by "serious" theater? Lengthy explications of literature on the stage through exhaustive emoting by the actors. In the old Yiddish theater, they denied not only its latter-day popular smut, but also what remained intact: the mobility, the popular trumpeting, the harlequinade, the ecstasy of the whole body. The ideal was at least some reflection of the Moscow Art Theater, where the twisted soul of the Russian intelligentsia would be transformed into the Jewish piety of a small town grandson of the Besht — in short, a kind of Yiddishist HaBima.

But instead they got the State Yiddish Chamber Theater!

And revolution, according to the petit-bourgeois caretakers of the spirit, is just asceticism, a kind of monkish withdrawal from the world. Poverty with no light or color, nakedness of body, and emptiness of soul.

But it turns out that the masses who make the revolution are much richer in life, light, colors, movement, and joy than the peripheral people-providers, for, precisely because they possess all that, can they go to revolution and triumph!

And the State Yiddish Theater came precisely as one expression of that mass ecstasy. It is the embodiment of "serving with joy" — serving art with joy, with impetus. And the ecstasy does not lie hidden in the soul, but gushes from every limb of the body.

A treasure of light, a wealth of colors, a chasm of movement, a richness of rhythms — this is what the Yiddish Chamber Theater has discovered for the Jewish working masses. A liberated body which is the organic collaborator of the liberated spirit. Both serve the red virgin soil of revolution, and are hostile to all vestiges of Jewishy junk. The Jewish grimace, which they tried for generations to transform into an idly Jewishy feature, the Jewish gesture, which was supposed to remain forever godly pious — here they have become new, free, sharp gestures of an epoch of "iron and concrete."

The ecstasy in the Yiddish Chamber Theater is not arbitrary, not spontaneous, but regulated, planned. For we live in an epoch when the spontaneous thrust of the masses is regulated by the genius of collective rationality — through the avant-garde of the working class, the Communist Party, planned economy, rationalized working processes. And as in political-economic life in general, so in the life of art is ecstasy not weakened by the progressive consciousness and calculation, but rather is strengthened and attains its greatest triumphs. An expression of that is the State Yiddish Chamber Theater.

In the *Sholem Aleichem Evening*, we see the mathematical fantastic. The generally known and almost banal Menakhem-Mendel is elevated by the artist Mikhoels to the level of an unforgettable art symbol; for the first time, an artistic, scenic embodiment is found for the popular-Yiddish Don Quixote, Reb Alter.

In *Uriel Accosta*, the unrest of Uriel's free thought merges wonderfully with the unrest of Al'tman's decorations; the enraged narrowness of the representatives of religious fanaticism is amazingly framed in Al'tman's ornate mannequins. An artistic-rational approach to the tragedy of the tottering free thought of the late Middle Ages was found here.

Not to mention *The Sorceress*! Such a plethora of colors, a treasure of movements, wealth of sounds — Jewish art has never before provided such a dizzying rush of folk masses, liberated from their Jewishy Diaspora essence.

Here an immense and joyous theatrical explosion was brought together, aiming its full blade against the social and the spiritual, and especially against artistic junk.

Mathematical conspicuousness of gesture, precisely calculated movements, with a rapid tempo, laying bare the skeleton of the theatrical narrative in the resonating interplay of sets and music (where the necessity of music is dictated by the organic logic of the scenic intention), white-hot rhythm, dazzling collaborations of light, provocative expressiveness of color, multifunctionality and vividness in every inch of the stage boards — such are the principle features of any spectacle of the Yiddish Chamber Theater. And it is all dominated by the liberated body and the firm and elastic spirit of the actor.

What is primary in the Chamber Theater — the whole ensemble or the individual comedian? It is hard to tell. One thing is clear — the Yiddish Chamber Theater created the new, free, joyous, agile Jewish comedian, the comedian of the liberated proletariat. It has also created a joyous ensemble — a new *kapelye* [orchestra], and "a *Kapelye* is more than a *minyan*" — according to one of Peretz's characters.

3. Theater of Organized Rationality.
Therefore, the State Yiddish Chamber Theater has many foes and even more friends. Each new production provokes, on the one hand, excited recognition, and, on the other hand, wild rage. But soon, many of the most "outraged" begin to attend the loathsome spectacle, declaring in embarrassment that "you have to get used to it."

This in itself shows that the Yiddish Chamber Theater is not just a theater where "the actor does an act, and the spectator casts a glance," but one of the institutions that does battle in the domain of art in Moscow, and, indeed, in the entire Soviet Union.

The success and triumph of the State Yiddish Chamber Theater was determined by its artistic essence.

First, this is the first and so far the only Yiddish theater with mastery of a European theater style. Before the State Yiddish Chamber Theater, Jewishy "culture-providers" only dreamed of a "real" Yiddish theater; small-town Talmudists, however, took great pains to realize this dream, through hair-splitting arguments about the theories and methods of an art theater. And here in the Chamber Theater true theatrical mastery came and declared, "I am!" And, though unexpected, it came full of *joie de vivre*, young, confident, like all the creations of October.

A new director and a new comedian arrived for whom "Jewishness" — that is, nationalistic smugness and folkloristic shmaltz — was totally alien. The key to the theatrical re-creation of Jewish folklore was found for the first time by the State Yiddish Chamber Theater — first in its performance of Sholem Aleichem's miniatures and then in the other works, especially in *The Sorceress*.

But the chief property of the Yiddish Chamber Theater, which attracts more attention than any other, I would say, is its "planned creation," or the rationalist methods of its artistic work.

The Yiddish Chamber Theater completely rejects the method of "experiencing," the cult of emotionality. Above the "kingdom of necessity" — above the spontaneous force of unregulated feelings — it puts the "kingdom of freedom" — the organized and determining understanding. Hence, in the productions of the Yiddish Chamber Theater, mathematical formulas were transformed into intuitive revelations, which, after the fact, when the habituated spectator begins to grasp them, appear as intuitive revelations, distinguished by the surprising obviousness of mathematical formulas.

This explains the interesting and "sensational" gestures of the Yiddish Chamber Theater, its groupings and pauses, which seem outlandish at first glance. The Sholem Aleichem spectacle initially provoked embarrassment, anger, even rage, and now it is already a canonized spectacle; many of the former protestors even tend to think that the theater condescended to them and "softened" its gestures. The same holds for *Uriel Accosta*, perhaps the best work of the Yiddish Chamber Theater: in *Uriel*, theatrical mastery, based on rationalist ecstasy or ecstatic rationalism, achieves a high level and tension.

And even in *The Sorceress*, in this most dynamic spectacle, filled with light, dance, brouhaha, notwithstanding the external emotionality of the staging and acting, there is a rigorous calculation and mathematical forging: precisely because of that, the emotional saturation is achieved, and not vice versa.

The same is true for Sholem Aleichem's *Great Prize* and other productions, from the most monumental to the smallest comedian skits, such as *Three Dots* and even *Warsaw Thieves* and *Comedians' Carnival*.

And not only is this theater inspired by the artists, but it also inspires them, mobilizing each of them for a specific work in the style and spirit of the given artist, yet still within the rigorous plan of the given piece. For Sholem Aleichem's sleepwalking characters, who see raging dreams in a quite calculated "reality," the theater found Chagall, who, for his part, found the Yiddish Chamber Theater. Such an ideal merger of a theater and an artist is rarely achieved. Sholem Aleichem's characters, embodied by the artists on the stage of the Yiddish Chamber Theater, in the costumes and framework of Chagall's designs, which, despite their fantastic mood, are structured rationally and calculated mathematically — this is a beautiful theatrical spectacle, which gives the Jewish spectator a new *literary* Sholem Aleichem. The same wonderful accord between the creative intention of the theater and its decorative realization by an artist is achieved in *Uriel Accosta*. In his design, the artist Al'tman expresses almost with genius the unrest of the struggling free thought in the context of religious fanaticism, indicated through a world of pompous mannequins. Al'tman's rationalist thinginess best matches Granovskii's methods.

And in *The Sorceress*, the bright, vivacious, Chagallized realism of I. Rabinovich proved itself a real revelation for the tasks of the Yiddish Chamber Theater.

And then comes the ideological revolutionary aspect of the theater: the merciless revelation of the Jewish lifestyle, and the constant exposure of the flaccidity of the past, the theater's biting, life-loving mockery of the elements of the religious-nationalistic milieu, its striving to October.

All this makes the State Yiddish Chamber Theater one of the first-rate contemporary European theaters, beloved and dear to the Jewish worker. . . .

4. Theater and Yiddish Mass Culture.
[Before October,] literature held the hegemony in our cultural creativity. It led, stimulated, organized, and clustered the forces in all other areas of art. And its creativity itself proceeded in the spirit of that epoch — in the spirit of internal Jewish narrowness. In a certain sense, Yiddish literature did not completely withstand the pressure of October, and now it struggles consciously to overcome the crisis stemming from the previous, unfinished epoch.

Our theater did not have the rich, though often difficult, traditions of literature — therefore, it was easier for the theater to absorb the thrust of October. So the Yiddish Chamber Theater was created.

The Chamber Theater did indeed emerge from the soil of massive accumulated creative energy, yet its impulse still came from outside. Dimensions never before seen in the Jewish milieu, rhythms, and tempos never before heard or felt, achievements never before experienced were the triumphs of this theater. For the first time in the history of Yiddish culture in general and of our mass culture in particular, there was a cultural creation that measured itself by — and was aligned

with — the frontline of European culture. For the Chamber Theater is indeed a Jewish theater, but it has attained its value outside the framework of purely Jewish art culture. In this very respect, it is the first and thus far the only October achievement of Yiddish mass culture.

But not only in this respect.

Usually, people imagine that October art is art that speaks directly about barricade battles, red banners, the hammer and sickle, shears and iron, bloodsucking capitalists, and oppressed proletarians. This is, of course, an over-simplified, vulgar position. If that were so, we should, for example, have renounced any proletarian or revolutionary music. For music speaks with tones and not with generally accessible words or paintings. Yet there is revolutionary music, and proletarian music is possible insofar as proletarian art in general is possible.

Revolutionary art in general, and October art in particular, is revolutionary not just in terms of its concrete themes and motifs, but in terms of its spirit, the moods it evokes, its play of colors, its rhythms, its tempos, the enchanted world into which it transposes us, the ideological thrust that dominates it. For art has methods of influence different from those of journalism. It remains art only when it leads to political conclusions, through its own ways and methods. If it is only journalistic it is not art, but simply agitation. If, however, it lacks agitational conclusions, it is socially dead even when it has purely formal achievements. And the Chamber Theater is the only theater here, and one of the few theaters in the whole Soviet Union, where a synthesis has been found between formal achievements and the ideological sediment of the October period.

5. In the Rhythm of October.
The Yiddish Chamber Theater is not a proletarian theater and does not claim to be. The Yiddish Chamber Theater, however, is the only theater that is *acceptable* for the proletariat.

Why?

The Yiddish Chamber Theater rejects the methods of internal emotings which are *explicated in a literary manner* on the stage; it provides *theatrical actions* that attain a colossal value even for purely literary works. The method of emoting cripples even collective actions and degrades them to the level of individualistic brooding, whereas the method of theatrical action elevates even the internal experiences of the individual to the level of a moment in the collective being.

This is because the Yiddish Chamber Theater bases its creation not on *emotion*, but on *rationality*; that is, not on the spontaneous force of unregulated feeling, but on the calculation of an organized understanding. It evokes feelings through the mathematical emphasis of rationality, through creation rather than spontaneous outbursts, which is entirely in the spirit of our October epoch.

Meierkhol'd in Moscow and Kurbas in Kiev follow the same path, but they turn the *material apparatus* of the theater into a *machine*, while Granovskii *rationalizes the living material* of the theater. Of course, we cannot feel the present epoch without revealing its industrialism, without technical constructions, and therefore Meierkhol'd's and Kurbas's work are a great achievement for the future theater of the proletariat. But through such a method, we may eventually be able to feel the technical milieu of the worker — though not the worker himself, and not his living nature. Therefore, in Meierkhol'd's and Kurbas's theaters we remember only technical construction, while in the Yiddish Chamber Theater we remember living figures and excited masses. Therefore, those theaters may be revolutionary only when they perform concrete revolutionary plays which speak for themselves, while the

Yiddish Chamber Theater is always revolutionary, regardless of its repertoire, because technique alone can also serve, did serve, and still serves the bourgeoisie, but living flesh and blood serves only itself.

The Sholem Aleichem Evening.
The Yiddish Chamber Theater was a true revelation in our cultural creation, and this revelation came from the wintry north, from Petersburg.

We had old centers of our mass cultural creation: Warsaw, Vilna, later Kiev. In the course of generations, our mass life was created there; there our literature emerged and developed, there too the first dreams took shape of a real, artistic Yiddish theater. They dreamed — but nothing came of it. Then active agitation was conducted for a "true" theater. The first who began to suffer and torment himself was Peretz Hirshbeyn; then Vayter began working toward this goal, and eventually Peretz himself took over the task.

Under the impact of this heroic company, the unhappiness with the "old Yiddish theater," indeed, grew deeper — some signs of a new theater culture even appeared, but no new theater came out of it.

Meanwhile, a kind of historio-cultural entanglement arose. For a long time, literature was the only element of our new culture. In time, literature also became the central organizational focus for all other domains of our artistic culture. And literature was the first to suffer in its isolation because of the actual lack of those other areas. Thus, from leading an active campaign to bring them to life, a damaging illusion emerged in literature that it was destined always to be the ruler, lawgiver, and tone-giver in those areas of art both during their emergence and after they had emerged. Writers became convinced that all other areas of art — painting, music, and especially theater — would and must be only appendices to literature and would have to follow its directives. And if literature was creative in its own domain, in its relation to those other areas, especially the theater, it became a pure culture-bearer, didactic, and Jewishly dilettantish.

And suddenly — Petersburg!
Petersburg?
The city of the "Disseminators of Enlightenment," of the Baron Ginzburg family, of *Voskhod*, of Slyozberg and Gruzenberg, of Vinaver and "Deputy Friedman," of Bramson and Pereferkovich — in a word, the city of Jewish plutocratic junk — how is it related to the cultural creation of the Jewish masses?

Hence everyone was skeptical about the Yiddish Chamber Theater made in Petersburg. We know the "Societies for the Encouragement of Jewish Art" that used to emerge in Petersburg, with doctors, lawyers, and often led by State Counsellors.

All of a sudden the Yiddish Chamber Theater moved to Moscow and gave its first performance: *Sholem Aleichem Evening*. It was an incredible sensation.

It was profanation enough that the theater was born without the midwifery of literature, but it also dared to manifest its independence in a Sholem Aleichem performance! Isn't Sholem Aleichem all "ours"? Don't we all know how he must be "interpreted" on the stage, what movements, gestures, and grimaces the performers must make, what decorative *illustrations* there must be — and here is everything topsy-turvy!

There was a hue and cry. Literature didn't recognize its dream image and began blocking the theater. . . .

Several years of literary-dilettantish siege passed, supported by the Jewishy petit-bourgeois small-mindedness of "everyday" Jews; and the Chamber Theater triumphed on the whole front.

Now the Yiddish Chamber Theater celebrates its fifth anniversary, crowned with general and full recognition. At its celebration, it will have completed 300 performances of the same, initially sensational, now canonized *Sholem Aleichem Evening*. . . .

Three hundred performances in four years! Not a small production program. . . .

Permit me to quote myself. I once wrote about Sholem Aleichem:

The major traits of Sholem Aleichem's writings are daydreaming and skepticism; their unique combination creates lyrical irony, the lyric-Jewish humor. The daydreaming endows the skepticism with a hopeful character; it leaves the door open for the eternal "perhaps yes." The skepticism brings "a fair in the sky" {castles in the air} down to earth and transforms tangible life itself into a dream, into a question-mark. This daydreaming that gives wings of hope to doubt, this doubt that is willing meanwhile to deny the dreams, give in their coupling the deep simplicity, the elementary force that often becomes the work of a genius. They undress the soul, taking off all the inherited socio-cultural layers, and show it in its original form at the "time of Creation."

Sholem Aleichem's lyricism, his lyrical humor, reveals the elementary force in the Jewish psyche. True, it is the psyche of certain Jewish strata in a specific historical epoch, but he succeeded in getting to the root, discovering our psychic skeleton. The unique coupling of daydreaming and skepticism in his lyrical work create the world of chaos in which his enchanted figures spin around like primitive marionettes. They say words that are so elementary and obvious, that are really on the tip of your tongue, that we are amazed that we didn't predict them ourselves, and yet they are always new, as an artistic discovery. Their movements and grimaces are the eternally old-new — and it often seems to us that we didn't see it first in Sholem Aleichem but that he copied it readymade from us.

(*In Umru*. Kiev: 1918, pp. 93–94.)

Daydreaming and skepticism, dream and doubt — those are the two basic areas of the human psyche: the areas of emotionalism and rationalism, spontaneity of feeling and the kingdom of rationality. We shall not enter into an argument about what causes what. I think that moving from the "kingdom of necessity" to the "kingdom of freedom" means that our future life will be regulated by rationality and not by spontaneous feeling, on condition that rationality itself will by then have the clairvoyance of feeling.

But the Yiddish Chamber Theater evokes in us clearcut conceptions about Sholem Aleichem's figures and their chaotic world through methods of rationalistic creation. Menakhem-Mendel Yakenhoz (Mikhoels) reaches us, after all, as living and feeling flesh and blood. But we can see tangibly that this is achieved through an iron band of mathematical movements and gestures. Only thus is his "psychic skeleton" revealed to us, from which, covered with skin and flesh, endless variations of Menakhem-Mendel can blossom. Or take Reb Alter in *Mazel Tov*. Here we see through the "bare mathematics," the "elementary simplicity that often becomes a work of genius." Dressed in Chagall's costumes and surrounded by Chagall's designs, which, with all their fantasy, are rigorously calculated, mathematically concrete, they become those "enchanted figures" that remind us of "almost primitive marionettes" that can give rise to a plethora of new types.

Or take the episode *It's a Lie!* Through the impulsive speech of two skeptical, daydreaming figures in Sholem Aleichem's Jewish world of chaos, confined in the iron grating of calculated movements and gestures and caged in Chagallized

Al'tmanish frames, we feel and palpably perceive, newly discovered, two Jewish *luftmentsh* figures.

Because of a misunderstanding, our literature initially negated the *Sholem Aleichem Evening*. But, in fact, it was and remained a powerful impetus for literature itself, for it created an entirely new key to understanding and grasping one of the founders of our modern literature. For the first time, Sholem Aleichem received the classical, truly artistic embodiment of his figures. In the Chamber Theater, Sholem Aleichem was just a beginning and a herald — *The Sorceress* proved what the new Yiddish Theater can make even of Goldfaden. . . .

It is good that the twin sisters in our art culture finally recognized each other and learned to live together. This is one of the best laurel wreaths for the Yiddish Chamber Theater on its fifth anniversary. . . .

The Yiddish Chamber Theater has found the secret of Jewish gesture, Jewish movement, Jewish plastics and dynamics, and, peeling the skin of Jewishy "wheeling-dealing" off it, the theater discovered the boundary where the national is transformed into the international. The theater created such a Jewish theater style, which can justly claim to be one of the styles which will in their ensemble construct the new style of the future international freedom-theater.

By the force of an immense socio-cultural leap, of which the theater is capable, it filled the gap in Jewish theater culture — the absence of artistic traditions. At one and the same time, the theater creates artistic traditions that bear the value of generations of culture, and also overcomes them, transforming them into only elements of an artistic tradition. The theater found the magic key to the treasures of Jewish folklore which it poetically reshapes into works of art of a new mass culture.

Agents: A Joke in One Act (1905) *Sholem Aleichem*

Agents was one of three plays performed at the Sholem Aleichem Evening, *the first production by the State Yiddish Chamber Theater. In this translation from the Yiddish, those phrases that were originally to be spoken in Russian are rendered in French.*

Cast

Menakhem-Mendel Yakenhoz'

A young man from a small town, dressed in a new outfit fresh from the needle, with a new fedora (which doesn't sit well on his head), and with a collar that squeezes his eyes out of his forehead. In his lap he holds a large briefcase, also new.

Mark Moyseyevich Lanternshooter

A young dandy. Also with a large briefcase.

Akim Isaakovich Bakingfish

A stout character who values eating. Also with a large briefcase.

Lazar Konstantinovich Turtledove

A character with a big beard and a big family: a wife with several children, each one smaller than the next.

Various characters, extras

The action takes place on the road, in a third-class train car.

Scene 1

[In a train. Several characters sit, some lie stretched out, some sleep. On the racks, packages, valises. Up front, alone on a bench, close to the window, sits Menakhem-Mendel, observing his new outfit, talking to himself]

Menakhem-Mendel

Have they piled up clothes on me — like a bridegroom! All dolled up — like a bride! One problem — the pants are just a little bit too snug; and the collar . . . Oy, the collar! Just made for choking! . . . I'm traveling on a train. Do I know where I'm traveling? You will be, they said, a good agent. Your name alone, they said, will do it! Isn't it something, the name itself: Menakhem-Mendel Yakenhoz, who is known, they say, like a bad penny, everywhere: in Yehupets, in Boyberik, in Mazepevke, and where not? Travel, they said, among your little Jews, and be a success! Condemnify, they said, people from death . . . . To condemnify people from death? How do you start to condemnify somebody from death? May I know such a bad supper! Though they crammed into me for two days the agent's Torah, and an "advance" they also gave me, and this is the main thing because all agents take "advances." If there were no "advances," they say, there would be no agents. . . . In addition to that, they filled me up a full briefcase with constitutions — institutions, I mean — how an agent should operate when he condemnifies somebody from death. I must start in right away on the constitutions — institutions, I mean. . . . [*Opens the briefcase and pulls out a letter*] Oh! Just mention Messiah — and you get a letter from Sheyne-Sheyndl! How does my mother-in-law put it: "When you look for scissors, you find a broom." . . . Still, you have to read again what she writes, your better half, may she have a long life. Anyway, it's boring on the train, nothing to do. [*Reads the letter*] "To my Honorable, Dear, Famous, Sage husband . . ." In short, "Our Teacher and Rabbi Reb Menakhem-Mendel, May his Light Illuminate. First of all, I come to inform you that we are all, thank God, in the best of health, may God let us hear the same from you, not worse, in the days to come . . ." [*Breaks off*] Thank the Almighty, blessed be He, at least in good health. [*Reads on*] "Second of all, I am writing to you that you should have as much strength, you piece of a convert . . ." [*Breaks off*] Already! She starts already with her blessings! [*Reads on*] "You should have as much strength, you piece of a convert, to wallow there in your disease, in the desolate, dark Yehupets, may it burn together with you in one fire, as much as I have strength to trip over my feet, for after all, the handsome doctor told me to lie in bed — may he lie in the cemetery next to you, as mama says . . ." [*Breaks off*] Aha! As mama says! [*Reads on*] " . . . as mama says, so it'll be cozier for you on the long winter nights. . . . What kind of new garbage — a new livelihood God sent down to him, my breadwinner! He will condemnify people to death! What does it mean, Mendel, that you will condemnify people to death? What for?" [*Breaks off*] She doesn't begin to understand what you write to her! [*Reads on*] "You're clean out of your mind — may you go out of your mind for all the Jews and for all the, not to put them in the same breath, Goyim, as mama says . . ." [*Breaks off*] There she goes again with mama! [*Reads on*] " . . . as mama says, a horse, when you let go of the reins, lifts its tail too. It's not enough, that is, that you followed over and over all pagan rites, you were everything in the book: a dealer — a wheeler, a buyer — a liar, a matchmaker — a heartbreaker, a pester — a jester, so that the whole world has to deal with you — you also have to try out trading with dead living corpses, as mama may she live says: wait a minute, he will soon dress you up as a wetnurse somewhere in Poland! . . . Wouldn't it have been a thousand times better if you should, for example, be now in the war with Jampony . . ." [*Breaks off*] Oh yes, of course! I'm flying right away! [*Reads on*] " . . . and return home in such a state, God forbid, like our Moyshe-Velvel Levi-Avrom came back, a dark night on me, with no arms and no legs and no body and no soul, as mama says, does the bullet know who it shoots? . . . So remember, Mendel, this time I'm saying it with good wishes: may a commotion, a fire, a plague fall on you. . . . "

Scene 2
[*Lanternshooter walks into the compartment with a big valise, looks for a place to sit down*]

Lanternshooter	*Permettez-moi?*
Menakhem-Mendel	[*Hides the letter in his briefcase*] Oh, *pourquoi non?* [*To himself*] A fine personage with a pretty valise . . . Maybe he'll let me condemnify him from death?
Lanternshooter	[*Tends to his valise, sits down next to Menakhem-Mendel, pulls out a cigarette*] *Avez-vous du feu?* [*To himself*] *Il faut examiner la terre* — a squeeze in the wagon.
Menakhem-Mendel	Oh! *Pourquoi non?* [*Gives him a match. Talks to himself*] Better he starts first.
Lanternshooter	[*Offers him a cigarette*] *S'il vous plait?* [*To himself*] *Un convenable* subject . . . A provincial with a new outfit . . . Maybe we can do business with him? Just a little insurance to cover expenses . . .
Menakhem-Mendel	[*Takes the cigarette*] Oh! *Pourquoi non?* [*Lights the cigarette. Talks to himself*] On the face of it, a pretty solid citizen. God willing, he will condemnify himself from death.
Lanternshooter	[*To himself*] With such a jerk you can talk Yiddish. [*Starts talking Yiddish*] A pleasure to travel by train. . . . Not like it used to be! When you traveled by wagon, you used to, *vous comprenez,* drag on and on and on.
Menakhem-Mendel	[*Repeats after him*] Drag on and on and on.
Lanternshooter	You were in Diaspora in the hands of the carter, like clay in the Maker's hand.
Menakhem-Mendel	Like clay in the Maker's hand.
Lanternshooter	He would pack a covered wagon with characters of various and sundry sort.
Menakhem-Mendel	Various and sundry sorts.
Lanternshooter	Jews, females, a sack of flour, and a cantor, and a goat, and a priest . . .
Menakhem-Mendel	And a goat, and a priest . . .
Lanternshooter	And as you went uphill, he told the characters to make the effort to get out, forgive the inconvenience.
Menakhem-Mendel	Forgive the inconvenience.
Lanternshooter	And today I'm a lord. I sit, *vous comprenez,* in a compartment and smoke a cigarette, et *je suis à mon aise!*
Menakhem-Mendel	*A mon aise!*
Lanternshooter	The old traveling did have one advantage — your life was safe. You weren't afraid, God forbid, of an accident, a catastrophe, that is, of turning over, *vous comprenez,* and flying like dumplings, upside down.
Menakhem-Mendel	Like dumplings, upside down.
Lanternshooter	It's good to be protected with several thousand rubles after your death, so your wife and children shouldn't, God forbid, *vous comprenez,* go begging in the streets
Menakhem-Mendel	Go begging in the streets . . . [*To himself*] He walks straight into it like a good horse. . . .
Lanternshooter	[*To himself*] He follows me like a good colt! [*Aloud*] For, *vous comprenez,* as long as the wheel turns, it turns.
Menakhem-Mendel	It turns.

Lanternshooter	And when it stops turning, it's — stop, machine!
Menakhem-Mendel	Stop, machine!
Lanternshooter	[*To himself*] He follows nicely. Let's go with him straight to the stable. [*Aloud*] The problem is, not everyone can protect himself with money. Today's expenses, *vous comprenez*, with today-ay-ay-ay . . .
Menakhem-Mendel	With today-ay-ay-ay . . .
Lanternshooter	So at least, *tout au moins*, *un petit insurance*.
Menakhem-Mendel	*Un petit insurance* . . . [*To himself*] It's really something right from heaven, my word!
Lanternshooter	I just now recalled something that happened in our town. One simple citizen who never had a thousand rubles in his life, *vous comprenez*, never saw the eyes of a hundred-ruble bill, still had the good sense to insure himself in time for several thousand rubles. Now he died, traveling, may it not happen to you, in a train, so they paid his wife in our town not much but five thousand rubles cash, one by one!
Menakhem-Mendel	Cash, one by one! Just the same as in our town. In our town too something happened — not with five, but with ten thousand rubles. May God so help me wherever I turn!
Lanternshooter	[*Excited*] Ten thousand rubles?
Menakhem-Mendel	Ten thousand rubles.
Lanternshooter	What did they do with such a sum of money?
Menakhem-Mendel	What should they do? They opened a store, a clever store!
Lanternshooter	Really? *Nu?* And they make some money?
Menakhem-Mendel	And how! A treasure of a fortune!
Lanternshooter	[*To himself*] This is the best moment. Let's take him for a ride. [*Aloud*] What can you say, envy a dead corpse; but when you remember the living, *vous comprenez*. . . . Everybody has a wife and children. . . . [*Sighs*] Everybody has to do it.
Menakhem-Mendel	[*Sighs*] Listen, this is what I'm talking about! [*To himself*] This is the best time. Let's rope him in.
Lanternshooter	[*Sighs*] Blessed be he who does it in time.
Menakhem-Mendel	[*Sighs*] If you have good sense, you put the cart before the horse, you . . . and it's not expensive either. How much can it cost?
Lanternshooter	[*Excited*] It depends on your years. I mean, can we indeed do it here?
Menakhem-Mendel	[*Excited*] Why not?
Lanternshooter	A doctor we can get later, submit an affadavit, *vous comprenez* . . .
Menakhem-Mendel	This is my last worry. The main thing is the sum.
Lanternshooter	[*Grabs his briefcase*] The main thing isn't the sum, the main thing is the years.
Menakhem-Mendel	[*Grabs his briefcase*] Normally, the years. For example, how old are you?
Lanternshooter	Me? What does it matter how old I am?
Menakhem-Mendel	What do you mean what does it matter? You said yourself the main thing is the years, didn't you?
Lanternshooter	What do you mean? You want to indemnify me ?
Menakhem-Mendel	What else? You want to condemnify me ?

Lanternshooter	Are you an agent too?
Menakhem-Mendel	And how! Not just an agent, a sup-agent!
Lanternshooter	[*Stands up, shakes his hand and introduces himself politely, but arrogantly*] Mark Moyseyevich Lanternshooter, Agent Acquéreur Régional of "Equitable."
Menakhem-Mendel	[*Stands up and introduces himself elegantly*] Menakhem-Mendel Yakenhoz, Sup-agent of "Yakir."

Scene 3
[*Bakingfish enters the compartment with two valises and looks for a place to sit down*]

Bakingfish	*Vous permettez?*
Lanternshooter	*S'il vous plait.*
Menakhem-Mendel	Play!
Bakingfish	[*Sits down opposite, spreads his valises around. He opens one valise and takes out bottles and boxes with various foods, puts the second valise upright, like a table, and starts eating*] On the road, you hear, it's good to carry everything with you, because you can't get what you need at every station, and I don't eat everything they give me. I'm afraid for my stomach. That is, not, God forbid, that I have a sick stomach, may it go on forever, but I'm afraid not to spoil it. The stomach, you hear, is a kettle. If, God forbid, the kettle stops cooking, then the whole machine is kaput. [*Opens a bottle and pours himself a drink*] L'Chaim, Jews, to your health. [*Pours another drink and offers it to Menakhem-Mendel*] Forgive me, will you have a little sip? My own home brew from orange peels.
Menakhem-Mendel	[*To himself*] A real friendly person. Maybe we could condemnify him from death? [*Aloud*] Thank you! Better offer it to him. [*Points to Lanternshooter*]
Lanternshooter	[*To Menakhem-Mendel*] Drink up. [*To himself*] A friendly subject. We could indemnify him, to cover expenses . . .
Bakingfish	[*Has another drink and offers one to Lanternshooter*] Have a sip, I beg you, of a good little drink and wash it down with these sardelles. Exquisite sardelles. Hah? What do you say? Aren't they good sardelles? Aren't they fresh? I don't move without sardelles. Don't ask, who knows what may happen on the road. On the road, you have to watch out for your food, because your health, you hear, is the most precious thing in the world. [*Opens a bundle of kishke (dried stuffed derma), eats, and offers them some*] Since you already tasted my sardelles, you have to taste my dried kishke too. Don't be scared, it's fresh and kosher, too. I, if I buy kishke, I don't buy just any old kishke. Health, you hear, is the most precious thing in the world. Because, if you think about death, you're not sure of your life, and especially if you left at home a wife with two little kids like two eyes in your head.
Lanternshooter	[*Eats*] No more than two?
Menakhem-Mendel	Only two?
Bakingfish	[*Chewing*] Not enough? And if, God forbid, you pick yourself up and drop dead?
Lanternshooter	[*Eats*] With your complexion?
Menakhem-Mendel	[*Eats*] Kenna-hora, no evil eye should see it, with your looks?
Bakingfish	[*Chewing*] Don't look at me that I'm so . . . If I hadn't supported myself with food, I would already have — Eh-heh-heh! [*Opens another bundle*] Come on, will you taste, forgive me, the smoked meat! It's cold but fresh. I, when I buy meat, I don't buy just any old meat. Why don't you have a pickle? It's an etrog, not a pickle. My wife, may she live long, before I leave home, when she starts to pack, she packs and packs and packs and packs . . . Take, I beg you, a glass of cherry brandy. It's our own cherry brandy, my wife's specialty.
Lanternshooter	[*Drinks*] A loyal wife you have.
Menakhem-Mendel	[*Drinks*] You have a loyal wife.
Bakingfish	A rarity. One in a whole Guberniia! What do you know?

Lanternshooter	It's not a wife, *vous comprenez*, but some treasure!
Menakhem-Mendel	A treasure, not a wife!
Bakingfish	What do you know? What do you know?
Lanternshooter	[*To himself*] Stepped on the right spot. . . . It looks like it'll go the right way. . . . [*Aloud*] Such a wife, you must appreciate.
Menakhem-Mendel	[*To himself*] He takes him in the right way. . . . [*Aloud*] Such a wife, you have to respect, such a wife!
Bakingfish	[*Peels an orange*] What do you know? What do you know? Take, I beg you, a piece of orange. Good oranges. I, when I go to buy oranges, I don't buy just any old oranges. This too she packed for me, my wife, I mean . . .
Lanternshooter	[*Peels an orange*] A wife like yours, you must not leave just like that, with no protection, God forbid, for the case of the worst case, in case, Heaven forfend, of a catastrophe. *Vous comprenez?* My way of doing it, that, *en principe*, a wife must be protected, let alone children, and let alone people like us, *vous comprenez*, road-people. . . .
Menakhem-Mendel	[*To himself*] Not bad, not bad, on my word! [*Aloud*] We are, after all, road-people, aren't we!
Bakingfish	My way of doing it too, that a wife you must protect, insure at least with a capital of some ten thousand rubles. There is only one recipe for that.
Lanternshooter	[*Excited*] To indemnify yourself?
Menakhem-Mendel	[*Excited*] To condemnify yourself from death?
Bakingfish	How did you guess what I mean? You took the words right out of my mouth!
Lanternshooter	Good sense. For how else could people like us, *vous comprenez*, protect our wives?
Menakhem-Mendel	Simple good sense!
Bakingfish	Absolutely right. If you can pay a little at a time, and it doesn't cost much . . . Which one of you would like to make a deal?
Lanternshooter	[*Grabs his briefcase*] Me, naturally. [*Looks down at Menakhem-Mendel*]
Menakhem-Mendel	[*Grabs his briefcase*] Naturally, me.
Bakingfish	You mean, both of you? My pleasure, even better. [*Bends down for his briefcase*] About a doctor, I think, there won't be any problem.
Lanternshooter	From a doctor, we can bring an affadavit later. The main thing is the years.
Menakhem-Mendel	A paper from a doctor you can furnish later. How old are you — this is the main thing.
Bakingfish	Me?
Lanternshooter	Who else?
Menakhem-Mendel	Who else, me?
Bakingfish	What do you mean? Didn't you want me to in—
Lanternshooter	You should us? We thought you!
Menakhem-Mendel	You, we thought!
Bakingfish	You? Me? Are you age— ?
Lanternshooter	Of course, agents! And you?
Menakhem-Mendel	Agents, naturally! And you, who are you?

Bakingfish	[*Stands off, dusts off the food. Stretches out his hand*] I have the honor to introduce myself: Akim Isaakovich Bakingfish, Inspector-Organizer of "New York."
Lanternshooter	Really? Our brother's keeper! Mark Moyseyevich Lanternshooter, Agent Acquéreur Régional of "Equitable." [*Looks down at Menakhem-Mendel*]
Menakhem-Mendel	Are you really, indeed, one of us?! [*Elegantly*] Menakhem-Mendel Yakenhoz, Sup-agent of "Yakir."

Scene 4
[*Turtledove enters the train with his clan, lots of suitcases, packages, and baskets covered with shawls. Looks for a place for himself and his family*]

Turtledove	*Est-ce que je peux entrer?*
Bakingfish	*Je vous en prie.*
Lanternshooter	*Enchanté.*
Menakhem-Mendel	*Dans chanté.* [*The new character sits down with his wife and children and they begin spreading their packages around. Commotion, tumult. One screams "Dinner! Mama, dinner!" Another wants a drink. The mother cracks nuts, and puts them into the little child's mouth; she holds another baby at her breast. The older ones push to the window, elbow each other aside. The father honors them — one with a slap, one with a poke, one with a smack on the back*]
Bakingfish	[*To himself*] Such a head of a family surely would need to be insured. [*Aloud*] No good with children on the road?
Lanternshooter	[*To himself*] *Un convenable* subject to indemnify himself with the children! [*Aloud*] On the road with children must, I'm sure, be hard?
Menakhem-Mendel	[*To himself*] Maybe this character would condemnify himself from death, maybe? [*Aloud*] It's hard, I'm sure, with children on the road?
Turtledove	As hard as death.
Bakingfish	They're jittery, your kids, aren't they?
Lanternshooter	You spoil them?
Menakhem-Mendel	Are they spoiled, your kids?
Turtledove	[*Pokes the oldest to move him away from the window*] Not so jittery as dear.
Bakingfish	Fine children you have.
Lanternshooter	No evil eye turned out good, *vous comprenez?*
Menakhem-Mendel	Turned out good, no evil eye.
Turtledove	Not bad. Learn very well. Well bred. Breeding is the main thing. [*Calls the oldest one*] Abrasha, come here! Give the uncle a hand. *Nu*, Abrasha! [*Abrasha doesn't want to come and gets a slap from father*] You see this brat? [*Points to the second one*] What a head! A genius, I'm telling you! But a hooligan! Oy, a hooligan! You argue with him, he'll mix you with mud. . . . And that snot-nosed boy, you see? — A sage! Listens to his mother like a tomcat. But for me they have some respect. That is, they wouldn't listen to me either, but I have a whip and I lash, oy do I lash! Children, you hear, have to be taught, educated. Education is the main thing. You see this little squirrel, whose mother feeds him nuts? A big mouth! Not yet four years old and talks every word, every word like an old man. Davidke! Come here, Davidke! [*The little squirrel called Davidke doesn't want to get out of his mother's arms, turns his head to father*] Tell me, Davidke, what's your name? [*Davidke answers "Tye, tye, tye."*] How old are you, Davidke? [*Davidke answers "Tye, tye, tye."*] Davidke! Ask your mother to give you jam. [*Davidke turns his head to his mother: "Tye, tye, tye!"*] What do you say to that? Every word, every word, like an old man!
Bakingfish	[*Enthusing*] For such children, you got to have a lot.
Lanternshooter	For them, *vous comprenez*, you got to gird your loins.

Menakhem-Mendel	Gird your loins, you got to.
Turtledove	What's to be amazed! You see my gray hair? [*Points to his beard*] Not yet fifteen years after the wedding.
Bakingfish	[*Shakes his head*] Ay-yay-yay!
Lanternshooter	No evil eye, such a company!
Menakhem-Mendel	Such a company, no evil eye!
Turtledove	To nourish, clothe, shoe, teach, educate! Education is the main thing. That is, I'm not complaining, God forbid. Thank God I have a fine job, I work out my few thousand rubles with these ten fingers. [*Shows them his fingers*] But as I take a look at my tribe, no evil eye, and it occurs to me, if, Heaven forfend, may God watch over, the hour should never come. . . . You understand? As long as the head serves, and the hands work. . . . You understand?
Bakingfish	Oh! We understand very well. We are also family men. We know the taste of raising children.
Lanternshooter	To protect children is, *vous comprenez*, one of the big things!
Menakhem-Mendel	A big thing to protect children, to protect!
Turtledove	I argue it all the time with my wife, and with everybody separately, wherever I come, I argue the same: What would people like us have done, middle-class people, if there were no means to —
Bakingfish	[*Takes the words out of his mouth*] To insure yourself?
Lanternshooter	To indemnify yourself, *pour le cas de mort?*
Menakhem-Mendel	To condemnify yourself from death?
Turtledove	[*Excited*] I see on your face that you all understand it very well, and that you are all ready to make a deal? So I can only congratulate you — you're doing a good thing.
Bakingfish	[*Very agitated*] We do what our duty tells us to do.
Lanternshooter	What our conscience dictates, *vous comprenez.*
Menakhem-Mendel	We are doing the just thing, we are.
Turtledove	May God help you, as you wish it for yourself, may you have long days and years, may God give you pleasure as you have given me pleasure, along with my wife and children; they, poor things, are looking for this, for I am their only breadwinner. [*Pulls out a briefcase*] How much do you want to make? For instance, what kind of a sum, that is?
Bakingfish	[*Busies himself with his briefcase*] How can we know what kind of a sum?
Lanternshooter	[*Busies himself with his briefcase*] Can we, *vous comprenez*, give you any advice?
Menakhem-Mendel	What do you mean, we should give you advice, we?
Turtledove	[*Amazed*] What do you mean, you me? It's I want you —
Bakingfish	[*Beside himself*] You want to make the spiel to us ?
Lanternshooter	You want to indemnify *us, en cas de mort?*
Menakhem-Mendel	*You* want to condemnify *us* from death? *You?*
Turtledove	What else? *You — me?* Are you agents too?
Bakingfish	Ha-ha-ha! Of course, agents. And how about you?
Lanternshooter	Agents, *vous comprenez.* And who are you?
Menakhem-Mendel	Agents, you bet! And you?

Turtledove	[*Elegantly*] Lazar Konstantinovich Turtledove, Inspector General and Agent Organizer of "Urban."
Bakingfish	[*Elegantly*] Akim Isaakovich Bakingfish, Inspector-Organizer of "New York."
Lanternshooter	Mark Moyseyevich Lanternshooter, Agent Acquéreur Régional of "Equitable." [*Looks down at Menakhem-Mendel*]
Menakhem-Mendel	[*Elegantly*] And I am Menakhem-Mendel Yakenhoz, am I, sup-agent of "Yakir." [*All four shake hands and exchange cards. Only Menakhem-Mendel pats all his pockets*] Oh dear! I haven't got any cards yet, I haven't!
Turtledove	[*Sighs*] A hard way to make a living. Eh?
Bakingfish	[*Sighs*] Like crossing the Red Sea! You travel, you sniff, you think — maybe?
Lanternshooter	[*Looks down at Menakhem-Mendel*] Vous comprenez? Maybe it would not have been so bad if there weren't so many agents. *Vous comprenez*, competition . . .
Menakhem-Mendel	What do I need competition-shmompetition? Say it in simple Yiddish: You lay in the ground and bake bagels.

CURTAIN

1. Yakenhoz: a mnemonic device to remember the order of the blessings said at the Kiddush of a holiday that falls at the end of the Sabbath. In Yiddish, Yakenhoz sounds like a funny name, and may suggest a kind of rabbit. In his introduction to the comedy *Yakenhoz, or the Great Stock Market Game*, Sholem Aleichem wrote, "Y. K. N. H. Z. [Yakenhoz] has five letters, the initials of five words: Yayin, Kiddush, Ner, Havdoleh, Zman [wine, blessing, candle, separation, time] — the five signs of a Jewish holiday. The word itself has no meaning. It is *something*, yet nothing; nothing to hold on to. He who knows the trade of stocks, papers, rates, etc., on the stock market will understand at once the taste of Yakenhoz; and he who is far from that business will digest it only after reading the whole work to the end."

Essays, Speeches, and Letters by Chagall

With the exception of Chagall's letter to the management of GOSEKT, which was written in Russian, the works in this section are translated from the Yiddish.

To the Management of GOSEKT

This letter, in Russian, is in the State Bakhrushin Museum, Moscow.

When I finished my work, I assumed, as was promised, that it would be exhibited publicly like many of my most recent works.

The management will agree that, as an artist, I cannot rest until the "masses" see it, etc.

Instead, the works appear to have been placed in a cage and can be seen, crowded (though happily so), by at most a hundred Jews. I love Jews very much (there is plenty of evidence for this), but I also love Russians and various other peoples and am used to painting serious work for many nationalities.

Hence, my demand and appeal to the theater are natural and legitimate; I am asking you to put at my disposal twenty-eight hours in the course of two weeks — two hours a day — for the organization of an exhibition and survey of my works for all interested parties. The expenses for the organization of the exhibition, such as posters, etc., will be borne by IZO NKP [Art Division, People's Commissariat of Enlightenment] or by me. I cannot give up this demand.

Expecting an official answer,

Marc Chagall
12/2/21

Leaves From My Notebook

Originally published in Shtrom, *Moscow, no. 1 (1922).*

A few words, comrades, on the topic you asked me to write about at length — my opinion on Jewish art.

Just recently in Jewish artists' circles a hot debate went on about the so-called Jewish art.

In the noise and fever, a group of Jewish artists emerged. Among them was Marc Chagall.

Still in Vitebsk when this misfortune happened — just returned from Paris — I smiled to myself.

I was busy then with something else.

On the one hand, Jews of the "new world" — that world so hated by Litvakov — my shtetl alleys, hunchbacked, herringy residents, green Jews, uncles, aunts, with their questions, "Thank God, you grew up, got big!"

And I kept painting them. . . .

On the other hand, I was younger then by a hundred years, and I loved them, simply loved them. . . .

I was more absorbed by this, this gripped me more than the thought that I was anointed as a Jewish artist.

Once, in Paris, back in my LaRuche room, where I worked, I heard through the Spanish screen the quarrel of two Jewish émigré voices, "So what do you think, after all, Antokolsky wasn't a Jewish artist, nor Israels, nor Liebermann!"

The lamp was dim and lit my painting standing upside down (that's how I work — now are you happy?!) and finally, when the Paris sky began to dawn, I laughed at the idle thoughts of my neighbors about the lot of Jewish art, "O. K., you talk — and I will work."

Representatives of all countries and nations! — To you — my appeal. (I cannot, I remembered Spengler.) Confess: Now, when Lenin sits in the Kremlin, there is no sliver of wood, smoke rises, the wife is angry — do you now have "national art?"

You, clever German Walden, and you, various others who preach international art, fine Frenchmen, Metzinger and Gleizes (if they're still alive), you will answer me, "Chagall, you're right!"

Jews, if they feel like it (I do), may cry that the painters of the shtetl wooden synagogues (why am I not with you in one grave?) and the whittlers of the wooden synagogue clappers — "Hush!" (I saw it in An-ski's collection, got scared) — are gone.

But what is really the difference between my crippled Mohilev great-grandfather Segal who painted the Mohilev synagogue, and me, who painted the Yiddish theater (a good theater) in Moscow?

Believe me, no fewer lice visited us as we wallowed on the floor and in workshops, in synagogues and in the theater.

Furthermore, I am sure that, if I stopped shaving, I would see his precise portrait. . . .

By the way, my father.

Believe me, I put in quite a bit of effort; no less love (and what love!) have we both expended.

The difference is only that he took orders for signs and I studied in Paris, about which he also heard something.

And yet. Both I and he and others (there are such) are not yet Jewish art as a whole.

Why not speak the truth? Where would it come from? God forbid it should have to come from some fiat! From Efros writing an article, or because Levitan will give me an "academic ration!" . . .

There was Japanese art, Egyptian, Persian, Greek. Beginning with the Renaissance, national arts began to decline. Boundaries are blurred. Artists come — individuals, citizens of this or that state, born here or there (blessed be my Vitebsk) — and one would need a good registration or even a passport specialist (for the Jewish desk) to be able to "nationalize" all the artists.

Yet it seems to me:

If I were not a Jew (with the content I put into that word), I wouldn't have been an artist, or I would be a different artist altogether.

Is that news?

For myself I know quite well what this little nation can achieve.

Unfortunately, I am too modest and cannot say aloud what it can achieve.

It's no small matter what this little nation has achieved!

When it wanted — it showed Christ and Christianity.

When it wished — it gave Marx and Socialism.

Can it be that it won't show the world some art?

It will!

Kill me if not.

How I Got to Know Peretz

Originally published in Literarishe bleter, *Warsaw, nos. 49–50 (1925). Reprinted in* Di goldene keyt, *Tel Aviv, no. 60 (1967).*

You asked me, dear colleagues, to write for the Peretz issue. You probably think it is enough to love something in order to be able to write about it — to write about Peretz. But is he who loves a critic?

Besides, I note with fear that I have recently lost, it seems to me, the talent for writing. . . . The pen betrays me. . . .

I didn't even know Peretz personally. Only when a publisher (I don't remember which) asked me to do drawings for one of Peretz's tales, "The Magician," did I start reading Peretz. I was surprised. You can certainly remember the impression when you walk in the street and turn into another street and, at that very corner, behind a fence, a Jewish moon with a dark horizon behind it suddenly leaps at your feet from the sky.

Just like that did poor and splendid Jewish images and figures float up from the little white pages. It is simple and new. It is that modest, hardly underlined noble technique, those already lived-out means that alone can make art national, independent of content.

And really, from childhood on, haven't they dangled anxiously inside us — those notes, Sabbath days, Friday evenings, velvet caps, girls of your first love, landscapes breathing with psalms, the last tones of the weary cantor, and Jews, Jews on the earth and in the sky?

I recall my strolls along the street on the riverbank. Past the sawmill and factory, far, far beyond the other side of the bridge — there, you stop at a tree next to the graveyard. Peretz murmured to my feet from below. Swam in the clouds above. Rustled among the little houses — the tombstones of the cemetery, where pieces and crumbs of his folklore stories were heaped up — various scraps of paper covered with writing. Wasn't the forsaken, mountainous and half-alive place good for the stage of his play, *A Night in the Old Market*?

I will not calm down until the collection of his folklore tales is illustrated by me. A dream!

I am sorry, dear colleagues, that on the day of the *Yortseyt*, I cannot be in a corner in a synagogue somewhere — where Jews will remember Peretz. In such moments our lives and our works pass before our eyes. . . . And years unknown are still there for us.

And you think: our epoch may be one of iron and cruelty, yet we have now rediscovered Peretz and Sholem Aleichem.

They were first to lay their hands on you and bless you — the new generations of Jewish poets and writers.

Letters to YIVO On a Jewish Art Museum

YIVO, the Jewish Scientific Institute, was founded in Vilna in 1925. For its Conference in 1929, Chagall wrote a letter initiating the creation of a Jewish Art Museum. The museum, supported financially by the Berlin psychoanalyst Eitingon, was officially opened by the eminent historian Professor S. Dubnov, on the tenth anniversary of YIVO, August 18, 1935. Jacob Sher, who greeted the delegates on behalf of the Vilna Jewish artists, remarked, "It is the greatest celebration for the young Jewish artists to see Chagall. Chagall is the dream of every young artist. The Vilna artists have lived to see Chagall with their own eyes and to hear him speak in the international language, the Esperanto, called Jewish art." Chagall delivered the opening address. The following letters were published in Journal for Jewish Art, *Vilna (YIVO), no. 1 (Nov.–Dec. 1936).*

Allow me to say a few words about the Jewish Scientific Institute. We Jews, scattered over the whole world, badly need cultural institutions to unite us. You absolutely must not postpone the organization of a Section for Art. It is as necessary as the whole Institute.

I admit, for quite some time a bitterness has been building up in me, since, even in the better Jewish circles, there is no discussion of the need to create a Jewish art museum. Few among us are aware of how important it is, and not just politically. The centers for collecting for the museum will be Vilna, Berlin, New York. I know it would have been easy to establish in Paris, for example, a society of "Friends of a Jewish Museum Foundation" with branches in all other cities. But I also know the fate of such societies dealing with the issues of Jewish art. The Jewish Scientific Institute, since it stands on its own two feet, and wants to take care of it, must do so as soon as possible.

You will tell me, "Be our guest, come work, help." Thus far, I haven't refused. If I had two lives, I would have given one to the Jews. But our art is a terrible art, it demands all of your soul, your entire devotion.

You will say, and the means? The means, as always, must be given by the Jewish government, that is, by the Jewish people as a whole. While we are wasting enormous sums on, I admit, important but temporary needs, we must especially find money for such a goal. We Jews have often been accused of not being capable of art. Now we could show the world what we really possess.

But we possess absolutely no connoisseurs of the visual arts, while we do have many specialists in Yiddish literature. Hence, the Institute should set up courses to study the problems of art in general and of Jewish art in particular.

This is more or less what I wanted to tell you. It may seem like an illusion, but illusions are often important and vital. I greet YIVO warmly and wish it success.

Your devoted,

Marc Chagall

Dear Dr. Schneid:

On the publication of the first issue of the *Journal for Jewish Art* by the Museum at YIVO, I send you my best wishes.

I have thought a lot about it.

Humanity today is far from both art and humanity. And I have often thought that my erstwhile talks and plans about a museum and about art are perhaps off the mark.

And after my trip to Poland, when I saw the Jews almost dying of starvation, I was even more upset.

But — no!

Let everyone help build our true Jewish art, our Jewish museum foundation, our science of art, our strength! Let your journal serve those goals successfully.

Paris, October 1936

Marc Chagall

Speech at the World Conference of the Jewish Scientific Institute, YIVO

Originally published in World Conference of the Jewish Scientific Institute: On the Tenth Anniversary of YIVO. *Vilna: YIVO, 1936. Reprinted in* Di goldene keyt, *no. 60 (1967).*

Actually, you might think I am out of place here. For I am an artist and you are scientists. But I am here exactly as you are, for we share the same weakness, the same passion: *Jews.*

And precisely now, in this terrible and ridiculous time, in the time of contemporary fashionable anti-Semitism, I would like to emphasize once more that I am a Jew. And by this very fact, I am even more international in spirit — not like the model of the professional revolutionaries who contemptuously shake off their Jewishness.

There are several reasons why I am here. I have known these little huts and fences around you by heart for a long time. But your house, the house of the Institute, though it seems to be as poor as a hut in one of my paintings, is nevertheless as rich as Solomon's Temple. So I greet it and I greet you who created it. I am filled with a special, bitter joy, by the thought that without means, with no state support, with only enthusiasm and love, you built a house with your own hands. In the future, in the period of our ascendance, this house will serve as a model of stubborn Jewish devotion to the idea of culture.

There is also a personal reason why I came here. A few kilometers from you, there is a land, actually just one city, which I haven't seen in a long time, and which won't let go of me. I used your invitation and came to meander here a while. I admit that the older I get, the lazier I get, and I don't move if I'm not called.

I don't know why, but between me and my homeland there is a one-sided affair, and nevertheless, such a land of genius, with such a revolution of genius, might have sensed what occurs in the heart of one of their own, and not just listened to and believed in the words and declarations of the confession letters. . . .

But the major reason for my coming here is to remind again not just you Vilna Jews (because you do do something in this respect), but the Jews of the whole world, that a Jewish Scientific Institute is indeed beautiful — but that a Jewish Art Museum is just as beautiful and just as important.

Indeed, since the end of the nineteenth century and the beginning of the twentieth, Jews have strained at their fetters and stormed into the world with their art; and it seems to me that this cultural contribution is the most important Jewish contribution of recent times. But most people have barely heard about it. The masses and the intelligentsia don't see it; everything is splintered, not concentrated, and I even feel awkward talking about it because I am myself an interested party.

But what can you do? We Jews don't have our own Baudelaire, Théophile Gauthier, Apollinaire, who powerfully forged the artistic taste and the artistic concepts of their time. Can we help it? In our Jewish society, we don't have a Diaghilev, a Morozov, a Shchukin, who collected and organized the art culture with such ardor and understanding.

And the fact that the intelligentsia in general, and Yiddish writers in particular, lack interest in the plastic arts indicates that art is alien and superfluous in their lives and work, and the world rests on literature alone.

If Yiddish poetry, Yiddish literature, were intertwined with other branches of art in general, and with visual art in particular, it would have been richer, it would have strengthened its upward thrust, both in spirit and in style.

If we take, for example, Russian literature — the connection between Pushkin and the pseudoclassicists of his time, between Gogol' and Alexandr Ivanov, Tolstoi and the "Itinerants," Chekhov and Levitan, or in our literature, Peretz and his fine sensibility for the modernism of his time — we will surely find that this connection filled their literary creation with an intensive plastic actuality, with a new source of richness, with a great freshness. And therefore their language is not ethnographic, but universal in a pure artistic sense. But this is a different problem, much more important than one might think, and perhaps also a scientific problem, so I hand it to the proper address, to you, scientists.

Simply, we new Jews who, thousands of years ago, created the Bible, the work of the Prophets, the basis of all religions of all peoples, we also want to create great art that will resound in the world.

But I am not amazed at the feeling toward us on the part of strangers or enemies. No, what amazes me is the relationship of all layers of Jewish society to its own artists, their treatment of the artists as second-class political activists, who don't deserve even part of that respect we grant artists of the pen or the theater, who often have to be grateful to the visual artists themselves. I am not talking just about the fact that Jews don't buy paintings, don't support the artists, though this is also important in today's time of crisis. What is important is the attention, the interest. And if this appears sometimes, it is directed to the least talented and most tasteless "kitsch."

Indeed, the reasons for that situation are well known. The Torah, which gave us the Ten Commandments, snuck in an eleventh commandment too: "Thou shalt not make unto thee any graven image."

Our monotheism was dearly bought — and, because of that, Judaism had to give up observation of nature with our *eyes*, and not just with our soul. On religious grounds, Judaism struggled with ancient idolatry, whose remnants are displayed today in all museums of the world, so that it remained with no share in the treasures of graphic art. We left nothing behind us in the world's museums except for Torah Scrolls and the abandoned synagogues that are no longer attended.

But we, the new Jews, have revolted against this, we no longer want to recognize such a state of affairs, we want to be not just the People of the Book, but also a people of art. This is the source of the birth pangs of our art, this is why its infancy is so sad. All this requires good organization and good will: to collect art among Jews and everything that is related to the history of art, to promote art not as a thing outside us, but as part of our internal life, and to encourage our artists.

Collecting paintings must not be only a matter of the artists' philanthropy. Keep in mind that even canvases and paints cost the artist more than a pen and paper for the writer; but no one would think of asking for a writer's manuscript — whether valuable or not — for nothing. At a time when we seem to complain everywhere that we have no advocates in the world, which persecutes us so much, and we dream of a congress where disbarred lawyers will appear, we forget that we have in our hands an immense shield; our cultural treasures must speak for us, must plead our case and defend us. The Scientific Institute is a valuable treasure, but we must also create an art institute, national art foundations, which will continue to nourish and build museums in the centers of Jewish life. You may say that this is an illusion, but the illusory and fantastic, as we often discover, are the most real. A proof is the YIVO. For the first conference of YIVO, six years ago, I wrote to you about creating a museum at the YIVO. I know how difficult it is. But better difficult than hurried, as they did in Eretz Israel, where, despite my warnings, they brought together anything they could, and the leadership went to inexperienced and not-very-artistic hands. The new Jewish people does not need a repetition of the Bezalels.

We don't need to reach the goal right away. There is a whole series of preparatory stages, moral and material: propagating the idea, training art historians and museum specialists, staging exhibitions in public institutions, workers' clubs, schools; organizing excursions to the European centers, to the great international exhibitions; instructing teachers, pupils, students in teachers' colleges and universities in understanding art; fostering their knowledge of art as you foster their taste in literature; publishing books and journals about art. For Jewish taste is horrible, backward; and their confidence in their own judgment is even greater. Young (and not so young) people, who travel to the great centers to study law, medicine, and other professions that often don't quite feed the body, might have thought a bit about art culture, about art that at least nourishes our spirit.

I close with the feeling that all I have said, and all I have not said, should have been said at a conference of writers and artists. But artists as a social element practically don't exist; artists can hardly talk to each other. Therefore, others, all of you here, have to look at us actively from the side, organize sensibly, tactfully, and with an internal empathy.

For a long time, I have wanted to say these few words about our role, about your role, about the role of all of us, not just artists, but scientists, and all Jews for the good of all humanity. In these days of crisis, not just a material but also a spiritual crisis, when world crises, wars, revolutions flare up over a piece of bread, and the Jews truly don't have the wherewithal or the where to live, there is still no sweeter mission than suffering and working for our goal, for our spirit, which lives in our Bible, which lives in our dreams about art, which can help bring the Jews to the true and right path, to achieve while other nations just spill blood — their own and that of others.

August 14, 1935

The Artist and the Poet

Speech delivered in New York on April 30, 1944, on the publication of Itsik Fefer's book, To Start Anew {Oyfsnay}, *which Chagall illustrated. Fefer, a Soviet Yiddish poet, visited the United States with Mikhoels in September 1943. The manuscript is in the YIVO archives (New York City).*

Thank you for your invitation to be with you at this assembly. I am just an artist struggling with himself and his art. What can I say, I who want to hear? Perhaps the folk proverb is right, that silence is golden and the word is silver.

But today it must be different. Keeping silent is not golden, and there are words that say nothing. For an artist, it is not enough today to live with nature, with himself. He must also live with and feel the people.

Today my people are those who let their life's road be illuminated by the young rays that emanate from our great homeland.

My people are those who strive toward the unity of all its parts.

And, like many of you, I want the realization of a just Jewish home for millions of Jews in Eretz Israel, which must be dear to everyone.

Those are the three points without which a Jew is today only half a man and only half a Jew. The more I strive toward them simultaneously — the fuller is my personality as a Jew and as a artist.

With those three points, we bring our Jewish face to the ideal that is possible today. The splintering of the Jewish people has long led to its deformation and unhappiness. What Paris once was for those who sought art — I admire my great homeland for its achievements and ambitions. It saves the world. Jewish America should have become the great movement of Jewish unity.

Three Jewish worlds need each other. Together they must create the strength of Jewish creativity and culture; together the Jewish people will become whole, morally and physically. Unity is our new Hasidism.

I come to greet you as a simple Jew from the people. My father was from the people, a worker. In his *shul*, he was for "unity"; when he heard the word Jerusalem, he cried. My father is my best academy.

A few days ago, the war in Europe ended. The Jewish people who remain rise emaciated, pale. They look around: what remains of the people?

What remains are their pain and scattered sacks of their limbs. I don't know if they will count our lost Jewish people's armies. If only Moses were here, he would have presented a bill.

I want to hope that "on the waters of another river" a new child will be found — a Moses who will heal the Jewish people both from satiation and hunger, will straighten the twisted ways, and twist the straight ones a bit. He will put us on our feet so we will become a people of dawn and not of sunset.

Now is the time. No world conferences can be successful until the Jewish people are taken down from the cross on which they have been crucified for two thousand years.

The world must do justice to itself. Temporary luck and wealth is not enough — a state, a land, also has a consciousness, a soul, like an individual person.

The Jewish people emerged from the war like a capsized ship at sea. We look in the water — torn legs and souls are floating, torn Torah scrolls disintegrate like bright, childish intestines. From the abyss you hear no divine or prophetic voices.

And as always the sun burns above and colors us and everybody with the color of red blood.

The war is over. But may peace not be like that painting that has everything except a soul.

I greet the Jewish folk masses. I always wanted to feel like one of them, to fill myself with the people's breath, as once upon a time in my home. It is good to come to the people, as a man who knocks at the door at night. Let us just not think that the door is like a wall. To go to the people . . . find in them a salvation from yourself, a way to a lost world.

I wish you and your children to seek not only a piece of bread, but primarily to strive to reach the source of Jewish and human culture, and thus we will attain general human value in our own eyes and in the eyes of others.

To the Paris Artists

The typed manuscript is the YIVO archives (New York City).

I send my word to you, my fellow painters of the Salon of Liberation.

Thirty-five years ago, as a very young man, like thousands of others, I came to Paris to fall in love with France and study French art.

In recent years I have felt unhappy that I couldn't be with you, my friends. My enemy forced me to take the road of exile.

On that tragic road, I lost my wife, the companion of my life, the woman who was my inspiration. I want to say to my friends in France that she joins me in this greeting, she who loved France and French art so faithfully. Her last joy was the liberation of Paris.

In the course of these years, the world was anxious about the fate of French civilization, of French art.

The absence of France seemed impossible, incomprehensible. Today the world hopes and believes that the years of struggle will make the content and spirit of French art even more profound. The world hopes and believes that the art of France will, more than ever, be worthy of the great art epochs of the past.

I bow to the memory of those who disappeared, and of those who fell in the battle.

I greet you, Picasso, Matisse, Bonnard. I greet you, Raoul Dufy. I greet you, the old and the young, who all fought with so much courage.

I would also like to greet my friends, the French writers who are so worthy to bear that name, Jean Paulhan, Jean Cassou, André Malraux, Paul Eluard, and so many others.

I bow to your struggle, to your fight against the foe of art and life.

Now, when Paris is liberated, when the art of France is resurrected, the whole world too will, once and for all, be free of the satanic enemies who wanted to annihilate not just the body but also the soul — the soul, without which there is no life, no artistic creativity.

Dear friends, we are grateful to the destiny that kept you alive and allowed the light of your colors and your works to illuminate the sky darkened by the enemy.

May your colors and your creative effort have the strength to bring back warmth and new belief in life, in the true life of France and of the whole world.

October 14, 1944

To the Jewish People in Paris

Originally published in Naye Prese, *Paris, June 15, 1946. Reprinted in* Di goldene keyt, *no. 60 (1967).*

From one soul to the other, from year to year, from country to country. . . .

I am back here again, where I spent my youth in art.

You, along with other peoples, brought me here.

Here is my beautiful and melancholy city. I still saw little of you. Just a few eyes, a few weary faces.

I saw how similar you are to me, to my art, but through your eyes I saw more — I saw the gun that liberated us, but also the smoke of the burning ovens, the forests and the villages where you hid and fought, and the heroism that is the greatest in our history.

It seems to me that you are standing before me, impoverished and naked, in tatters.

But be calm, this reminds me of those paintings by Rembrandt, where naked and barely covered figures appear, and are therefore as pure as gold. . . .

We lived to see that our life is like the torn tatters on those paintings of genius, but our spirit still shines.

Only one woe: We lost our dear ones. Our house is empty, even when we are in it.

We are crying and cannot cry them out enough. We are seeking them up above in the clouds. We are seeking them down below in the corners. We are seeking them in ourselves. . . .

We touch ourselves and push ourselves away. It is only us — without them.

We are desolate, not just because we are missing our near ones, but because many "near ones" here and there look like strangers. . . .

We are amazed that the more we break through to light — the deeper we see the "shadow."

But where was the real "foe"? The barbarian who accidentally has a human face, who destroys a child and a woman and robs in broad daylight, cannot be called "foe." He could not present to us any important philosophical or moral proof — against our philosophy and morals.

We won.

In my personal life, I want to see some consolation in that: that we will remain what we were before. We don't want to flee from the depths of our culture and belief, for through them lies the road to the world.

And we still want to create our form and content.

And it seems to me that out of the fire, breaking the boundaries of factionalism, Jews will find a language of unity.

A. Sutzkever — Poet and Symbol

Speech at a celebration in Paris honoring the Yiddish poet and partisan A. Sutzkever.

I am happy to be among Jews and greet my friend and poet Sutzkever, who is not only a great poet, but also a symbol of that tragic and heroic time when our people still lived in their old homes. He was among those who, in the locked-up ghettoes, fevered and fought our enemy. His young eyes saw that reality which we didn't know in our youth. Therefore, his poems, no matter with what color they are painted or what they sing about, often take on that tragic tone of our yesterday. While we dreamed once upon a time about such fantastic, sweet fires and broken *khupa* houses, he saw ugly man in his physical and spiritual mire.

Therefore, I feel a kind of obligation to Sutzkever and his friends the other heroes. Moreover, Sutzkever the poet is also often close to me. Pieces of his young poetry remind me of pieces of my Vitebsk streets, when I walked over them, over the roofs and chimneys, believing that, outside of me, no one lived in the city, that all the girls were waiting for me, that from the graves in the cemetery, the dead were listening to me, that the clouds and the moon turned with me into another street.

But there is no more Vitebsk nor Vilna, and together with them, the Yiddish language has shuddered, and what not? Only a distant sound remains, such an unclear taste on the tip of your tongue.

Sometimes the familiar tombstone with its torn Torah Scrolls appears from afar — the thin Yiddish poet and painter who writes and paints. For whom, for what?

But if Sutzkever saw the face of that last day, in a happy day he started a new day. He hovered over to the land of the Jewish natural dream, to the biblical land. He lives in Israel. I cannot help but recall here my old friend the national poet Bialik, walking around the streets of Tel Aviv like a prophet and suddenly, quietly, on the side, asking my little daughter and my wife (apparently, he thought women were closer to God . . .) to pray for him to be able to write poems — he had in mind the city of Odessa, where he had previously created his monumental poems. . . .

My dear friends, you feel that the time has come for us Jews to be born again. We are not a people that dies. And may your art attain even more the new shine we have recently seen on the faces of the "sabras" born in our land.

May you find the harmony of yesterday and today. I know it is difficult to find such a balm to heal and renew our body and soul. Perhaps this is a good means: to let your own diamond shine and illuminate freely, if you have one, let the colors sink freely inside you if you are born with them. And the form of a world will follow us like a shadow, but the shadow is not a shadow, it is the Jew in us.

It becomes ever clearer that the freer we are, the more Jews we are; and the more Jew — the more man we become.

We are stronger now, though smaller in number, and may our enemies understand little by little that it is superfluous and dangerous to touch us. For our strength is our *internal* truth, a truth like the purest hue of a painting, as freedom itself.

Art, poetry, is built on such a fiery base. It envelops the man and the people. May you so Jewishly stream into our people as into a river, a river that flows into the sea of the world.

1955

Summary Translation of Chagall's Letter to President Weitzman

This summary, in English, was discovered among Chagall's correspondence in the YIVO archives (New York City). It is reprinted with only minor spelling corrections. The original is not in the Weitzman archives in Rehovot.

. . . I write to you as our fathers in Russia used to write to their Rabbis for help in solving problems of conscience.

I have been asked to execute mural paintings in a 16th-century chapel in Vence, which is a historical, cultural, and religious center on the Riviera. I have not yet accepted.

. . . Of course I shall be left entirely free to paint whatever I wish and if I accept I intend to do Biblical scenes such as appear in some of my paintings, strictly in my own manner and from my own point of view, symbolizing the suffering of the martyred Jewish people.

To decorate a chapel might give me the chance to do work that is only possible on large walls, instead of having to limit myself to relatively small canvases destined to hang in private houses. To decorate walls in public buildings has long been my dream. If it were possible to decorate a synagogue my dream would be completely fulfilled.

If I decide to decorate this chapel I would not want the people of Israel to think that in my heart or mind — not to speak of my art — I have anything in common with non-Judaism. With my ancestors I shall always be bound to my people.

On a more temporal basis I do not know whether I should decorate a Catholic church at a time when the Vatican is not favorably disposed to Israel. At the same time, I wonder if the presence of a Jewish painting in a church might be good propaganda for our people.

In other situations I have solved similar cases myself. I refused my friend Jacques Maritain's request to donate a picture to the Vatican's museum of modern art. I refused to exhibit in German museums after the war, in spite of the official invitation of the French Cultural Services. An exhibition that has recently taken place in Düsseldorf was organized without my consent and consisted of pictures from German and Dutch collections. I refused to be present at the opening of my exhibition in London at a time when British policy was unfavorable to our interests.

But today I have neither the strength nor the capacity to reply, and all the more because I have been asked to do work in other churches and in other towns.

But with the renaissance, after 2,000 years, of the spiritual and political center of the Jewish people, I cannot help turning with all my doubts toward its most eminent representative.

A Word at the Celebration in Jerusalem

Published in Di goldene keyt, *no. 60 (1967).*

How did the air and earth of Vitebsk, my hometown, along with thousands of years of Diaspora, blend with the air and earth of Jerusalem?

How could I have known that it was not only my hands and colors that would lead me in my work, but also the dear hands of my father and mother, and of others and yet others, with their mute lips and closed eyes, who whispered behind me as if they wanted to take part in my life?

It seems to me that your tragic and heroic resistance movements in the ghettos, and your war here, in this country, have merged with my flowers and animals and fire-colors. . . .

Insofar as our age refuses to see the whole figure of the world and is content with a very small part of its skin, my heart aches when I observe this figure in its eternal rhythm, and my will to go against the general stream is strengthened.

It seems to me that the colors and the lines flow out, like tears from my eyes, though I am not crying. — And do not think I am talking here in a moment of weakness. On the contrary, the more years I pile up, the more certain I am of what I want and what I say.

I know that my life's path is eternal and brief. And I learned, back in my mother's womb, to walk that path more out of love than out of hatred.

The thoughts have nested in me for many years, since the time when my feet walked on the Holy Land, when I prepared myself to create engravings of the Bible. They strengthened me and encouraged me to bring my modest gift to the Jewish people — that people that lived here thousands of years ago, among the other Semitic peoples.

And what is now called religious art I created when I recalled also the great and ancient creations of the surrounding Semitic peoples.

I hope that, thereby, I stretch out my hand to the neighboring peoples, their poets and artists, to whom human culture is dear. I saw the mountains of Sodom and the Negev, and the shadows of our Prophets, in their garb the color of dried bread, shine from those mountains. I heard their ancient words. . . .

In their words they marked the path for behavior on the earth and pointed out the moral essence of our life.

I draw hope and courage from the thought that my modest work will remain on their-your land.

Color, Which Is Love (A Word for America)

Published in Di goldene keyt, no. 50 (1964).

My friend, Professor Neff, asked me to come to you, listen to you, and say a few words to you.

In truth, I would have preferred to listen to you, for all my life I have preferred to listen to what others say, to learn something from them, as far as I can.

Not for the first time do I come to you, for it seems to me that the idea of your association deserves much interest.

Rationally, I should have stayed at work in my atelier, for this is the main goal of my life, when I am daring enough to hope that I work not just for myself. But it is good to think that people in our time come together to share their thoughts about the main goals of life.

What can be more moving in our society, on this planet, than the striving to listen to the human heart, to hear in it the pulse of a world, the sighs and the dreams.

For hundreds and thousands of years, it was morally easier for a man to live. He had this or that moral ground, deeply anchored in himself. His life and his creative activity were the deep and precise result of his world view. We see it clearly sealed in the works of distant epochs of the past.

Gradually, however, in the course of time, those old conceptions became powerless to inspire a living breath in people and fill them with an internal life, not only for their creativity but simply for their life.

I am not sad at all when I speak about it, and I'm not a pessimist. Forces do not exist that could influence me to believe no longer in the human personality, for I believe in general in the greatness of nature. But I also know that human will and human behavior often result from cosmic influences of that nature, just like the unfolding of history and human destiny. Yet we cannot refrain from always asking the same question: why are we so sad in recent years?

The more boldly man liberates himself from his chains, the more man feels alone, and among the masses he is left alone with his destiny.

As always, however, I shall shift to art.

With Impressionism, a window opened for us. A bright rainbow rose on the horizon of our world. And though this world was different and more intensively colored, it seems to me that, on the whole, it was narrower than the Naturalistic world of Courbet, for example. Just as the Naturalism of Courbet was, in his time, narrower than the world of Romanticism of Delacroix. And the world of Delacroix was more declamatory and narrower than the Neoclassical world of David and Ingres. I don't want to go on. . . .

After Impressionism came the Cubist world, which led us into the geometrical underground of things. Afterward, abstraction led us into a world of tiny elements and matter. Thus we see the diapason and the size of the stage growing narrower and narrower. Going on, you have the impression that you are going toward a constantly progressive shrinking. What did happen? Let us see what is authentic in our life-baggage.

The world belongs to us from the moment we are born, and it seems to us that we are prepared for it from the very beginning of our life.

For about two thousand years, a reservoir of energy has nourished us, supported us, given us a certain content in life. But in the last century, a crack has opened in that reservoir. And its elements have begun to fall apart.

God, perspective, color, the Bible, form, lines, traditions, the so-called humanistic theories, love, loyalty, family, school, education, the Prophets, and Christ himself.

Perhaps I was once skeptical? I made pictures topsy-turvy. I decapitated my characters, cut them to pieces, and in my paintings they hovered in the air. All this in the name of a different perspective, a different construction of paintings, and a different formalism.

And gradually our world appeared to us as a small world where we small people hover in the air, grasping onto the small elements of our nature, until the moment when, through very small elements of nature, we approached the atom itself.

This so-called scientific control of nature — doesn't it limit the source of poetry, doesn't it empty the soul? Doesn't it deprive man of calm, even of purely physical rest? Doesn't all this deprive the organism of the moral concept of life and creation?

In recent years, I have often spoken about the chemistry, about authentic color, and about painterly matter as a barometer of authenticity.

A particularly sharp eye can see that authentic color and authentic matter contain in themselves every technical possibility as well as moral and philosophical content.

If there is a moral crisis, there is also a crisis of color, of the moral material, the blood, and of the elements of the word, of sound, of all the components of art and life as well.

And even if you have mountains of color in a painting, if you see something there or not, if there are lots of words and sounds — it still means that the work is also authentic.

In my opinion, the color and the matter of Cimabue itself stimulated an upheaval in the art of the Byzantine period. In the same way, another color of Giotto, also absolutely authentic — and I emphasize this word from a chemical point of view — stimulated a different moral and artistic upheaval. Just as later, it was done by Masaccio and others. . . .

I repeat: it is not the world view that is a literary or symbolic issue, that brings this change, but the blood itself, a certain chemistry of nature, objects, and human concentration itself. You can see the conception of this authenticity in all domains.

How was it born, how is it built up, this chemistry through which art is created, the true conception of the world and of life?

It consists of elements of love and of a certain natural attitude, just as nature itself, which cannot stand evil, hatred, indifference. . . .

If, for example, we are seized to the quick by the soul of the Bible, it is primarily because, even chemically, the Bible is the greatest work of art in the world, which includes the highest life-ideal on our planet.

Let another chemical genius come, and humanity will follow him as a new world view, a new light in life.

I don't pretend in these few words to reveal to you the various other values of our history.

But those who think this chemistry can be found somewhere in scientific laboratories, in a factory, are mistaken; nor can you learn it in ateliers or from theories.

No, it is in us, in our hands, in our souls; it is both inherent in us and the result of education.

Not, however, to remain with general meditations, I will tell you what I am doing now: I intend to continue the biblical series planned for a building — not a church, not a museum, but a place for people seeking this new plastic spiritual content I talked about. It seems to me that there are people among us seeking it. Perhaps today you, tomorrow — others. . . .

Though I don't sense in myself any philosophical mission, I cannot avoid sensing what currently stifles art and culture, and sometimes even life itself.

On the other hand, precisely in a time of constant sapping of religiousness — not to go into the reasons for that — we must see how the art of the nineteenth and twentieth centuries up to now has been a weak reflection of scientific discoveries, whereas, before this period, including the Renaissance, art always mirrored the religious spirit or, at least, illustrated the religiousness of its time.

I cannot refrain from saying that art of a scientific nature or art for enjoyment's sake, like nourishment, is not a living value. Historically, such art may gradually wither. They say that a "good" man can be a bad artist. But there is not and never will be an artist who is not a great and indeed good man.

I know that certain people today discredit nature. After Cézanne, Monet, Gauguin, there seems to be no genius who would reflect it.

Today, it is common to avoid nature as far as possible; this looks to me like people who avoid looking into your eyes. I am afraid of it, and turn my gaze away from such people.

Certain revolutionaries wanted, scientifically, to introduce order into the social and economic life of the world. But after a certain time, these scientific theories are contradicted in part by other theories.

Perhaps the change in the social order, as well as in art, would have been more certain if it also emerged from our soul, not just from our head. If people read more deeply the writings of the Prophets, they could have found there some keys to life.

Are there no other revolutionary methods aside from those we experienced?

Is there no other basis for art aside from the decorative art to please, or the experimental art, or ruthless art that wants to scare others? It is childish to repeat the long-known truth: the world in all its domains will be saved only through love; without love it will gradually decline.

If we could add love to the theoretical and scientific sources I spoke of, their result could have been more valuable and just.

It seems to me that, in our atomic epoch, we are approaching certain boundaries. What boundaries? But we don't want to fall into that world abyss.

I had to live for many years to see many mistakes in life, and to understand that it is easier to climb Mont Blanc than to change man.

As for art, I often talked about color, which is love.

Joyfully I think about young people among whom we hope to find a resonance.

I think that you too think about the same things.

And I love to dream that it won't be a voice crying in the wilderness.

May 1963

On the First Day of War

Letter to Di goldene keyt. *Published in* Di goldene keyt, *no. 60 (1967).*

Would that I were younger, to leave my paintings and brushes, and go, fly together with you — with sweet joy to give up my last years.

I have always painted pictures where human love floods my colors.

Day and night I dreamed that something would change in the souls and relationships of people.

I have always thought that, without human or biblical feelings in your heart, life has no value. Now the Semitic nations have arisen, jealous of our hard-earned piece of bread, our burning national ideal, our national soil. They want to show that, like other nations, they are also anti-Semites. They want to choke us as did the Pharoahs of old. But we crossed the sea of the ghettos, and our victory was eternalized in the {Passover} Hagada.

We now stand before the great world trial of the human soul: will all dear visions and ideals of two thousand years of human world culture be blown away with the wind?

History again puts the torch and sword in our hand, for the world to tremble when it hears our prophetic voice of justice.

Thousands and thousands of simple people here and everywhere are with you. Only "leaders" with no heart are with our enemies.

Perhaps I am of an age to bless you, and, instead of crying, to comfort you.

I want to hope that the land of the great French Revolution, the land of Zola, Balzac, Watteau, Cézanne, Baudelaire, Claudel, Péguy, will soon raise its voice to stop the world shame.

I hope that America with its democracy, the land of Shakespeare, and also the land of Dostoevskii, Moussorgskii — the land of my birth — will begin to scream that the world must stop its "manners" and give the people of Israel one chance — to live free and create freely in its own land.

Anyway, no one will be able to create freely anymore if the nations let their consciences go to sleep. The last drop of talent will evaporate and their words will remain hollow.

To let Israel and the Jews be choked — means to kill the soul of the whole biblical world.

No new "religion" can be created without this drop of the heart's blood. And we will see if we are worthy of continuing to live or of being destroyed by the atomic bomb.

My word of consolation is in my eyes, which you cannot see now.

And my blessings are embossed in my windows of the Twelve Tribes, now hidden in Jerusalem. . . .

June 6, 1967

About the Yiddish Poet Elkhonon Vogler

Published in Di goldene keyt, *no. 60 (1967). Vogler (1907–1969) emerged as a poet in Vilna in the 1930s and lived in Paris after World War II. This was written on the occasion of the publication of Vogler's book* Spring on the Highway.

For hundreds of years in cities and shtetls, on streets and squares, in houses and schools, your language has been heard.

Sky and clouds, fields and forests have listened to your language.

Our fathers and mothers cried their lives out in Yiddish.

In *heder*, with the rebbe, the flies dashed to the window, begged, shuddered — when we children repeated Yiddish lines.

And you stood at a distance, and saw it all painted and registered it close up.

The world finally perceived that all the cities and shtetls it destroyed have remained only in our dreams, paintings, and songs.

Our foes wanted to put a candle at our head as at the head of a dead person; they assumed we would stop singing and painting, we would not even have any more tears to weep.

Our house of wood and bricks is destroyed, but not the Jewish people. And there is no force in the world that would prevent us from believing in miracles.

And you, Yiddish poet and artist, know that new cities and shtetls, new parents, dear and our own, descend to us as from Jacob's Ladder.

As great as your genius — so great is the miracle. As pure as your paint and your word — so great is your world.

And if you weep — they are tears of joy and creation.

Our streets of Vitebsk and Vilna arise somewhere else — in Tel Aviv and Jerusalem. They arise in our hearts and wherever the Jewish truth, the human truth, lives free.

May our spirit be strong and clear, holy as the music of our books, as the look of a child, may we be able to go our own way which has been, from the beginning, both a Jewish and a human way.

On the Death of Elkhonon Vogler

Published in Di goldene keyt, *no. 66 (1969).*

It may be late or not too late to express my grief at the death of poor Elkhonon Vogler. Why poor? After all, he was a genuine Yiddish poet, but so lonely among Jews.

A stranger to others and perhaps even to himself.

How many times did I want to make him happy — and I didn't know how. I tried to make a few drawings for his book and I don't even know if the book appeared.

Everything around him was delayed. He didn't know how to recover. Deep in me lies a thought that he made a mistake: he didn't go to Israel, at least for a short time — to draw another strength from there.

His poetry was without beginning and without end, as genuine poetry must be (and all that in Vilna — harder in Paris).

To whom shall I convey my grief? He had no family of his own. I send my grief to all of you.

Speech at the Unveiling of the Tapestries in the Knesset in Jerusalem
Published in Di goldene keyt, *no. 66 (1969).*

Over forty years ago, I was invited by the French publisher Vollard to paint motifs of the Bible. Then, I was confused: I didn't know how to begin the work. I was so far from the biblical spirit, in a strange land. . . .

Fortunately for me, the Mayor of Tel Aviv, Meir Dizengoff, appeared before me like a flying angel. He invited me to come to Eretz Israel. Since then, I have grown close to the land and have created on biblical motifs; since then, I am newborn; I have become a different person. It is difficult for me to explain it in words. Why? I only know that, since then, I have always had the desire to express signs of devotion, however and whenever I can.

I have made many voyages through the land. And every time, it meant an even-greater closeness; and here and there I left a sign of it.

Finally, I am in the new building of the parliament of Israel in Jerusalem — the Knesset — on its floor and on its walls; I am in the Knesset with its dear Speaker Kaddish Luz, who has so inspired me.

But it is not for me to talk about myself and my work. My goal, as I said, was to get closer to the land, to the biblical homeland of the Jewish people, to the land where there is an understanding of life and a right to life — a creation in the spirit of that which hovers over every page of the Bible and hovers here in the air, in the fields, in the sky, and in the souls of the inhabitants. When the world, including our so-called "foes" (who are rather their own foes), understands this; when the world feels this — a new peace will come, as envisaged by our Prophets. But, in the meantime, the reality is tragic: the vision of peace is still a mirage.

Art of genius and its luminaries are so rare. . . . People prefer to be content with evil and injustice rather than to clutch onto love.

I pity our enemies, who waste their time and their lives on byways and try to burst through closed doors that are actually open. The straight road and the key to the doors is love, which is sown here at every step by our forefathers, by the people who returned here two thousand years later, from all the ghettos; returned to live with a renewed love and brotherhood with the surrounding Semitic peoples.

From my whole heart, I would call to friend and non-friend, whose soul is shining, to open their eyes and stretch out a hand to give content to our short life, elevate our life, and create at the height of the genius of nature.

Some may not understand my fragmented words, but perhaps you will sense the pulse of life throbbing in them and the breath of truth permeating them: that our would-be enemies would reject their weapons of annihilation, for they destroy first of all their own souls.

My voice echoes the voices of my parents and forefathers: the world must listen to the voice of that people who gave content to life — and thereby the world will endow itself with content.

There is no art or creation in a life without love. Love lives in this land, and everything that comes with love is great and sublime.

Let my work here, whatever it may be, serve as an expression of my soul's devotion to the land — this land of justice and biblical peace.

August 1969

Letter to the President of Israel
Published in Di goldene keyt, *no. 66 (1969).*

Dear friend Zalman Shazar,

You have to be a Shakespeare or a poet of our Bible to be able to express what I would like to tell you —

Fate put you at the head of our biblical land — today when humanity wants even less to recognize our spirit and right to life —

I kiss you and wish you and all of Israel happiness — to live through and live to see.

Marc Chagall

Poems by Chagall

With the exception of "My Land," the following poems were translated from the original Yiddish. "Bella" is translated from a manuscript found in the Joseph Opatoshu archive at YIVO (New York City). It has also been published, in Yiddish, in I. E. Ronch, The World of Marc Chagall *(Los Angeles, 1967). All others have been published, in Yiddish, in* Di goldene keyt, *Tel Aviv, no. 60 (1967). Some titles are Chagall's own, others were given by A. Sutzkever.*

"And now, in conclusion — since I am among poets — allow me to become a bit of a poet for a moment and read you a few of my poems, which I stray into from time to time.

"You must not be amazed that an artist writes poems, for in the past, some artists, very great ones like Michaelangelo, Leonardo da Vinci, Delacroix, wrote poems and prose, as well as, recently, Gauguin and van Gogh, and, in our time, Picasso and others."

Marc Chagall
(from the Joseph Opatoshu archive, YIVO)

My Land

Translated from Russian and Yiddish manuscripts found in the Sutzkever archive. Chagall noted that the Yiddish is a translation from the Russian, but, comparing the two versions, it is difficult to determine which came first. "My Land" has no rhymes in either language, whereas all of Chagall's other Yiddish poems are rhymed. The title is written on the Russian version, in Chagall's hand, in Yiddish.

Only that land is mine
That lies in my soul.
As a native, with no documents,
I enter that land.

It sees my sorrow
And loneliness,
Puts me to sleep
And covers me with a fragrance-stone.

Gardens are blooming inside me,
My flowers I invented,
My own streets —
But there are no houses.

They have been destroyed since my childhood.
Their inhabitants stray in the air,
Seek a dwelling,
They live in my soul.

That's why I smile sometimes
When the sun barely glimmers,
Or I cry
Like a light rain at night.

There was a time
When I had two heads,
When both faces were covered with a film of love —
And evaporated like the scent of roses.

Now I imagine
That even when I walk back
I walk forward —
Toward high gates,
Beyond them, walls are strewn about,
Where worn-out thunders sleep,
And broken lightning — —

Paris 1946
(The date is changed, in Chagall's hand, from 1947 to 1946.)

My Old Home (Autobiographical Poem)

Originally published, simultaneously, in Tsukunft, New York, *vol. 16, no. 12 (December 1937), and* Literarishe bleter, *Warsaw, no. 9 (February 25, 1938). Chagall's manuscript for the* Tsukunft *version is in the YIVO archive (New York City). In both the manuscript and the* Tsukunft *version, the strophes of the last two parts are confused, and two are omitted. This translation is from the* Literarishe bleter *version.*

I

It rings in me —
The distant city,
The white churches,
The synagogues. The door
Is open. The sky is blooming.
Life flies on and on.

It yearns in me —
The crooked streets,
Gray tombstones on a mountain,
Deep lie the pious Jews.

In colors and daubs,
In light and shadow,
My picture stands at a distance.
I want to cover my heart with it.

I walk flowing and flaming,
The years flash.
My world comes to me in a dream —
I am lost.

Don't look for me today, don't look for me tomorrow.
I have run away from myself.
I will make a grave for myself
And will melt in tears.

II

I imagine I see my father
Lying far away in the earth.
All night long he prayed.
He threw off all earthly things,
A cold sword slew him.

In synagogue, you waited for miracles,
A bitter tear would fall on your beard.
From the depths of your heart you cried a word
To Abraham and Isaac, to sweet Jacob.

In the sweat of your brow you toiled all your life,
The weeping was the weeping of your hands.
Pale and mute, you fed us all —
Your children in the poor four walls.

You left me a legacy —
Your old, evaporated smell.
Your smile flows in all my senses.
Your strength moved into me.

My dead mother hovers in the air,
Barely breathing, crying alone.
"Where is my son, what is he doing now,
Once I rocked him in his trough,
May his path be blessed and pure.

"In travail I carried him, nursed him,
He sucked my first strength.
I taught him to say the She'ma at bedtime,
I led him by the hand into the world.

"Where are you now, my son?
You're in my memory.
Deep inside me sleeps a starry night,
Quietly it closed my eyes."

Only bones remained of you.
The young beauty is no more.
You lie alone among stones,
You abandoned me here.

I would have kissed your sand and grass,
Like your stone I would have cried.
I would have left my soul to you
And crowned you as a queen.

My old Rebbe's head is flying
Toward me with regards:
"I gave you my Torah,
You will not set foot in my home again."

No more my teacher with his brush, no more his little beard.
A robber killed him for two cents.
A black horse carried him away
To the other world through the gate.

His lamp went out.
A cloud peeps into his home.
Facing it, like a dolt,
Stands the church, bolted shut.

Your Jewish painting in the mud
A pig's tail daubed it over —
My teacher, I'm sorry
I left you long ago.

Let your name be mentioned, David,
My young brother is deceased.
Left life with no honor
And no one knows where he lies.

My sisters laugh and cry.
They stand together in the door,
Look for something in the window
And seek happiness forever.

An old house with no window,
Inside it is dark at night.
I came out first
And stretched out my hand.

I see the river, the cool water.
At dusk, I walk to its bank.
It flows into me a prayer
Singing in calm, in the abyss.

You walk with your long hair,
With love, trembling, toward me.
You bestow on me a pair of eyes.
And I always want to ask you:

Where are my white flowers
From our *khupa* on the roads?
For the first time I came to you,
The whole night I lay with you.

We put out the moon
And ignited white candles.
My love flowed to you
And opened your face.

You became a wife to me,
For long years, as sweet as almonds,
Your belly gave me a gift —
A daughter pretty as a new year.
Thank you, God from the Ark of the Covenant,
For that day and in that month.

III
Oh, descend, my white cloud
And raise me up to you!
I hear the bells ring down below
And smoke rises from the houses.

My mouth wants to say a word
To them, covered in snow.
As long as my breath carries me,
My soul will be with them.

Did you forget me, my city?
Your water flows in my body.
On your benches, I sat
And waited for my calling.

Where houses stand crooked,
And a road leads to the graveyard,
Where a river overflows its banks —
I dreamed my days.

At night an angel flies in the sky,
Flashing the roofs with white.
He tells me from far away:
He will exalt my name.

I sang to you, my people.
Who knows if you like my song.
A voice rises from my lungs
And makes me sad and weary.

I made my paintings from you,
The flowers, forests, houses, people.
Like a wild man, I paint your face
And day and night, I want to bless you.

I painted the bright walls,
The klezmers, dancers on the stage,
With colors blue, red, yellow,
I adorned them like the Holy Spirit.

You played, sang and frolicked,
You played an old king,
You played with me and swallowed me.
It was a jolly caper.

The moon comes over
From that land to me, a guest.
A red flag waves to me.
I wake up on our street.

The world there is renewed.
Families, close and far,
Made a wedding without me.
Winds blow from there.

I hear the voices from afar
Of people crowding together in joy.
They possessed a life, liberated
With hot rifles and with words.

Oh, crawl out of deep graves,
Aunts, uncles, grandfathers.
You are free citizens, congratulations!
I am your witness from afar.

You are silent, my homeland.
Do you want my heart to break?
Shall I beg on bended knee for my days?
Should a fire boil inside me,
Should I leave you all I have?

I will send you my dreaming blood,
My breath will gradually drip like tears.
The air will sway blue
And I will lie quietly at the fence.

Are you, my homeland, angry at me?
I am open to you like water in a bottle.
Long ago, you hurled me into the distance,
I will come to you to sleep forever
And you will cover my grave with ash.

IV

My people, poor people, you have no more tears.
No cloud walks before us, no star.
Our Moses is dead. He has long been lying in sand.
He brought you to our land and exiled you from it.

Our last prophets are silent, mute,
They have shouted out their throats for you.
You no longer hear the melody of those songs
Flowing from their mouth like a river.

Everyone wants to break your tablets in your heart,
Trample your truth and your God.
A guilty world wants to sap your strength
And leave you a place only in the earth.

They pursue, they beat my people from all sides.
Its crown is falling.
Its Star of David is falling.
Where is its light?
Where is its honor?

My people rends the scarlet sky,
Hurls its exile down to the ground.
A lightning burns its old mold,
It runs at it with a sword.

And if you have to be destroyed
For old sins of the last Destruction,
In your place, perhaps, another star will rise,
Doves will fly out of your eyes.

I want to eternalize your wish,
To engrave a new truth.
Of life, let art remain —
The sound of thunder and lightning.

1937

My Tears

My tears fall like stones,
Melt and flow into a river,
Float like flowers on the water,
Thus I live, my God. Why?

I live and I breathe.
I seek you, I seek.
For you are with me
And far from me, my God. Why?

I hear no word around me.
Roads and forests crisscross.
I begin my day with a smile
And wait for you, God. Why?

I bear the cross every day,
Pushed and led by the hand,
Night grows dark around me,
Have you forsaken me, my God? Why?

I am your son,
Born on the earth to crawl,
You put paint and brush in my hand —
I don't know how to paint You.

Should I paint the earth, the sky, my heart?
The cities burning, my brothers fleeing?
My eyes in tears,
Where should I run and fly, to whom?

There is someone who gives us life,
There is someone who gives us death —
He could have helped me,
To make my painting bright with joy.

My hour, my day, my last year.
How sweet is my hot tear.
My heart is silent, waiting.
I see the sun flowing above —
Covering my face with red beams.

It promises me consolation:
I shall not shed more tears,
I shall go along with my luck,
My hope hidden deep inside me,
And hear your distant call.

In Lisbon Before Departure

A wall grows up between us,
A mountain covered with grass and graves,
The hand that creates paintings and books
Has separated us.

Have you ever seen my face —
In the middle of the street, a face with no body?
There is no one who knows him,
And his call sinks into an abyss.

I sought my star among you,
I sought the far end of your world,
I wanted to grow stronger with you,
But you fled in fear.

How shall I tell you my last word,
You — when you are lost.
I have no place on earth
To go.

And let the tears dry out,
And let the name on my stone be wiped out,
And I, like you, will become a shadow,
Melt like smoke.

1941

On the Ship

I came to the ship,
Told you farewell —
You took over my earth,
The graves on the river.

But you wiped out my grief,
Veiled my home from me,
Opened a new page for me,
Revealed a new land.

Don't leave me adrift in mid-sea,
Where hordes of weary brothers, pitiless,
Reminded me of my pedigree and my race.

Let my road stretch without menace —
How shall I bless you, my God,
And on what day shall I fast?

The Vilna Synagogue

The old *shul*, the old street,
I painted them just yesteryear.
Now smoke rises there, and ash
And the *parokhet* is lost.

Where are your Torah scrolls?
The lamps, menoras, chandeliers?
The air, generations filled with their breath?
It evaporates in the sky.

Trembling, I put the color,
The green color of the Ark of the Covenant.
I bowed in tears,
Alone in the *shul* — a last witness.

Jacob's Ladder

I walk in the world as in a woods.
On my hands and feet do I crawl.
Every tree sheds its leaves,
They wake me. I am scared.

I paint my world as sleeping in a dream;
And when the woods are filled with snow,
My painting is from another world,
But for a long time, I alone stand on it and stand.

I stand and wait for a miracle to embrace me from afar,
To warm my heart and drive out my tremor,
I wait for you to come to me from all sides.

And I shall stand no more, but fly —
And rise with you on Jacob's Ladder.

The Painting

If only my sun had shone at night.
I sleep — steeped in colors,
In a bed of paintings,
Your foot in my mouth
Presses me, tortures me.

I wake up in pain
Of a new day, with hopes
Not yet painted,
Not yet daubed with paint.

I run up
To my dry brushes,
And I'm crucified like Jesus,
With nails pounded in the easel.

Am I finished?
Is my picture done?
Everything shines, flows, runs.

Stop, one more daub,
Over there — black paint,
Here — red, blue, spread out,
Calmed me.

Can you hear me — my dead bed,
My dry grass,

My departed love,
My new come love,[1]
Listen to me.

I move over your soul,
Over your belly —
I drink the calm of your years.

I swallowed your moon,
The dream of your innocence,
To become your angel,
To watch you as before.

1. An allusion to Virginia Haggard.

Your Call

I do not know if I lived. I don't know
If I am alive. I watch the sky,
I don't recognize the world.

My body sets toward night.
Love, the flowers in paintings —
They call me back and forth.

Don't leave my hand without light
When my house is dark.
How will I see your shine in the whiteness?

How will I hear your call
When I remain alone in my bed
And cold and calm is my body.

Bella: On the Fourth Anniversary of her Death

Your white dress swims over you,
My flowers untouched,
Your stone glimmers, gets wet,
I get gray as ash. . . .

Today, like yesterday, I ask you:
Are you staying here, are you following behind me?
See — my steps swathed in tears.
What are you saying to me? I want to listen.

" . . . As red as our *Khupa*,
So is our love for our people and our homeland,
Go and wake them up with our dream — —

"How green the fields lie on my body,
Every night the stars wink at me.
So you will someday return to me."

August 16, 1948

For the Slaughtered Artists

Did I know them all? Did I visit
Their atelier? Did I see their art
Close up or from afar?
And now I walk out of myself, out of my years,
I go to their unknown grave.
They call me. They pull me into their grave —
Me, the innocent, the guilty.
They ask me: Where were you?
— I fled. . . .

They were led to the baths of death
Where they knew the taste of their sweat.
Then they saw the light
Of their unfinished paintings.
They counted the unlived years,
Which they cherished and waited for
To fulfill their dreams —
Not slept out to the end, overslept.
In their head, they sought and found
The nursery where the moon, circled
With stars, promised a bright future.
The young love in the dark room, in the grass,
On mountains, in valleys, the chiseled fruit,
Doused in milk, covered with flowers
Promised them paradise.
The hands of their mother, her eyes
Accompanied them to the train, to the distant
Fame.

I see: now they drag along in rags,
Barefoot on mute roads.
The brothers of Israels, Pissarro and
Modigliani, our brothers — they are led
With ropes by the sons of Dürer, Cranach
And Holbein — to death in the crematoria.
How can I, how should I, shed tears?
They have been soaked in brine —
The salt of my tears.
They were dried out with mockery. Thus I
Lose my last hope.

How should I weep,
When every day I heard:
They tear the last board off my roof,
When I am too tired to make war
For a piece of earth where I remain,
Where I will later be laid to sleep.
I see the fire, the smoke and the gas
Rising to the blue cloud,
Turning it black.
I see the torn-out hair and teeth.
They overwhelm me with my rabid
Palette.
I stand in the desert before heaps of boots,
Clothing, ash and dung, and mumble my
Kaddish.

And as I stand — from my paintings
The painted David descends to me,
Harp in hand. He wants to help me
Weep and recite chapters
Of Psalms.
After him, our Moses descends.
He says: Don't fear anyone.
He tells you to lie quietly

Until he comes again to engrave
New tablets for a new world.
The last spark dies out,
The last body vanishes.
Quiet as before a new deluge.
I stand up and say farewell to you,
I take the road to the new Temple
And light a candle there
Before your image.

1950

To Israel

Should I pray to God, Who led my people to the fire,
Or should I paint Him in image of flame?
Should I get up from my place a new Jew
And go fight along with my race?

Should my eyes lament without a halt,
So the tears drown in a river?
I won't let my grief approach
When I swim to your shore.

And when my weary foot gropes on the sand —
I shall lead my bride by the hand.
For you to see her — the holy bride in the sky,
As I will dream with her our last dream.

1950

The Ship

Two thousand years — my Exile,
My land is just a few years old.
Young as my son David.
I crawl on my knees with spread-out hands
And seek the stars and the Magen-David.

The Prophets swim past me,
Moses shines to me from afar.
I have long been enraptured by his beams
And by the wind blowing from him.

All those years I counted the tears,
Sought you in the sky, on the earth,
Two thousand years have I waited
For my heart to calm down and see you.

Like Jacob, I lay sound asleep,
I dreamed a dream:
An angel raises me on a ladder,
Extinguished souls sing around me.

About the new land Israel,
About two thousand years of our Exile,
And about David — my son,
They sang sweeter than Mozart and Bach

When will you come, my hour,
When I shall go out like a candle,
When will I reach you, my distant one,
And when will my rest come?

I don't know if I'm walking,
I don't know who I am,
I don't know where I stand,
My head and my soul — where they are.

Look, my dear mother,
At your son going down,
Look, my dear crown,
How quiet and deep my sun sets.

1960

Bibliography

Benjamin Harshav

Abramovitsh, Dina. "Marc Chagall's Memoirs of his Youth in *Tsukunft* and his Letters to A. Lyesin" (in Yiddish). *Tsukunft*, vol. 95 (1988), nos. 5–8, pp. 58–63.

———. "Marc Chagall" (in Yiddish). *Tsukunft*, vol. 95 (1988), nos. 9–12, pp. 123–28.

Alexander, Sidney. *Marc Chagall: An Intimate Biography*. New York: Paragon House, 1989.

Al'tman, Natan. "The State Yiddish Chamber Theater (After the Premiere)" (in Yiddish). *Der Emes*, Sept. 29, 1921.

Al'tman, Natan, Marc Chagall, and David Shterenberg. *Kultur-Lige*. Moscow: Kultur-Lige, 1922.

Amiard-Chevrel, Claudine. *Le Théâtre artistique de Moscou (1898–1917)* (The Moscow Art Theater [1898–1917]). Paris: Centre national de la recherche scientifique, 1979.

Amishai-Maisels, Ziva. "Chagall's Jewish In-Jokes." *Journal of Jewish Art*, vol. 5 (1978), pp. 76–93.

———. "Chagall and the Jewish Revival: Center or Periphery?" In Ruth Apter-Gabriel, ed., *Tradition and Revolution: The Jewish Renaissance in Russian Avant Garde Art 1912–1928.*

———. "Chagall's Murals for the Jewish State Chamber Theater." In Christoph Vitali, ed., *Marc Chagall: The Russian Years: 1906–1922.*

Antonova, Irina, Andrei Voznesenskii, and Marina Bessonova. *Chagall Discovered* (trans. from the Russian by John Crowfoot and Alex Miller). New York/Moscow: Hugh Lauter Levin/Sovietskii khudozhnik, 1988.

Apter-Gabriel, Ruth, ed. *Tradition and Revolution: The Jewish Renaissance in Russian Avant Garde Art 1912–1928*. Jerusalem: The Israel Museum, 1987.

Arnheim, Rudolf. *The Genesis of a Painting: Picasso's* Guernica. Berkeley and Los Angeles: University of California Press, 1962.

Aronson, B. *Mark Shagal* (in Russian). Berlin: Petropolis, 1923. *Marc Chagall* (in German; trans. from the Russian by R. von Walter). Berlin: Razum-Verlag, 1924. *Marc Chagall* (in Yiddish; trans. from the Russian by Ben-Baruch). Berlin: Idisher literarisher farlag — Petropolis, 1924.

———. *Sovremennaia evreiskaia grafika* (Contemporary Jewish graphic art). Berlin: Petropolis, 1924.

Atkinson, J. Brooks. "The Play" (review of *The Dybbuk*). *The New York Times*, Dec. 14, 1926.

B. "The Opening of the Yiddish Chamber Theater" (in Russian). *Pravda*, Oct. 5, 1923.

Bablet, Denis. *The Revolutions of Stage Design in the Twentieth Century*. Paris: Léon Amiel, 1977.

Baer, Nancy van Norman, ed. *Theatre in Revolution: Russian Avant-Garde Stage Design 1913–1935*. New York: Thames and Hudson/The Fine Arts Museums of San Francisco, 1991.

Ben-Ari, R. *Habima* (in Yiddish). Chicago: L. M. Shteyn, 1937.

Berezkin, V. I. *Sovetskaia stsenografiia* (Soviet stage design). Moscow: Nauka, 1990.

Bergelson, Dovid. "Dovid Bergelson On the Theater" (in Yiddish). *Literarishe bleter*, April 27, 1928.

Bernstein, Ignaz. *Yudishe shprikhverter un rednsartn* (Yiddish proverbs and expressions). Collected and edited with B. W. Segal. Warsaw/Frankfurt: J. Kaufmann, 1908.

Beyder, Chaim. "Marc Chagall Returned to Russia" (in Yiddish). Unpublished.

Bir., O. "The Al'tman, Chagall, and Shterenberg Exhibit" (in Russian). *Teatral'naia Moskva*, no. 35 (April 17–23, 1922), pp. 13–15.

Bojko, Szymon. "Three Waves of Emigration." In Charles Doria, ed., *Russian Samizdat Art.*

Bowlt, John E. *The Silver Age: Russian Art of the Early Twentieth Century and the "World of Art" Group*. Newtonville, Mass.: Oriental Research Partners, 1978.

———. *Russian Stage Design: Scenic Innovation, 1900–1930*. Jackson: Mississippi Museum of Fine Arts, 1982.

———. *Khudozhniki russkogo teatra 1880–1930: Sobranie Nikity i Niny Lobanovykh-Rostovskikh* (Artists of the Russian theater 1880–1930: The Nikita and Nina Lobanov-Rostovsky Collection). Moscow: Iskusstvo, 1990.

Bozo, Dominique, ed. *Marc Chagall: Oeuvres sur papier* (Marc Chagall: Works on paper). Paris: Centre Georges Pompidou, 1984.

Brockett, Oscar G. *Modern Theatre: Realism and Naturalism to the Present*. Boston: Allyn and Bacon, 1982.

Buber, Martin. "Jüdische Renaissance." *Die jüdische Bewegung* (The Jewish movement). Berlin: Jüdischer Verlag, 1916.

———. "Von jüdischer Kunst." *Die jüdische Bewegung* (The Jewish movement). Berlin: Jüdischer Verlag, 1916.

Bunkamura Museum of Fine Arts. *Chagall* (in Japanese and French). Tokyo: Bunkamura Museum of Fine Arts and Tokyo Shimbun, 1989.

Burko, Faina. *The Soviet Yiddish Theatre in the Twenties*. Ph.D. diss., Southern Illinois University, Carbondale, 1978.

Burrus, Christina, ed. *Marc Chagall*. Martigny, Switzerland: Fondation Pierre Gianadda, 1991.

Carter, Huntley. *The New Theatre and Cinema of Soviet Russia*. New York: International Publishers, 1935.

———. *The New Spirit in the Russian Theater: 1917–28*. New York: Benjamin Blom, 1970.

Centro Cultural/Arte Contemporáneo. *Chagall en nuestro siglo* (Chagall in our century). Mexico City: Centro Cultural/Arte Contemporáneo, 1991.

Chagall, Bella. *Brenendike licht* (Burning candles). New York: Book League of the Jewish Fraternal Order, 1945.

———. *Di ershte bagegenish* (The first meeting). New York: Book League of the Jewish Fraternal Order, 1947.

Chagall, Marc. "My Own: Autobiography" (in Yiddish). *Tsukunft*, vol. 30 (1925), pp. 158–62, 290–93, 359–61, 407–10.

———. *My Life* (trans. from the French by Elizabeth Abbott). New York: Orion Press, 1960.

———. *Angel nad kryshami* (An angel above the roofs; translated from the Yiddish by L. Berlinsky). Moscow: Sovremennik, 1989.

———. *Die Bibel: Gouachen, Aquarelle, Pastelle und Zeichnungen aus dem Nachlass des Künstlers*. Bundeskanzleramt Bonn: Landesmuseum Mainz, 1990.

————. "Two Letters of M. Chagall" (in Russian). *Shagalovskie dni v Vitebske* (special issue of *Vit'bichi*), July 3–5, 1992.

Chagall, Marc, and Klaus Mayer. *Der Gott der Väter: Das Chagall-Fenster zu St. Stephan in Mainz*. Würzburg: Echter Verlag, 1978.

Charney, Daniel. *A yortsendlik aza* (Such a decade). New York: CYKO, 1943.

Chipp, Herschel B., with Peter Selz and Joshua C. Taylor. *Theories of Modern Art: A Source Book by Artists and Critics*. Berkeley and Los Angeles: University of California, 1968.

Compton, Susan. *The World Backwards: Russian Futurist Books 1912–16*. London: The British Library Board, 1978.

————. *Chagall*. London: Royal Academy of Arts, 1985.

————. *Marc Chagall: My Life — My Dream*. Munich: Prestel-Verlag, 1990.

Däubler, Theodor. *Marc Chagall*. Rome: Ed. Valori plastici, 1922.

Deytsh, Aleksandr. *Maski evreiskogo teatra* (Masks of the Yiddish Theater). Moscow: Russkoe teatral'noe obshchestvo, 1927.

————. "The Paths of GOSET" (in Russian). *Teatral'naia dekada*, no. 5 (1935), pp. 4–10.

Dobrushin, Y. "From Cloud to Fire" (in Yiddish). *Der Emes*, Jan. 21, 1923.

————. "The German Press About the Guest Performances of the Moscow State Yiddish Theater" (in Yiddish). *Der Emes*, May 10, 1928.

————. *Mikhoels der aktyor* (Mikhoels the actor). Moscow: Der Emes, 1941.

Doria, Charles, ed. *Russian Samizdat Art*. Essays by John E. Bowlt, Szymon Bojko, Rimma, and Valery Gerlovin. New York: Willis, Locker and Owens, 1986.

Efros, Abram. "Remarks about Art: Chagall, Al'tman, Fal'k" (in Russian). *Novy put'*, nos. 48–49 (1916), pp. 58–64.

————. "The Artist and the Stage" (in Russian). *Kul'tura teatra*, no. 1 (1921), pp. 11–12.

————. "Before the Opening Curtain: The New Season at the Jewish Theater" (in Russian). *Teatr i muzyka*, no. 9 (Nov. 1922), pp. 110–11.

————. "On the Rise: The Jewish Chamber Theater" (in Russian). *Novaia Rossiia*, no. 1 (1924), pp. 18–19.

————. "The Artists of Granovskii's Theater" (in Russian). *Iskusstvo*, vol. 4 (1928), books 1–2, p. 74. (Reprinted in *Kovtsheg: Almanakh evreiskoy kul'tury* [The Ark: Almanac of Jewish culture]. Moscow/Jerusalem: Tarbut/Khudozhestvennaia literatura, 1991.)

————. *Profili* (Profiles). Moscow: Federatsiia, 1930.

Efros, A., and Ia. Tugendkhol'd. *Iskusstvo Marka Shagala* (The art of Marc Chagall). Moscow: Helikon, 1918. *Die Kunst Marc Chagalls* (trans. from the Russian by Frieda Ichak-Rubiner). Potsdam: Gustav Kiepenheuer Verlag, 1921.

Erben, Walter. *Marc Chagall*. New York and Washington: Frederick A. Praeger, 1957. Rev. ed. 1966.

Even-Zohar, Itamar. *Polysystem Studies* (special issue of *Poetics Today*), vol. 2 (1990), no. 1.

Evreiskaia entsiklopediia (Jewish encyclopedia). St. Petersburg: Brockhaus and Ephron, 1915.

Evreiskoe shchast'e (Jewish luck; brochure for the film). Moscow: Kino-petshat', 1925.

Felitsin, Y. "The Moscow State Yiddish Chamber Theater: On Its Fifth Anniversary" (in Yiddish). *Literarishe bleter*, no. 12 (1924).

Fletcher, Valerie, ed. *Crosscurrents of Modernism: Four Latin American Pioneers*. Washington, D. C.: Smithsonian Institution Press, 1992.

Frost, Matthew. "Marc Chagall and the Jewish State Chamber Theater." *Russian History*, vol. 8 (1981), parts 1–2, pp. 90–107.

Gay, Peter. "Sigmund Freud: A German and his Discontents." *Freud, Jews and Other Germans: Masters and Victims in Modernist Culture*. New York: Oxford University Press, 1978.

Geyser, M. *Solomon Mikhoels* (in Russian). Moscow: Prometheus, 1990.

————. "Gifts of Fate" (in Russian). Unpublished.

Gnessin, M. *Darki im ha-teatron ha-ivri* (My road with the Hebrew theater). Tel Aviv: Hakibutz Hameuchad, 1946.

GOSET (State Jewish Theater). *Moscow State Jewish Theater* (playbill for GOSET's 1926 tours to Minsk, Kiev, Homel, Odessa, and Leningrad; includes short play reviews; in Russian and Yiddish). 1926.

————. "Biographical Note on the Moscow Actors" (in Yiddish). *Jiddisch*, vol. 1, nos. 5–6 (Aug.–Sept. 1928).

Granach, Aleksander. "Granovskii, Mikhoels, and Zuskin — Congratulations!" (in Yiddish). *Literarishe bleter*, no. 20 (1928), p. 390.

Granovskii, A. "The Yiddish Theater" (in Russian). *Zvezda*, July 31, 1923.

————. "Our Theater" (in Yiddish). *Literarishe bleter*, April 27, 1928.

Gregor, Joseph, and René Fülop-Miller. *Das russische Theater* (The Russian theater). Vienna: Amalthea-Verlag, 1927.

Grinbal'd, Ia. *Mikhoels* (in Russian). Moscow: OGIZ, 1948.

Güse, Ernst-Gerhard, ed. *Marc Chagall: Druckgraphik* (Marc Chagall: Works on paper). Landesmuseum Münster/Mittelreinisches Landesmuseum Mainz: Hatje, 1984.

Haftmann, Werner. *Marc Chagall*. New York: Harry N. Abrams, 1973.

————. *Marc Chagall: Gouaches, Drawings, Watercolors*. New York: Harry N. Abrams, 1975.

Harshav [Hrushovski], Benjamin. "The Meaning of Sound Patterns in Poetry: An Interaction Theory." *Poetics Today*, vol. 2 (1980), no. 1a, pp. 39–56.

————. "Poetic Metaphor and Frames of Reference: With Examples from Eliot, Rilke, Mayakovsky, Mandelshtam, Pound, Creeley, Amichai and *The New York Times*." *Poetics Today*, vol. 5 (1984), no. 1, pp. 5–43.

————. "Fictionality and Fields of Reference: Remarks on a Theoretical Framework." *Poetics Today*, vol. 5 (1984), no. 2, pp. 227–51.

————. *The Meaning of Yiddish*. Berkeley and Los Angeles: University of California Press, 1990.

————. *Language in Time of Revolution*. Berkeley and Los Angeles: University of California Press, 1993 (forthcoming).

Harshav, Benjamin and Barbara, eds. and trans. *American Yiddish Poetry: A Bilingual Anthology*. Berkeley and Los Angeles: University of California Press, 1986.

Hofshteyn, Dovid. *Troyer* (Sorrow). Kiev: Kultur-Lige, 1922.

Hume, Samuel A., and Walter Rene Fuerst. *Dos Idishe Kamer Teatr* (The Yiddish Chamber Theater). Petrograd: Jewish Theater Society, 1919.

———. *Idisher Kamer Teatr* (The Yiddish Chamber Theater). Kiev: Kultur-Lige, 1924.

———. *Twentieth Century Stage Decoration*, vol. 1. New York: Alfred A. Knopf, 1929.

Jakobson, Roman. "Linguistics and Poetics." *Language and Literature*. Cambridge, Mass.: Harvard University Press, 1987.

Jencks, Charles. *The Language of Post-Modern Architecture*. New York: Rizzoli, 1987.

———. *Post-Modernism: The New Classicism in Art and Architecture*. New York: Rizzoli, 1987.

Jiddisch: Monatsschrift für jüdische Kultur in Wien (special issue of *Jiddisch* on the Moscow Yiddish Theater), vol. 1, nos. 5–6 (Aug.–Sept. 1928).

Jouffrey, Alain. "Theater and Revolution." In G. di San Lazzaro, ed., *Chagall Monumental Works* (special issue of *XXe siècle Review*). New York: Tudor Publishing Company, 1973.

Kagan, Andrew. *Marc Chagall*. New York: Abbeville Press, 1987.

Kamensky, Aleksandr. *Chagall: The Russian Years 1907–1922* (trans. from the French by C. Phillips). New York: Rizzoli, 1989.

Kampf, Avram. "In Quest of Jewish Style in the Era of the Revolution." *Journal of Jewish Art*, vol. 5 (1978), pp. 48–75.

———. "Art and Stage Design: The Jewish Theatres of Moscow in the Early Twenties." In Ruth Apter-Gabriel, ed., *Tradition and Revolution: The Jewish Renaissance in Russian Avant Garde Art 1912–1928*.

———. *Chagall to Kitaj: Jewish Experience in Twentieth Century Art*. London: Lund Humphries, with the Barbican Art Gallery, 1990.

———. "Chagall and the Yiddish Theater." In Christoph Vitali, ed., *Marc Chagall: The Russian Years 1906–1922*.

Kann, E. "Music at GOSET" (in Russian). *Teatral'naia dekada*, no. 5 (1935), p. 10.

Kasovsky [Kazovskii], Grigori. "Chagall and the Jewish Art Programme." In Christoph Vitali, ed., *Marc Chagall: The Russian Years 1906–1922*.

———. "Chagall and the Yiddish Artistic Programme" (in Russian). Unpublished.

Kerr, Alfred. "The Moscow Yiddish Theater (1928)" (in German). *Mit Schleuder und Harfe: Theaterkritiken aus drei Jahrzehnten*. Berlin: Henschelverlag, 1981.

Keshet, Yeshurun. "Marc Chagall" (in Yiddish). *Di goldene keyt*, no. 60 (1967), pp. 34–53.

Kloomok, Isaac. *Marc Chagall: His Life and Work*. New York: Philosophical Library, 1951.

Kornfeld, Eberhard W. *Marc Chagall: Catalogue raisonné de l'oeuvre gravé*, vol. 1: 1922–1966. Bern: Kornfeld und Klipstein, 1971.

Kornhendler, Yikhezkel. "About the Moscow Yiddish Chamber Theater" (in Yiddish). *Fraye Arbeyter Shtime*, 1928.

Kultur-Lige: A sakh hakl (The Culture League: A stocktaking; publication of the Central Committee). Kiev: Nov. 1919.

Lassaigne, Jacques. *Chagall* (in French). Paris: Edition Maeght, 1957.

Levy, Emanuel. *Ha-teatron ha-leumi Ha-Bima: Korot ha-teatron ba-shanim 1917–1979* (The National Theater HaBima: History of the theater in the years 1917–1979). Tel Aviv: Eked, 1981.

Lirov, M. "The Jewish State Chamber Theater" (in Russian). *Prozhektor*, Dec. 31, 1924.

Lissitzky, El. "The Synagogue of Mohilev" (in Yiddish). *Milgroym*, no. 3 (1923), pp. 9–13.

Lissitzky, El, and Hans Arp, eds. *Die Kunstismen. Les Ismes de l'art. The Isms of Art*. Erlenbach-Zurich: Eugen Rentsch Verlag, 1925.

Litvakov, M. "Of the October Miracles" (in Yiddish). *Der Emes*, April 13, 1922.

———. *"The Sorceress* in the Yiddish Chamber Theater" (in Yiddish). *Der Emes*, Dec. 16, 1922.

———. "Sholem Aleichem in the Yiddish Chamber Theater" (in Yiddish). *Der Emes*, Jan. 21, 1923. Also in *Literarishe bleter*, no. 4 (1924).

———. *Finf yor melukhisher yidisher kamer-teater* (Five years of the Yiddish State Chamber Theater). Moscow: Shul un bukh, 1924.

Liubomirskii, I. [O.] *Der revolutsyonerer teater* (The revolutionary theater). Moscow: Shul un bukh, 1926.

———. *Mikhoels* (in Russian). Moscow: Isskustvo, 1938.

Lozowick, Louis. "Moscow Theatre, 1920s." *Russian History*, vol. 8 (1981), nos. 1–2, pp. 140–44.

Lynton, Norbert. "Chagall 'over the Roofs of the World.'" In Susan Compton, *Chagall*.

Mandelshtam, Osip. "Mikhoels (1926)" (in Russian). In G. P. Struve and B. A. Filipoff, eds., *Sobranie sochinenii v trex tomax*, vol. 3. New York: Inter-Language Associates, 1969.

———. "On the Nature of the Word (1922)" (in Russian). In G. P. Struve and B. A. Filipoff, eds., *Sobranie sochinenii v trex tomax*, vol. 2. New York: Inter-Language Associates, 1972.

Manteyfel, A. N. "The First Theater of the Revolution" (in Russian). *Moskva*, no. 1 (1968), pp. 192–94.

———. "The Theater of Revolutionary Satire (TEREVSAT)" (in Russian). *Teatral'noe iskusstvo*.

Margolin, S. [S. M.] "Tragic Carnival: 'A Night at the Old Market' at the Jewish State Theater" (in Russian). *Vsemirnaia illiustratsiia*, no. 3 (1925).

———. "The Artist and the Theater: GOSET Performances" (in Russian). *Teatral'naia dekada*, no. 5 (1935), pp. 8–9.

Markov, P. A. *The Soviet Theatre*. New York: G. P. Putnam's Sons, 1935.

Mayzel, Nakhman. "Five Years of the Yiddish Chamber Theater in Russia" (in Yiddish). *Literarishe bleter*, no. 46 (March 20, 1925).

———. "The Great Miracle of the Stage" (in Yiddish). *Literarishe bleter*, April 27, 1928.

Meyer, Franz. *Marc Chagall: Life and Work*. New York: Harry N. Abrams, 1963.

Mikhoels: 1890–1948 (in Yiddish). Moscow: Der Emes, 1948.

Mikhoels, S. "The New Jewish Comedian" (in Yiddish). *Der Veker*, July 19, 1923.

———— [Vofsi-Mikhoels]. "Our Comedians' Parade in the Ukraine." *Idisher Kamer Teatr* (The Yiddish Chamber Theater). Kiev: Kultur-Lige, 1924.

————. "Mikhoels Vofsi On the Theater" (interview; in Yiddish). *Literarishe bleter*, April 27, 1928.

————. "What a Question!" (interview; in Yiddish). *Jiddisch*, vol. 1, nos. 5–6 (Aug.–Sept. 1928).

————. *Stat'i, desedy, rechi* (Articles, conversations, and lectures). Moscow: Iskusstvo, 1965.

Mikhoels, S., and Y. Dobrushin. "Yiddish Theater Culture in the Soviet Union" (in Yiddish). In S. Dimanshteyn, ed., *Yidn in FSSR* (Jews in the USSR: A symposium). Moscow: Mezhdunarodnaia Kniga and Emes, 1935.

Milhau, Denis. *Chagall et le Théâtre* (Chagall and the theater). Toulouse: Musée des Augustins, 1967.

————. "Chagall and the Theater." In G. di San Lazzaro, ed., *Homage to Marc Chagall*. New York: Tudor Publishing Company, 1969.

Musée National Message Biblique Marc Chagall Nice: Catalogue des collections. Nice and Milan: Ministère de la Culture, 1985; Paris: Editions de la Réunion des Musées Nationaux, 1990.

Nekliudova, M. G. *Traditsii i novatorstvo v russkom iskusstve kontsa XIX–nachala XX veka* (Tradition and innovation in Russian art from the end of the nineteenth to the beginning of the twentieth century). Moscow: Isskustvo, 1991.

Norman, Itzhak, ed. *Be-reyshit Ha-Bima: Nahum Zemach meyased Ha-Bima be-hazon u-ve-ma'as* (The birth of HaBima: Nahum Zemach, founder). Jerusalem: Ha-Sifriya ha-Zionit, 1966.

Orsahnski, B. *Teater-shlakhtn* (Theater battles). Minsk: 1931.

Osborn, Max. "Marc Chagall" (in Russian). *Zhar-ptitsa*, no. 11 (1923).

————. *Jüdische Graphik* (Jewish graphic art). Berlin: Petropolis, 1923.

Pavel, Thomas G. *Fictional Worlds*. Cambridge, Mass.: Harvard University Press, 1986.

Payne, Darwin Reid. *The Scenographic Imagination*. Carbondale and Edwardsville: Southern Illinois University Press, 1981.

Petrow, Wsewolod, and Alexander Kamenski. *Welt der Kunst: Vereinigung Russischer Künstler zu Beginn des 20. Jahrhunderts* (trans. by Hans-Joachin Grimm and Galina Bajeva). Leningrad and Helsinki: Aurora-Kunstverlag, 1991.

Petrova, Evgeniia, and Jürgen Harten, eds. *Pavel Filonov i ego shkola* (Pavel Filonov and his school). Cologne: Buchverlag, 1990.

Picon-Vallin, Béatrice. *Le Théâtre juif soviétique pendant les années vingt* (The Soviet Jewish Theater in the nineteen-twenties). Lausanne: La Cité, 1973.

Rischbieter, Henning, ed. *Art and the Stage in the Twentieth Century* (trans. from the German by Michael Bullock). Greenwich, Conn.: New York Graphic Society, 1978.

Romm, Aleksandr. "Marc Chagall" (in Russian). Unpublished.

Ronch, Itzhak Elchanan. *Di velt fun Marc Shagal* (The world of Marc Chagall). New York: YIKUF, 1967.

Roose-Evans, James. *Experimental Theatre: From Stanislavsky to Today*. New York: Universe Books, 1970.

Rost, Nico. *Kunst en Kultur in Sowjetrusland* (Art and culture in Soviet Russia). Amsterdam: Querido, 1924.

Rudnitsky, Konstantin. *Meyerhold the Director* (trans. by George Petrov). Ann Arbor: Ardis, 1981.

————. *Istoriia russkogo sovetskogo dramaticheskogo teatra*, vol. 1: 1917–1945. Moscow: 1984.

————. *Russian and Soviet Theater 1905–1932* (trans. from the Russian by Roxane Permar). New York: Harry N. Abrams, 1988.

Russian Painters and the Stage: 1884–1965. Austin, Texas: University of Texas Art Museum, 1978.

Sandrow, Nahma. *Vagabond Stars: A World History of Yiddish Theater*. New York: Harper and Row, 1977.

Schein, Yosef. *Arum moskver yidishn teater* (Around the Moscow Yiddish Theater). Paris: Les éditions polyglottes, 1964.

Shatskich, Alexandra [Aleksandra Shatskikh]. "Chagall and Malevich in Vitebsk." In Christoph Vitali, ed., *Marc Chagall: The Russian Years 1906–1922*.

————. "Marc Chagall and the Theater." In Christoph Vitali, ed., *Marc Chagall: The Russian Years 1906–1922*.

————. "When and Where Was Marc Chagall Born?" In Christoph Vitali, ed., *Marc Chagall: The Russian Years 1906–1922*.

————. "Marc Chagall and Kazimir Malevich" (in Russian). *Shagalovskie dni v Vitebske* (special issue of *Vit'bichi*), July 3–5, 1992.

————. "Aleksandr Romm and his Memoirs of Mark Chagall" (in Russian). Unpublished.

————. "Copies of Mark Chagall's Theatrical Sketches in the Bakhrushin Museum" (in Russian). Unpublished.

————. "Mark Chagall and the Jewish Chamber Theater" (in Russian). Unpublished.

————. "The Theatrical Phenomenon of Mark Chagall" (in Russian). Unpublished.

Shazar, Zalman. "Homage to Chagall" (in Yiddish). *Di goldene keyt*, no. 60 (1967), pp. 27–33.

Shklovskii, Viktor. "Jewish Luck" (in Russian). In *Evreiskoe shchast'e* (Jewish luck).

Sorlier, Charles, ed. *Chagall by Chagall* (trans. from the French by John Shepley). New York: Harry N. Abrams, 1979.

————. *Marc Chagall: The Illustrated Books*. Paris: André Sauret/Michèle Trinckvel, 1991.

Spencer, Charles. *Leon Bakst*. New York: Rizzoli, 1973.

Sutzkever, Abraham. *Di fidlroyz* (The fiddle-rose). Tel Aviv: Di Goldene Keyt, 1974.

————. *Selected Poetry and Prose* (trans. by Barbara and Benjamin Harshav). Introduction by Benjamin Harshav. Berkeley and Los Angeles: University of California Press, 1992.

Sweeney, James Johnson. "Art Chronicle: An Interview with Marc Chagall." *The Partisan Review*, no. 11 (Winter 1944), pp. 88–93.

————. *Marc Chagall*. New York: Museum of Modern Art, 1946.

Swett, Herman. "German Jews, German Press, and the Granovskii Theater" (in Yiddish). *Literarishe bleter*, April 27, 1928.

————. "The Theater World in Berlin" (in Yiddish). *Literarishe bleter*, no. 41 (1928).

————. "Meierkhol'd and Granovskii" (in Yiddish). *Literarishe bleter*, no. 19 (1930), p. 344.

Szmeruk [Shmeruk], Ch. *Ha-kibutz ha-yehudi ve-ha-hityashvut ha-khaklayit ha-yehudit be-byelorusya ha-sovietit (1918–1932)* (The Jewish community and Jewish agricultural settlement in Soviet Byelorussia [1918–1932]). Ph.D. diss., Hebrew University, Jerusalem, 1961.

Tairov, Aleksandr. *Zapiski rezhisera* (Notes of a theater director). Moscow: Kamernyi Teatr, 1921.

Tarabukin, Nikolai. "Art Exhibits: Al'tman, Chagall, Shterenberg" (in Russian). *Vestnik Isskustv*, no. 5 (1929), pp. 27–28.

Teatral'naia Moskva (a theater, music, and film guide), 1926.

Teatral'naia zhizn' (special issue on GOSET), no. 10 (1990).

Toller, Ernst, Joseph Roth, and Alfons Goldschmidt. *Das Moskauer Jüdische Akademische Theater* (The Moscow Jewish Academic Theater). Berlin: Verlag Die Schmiede, 1928.

van Gyseghem, Andre. *Theatre in Soviet Russia*. London: Faber and Faber, 1943.

Venturi, Lionello. *Chagall: A Biographical and Critical Study* (trans. by S. Harrison and J. Emmons). Paris: Editions d'Art Albert Skira, 1956.

Vetrov, A. [Arkin, David]. "On Chagall" (in Russian). *Ekran*, no. 7 (1921).

————. "Exhibition of Three" (in Russian). *Ekran*, no. 28 (1921).

Vevyorke, A. "A Jewish Theater Style: On the Sholem-Aleichem Evenings in M.Y.C.T." (in Yiddish). *Der Emes*, no. 78 (1921).

————. "A Holiday" (in Yiddish). *Der Emes*, April 13, 1922.

Vitali, Christoph, ed. *Marc Chagall: The Russian Years 1906–1922*. Frankfurt: Schirn Kunsthalle, 1991.

Vlasova, R. I. *Russkoe teatral'no-dekoratsionnoe iskusstvo nachala XX veka* (Russian theatrical design of the early twentieth century). Leningrad: Khudozhnik RSFR, 1984.

Vofsi-Mikhoels, Natalia. *Avi Shlomo Mikhoels* (My Father Shlomo Mikhoels). Tel Aviv: Hakibutz Hameuchad, 1982.

Walden, Herwarth. "The Moscow Yiddish Chamber Theater" (in German). *Der Sturm*, vols. 2–3 (1928–29), p. 229.

Walt, Abraham [A. Lyesin]. *Lider un poemen (1888–1938)* (Poems and long poems, 1888–1938), vols. 1–3. With illustrations by Marc Chagall. New York: Forwerts Association, 1938.

Weinreich, Uriel. "Problems in the Analysis of Idioms." *On Semantics*. Philadelphia: University of Pennsylvania Press, 1980.

Worrall, Nick. *Modernism to Realism on the Soviet Stage: Tairov-Vakhtangov-Okhlopov*. Cambridge: Cambridge University Press, 1989.

YIVO. *Barikht fun der konferents fun dem yidishn visnshaftlekhn institut, opgehaltn in vilne 1929* (Report on the conference of the Yiddish Scientific Institute in Vilna, 1929). Vilna: YIVO, 1930.

Yudovin, Sh. *Idisher folks ornament* (Jewish folk ornamentation). Vitebsk: 1921.

Yudovin, Sh., and B. Malin, eds. *Idishe ornamentale folks kunst* (Jewish ornamental folk art). Vitebsk: 1921.

Zagorskii, M. *Mikhoels* (in Russian). Moscow and Leningrad: Kinopechat', 1927.

————. "Mikhoels" (in Russian). *Teatral'naia dekada*, no. 5 (1935), p. 7.

Zingerman, B. "Russia, Chagall, Mikhoels, and Others" (in Russian). *Teatr*, vol. 2 (1990), pp. 35–53.

————. "About Mikhoels" (in Russian). *Moskovskii nabliudatel'*, no. 2 (Jan. 1991).

Znosko-Borovsii, Evg. *Russkii teatr nachala XX veka*, vol. 1. Prague: Plamya Press, 1923.

Zrelishcha (special issue on the fifth anniversary of GOSET), no. 89 (1924).

Zuskin, B. "Actor B. Zuskin On the Theater" (interview; in Yiddish). *Literarishe bleter*, April 27, 1928.

Zylbercwaig, Zalmen. *Leksikon fun yidishn teater* (Lexicon of the Yiddish Theater), vol. 2. Warsaw: Elisheva, 1934; vol. 4. New York: Elisheva, 1963.

Afterword

Gregory Veitsman

During the fifteen years that I worked at the State Tret'iakov Gallery, in Moscow, I participated in and witnessed many interesting events, including the visit of Marc Chagall in 1973. As Assistant Director for Technical Services and a member of the Directorate I was involved in every aspect of the museum's operation.

I was fortunate to work with a group of remarkable people, genuine experts of the old school, such as E. V. Silversvan, A. N. Svirin, S. I. Bitiutskaia, and others, who spent their entire careers at the museum. They passed down to the next generation those special curatorial skills that helped us to save and preserve great works of art, including Chagall's murals of 1920 for the State Jewish Chamber Theater, in Moscow. Those canvases were kept rolled up and hidden in a storage space in what had once been an old church, adjoining the Tret'iakov building on Tolmachevskii Lane. In 1966, a small group, which included Director P. I. Lebedev, curator L. I. Romashkova, restorer A. P. Kovalev, V. M. Volodarskii, and myself, performed the so-called "secret" examination of Chagall's paintings. Room 45, which directly adjoined the church storeroom, was closed off and we unrolled and spread out the murals on the floor. I remember what a strong impression they made on us. I took measurements and then constructed special, large drums on which to roll the oversized murals in order to better preserve them.

While we were examining them, Lebedev mentioned that it would be good to find someone who could read the paintings' Yiddish inscriptions. I almost jumped up to offer my services. Although I knew Yiddish, I had concealed this knowledge ever since a certain incident that occurred in the late 1950s during Khrushchev's "thaw." My brother and I were at the theater in Moscow's Zhuravlev Square, where the Jewish actress Anna Guzik was appearing. In the interval between acts a man sitting two rows in front of us pulled out a newspaper that was either in Hebrew or Yiddish. At that time the presence of a Jewish newspaper in Moscow was so unexpected and so improbable that we leaned slightly forward just to read its title. This gesture was enough for KGB agents to start following us. Although it was probably only someone from the Israeli consulate who had opened the newspaper, we were closely followed for three days and nights. After that I never revealed that I knew Yiddish. Thus, in 1966 (it was now the Brezhnev era) I resisted the temptation to read the inscriptions on Chagall's murals for my colleagues. Several months later, after the Arab armies, who were equipped by the Soviets, suffered a crushing defeat in the Six-Day War with Israel, the Kremlin geared up its propaganda machine in a desperate anti-Zionist campaign. Newspapers, magazines, television, and radio proclaimed the Zionists' subversive activities; numerous books about the threat of Zionism were published and printed in large runs. The tactics were designed to incite anti-Semitism and to put pressure on and demonstrate hostility toward Jews. The Soviets had kept silent about Chagall's existence since he had left Russia more than fifty years earlier. In the early 1970s, I came across Chagall's name in one of those contemptible books, among the names of those who had sympathized with Israel. He was identified as the "bard of Zionism."

In the spring of 1973, I was summoned to a meeting at the Ministry of Culture of the USSR, at which I was informed that Chagall himself was coming to Moscow and at which the mounting of some kind of exhibition during his visit was proposed. The head of the Department of Culture of the Central Committee of the Communist Party of the Soviet Union, who was at the meeting, did not conceal his contempt when Chagall was mentioned. With the exception of its appearance in the anti-Zionist publication discussed above, his name, it seemed, had actually been forgotten until that time.

*Marc Chagall — surrounded by, from left to right, A. P. Kovalev,
L. I. Romashkova, Gregory Veitsman, V. M. Volodarskii, L. Lifshitz,
and P. I. Lebedev — as he signed* Introduction to the Jewish Theater
*at the State Tret'iakov Gallery in 1973. Photo courtesy Gregory
Veitsman.*

On June 5, rooms 17A and 17B were closed off from the rest of the museum, and an exhibition of sixty-three of Chagall's lithographs was hung. No announcement of the day or time of his visit to the Tret'iakov had been made, but a crowd gathered in the side streets around the museum. Three rows of policemen prevented anyone from approaching Chagall. He, his wife Vava, and Nadia Léger were not brought in through the main gates but by a service entrance. They came up to the Director's study on the second floor for a champagne toast and then walked through the library to rooms 17A and 17B. Chagall went first, escorted by Minister of Culture E. A. Furtseva, Director Lebedev, and several other officials. With Vava holding my arm, she and I followed a few steps behind. I was observing Chagall, who was smartly dressed and looked magnificent. He seemed quite happy and excited and was cordial to all. We went upstairs to the Repin room and then to the galleries where the lithographs were displayed. They were not even framed but under glass in cases that had been slapped together for the occasion. The entire viewing lasted only a very short time. It was packed with KGB agents; there were no members of the press present except for the *Paris-Match* correspondent, at Chagall's personal request. The sculptor I. M. Chaikov pushed his way through the crowd to me and started lamenting how quickly the years had flown by. He recalled the time of his youth when he and Chagall had worked and exhibited together in Berlin. We were waiting for the viewing to end when Chagall came over; a museum photographer captured the touching meeting of the two former students as I stood between them. When Chagall came to the museum again on June 8 to see the GOSEKT panels, I handed him the photograph, which he kindly signed with the date, "8/6 1973," his name, "Chagall," in French, and the place, "Moscow," in Russian.

On this second visit, Chagall seemed more at ease. The moment we entered room 21 (the Valentin Serov room), where all of Chagall's huge murals for the Jewish Theater were unrolled on the floor, he grew quiet; I saw delight and astonishment in his face. We — there were only a few people in the room — stood to one side while Chagall walked back and forth beside the painted canvases spread out on the floor, the works that he had created more than a half-century before. His eyes shone, and he was silent for a few minutes before saying something quietly to himself. Then he drew himself up proudly as if to communicate, "Look, *I* created this." He started to say something about how nice it would be to exhibit the murals, and that he was glad they were still together and had been so well preserved. After a short discussion it was decided he should sign the murals. Brushes and paint were brought in, along with a chair. Chagall sat down, laid a corner of a canvas on a drum, and began to sign them, not knowing which language it would be best to use, but finally deciding on Russian. Vava called to him from the other end of the room. Chagall, engrossed in his beloved murals, did not even hear, although he did say something to her like, "What a good artist I am." And then he began dreaming aloud about exhibiting them, displaying them there at the museum, in Russia. While glancing at Lebedev, who was maintaining a careful official expression, and then at one KGB agent and another KGB agent, I remembered the words in that anti-Zionist book calling Chagall the "bard of Zionism." Indeed, the time when the murals for the Jewish Theater could be exhibited was distant.

The day after the departure of Chagall, who was hurrying back to France for the opening of the museum dedicated to him, we were obliged to take down everything connected with him and hide it in the storeroom once again.

Many years later, in the early 1980s, I spoke with Marc and Vava at their home in St. Paul de Vence. He remembered every single detail about the visit to Moscow. He asked me if I remembered how Furtseva, the Minister of Culture, repeatedly asked him not to speak ill of the Soviet Union and the Communist government. With twinkling eyes, he said, "And why were they so certain that there was anything bad to say about them?" After a brief pause he continued, "Of course, they destroyed such a rich, beautiful Jewish culture." Perestroika and the fall of the Soviet empire were yet to come. I know how happy Chagall would have been to see the murals exhibited in New York.

—Translated, from the Russian, by Judith Vowles

The Solomon R. Guggenheim Foundation